'AN ARISTOCRACY OF EXALTED SPIRITS'

'An aristocracy of exalted spirits'

THE IDEA OF THE CHURCH IN NEWMAN'S *Tamworth Reading Room*

David P. Delio

GRACEWING

First published in England in 2016
by
Gracewing
2 Southern Avenue
Leominster
Herefordshire HR6 0QF
United Kingdom
www.gracewing.co.uk

No part of this publication may be reproduced, stored in a retrieval system, or transmitted in any form or by any means, electronic, mechanical, photocopying, recording or otherwise, without the written permission of the publisher.

The right of David P. Delio to be identified as the author of this work has been asserted in accordance with the Copyright, Designs and Patents Act 1988.

© 2016 David P. Delio

ISBN 978 085244 882 3

Cover design by Bernardita Peña Hurtado

Typeset by Word and Page, Chester, UK

Dedicated to my beautiful daughters Naomi and Cecilia
May they find in Newman what I have—
A way to know Truth and Christ's Church in this world.

CONTENTS

Foreword by the Rev. John T. Ford, CSC, STD	xi
Abbreviations	xvii
Preface	xix
Introduction	1
1. Newman and Peel in Nineteenth-Century Britain	7
Revolution, Recovery, and the Young Robert Peel	8
The Newman Family and the Napoleonic Wars	10
Peel and the Reaction to Revolution	11
Newman's 'Great Change of Thought'	13
Peel, Member of Parliament for Oxford	17
Newman at Oxford	19
Catholic Emancipation	21
The Reform Act and the Oxford Movement	26
Peel and the Conservative Ascendency	29
Newman's *Experimentum Crucis*	34
Newman and Peel: Idealists and Reformers	41
2. Adult Education and Peel's Tamworth Address	43
Britain's Adult-Education Movement	44
Sir Robert Peel's Tamworth Address	49
Press Reaction to the Address	60
From Address to Pamphlet	63
Looking Back and the Advent of Catholicus	64
3. The Background, Offer to Respond, and Letter 1	67
The British Critic	69
Tract 90	77
'The Duty of Christian Educators'	81
Avoiding Controversy	88
The Walters' Offer	90
The First Letter: An Anonymous Venture	92

'An aristocracy of exalted spirits'

4.	The Catholicus Letters 2–4	103
	Letters to the Editor and the 'Leading Article': from Anonymous to Catholicus	105
	The Second Letter: Catholicus Appears	107
	The 'E' Critique	115
	The Third Letter: Grace and the Church	118
	A Note of Panic from Walter II	128
	Newman's 'Incendiary' Response	129
	'Errata' in the Second and Third Letters	131
	The Leading Article: Praise for Peel	132
	The Fourth Letter: Rising from the Ashes	133
	The Times' Volte-Face	139
	Hiatus between Letters Four and Five	141
5.	The Catholicus Letters 5–7	147
	The Fifth Letter: 'Christianity is Faith'	147
	The Sixth Letter: Heart Knowledge and Scientific Reasoning	156
	Letter to Henry Wilberforce: The Identity of Catholicus	167
	The Seventh Letter: The Perils of Knowing God, and Summary	168
6.	The Reception of the Catholicus Letters	177
	The Areopagus: 'The wise men of Athens heard the Apostle and despised him'	177
	Press Reaction to the Catholicus Letters	183
	Newman's View of the Controversy	191
	Peel's Counter-attack	195
	The Tamworth Reading Room in *The British Critic*	201
7.	The Legacy of Newman's Letters and Tamworth Pamphlet	211
	The 1842 Tamworth Report	213
	The Trajectory of Catholicus	213
	Correspondence with the Froudes 1844; The Oratory at Birmingham 1847	214
	Peel at Tamworth in 1849	217
	Correspondence between Newman and Frederick Faber	218
	Correspondence between Newman and John Moore Capes	219
	The Idea of a University	221
	Catholicus in the *Catholic Standard*	223
	The Apologia pro Vita Sua	224

Contents

	An Essay in Aid of a Grammar of Assent	225
	Discussions and Arguments	228
	The Times' Obituary and Conclusion	231
8.	The 'Idea' of the Church: From Tamworth to Rome	233
	From Anglican 'Fundamentals' to Faith 'in the Bosom of the Church'	235
	The Form and Method of Newman's Sermons in *The Tamworth Reading Room*	239
	Aspects that Reveal Newman's 'Idea'	246
	The 'Idea' of the Church in *The Tamworth Reading Room*	253
	Coda: An Oratory for 'Exalted Spirits'	256

Appendices   261

Appendix I.
Peel's Address and the Catholicus Letters   261
Sir Robert Peel's Address   261
Newman's Letters of Catholicus   278
Appendix II.
Material Relevant to *The Tamworth Reading Room*   315
Appendix III.
Sample Press Reception of Peel's Address and the Catholicus Letters   329
Appendix IV. Biographical Entries   331

Bibliography   341

Index   353

FOREWORD

Newman the Journalist?

As a result of his beatification by Pope Benedict XVI on 19 September 2010, more people than ever are familiar with the life of John Henry Newman (1801–90). Yet many of those who have read some of his writings have different impressions of him. To those in higher education—both professors and administrators—Newman is the author of a much-admired as well as much-debated collection of essays: *The Idea of a University*. Among philosophers, Newman is regarded as the writer of a thought-provoking programmatic treatise: *An Essay in Aid of a Grammar of Assent* (1870). To avid readers of Victorian literature, Newman is recognized as the author of one of the most widely read autobiographies of all times: *Apologia pro Vita Sua* (1864). Among theologians, Newman is considered one of the most creative thinkers of the nineteenth century, whose seminal ideas in *An Essay on the Development of Christian Doctrine* (1845) have gained almost universal acceptance. In addition, since he wrote and delivered hundreds of sermons—many of which were published and widely read during his lifetime and continue to provide spiritual insight to readers today—Newman is a revered as a spiritual guide.

Given his wide-ranging interests, Newman might be characterized as a renaissance person—an individual who is outstandingly talented in different fields of endeavor. Their contemporaries regard such persons as authorities, if not celebrities, whose activities and writings have a considerable following yet sometimes occasion controversy: every genius has both disciples and detractors. Newman was such a person—an incredibly prolific writer who attracted numerous devoted followers, yet also aroused considerable opposition. In part, this was due to the fact that he was willing to discuss the controversial issues of his day: political and ecclesiastical, philosophical and theological, literary and spiritual—sometimes separately, but frequently collaterally, since such issues are interwoven into the texture of life.

'An aristocracy of exalted spirits'

Not only did Newman discuss a wide variety of issues; he treated them incredibly well. Most authors would be more than content if they could write even one "classic"—one outstanding book of the highest quality both in style and in content that continues to be worth reading decades after the time when it was originally published. Newman was an author who wrote "classics" not only in one, but in at least five different areas. What is even more unusual is that Newman's classics were not part of a literary master-plan, like a trilogy or series, but were produced by dint of circumstances—to address controversies of his day—which have an uncanny resemblance to many issues of our day. Though written in the nineteenth century, Newman's writings provide ample lessons for the twenty-first.

In contrast to those professional authors who plan a series of projected best-sellers, Newman needed a "call" to write: "What I have written has been for the most part what may be called official, works done in some office I held or engagement I had made ... or has been from some especial call, or invitation, or necessity or emergency". In fact, many of his "official" writings were regular and routine; both as an Anglican cleric and later as a Roman Catholic priest, Newman had the responsibility of preaching—a task that he accomplished so well that his audiences wanted copies of his sermons for spiritual reading and reflection; he obliged with more than a dozen volumes of sermons.

Newman also responded to other "calls": he wrote in whole or in part a third of the ninety *Tracts for the Times* (1833–41), the series of multi-authored publications supporting the Oxford Movement, setting its agenda and specifying its theology. He was also the author of numerous essays and reviews for periodicals, such as the *British Critic* and the *Rambler*: his essays often commented on the hotly debated questions of his day: both historical and theological, both political and ecclesiastical; his reviews critiqued a broad range of authors and their writings, especially, though not exclusively, concerning religious and spiritual topics. When either university professors or political figures took stances that ran counter to what Newman considered historically true or politically fundamental, or doctrinally sound, he did not hesitate taking issue with the offender via public critiques that were rhetorically masterful and polemically devastating. Newman adroitly demonstrated that the pen is mightier than the sword; his targets often felt offended publicly, damaged professionally, even wounded psychologically.

Newman's literary attractiveness and rhetorical effectiveness stemmed from the fact that his writings were multi-tiered. The ground floor was usually factual or historical: a particular person or current event that effectively "called" him to write. Building on this basis—in an era and country, where Church and state overlapped—Newman skillfully examined the political positions of persons and the ecclesiastical implications of events. Simultaneously, he teased out both the implicit philosophical assumptions and the collateral doctrinal stances of his opponents: he was an effective, at times annihilating, polemicist precisely because he made the effort to understand the views of his adversaries, sometimes presenting their positions more precisely and perceptively than they themselves had done—with the avowed intention of refuting them. Finally, Newman realized that people are not convinced by logic alone; he astutely caricatured the untenable aspects of his opponents' positions, while rhetorically captivating his audience with the persuasive reasonableness of his own.

In the case of his more circumstantial publications—articles, essays, reviews—Newman well might be described as a journalist—much to the chagrin of his antagonists, much to the delight of his admirers. Although there are Schools of Journalism in modern universities, such did not exist in Newman's time. The Oxford curriculum in his day consisted of mathematics and Greek and Latin classics, read in the original languages. Yet this seemingly obtuse combination had amazing benefits in Newman's case: he learned to think both logically and realistically and to express his thoughts succinctly and concretely. His literary talents were soon recognized by his Oxford contemporaries. As a youthful fellow of Oriel College, he was invited to contribute essays to various publications and to write a history of the councils of the Church. Like many a scholar, he quickly became so fascinated by the dramatic events surrounding the First General Council of Nicaea (325) that he never completed the assigned project; nonetheless, he managed to publish the major portion of his research in his first book, *Arians of the Fourth Century*.

Admittedly, *Arians* was and is not widely read—even by Newman devotees. Yet the challenge of writing this work seems to have been pivotal in his development as an author. First, he did not organize his presentation merely in chronological order; he saw such facts as events that shaped both the participants involved and the decisions that they made. The *dramatis personae* in the Arian controversy did not simply strut and fret their hour on the stage of history, but were wholeheartedly committed to their positions and fought strenuously to influence the doctrinal teaching of the Church. In his *Arians*, Newman effectively made a long-dormant doctrinal controversy come to life. In the Arian controversy, he saw salutary lessons for his day: just as the Arians were guilty of distorting the teaching of Christ, so too were some of his fellow Anglican clerics, including some of his Oxford colleagues. History can be instructive, if one recognizes the parallels between past and present. The reverse can be true. The present may resurrect the past and portend the future.

Such was the case in 1841 with a relatively obscure event that "called" Newman to write. The occasion was the dedication of a new public library and reading room in a modest-size town in the English Midlands. The population of Tamworth, which had once been a medieval market village some one hundred miles northwest of London, was swelling—thanks to the Industrial Revolution. The library-project exemplified an emerging philanthropic trend to provide educational opportunities for the working class—a legacy that was replicated in the American Mid-West with numerous Carnegie-funded libraries. The Tamworth Library was also a political benefaction—thanks to the influence of Tamworth's Member of Parliament, Sir Robert Peel (1788–1850), former and future prime minister. Even so, news about events in Staffordshire usually garnered scant space in the London *Times*.

Peel's speech on 26 January 1841 was not only an exception in terms of newspaper coverage; its contents were part of a political platform designed to appeal to workers, shopkeepers and entrepreneurs—all of whom were probably pleased with the benefits that the new library would presumably bestow. Yet one may wonder how many in the actual audience recognized the complex of problems—political, ecclesiastical, philosophical, theological— inherent in Peel's speech. The average reporter could describe the event; the average journalist could paraphrase Peel's address. However, the editors of *The Times* seemingly sensed the neuralgic nature of the underlying theoretical questions and so turned to Newman to tease out these issues and respond appropriately. Although preoccupied with writing what was to be the last of the *Tracts for the Times*, Newman agreed. The result was a series of seven letters that were published pseudonymously in *The Times*.

At the time of their publication, the letters created a flurry of interest about their contents and speculation about the identity of their author. But interest waned rapidly: in general, the customary fate of journalists is that today's news is quickly passé; in particular, with the publication of *Tract 90*, the British public had a more provocative political-ecclesiastical topic to debate: the alleged Catholicity of the Church of England proposed in *Tract 90* prompted more prolonged polemics than the more arcane philosophical discussion of the nature of faith and reason in the seven Letters in *The Times*. Moreover, instead of the cryptic Catholicus, the public had a well-known target in John Henry Newman.

Given both the historical—and dramatic—importance of *Tract 90*, it is perhaps not surprising that Newman scholars have generally by-passed the Catholicus Letters or at most given them short shrift. Students of Peel have done the same—mentioning Newman's Letters only in passing, if at all. Although Newman did not re-publish all his Anglican writings, he considered these Letters important enough to include in *Discussions and Arguments* (1872), though he over-modestly introduced them as "necessarily immethodical in composition". Such self-deprecation, however, was characteristic. Newman described his *Essay on Development* as "an hypothesis to explain a difficulty"; he said of his *Idea of a University* that "there is nothing novel or singular in the argument which I have been pursuing"; his *Apologia* was "doing no more than explaining myself, and my opinions and actions"; his *Grammar* "can only bring his own experiences to the common stock of psychological facts". Yet, however ambiguous his personal endorsement of his writings, Newman's major classics have stood the test of time on their own merits.

Unfortunately, many of Newman's other works have been ignored or forgotten. David Delio's study has rescued *The Tamworth Reading Room* from unmerited obscurity. Delio's study of Newman's letters provides three different but inter-locking components. First is the historical background: by a careful treatment of primary and secondary materials,

Delio has reconstructed the events surrounding the composition of the Letters; if the actual task of writing was solitary and onerous, the surrounding scenario was volatile and fascinating. Second, insofar as readers, then and now, could be mesmerized by Peel's enthusiastic and exuberant dedication without recognizing the fundamental issues at stake, Delio's careful analysis of both Peel's speech and Newman's Letters clearly surfaces what was central to the controversy. Delio might well have been satisfied with this dual contribution—historical and analytical—but he takes an additional important step.

Delio relates Newman's Letters to his ecclesial concerns and to the broader corpus of his writings—especially to *The Idea of a University* and *An Essay in Aid of a Grammar of Assent*. Newman's Letters are a prelude to positions that he later developed in greater detail. But what is more relevant is that the questions that Newman addressed—initially in these Letters and later in his *Idea* and his *Grammar*—are still much debated and much worth debating in the public forum today, especially: the relationship of faith and reason, the nature and goals of education, the relationship of Church and state. (One might add that *The Times* would do well to continue to publish articles of the caliber of the Catholicus Letters.)

In sum, Delio has retrieved and restored a mini-classic: *The Tamworth Reading Room*; simultaneously he has rediscovered a forgotten portrait: Newman the Journalist.

Rev. John T. Ford, CSC, STD

11 July 2016

ABBREVIATIONS

Burgis, TRR   Nina Fay Burgis, 'An Edition of Newman's *Tamworth Reading Room*, with Introduction and Textual and Expository Apparatus', MA diss., University of London, Birkbeck College, 1964. Permission to use Burgis's dissertation has graciously been granted by her estate executor.

DA   John Henry Newman, *Discussions and Arguments*. London: Longman, Green, & Co., 1907 [1872].

DNB   *The Oxford Dictionary of National Biography*, online edition, edited by Lawrence Goldman, Oxford: Oxford University Press. http://www.oxforddnb.com/

GA   John Henry Newman, *An Essay in Aid of a Grammar of Assent*. Notre Dame: University of Notre Dame Press, 1979.

LD   John Henry Newman, *The Letters and Diaries of John Henry Newman*, ed. Charles Dessain *et al.* 32 vols. Various Publishers, 1961–2009.

OUS   John Henry Newman, *Fifteen Sermons Preached before the Oxford University between A.D. 1826 and 1843*, ed. James David Earnest and Gerard Tracey. Oxford: Oxford University Press, 2006. Two sets of numbers are given for all references to the *Oxford University Sermons*, the first from the edition of Earnest and Tracey, the second from the uniform edition of the sermons published in 1871

PPS   John Henry Newman, *Parochial and Plain Sermons*. 8 vols. London: Longman & Co., 1907.

SMB   Eric J. Evans, *The Shaping of Modern Britain: Identity, Industry and Empire, 1780–1914*. Harlow: Pearson Educational, 2011

PREFACE

In February 1841 John Henry Newman responded in *The Times* of London to an address given by a leading Tory, Sir Robert Peel. Newman assumed the penname Catholicus and composed seven letters, clever and woven together by several theological and philosophical themes. Newman's search for an idea of the Church animated the letters. This was not an idea in his head but rather how the Church appeared in the world: a Church catholic and apostolic, broad enough to encompass many different Christians and yet unfinished. The Church, as it appeared through this idea, was concrete yet flexible and inclusive enough to elevate the truths and institutions arising in the modern world. However, it remained distinct in its divine *telos* as the means for human salvation. Newman also drew on Paul's thought leavened by faith in the Risen Lord and the Holy Spirit guiding his one Body spread throughout the world (1 Co 12:12–27). Newman, an apostle to the modern age, shared Paul's desire to confront the wise and learned, and also to draw persons deeper into the faith born of the Church.

Yet after almost two millennia of ecclesial development and schism, Newman faced a different series of challenges from Paul. For him, the most pressing questions were not what the nascent Church was to be, but where it was to be found and how she would encounter modern science, democracy, industry, and education. Newman's letters were laconic attempts to answer these and further questions, for himself and for others. Together they presented a unique a distillation of Newman's Anglican thought on education, faith and reason, in relation to the Church while anticipating his later works as a Roman Catholic including *The Idea of the University* and *An Essay in Aid of a Grammar of Assent*.

The Tamworth Reading Room's combination of rhetoric, philosophy, and theology challenged Newman's contemporaries and continues to challenge readers today. Themes, ideas, and the context of the letters have been treated by a variety of scholars with different interpretative agendas and abilities. This book seeks to clarify the history and interpretations of

'An aristocracy of exalted spirits'

The Tamworth Reading Room, for these oft-forgotten letters are indeed still relevant for our time. Most importantly, the book culls from the letters Newman's deeper ecclesiological concerns, which have been overlooked. For him, the Church and the faith she proclaimed were distinct from Peel's vision of knowledge in modern institutions. Newman's search for this Church animated the letters. What he imagined the Church to be was surprising: a Church catholic and apostolic, broad enough to encompass many different Christians, and yet unfinished. The faith of the Church, however, was not an ideal but concrete: it was flexible and inclusive enough to elevate the truths found in new establishments and innovations in knowledge, yet remained distinct in its divine origin and *telos* as the means for human salvation. The story of *The Tamworth Reading Room* helps to complete the picture of the Church and of a Christian trying to negotiate the emerging democratic, scientific, and industrial world. This story is still with the Church today over fifty years from the Second Vatican Council, forty from Lausanne, through the Lambeth Conferences and other ecclesial movements. The drama of *The Tamworth Reading Room* may help the Church as she negotiates perils and promise of the third millennium.

Introduction

FAITH, VIEWED IN ITS HISTORY THROUGH PAST AGES, presents us with the fulfilment of one great idea in particular—that, namely, of *an aristocracy of exalted spirits*, drawn together out of all countries, ranks, and ages, raised above the condition of humanity, specimens of the capabilities of our race, incentives to rivalry, and patterns for imitation. (John Henry Newman, *The Tamworth Reading Room*)[1]

On 19 January 1841, Sir Robert Peel delivered a speech on the 'Establishment of a Library and Reading Room at Tamworth'. As Member of Parliament for Tamworth and leader of the Tory (Conservative) party, Peel had a vested interest in this project. The working public in nineteenth-century England generally did not have access to libraries. Peel believed that inaugurating such an institution would broaden his party's base and contribute to the betterment of Tamworth's inhabitants and to English society in general. The library would provide the people of Tamworth access to the latest trends in science and technology, thereby enabling them to become more productive citizens. Peel also believed that scientific and technological knowledge, as well as literature, would inspire persons to improve their lives intellectually, economically, while strengthening their moral and religious lives. In turn, this knowledge would help mitigate class conflict and further propel England into the modern age.

Peel's speech provoked a flurry of debate in newspapers and periodicals. *The Times* of London contacted John Henry Newman, an Anglican priest involved in the Oxford Movement, to critique the address.[2] Initially Newman balked at the offer; however, he had opposed Peel's actions and ideas for over a decade[3] and reluctantly accepted the

---

1 'Catholicus', Letters to the Editor, *The Times*, 20 February 1841.
2 *LD*, VIII, 25–6.
3 John Henry Newman, *Apologia pro Vita Sua*, ed. David J. Delaura (New York:

1

invitation. He sensed that this speech indicated a broader crisis in the Church and of faith in England.

Newman responded to Peel's speech with a series of seven letters to the editor of *The Times*—six under the pseudonym Catholicus.[4] The central argument of his letters concerned the role of the Church in the religious and intellectual formation of persons and society. Newman contended that one could not truly develop either as a human being or as a citizen merely by the acquisition of scientific or literary knowledge. Such knowledge could provide neither the basis for true religious belief nor satisfy human intellectual and moral longings. Newman embraced scientific learning and literature, although subsequent to the principles of divine faith and the dictates of one's conscience nurtured in the Church. He envisioned these principles and the Church as essential for the assimilation of knowledge and technology generated by the burgeoning modern world.

Newman's Catholicus letters, which later would be collectively published as *The Tamworth Reading Room* (1841; 1872), were analogous to St. Paul's speech at the Areopagus (Ac 17:16–34) and several of his epistles.[5] Newman's letters reflected the Pauline desire to correlate the Gospel message and contemporary learning. Just as Paul preached 'strange notions' about the Christian God in Athens, or exhorted the Corinthians and the Romans, Newman was able to use the pages of a prominent newspaper to represent the Church and Christian faith in English life.

Peel was the catalyst for Newman's apostolic venture. Following certain ideals of the Enlightenment, Peel sponsored an institution that sought to efface religious conflicts between Churches through emphasis on the fruits of science and literature. Newman countered with the 'idea' of the Church, which he loosely termed Christianity in his letters. The Church was faith incarnate, able to compliment and

---

W. W. Norton & Co., 1968), 14–15.

4 Catholicus, Letters to the Editor, *The Times*, 5 February, 9 February, 10 February, 12 February, 20 February, 22 February, 27 February, 1841. Peel's address and the letters as they appeared in *The Times* can be found in Appendix I. Additionally, all seven letters were revised and republished in *DA*, 270.

5 Biblical references throughout will be from the King James version as this was the version read by both Peel and Newman.

Introduction

fulfill human establishments and knowledge, by being distinct in her divine origin and end:

> Christianity is faith, faith implies a doctrine, a doctrine propositions, propositions yes or no, yes or no differences. Differences, then, are the natural attendants on Christianity, and you cannot have Christianity, and not have differences.[6]

The assertions and imagery advanced in Newman's Catholicus letters generated much speculation and comment in the press; they were denounced by Peel and other Tories. The controversy reverberated across political and religious factions throughout British society. For some readers, Newman's ideas were considered significant—a part of the Oxford Movement's call for a return to the teachings of the Catholic and Apostolic Church. The majority, however, viewed the letters either as a partisan assault on an important political leader who had embraced tenets of modern education or an unenlightened return to religious tyranny. These reactions—for and against the letters—flowed from churchmen, politicians, and *literati*. They were indicative of the partisan battles in the Church, in the State and between Church and State being waged in early Victorian England. Although 1841 is now a foreign world, Peel's vision for learning, and its underlying Enlightenment tradition, has become the dominant veneer of Western civilization. Yet, the power of Newman's response in the letters and beyond, and especially the interpretation of Newman, have continued to show that beneath the veneer questions subsist.

Several recent studies of *The Tamworth Reading Room* have characterized Peel's speech and Newman's letters as a controversy between these two men.[7] This was impossible in 1841, as Newman crafted his letters in anonymity, and Peel never knew his adversary. More than a decade would pass before Newman as Catholicus was made public—

---

6 Catholicus, Letters to the editor, *The Times*, 20 February 1841, *DA*, 284.
7 For example, Wendell V. Harris, 'Newman, Peel, Tamworth, and the Concurrence of Historical Forces', *Victorian Studies* 32 (1989): 189–208, at 206. While Harris adequately detailed the historical context of *The Tamworth Reading Room*, his primary hermeneutic placed Newman and Peel in opposition; Harris's treatment of the broader, philosophical and theological realities was inadequate, as will be noted in later chapters.

after Peel's death and with the controversy all but forgotten. Although these letters would have never happened had Peel not given the address and had Newman not accepted *The Times*' commission, it would be a mistake to reduce this story to a contest between two men. Rather it was the contest of two rival traditions, which Peel could not fully appreciate and Newman gleaned all too clearly.[8] For Peel, the Tamworth Library and Reading Room decoupled from religious life and thought represented Enlightenment ideals and a practical path forward. His vision would become a microcosm of the political and economic future of the nation. For Newman, the Church distinct from and yet absorbing the best the world had to offer signaled an alternative way.

Both Peel and Newman were renowned and reviled figures in nineteenth-century Britain. They represented many of the ideas that characterized their age, and yet they exceeded them. Peel's opinions imaged a triumphant humanism that has arisen in various ages, captured in the Babel narrative: 'Let us build us a city and a tower, whose top may reach unto heaven; and let us make us a name' (Gn 11:4). Newman's response accented the divine transcendence, reminding his readers that 'the LORD went before them by day in a pillar of a cloud to lead them the way' (Ex 13:21).[9] These rival positions were at the heart of the controversy in 1841.

The Tamworth Reading Room has received relatively brief but honorable mentions in many biographies and studies about Newman. Some commentators have focused on aspects of the letters as original ideas—or anticipations for his later works—regarding education, politics, science, faith and reason, or his satirical prowess.[10] There is only one

---

8 This indeed was how Newman thought; for example, in explaining to his mother in 1829 about the forces he saw arrayed against the Church, he wrote: 'Now you must not understand me as speaking harshly of individuals; I am speaking of bodies and principles' (*LD*, II, 130).

9 This verse became the title of one of Newman's most famous poems, published with the title 'The Pillar of the Cloud' but popularly known as 'Lead, Kindly Light' (*Verses on Various Occasions*, 156–7; available at: http://www.newmanreader.org/works/verses/verse90.html). Newman composed this poem while sailing from Sicily to England. See Ian Ker, *John Henry Newman: A Biography* (Oxford: Oxford University Press, 1988), 79–80.

10 Education: James Authur and Guy Nichols, *John Henry Newman*, Continuum

Introduction

scholarly monograph on the letters, by Nina Fay Burgis, who analyzed some of the historical background of *The Tamworth Reading Room* as well as offered a remarkable account of the initial reception of the letters in the British press.[11] Her thesis, however, concentrated upon Newman's literary style, his methodological approaches, and textual variants between the several editions of the letters. Apart from her work, scholars from various disciplines—Victorian studies,[12] political histories of the Oxford Movement,[13] and so forth, have canvassed *The Tamworth Reading Room* with varying degrees of accuracy and insight. Finally, it is important to note that no biography of Sir Robert Peel has treated the Tamworth event at length and only a few studies of Peel give any indication that he was involved in this event.[14]

This book accounts for the many studies of *The Tamworth Reading Room*, but focuses on the theological idea(s) undergirding the letters. Newman did not endeavor merely to critique secular knowledge and institutions but to offer an idea of the Church to engage British modernity as it was coming into its own. In order reveal this idea, Newman's voice and words will be the centerpiece of several chapters,

---

Library of Educational Thought, ed. Richard Bailey (London: Continuum, 2007). Politics: Terrence Kenny, *The Political Thought of John Henry Newman* (Westport, CT: Greenwood Press, 1974). Science: Stanley L. Jaki, 'Newman and Science', *The Downside Review* 108 (1990): 282–94. Faith and reason: Kenneth Beaumont, 'The Tamworth Reading Room: rapports entre «savoir profane» et foi Chrétienne', *Études Newmaniennes* 16 (2000), 55–68. Satirical prowess: Ian Ker, 'Newman the Satirist', in *Newman after a Hundred Years*, ed. Ian Ker and Alan G. Hill (Oxford: Clarendon Press 1990), 7–14.

11 Nina Fay Burgis, 'An Edition of Newman's *Tamworth Reading Room*, with Introduction and Textual and Expository Apparatus' (MA diss., University of London, Birkbeck College, 1964). Permission to use Burgis's dissertation has graciously been granted by her estate executor.

12 Jerry Coats, 'John Henry Newman's "Tamworth Reading Room": Adjusted Rhetorical Approaches for the Periodical Press', *Victorian Periodicals Review* 24 (1991): 173–80.

13 John Henry Lewis Rowlands, *Church, State, and Society: The Attitudes of John Keble, Richard Hurrell Froude, and John Henry Newman, 1827–1845* (Worthing: Churchman Publishing, 1989), 166–73.

14 For example, Norman Gash, *Sir Robert Peel: The Life of Sir Robert Peel after 1830* (London: Longman, 1972); Donald Read, *Peel and the Victorians* (Oxford: Blackwell, 1987).

often in lengthy quotations. This may seem cumbersome for the reader. However, it has been this author's experience that often his critics paraphrase or provide snippets of his thought in order to denigrate a particular idea or to highlight one of their own. This method not only erodes the beauty of his prose and thought and also leads to endless misinterpretation. For the contemporary reader, many of whom like discrete packets of information, Newman's writing may seem florid or drawn out. Nevertheless, whole and complete thoughts should be allowed to bloom on a page, as wine must be allowed to develop its proper bouquet. Patiently sipping Newman's words will be at times thrilling, maddening, and hopefully satisfying!

In the historical narrative that follows, a dramatic tension unfolds between a modern institution and the ancient Church. The first chapter examines the context preceding and surrounding *The Tamworth Reading Room* and includes biographies of Peel and Newman. A fairly detailed historical background in Chapter 1 is important in order to understand their respective viewpoints as well as various contemporary allusions and ideas found in Peel's address and Newman's letters. Chapter 2 briefly details the history of adult education in England in order to frame Peel's inaugural address of the Tamworth Library and Reading Room. The intent and content of Peel's speech are explored, along with a summary and annotated analysis of the address published in *The Times*. Chapters 3 through 5 summarize each of the Catholicus letters in light of Newman's activities, correspondences, and other theological works of his that were contemporary with the letters. Chapters 6 and 7 provide an explanation of the reception of the letters in Victorian society and the way that Newman continued to develop them as a Roman Catholic. The concluding Chapter 8 situates *The Tamworth Reading Room* within the broader context of Newman's developing ecclesiology. Newman had recently been convinced of a faith shared by the whole Church—Catholic, Protestant, and Orthodox. Although a member of the Church of England, by 1841 he had gravitated toward this view of faith and an idealized Apostolic and Catholic Church. This view guided *The Tamworth Reading Room*, providing the key distinction between secular educational institutions and the Church.

✠ I ✠

Newman and Peel in Nineteenth-Century Britain

BY THE MIDDLE OF THE NINETEENTH CENTURY, Sir Robert Peel and John Henry Newman had become eminent public figures in Britain. Peel had twice been prime minister and had staged an important revival of the Tory party in the 1830s and 1840s. He was a model of effective government and economic liberty that in turn shaped the politics of the Victorian era; however, in spite of his shrewd abilities, Peel's inability to grasp certain political constituencies ultimately shattered the party's core by 1846. He retired from politics and died tragically in 1850.

In 1841 Newman was a Fellow of Oriel College, Oxford, as well as an Anglican priest and a leading voice of the controversial Oxford Movement. In 1845 he left Oxford and the Church of England for the Roman Catholic Church. He re-emerged as a prominent and influential Catholic leader—serving Britain and Ireland as an Oratorian priest and eventually a cardinal until his death in 1890.

Although both Newman and Peel were influential and controversial in their respective vocations, neither man actually met the other. Peel took notice of Newman on only one occasion—his departure from the Anglican Church.[1] However, Peel was quite aware of the Oxford Movement and at times referred to the 'Puseyites,'[2] as adherents of

---

1 Peel to Reverend T. Henderson (18 November 1845), Peel Papers, 40578:345, The British Library, London.

2 John R. Griffin (*The Oxford Movement: A Revision* [Edinburgh: Pentland Press, 1984], 56) has stated, 'The name of Dr. Pusey is so closely associated with the Oxford Movement that even the greatest of scholars have forgotten the lateness of his entry into the movement'. Griffin, commenting on Owen Chadwick's *The Victorian Church* (Vol. I [London: A & C Black, 1964], 168), pointed out that although the

the Movement were disparagingly known.³ Conversely, Newman was much more aware of Peel, whom he first observed at Oxford in 1817.⁴ Newman contested Peel over his vote for Catholic emancipation in 1829 and referred to him in his letters and writings.

Revolution, Recovery, and the Young Robert Peel

The world in which Peel and Newman were born and thrived was influenced by the events of the late eighteenth century. Indeed, 'Britain's commercial activity and industrial production, the prime agents of its nineteenth-century supremacy', substantially quickened in the last quarter of the eighteenth century.⁵ These 'prime agents', as well as the wars with colonial America and France, had far ranging impacts on Britain's political, religious, and social life in the following century. In 1783, Britain ceded sovereignty to American colonists who had led 'the first successful rebellion in modern history'.⁶ Britain recovered unevenly after the colonial revolution. George III dismissed the government that presided over the war and promoted the twenty-four-year-old William Pitt the Younger to head a new government.⁷ Apart from the shame that followed the American Revolution, there were urgent domestic problems that had to be addressed—a swollen national debt and governmental inefficiencies and corruption. Pitt governed smartly and with aplomb—he implemented intelligent, efficient fiscal and governmental reforms which in time took effect. He was aided by a recovering economy strengthened by commercial expansion

---

movement's opponents concocted the label 'Puseyites', Newman was its real leader and thus 'the name Puseyite was quite misleading'.

3 *The Private Letters of Sir Robert Peel*, ed. G. Peel (London: John Murray, 1920), 475.

4 *LD*, I, 37.

5 Eric J. Evans, *The Shaping of Modern Britain: Identity, Industry and Empire, 1780–1914* (Harlow, England: Pearson Educational Ltd., 2011), 3.

6 Evans, *Modern Britain*, 85.

7 According to Evans (*Shaping of Modern Britain*, 95) Pitt had a clear path to political leadership. He was the son of a former Prime Minister, William Pitt the Elder (1708–88); however, Robert Pitt's appointment at such a young age depended more upon George III's desire to increase his own influence than Pitt's abilities.

and industrialization.⁸ The key to Pitt's success was that he was not indebted to party interests but rather envisioned himself as servant to Church, king, and country.⁹

Peel was born in 1788, during the Pitt recovery. His family had 'considerable wealth', but was not landed or titled; rather the family was a direct beneficiary of Britain's commercial and industrial revolutions.¹⁰ Peel's father, Robert senior, had inherited a textile business and prospered in the post-war era: 'The business flourished as the industrial revolution "took off" in Lancashire in the 1780s and Peel senior expanded his operations into Bolton. By the time of his eldest son's birth in 1788, he was employing more than 7,000 workers and the firm's profits were exceeding £70,000 (nearly £6m at current values) in good years.'¹¹ The elder Peel translated the family's fortune into a political career, becoming Member of Parliament for Tamworth in 1790. His political tenure was marked by a concern to improve the lives of factory workers and education in society.¹² He was made 'a baronet on William Pitt's recommendation in 1800, the result of staunch loyalty to the government during the French wars … It was that title—the lowest titled hereditary rank but a substantial achievement nevertheless for an industrial family—which Peel the future prime minister inherited'.¹³ The young Peel grew up during the wars that sprang from the chaos of revolutionary France.¹⁴ From 1793 to 1801, Britain was intermittently engaged in war with the new French Republic. Although Pitt had been adept in helping Britain to heal after the American Revolution, he was not a strong wartime leader.¹⁵ Moreover, the decade of martial conflict with France adversely affected the British people. Much of what had been gained in his first decade in office was suspended; fiscal, governmental, legal,

---

8 Ibid., 3; 99; 104.
9 Ibid., 99–106.
10 Ibid., 5.
11 Ibid.
12 Ibid., 6.
13 Ibid.
14 L. E. Elliott-Binns, *Religion in the Victorian Era* (London: Lutterworth Press, 1946), 11.
15 Evans, *Modern Britain*, 126.

and religious reforms were subordinated to the war efforts.[16]

During this turbulent period, Peel entered the world of the landed gentry. His entrée was facilitated by his father's money and political prestige. As part of the upper tier in the commercial middle class, Peel's family, like others in his rank, 'put a premium upon the acquisition of education.'[17] By 1800, the Peel family had become a part of the nobility yet had not abandoned certain middle-class attitudes. For the emerging middle class, 'education was both a "socially selective process" and "a fundamental tool of improvement"'.[18] This attitude would remain with Peel all his life. Peel attended the elite Harrow School from 1800 to 1804, which served as the bridge between elementary and university education and was reserved for sons of affluent families.[19]

The Newman Family and the Napoleonic Wars

John Henry Newman was born in London in 1801—the year that Pitt's long-serving government collapsed because of his mishandling of the conflicts with France. Pitt also had lost George III's favor because he had advocated Catholic emancipation during the negotiations for the Act of Union[20] with Ireland in 1800.[21] A new government was formed; fighting between England and France subsided with the Peace of Amiens in 1802. However, domestic instability—debt, inflation, a shrinking middle class, and a people weary of war—remained.[22]

---

16 Eric J. Evans, *Sir Robert Peel: Statesmanship, Power and Party* (London: Routledge, 2006), 12–13; 40.

17 Evans, *Modern Britain*, 36.

18 Quoted in Evans, *Modern Britain*, 36. See Peter Borsay, 'The Culture of Improvement', in *The Eighteenth Century, 1688–1815*, ed. Paul Langford (Oxford: Oxford University Press, 2002), 194.

19 W. H. G. Armytage, *Four Hundred Years of English Education* (Cambridge: Cambridge University Press, 1964), 62.

20 G. I. T. Machin (*Politics and the Churches in Great Britain: 1832–1868* [Oxford: Clarendon Press, 1977], 12) explained that Catholic emancipation, including 'the right [for Catholics] to sit in Parliament' became a major issue during the French Revolution; the denial of political equality led to an Irish rebellion in 1798, and eventually to the Act of Union (1800) which unfortunately codified Catholic inequality.

21 Evans, *Modern Britain*, 126; 95.

22 Ibid., 123–5.

During this period, the Newman family achieved some success. The Newmans belonged to the professional middle class, whose ideals, though tempered, were similar to the Peels', especially in regards to education. The Newmans' class 'depended, to a greater or lesser extent, on education, training, literacy and the acquisition of specialist skills'.[23] John Henry was the first child of John and Jemima Newman.[24] John Newman rose from humble beginnings and worked his way into the professional class as a banker. Jemima, who came from a family with 'a slightly higher social standing' than his father, was a woman of faith who 'encouraged her son to read' the Bible.[25] The Newmans seemed to have cultivated a happy home, despite living with the threat of war. One of John Henry's earliest memories came from this period; he recalled 'seeing lighted candles in the windows of his and other houses to celebrate victory in the battle of Trafalgar' in 1805.[26]

Peel and the Reaction to Revolution

After leaving Harrow, Peel matriculated at Christ Church, Oxford, in 1804–5. Peel, an excellent student, graduated in 1808 with a double first in classics and mathematics, 'the first person known to have achieved this intellectual feat'.[27] Soon after graduating, Peel followed his father into politics, although as a Tory. Through the influence of his father and Arthur Wellesley, later the Duke of Wellington, Peel was elected MP of a rotten borough, Cashel City in Ireland.[28]

---

23 Ibid., 32. Newman's background differed from that of Peel who had risen from the commercial middle classes into the aristocracy.

24 Newman had five siblings: Charles (1802–84), Harriet (1803–52), Francis (1805–97), Jemima (1808–79), and Mary (1809–28); Francis became a rival, while Mary was a close favorite.

25 Brian Martin, *John Henry Newman: His Life and Work* (Leominster: Gracewing, 2012), 10.

26 Martin, *Newman*, 11. As Evans (*Modern Britain*, 130) has pointed out, this battle, in which Horatio Nelson defeated Bonaparte's 'Franco-Spanish fleet off Cape Trafalgar' in 1805, was an important turning point in the Napoleonic wars.

27 Evans, *Peel*, 6.

28 Ibid. Evans (*Peel*, 100) defined 'rotten borough' as a 'term used often quite vaguely, to denote Parliamentary constituencies with few voters and usually controlled ("managed") by a large land owner or the Crown'.

'An aristocracy of exalted spirits'

Peel's choice of political party revealed the tenor of the times. Movement between the political parties, Tory and Whig, had been fluid in the latter half of the eighteenth century. The Whigs were ascendant, at least nominally, for most of that period. During the Napoleonic Wars, however, partisan lines began to be redrawn and British political radicalism, inspired by Thomas Paine, revolutionary France, and economic unrest, became prominent.[29] Both parties were populated by the wealthy and the landed and were concerned at the protests, speeches, and events triggered by international and domestic strife. However, one faction of the Whigs had been consistently sympathetic to the ideals of the French Revolution and remained so. Other Whigs, such as votaries of Burke and of Pitt, migrated to and aided in the resurgence of the Tory party. The Tories gradually emerged as the conservative party that responded to revolutionary challenges of the day;[30] and 'Peel was easily persuaded of the justice of the Tory cause. Its anti-reformist ideology and the reputation of order and administrative efficiency built up by Pitt [who was a Whig] suited both Peel's talents and his temperament'.[31]

By fortune and by political skill—in debate and in administration—Peel the backbencher advanced through the ranks quickly. In 1810, he was Under-Secretary of War and the Colonies. By 1812, he was appointed Chief Secretary for Ireland in the Liverpool administration (1812–27). This was an important post for the young man: 'Peel remained Chief Secretary for six years, the longest tenure of the post in the nineteenth century, during which time his resilience and his political skills were fully tested'.[32]

Peel worked tirelessly to consolidate the differences between the recently unified nations. One approach to bridging differences concerned Irish education. The Liverpool Administration pushed the imposition of a nationally administered 'mixed' Catholic and Protestant

---

29 Evans, *Modern Britain*, 153.

30 *Ibid.*, 108–9; 153–5; 165–9. Because 'Tory' connoted a variety of meanings, some positive, some negative, it was 'not regularly used as a descriptor of political attitudes until the late 1820s'.

31 Evans, *Peel*, 6–7.

32 Evans, *Peel*, 7.

education system. This endeavor was supported by Peel, who in a speech concerning the Irish budget in 1815, expressed his views on education:

> No man can be more sensible than I am of the advantages that would result to Ireland from the general diffusion of education ... I am confident that it is the only measure to which parliament can look for the introduction of habits of industry and morality among the lower orders in Ireland ... I am convinced ... that the only rational plan of education in Ireland, is one which should be extended impartially to children of all religious persuasions ... one which, while it imparts general religious instruction, leaves those who are its objects to obtain their particular religious discipline elsewhere ... Conclusive proofs have been afforded that the manner, character, and habits of a people are improved precisely in proportion to the diffusion of knowledge amongst them by a rational education ... I can conceive no more certain mode of effecting this most important object, than by adopting a judicious plan of general education.[33]

Peel's argument for national education did not become policy—the British government was not ready to organize a social project on such a large scale. A 'mixed' system in Ireland which effaced religious differences between Catholics and Protestants did not become reality until the 1830s. However, Peel's speech showed his early attempt at a politically expedient solution to an apparently intractable problem. It also anticipated a position that he would take on education in the late 1830s and his search for a national solution in 1841.

Newman's 'Great Change of Thought'

While Peel was making a name for himself in the Liverpool administration, Newman was coming of age. From 1808 to 1816 he attended Dr. Nicholas's school at Ealing. He was a very bright boy, given to reading, writing, acting, and playing music.[34] At school, Newman read Locke, Hume, and Paine, and briefly flirted with skepticism and radical ideas.[35] However, he also fell under the influence of an Evangelical Anglican

---

33 W. T. Haly, *The Opinions of Sir Robert Peel: Expressed in Parliament and in Public* (London: Whittaker & Co., 1843), 216.
34 Martin, *Newman*, 11–13.
35 Newman, *Apologia*, 15–16.

minister, Walter Mayers, whom he would later recall as 'the human means of this beginning of divine faith in me.'[36] He further attributed his religious growth to the writings of Thomas Scott, whose practical spirituality impressed upon him the importance of holiness.[37]

Newman was summoned home from Ealing in 1816, a year that altered the course of his life. After Napoleon's defeat at Waterloo in 1815, Britain experienced post-war economic and social turmoil and the Newman family was adversely affected as 'the Bank House of Messrs Ramsbottom, Newman & Co. [were compelled] to stop payment.'[38] Although the bank eventually paid its creditors, Mr. Newman decided to leave the business. The Newman family was forced to liquidate property and send the younger children to live with relatives for a time.[39] This experience deeply affected John Henry, who temporarily felt the sting of poverty and uncertainty.

Newman returned to Ealing for the summer, where he experienced a profound religious conversion. He described it a half-century later in his *Apologia pro Vita Sua*:

> When I was fifteen, (in the autumn of 1816,) a great change of thought took place in me. I fell under the influences of a definite Creed, and received into my intellect impressions of dogma, which, through God's mercy, have never been effaced or obscured... I received it [the doctrine of final perseverance] at once, and believed that the inward conversion of which I was conscious, (and of which I still am more certain than that I have hands and feet,) would last into the next life, and that I was elected to eternal glory.[40]

His family's crisis as well as Mayers's influence seemed to open Newman to God in new way. As a child Newman had been aware of God's presence as well as of certain Christian doctrines derived from Scrip-

---

36 Ibid., 16.
37 Joseph A. Komonchak, 'John Henry Newman's Discovery of the Visible Church (1816–1828)' (Ph.D. diss., Union Theological Seminary, New York, 1976), 370.
38 Louis Bouyer, *Newman: His Life and Spirituality*, trans. J. Lewis May (San Francisco: Ignatius Press, 2011), 10.
39 Dwight Culler, *The Imperial Intellect* (New Haven: Yale University Press, 1955), 4.
40 *Apologia*, 16.

ture.⁴¹ His adolescent intellectual travails had eclipsed this awareness, and yet, 'It would not only reawaken; it would transform, what in the child, was merely a passive impression, into a reasoned belief that was destined to remain an enduring factor in the life of the man.'⁴² Newman's conversion led him to recognize a disordered form of 'reason', a type of skepticism that had recently taken hold of him,

> in which self-reliance amounts to pride, and which refuses, on principle, to rely on any power external to itself. It was reason in this sense of the word, and reason very much alive in the boy John Henry, that led him to turn away from Christ, not indeed in order to live a life of sensual indulgence, but rather to entrench himself in a virtuous independence that refuses to bow to anything or anybody.⁴³

The particular notion of predestination that consumed him, conspired with his reason and yielded a kind of religious solipsism that placed the divine spirit and interior self over material creation and the body. He underscored this solipsism in his *Apologia*, recounting that he could 'rest in the thought of two and two only absolute and luminously self-evident beings, myself and my Creator.'⁴⁴ However, these errors eventually faded as he matured: Newman's encounter with the divine produced a new awareness and abolished his vain 'reason'. Newman distinctly recognized that his faith must have doctrine, which he did not self-imagine and project. For him religion must have a relational other to whom worship is directed, and that worship must be grounded in a sacred and visible community:

> First ... from the age of fifteen, dogma has been the fundamental principle of my religion: I know no other religion; I cannot enter into the idea of any other sort of religion; religion, as a mere sentiment, is to me a dream and a mockery. As well can there be filial love without the fact of a father, as devotion without the fact of a Supreme Being. What I held in 1816, I held in 1833, and I hold in 1864. Please God, I shall hold it to the end.

---

41 Bouyer, *Life and Spirituality*, 10–21.
42 Ibid., 21–2.
43 Ibid., 19.
44 Newman, *Apologia*, 16.

> Secondly, I was confident in the truth of a certain definite religious teaching, based upon this foundation of dogma; viz. that there was a visible Church, with sacraments and rites which are the channels of invisible grace. I thought that this was the doctrine of Scripture, of the early Church, and of the Anglican Church. Here again, I have not changed in opinion; I am as certain now on this point as I was in 1833, and have never ceased to be certain.[45]

This distinction that he discovered between a hubristic reason and a faith utterly dependent on God through the Church's creed formed the basic argument that he leveled against rationalistic forms of religion for the rest of his life. His conversion experience and the distinction he discovered between a faith and Church would develop significantly in the 1830s and were essential to Newman's letters to *The Times* in 1841.

Following his conversion, and in spite of his family's economic situation, Newman's father was able to find work as a brew master and the means to enroll his son at Trinity College, Oxford, in December 1816. However, Newman did not enter the college until the summer of 1817, when rooms became available. Soon after arriving at Oxford, Newman sent word home to his father about his new life at Oxford; he assured his parents that he was in good stead. A week after he had settled in, Newman sent his father an update that contained several amusing observations plus a comment about the rising star of Robert Peel:

> Almost all the—boys I was going to say, have left or are leaving College. Next week I suppose it will be quite a rare sight for a Collegian to be seen in the streets. Among the rest Thresher goes tomorrow. I suppose I shall leave next Monday week.
>
> Tell Mama, that having had for these last two or three days a cold, I have not immerged myself, that the said 'Commoner's' name is Bowden, and that he went this morning, and lastly that H. [Hans Henry Hamilton] has squeezed through his examination. I was in a very good place in the theatre yesterday. Tell Charles he would have liked to have seen the noblemen's dresses, as also the I-do-not-know-what-they-were, very fat men, I suppose DDs, in red robes, or scarlet, and the Proctors with sheepsskins. Mr Peel was made a Doctor of Laws by the Vice Chancellor.[46]

---

45 Ibid., 49–52.
46 LD, I, 37.

Peel, Member of Parliament for Oxford

Newman, who had watched Peel receive his honorary degree from the balcony of Oxford's Sheldonian Theatre, did not elaborate on the significance of this conferral. Peel was granted the degree two weeks after being elected MP for Oxford—a coveted political position. He had been invited to represent Oxford, in part, because of his recent stand against Catholic emancipation.

Peel's difficult tenure in Ireland included attempts to reform economic and fiscal problems endemic to the country; however, British oppression of Catholics remained the most significant issue which he confronted.[47] Peel continued to support the Act of Union (1800) which had codified religious discrimination and thus could not accept Irish Catholics' desire for greater political equality. In May 1817, Peel responded on the floor of Parliament to a new call by the Whigs for Catholic emancipation. He offered an impassioned defense against extending political liberty to Ireland: if Irish Catholics achieved parity they would disrupt the delicate political balance of Church and State in Britain; indeed, they would usurp the Church of England's favored status.[48]

Peel's speech, and overall leadership in Ireland, raised his political stature and established his reputation as a defender of Anglican orthodoxy—and Oxford noticed. This reputation was not the only reason for Peel's election by the university; rather, it was dissatisfaction with the other candidates. Nevertheless, the appearance of religious conviction won him the seat.[49] However, 'His policies on law and order in Ireland and against Catholic emancipation... conveyed the impression that he was a natural leader for the more extreme anti-Catholic Tories in Westminster. In reality, Peel was too ambitious and too shrewd to hitch himself irredeemably to a cause which might well be a political dead-end. Ultimately, however, he was to pay a heavy price for his reputation as an unswerving Protestant.'[50]

---

47 Evans, *Peel*, 10.
48 Norman Gash, *Mr. Secretary Peel: The Life of Sir Robert Peel to 1830* (Longman, Green, & Co., 1961), 208.
49 *Ibid.*, 214–16.
50 Evans, *Peel*, 11.

'An aristocracy of exalted spirits'

Although Newman did not recognize Peel's significance early on, over the years he embraced Peel's reputation as a dogged champion of the Church of England until his disastrous support of Catholic emancipation in 1829. However, in the 1820s, Peel enjoyed tremendous political success. Soon after he became MP for Oxford, he resigned from his secretariat and transformed his career by becoming an expert in fiscal policy and legal reform. Peel supported *laissez-faire* economics and adopted Adam Smith's and David Ricardo's notions of free markets and worked in concert with William Huskinsson.[51] Peel also led a committee that reformed banking practice that put the country back onto a gold standard. His work marked 'What was to become the dominant financial wisdom of the Victorian age—a sound, metal-based currency, buttressed by cheap government, balanced books and eventually low rates of direct and indirect taxation.'[52]

In 1820 Peel married Julia Floyd, and by 1822 had risen to a cabinet post, becoming Liverpool's Home Secretary. His ascent in concert with other like-minded men initiated what became known as Liberal Toryism. Reformist and forward-looking, Liberal Toryism was also a return to Pitt's policies, which had been interrupted as a result of the events of 1789:

> The French Revolution had a ... profound, polarizing effect on the generations of Liverpool and Peel. Wealthy politicians born between about 1770 and 1800 sincerely believed that they were engaged in a desperate struggle to uphold the old order, hereditary privilege and civilized values against what that quintessentially anti-French Revolutionary warrior Edmund Burke called the 'rash and speculative' opinion threatening to destroy the world they knew. Liberal Toryism in the 1820s might more appropriately be seen as the first, cautious recognition that the old world had not been destroyed and that, after Napoleon's defeat, ... governments could safely adapt to change rather than manning what some were beginning to see as anachronistic barricades.[53]

---

51 *Ibid.*, 12–13. Biographical entries for Ricardo and Huskinsson as well as for most other prominent individuals can be found in Appendix IV.
52 Evans, *Peel*, 14.
53 Evans, 15–16.

Following Pitt's line, Peel sought effective ways to reduce legal redundancies that had accumulated during the wars, streamline jury selection, reform prisons, and establish a police force in London.[54] In order to accomplish these reforms, Peel came to depend on some radical thinkers. Although he detested political radicalism, he was not so ideologically rigid as to reject ideas which he believed were rational and effective. For Peel, rationality and efficiency trumped ideology and party. This was especially true when Peel became acquainted with work of Jeremy Bentham, the radical reformer and architect of modern utilitarian thought. Peel eschewed Bentham's politics, yet he was interested in Bentham's proposals for a rational approach to law and government. The two men corresponded throughout the 1820s, forging a personal relationship up to Bentham's death in 1832.[55]

Newman at Oxford

Newman was affected, at least indirectly, by this political climate. Because of his parents' social standing and his father's profession, he seemed to have assimilated a basic British conservatism—respect for 'Church and king'. For much of the late eighteenth and early nineteenth centuries, this conservatism was shared by both Whigs and Tories, the upper and the middle classes. Newman also imbibed post-war Liberal Toryism, but not radicalism, espoused and practiced at Oxford, especially by its new MP, Robert Peel. Yet, as the 1820s unfolded, Newman found that there were limits to how far this Toryism could extend.

In the wake of his conversion, Newman was intent on developing his religious life and focusing on his studies rather than becoming involved with the politics of the day. He competed for and won a scholarship to Trinity College. As a student, he was known for eschewing the usual carousing of the Oxford gentry and committing himself to serious study under his tutor, Thomas Short.[56] During his final examinations for the baccalaureate, however, he imploded from his arduous habits of study and expectations: 'When the result list came out, Newman's

---

54 Ibid., 16–19.
55 Gash, *Secretary Peel*, 332–4.
56 Martin, *Newman*, 20–2.

name did not appear on the Mathematical side at all, and in Classics it was in the lower division of the second class, known contemptuously as being "under-the-line".[57]

After his near-collapse, Newman reconsidered his father's wish that he should embark on a career in law—he had already entered Lincoln's Inn in 1819. However, in light of his academic and religious experiences he 'persuaded' his father to allow him to enter ministry for the Church.[58] In 1821, Newman audited classes and privately tutored pupils. That same year his father declared bankruptcy and again the Newman family was singed by poverty and uncertainty. Despite these hardships, or because of them, Newman devised a bold move to stand for an Oriel College fellowship. Unlike his Trinity exams, Newman showed deft academic ability, and in 1822, was elected a Fellow at Oxford's most prestigious college—which ensured his own financial stability and enabled him to help his family.[59]

While an Oriel Fellow, Newman began to migrate away from the Evangelical doctrines that had so impressed him. In 1824, he was ordained a deacon and obtained a curacy at St. Clement's parish, Oxford. Working with the poor and sick, Newman soon abandoned the Calvinist notion that divided 'humanity into the saved and reprobate'.[60] Rather, he discovered the parishioners of St. Clement's were 'more or less converted to God'.[61] He also fell under influence of the prominent

---

57 Ibid., 23.
58 Ibid., 25.
59 Ibid., 25–7.
60 James K. Tolhurst, 'The Idea of the Church as a Community in the Anglican Sermons of John Henry Newman', *The Downside Review* 101/343 (July 1983): 140–64, at 142–4. Robert Christie ('The Clash of Evangelical Doctrine with Parish Experience: The Overlooked Catalyst to Newman's "Great Change in his Religious Opinions" in 1824–25', *Newman Studies Journal* 1/2 [Fall 1995]: 90–101, at 100–1) has recounted Newman's movement away from evangelical doctrines and practices because of his ministry with local parishioners as a young pastor: 'We find that Newman entered parochial ministry with a strong evangelical predisposition, but through the personal experiences of his parishioners' conversions, combined with the intellectual effects of his interpersonal relationships with his Oxford friends ... he was moved to question major tenets of evangelical doctrine, finally rejecting them'.
61 Martin, *Newman*, 30. Tolhurst, 'Idea of the Church', 146–8.

Oriel 'Noetics', Richard Whately and Edward Hawkins.[62] Whately befriended Newman, while also teaching him the language and method of empiricist epistemology and Aristotelian logic. Hawkins challenged Newman theologically to see the important role of history and tradition as well as apostolic teaching and the visible Church.[63] Newman later recounted that it was Hawkins who 'routed out evangelical doctrines' from his creed.[64] On 29 May 1825, Newman was ordained a priest of the Church of England.

The following year Newman was appointed a tutor at Oriel College. This position afforded him financial stability and allowed him to continue his pastoral work. Newman pursued his new role with vigor. His exuberance and personalist pedagogy, however, were not appealing to all of the students at Oriel. Nor did Oriel's newly elected provost and his former mentor, Edward Hawkins, agree with Newman's handling of the tutorship.[65] Newman was eventually relieved of his tutorial duties. Before this happened, however, Newman was installed as vicar of the church of St. Mary the Virgin, High Street, Oxford, in 1828.

Catholic Emancipation

As Newman attained greater prominence at Oxford, Peel's fortunes shifted. In 1827, after Liverpool suffered a stroke, George IV appointed George Canning to head a government. Canning advocated Catholic emancipation and Peel resigned in protest. However, Canning's government was short lived and George IV summoned the hero of Waterloo, Arthur Wellesley, Duke of Wellington, to form a new government. Peel had long been an ally of Wellington and returned to the cabinet as Home Secretary.[66]

---

62 See William Tuckwell, *Pre-Tractarian Oxford: A Reminiscence of the Oriel 'Noetics'* (1909), available at: http://archive.org/details/pretractarianoxfootuckrich.
63 Martin, *Newman*, 31. See Tolhurst, 'Idea of the Church', 159–60; 232.
64 Newman, *Apologia*, 19–20.
65 John T. Ford, 'Newman's View of Education: The Oxford Background', in *The Literary and Educational Effects of the Thought of John Henry Newman*, ed. Michael Sundermeier and Robert Churchill (Lewiston, New York: The Edwin Mellon Press, 1995), 27–47.
66 Evans, *Modern Britain*, 205–6.

'An aristocracy of exalted spirits'

Wellington was a military man and did not adapt well to a position that required tact and delicacy. His Whig opponents knew this and immediately challenged him. The issue upon which they made their stand was political equality for Dissenters or Nonconformists—people who were not members of the Church of England. The Whigs proposed to repeal the long-standing Test and Corporation Acts, which had prohibited those who did not explicitly adhere to the doctrines of the Church of England from holding political office.[67] In calling for change, the Whigs exploited the main weakness of Liberal Tories. While they had made modest economic and legal reforms, the Tories left untouched the crises of religious and political equality, 'and, in doing so, set Peel's career on a course at once more prominent and yet more contentious.'[68]

Peel and Wellington let the repeal pass. Soon after, they were caught unawares as 'Whig politicians ... wished to bring about the repeal of the Test and Corporation Acts in order to form a breach in the constitution so that Catholics might more fully enter in'.[69] However, the Whigs did not have to initiate proceedings for emancipation. Rather, they allowed Wellington's impetuousness to do it for them.

In 1829, Wellington's cabinet splintered. There had been a standing rivalry between Wellington and Husskinson, and the latter lost out. Several other Liberal Tories departed in protest: 'At a stroke Wellington had lost the balance which Peel considered vital for the ministry's survival ... The law of unintended consequences links the departure of the Huskinssonites with Catholic Emancipation. Peel suggested that Wellington replace [one of them] with Vesey Fitzgerald ... By the convention of the times, MPs accepting ministerial office had to submit themselves to their constituents for re-election.'[70] Fitzgerald, whose seat was in Ireland, was challenged by the Catholic nationalist and Peel adversary, Daniel O'Connell. O'Connell won in a land-slide; however, he could not join Parliament because he was Catholic. A crisis ensued and Wellington and Peel had inflicted this wound upon themselves.

---

67 *Ibid.*, 108.
68 Evans, *Peel*, 20.
69 Machin, *Politics and the Churches*, 20.
70 Evans, *Modern Britain*, 208.

Ireland became inflamed and the granting of Catholic emancipation was soon inevitable: 'The Emancipation Act of 1829 satisfied neither side." Protestants" screamed "betrayal", mostly at Peel, whom the Ultras[71] never fully trusted again ... Tory unity was shattered. The Catholics believed that what Emancipation had granted with one hand had been taken away with the other because they were still denied key positions and lacked certain rights.'[72] Peel's constituents at Oxford 'screamed betrayal'; one of those who protested at Peel's reversal was Newman. He was an impressionable boy of sixteen when he had seen Peel inaugurated as a champion of the University and of the Church. Peel's 'betrayal' shocked Newman, who relished the part he played in ousting Peel—now seen by him as a 'Rat'—from Oxford.[73] Indeed, this marked Newman's entry into political activism; as he recounted to his mother:

> We have achieved a glorious Victory. It is the first public event I have been concerned in, and I thank God from my heart both for my cause and its success. We have proved the independence of the Church and of Oxford. So rarely is either of the two in opposition to Government, that not once in fifty years can independent principle be shown; yet in these times, when its existence has been generally doubted, the moral power we shall gain by it cannot be overestimated ... No wonder that such as I, who have not, and others who have, definite opinions in favour of Catholic Emancipation, should feel we have a much nearer and holier interest than the pacification of Ireland, and should with all our might resist the attempt to put us under the feet of the Duke and Mr Brougham.
>
> Well, the poor defenceless Church has borne the brunt of it—and I see in it the strength and unity of Churchmen—An hostile account in one of the Papers says, 'High and Low Church have joined, being set on ejecting Mr Peel.'[74]

Following Peel's defeat, Newman again wrote to his mother about his concerns over State intervention in the Church. He made an insightful

---

71 'Ultra-Tories' were considered reactionaries, who did not want or accept social or political change, especially in the Church–State alliance.
72 Evans, *Modern Britain*, 208.
73 *Ibid.*
74 JHN to Mrs. Newman (1 March 1829), *LD*, II, 125–6. For the entire text of this and other significant letters from this period see Appendix II.

connection between the politics of Catholic emancipation and universal education; if radical reformers like Henry Brougham supported emancipation, it meant that other policies—like expanded suffrage, nationalized education (which was in line with Peel's 1815 prescription), and Church reform—were close behind. Writing to his mother on 13 March 1829, Newman concentrated on the difference between communal tradition bound education and individualist and Enlightenment education that had seemed to be ascendant:

> We live in a novel era—one in which there is an advance towards universal education.[75] Men have hitherto depended on others, and especially on the Clergy, for religious truth; now each man attempts to judge for himself. Now, without meaning of course that Christianity is in itself opposed to free inquiry, still I think it in fact at the present time opposed to the particular form which that liberty of thought has now assumed. Christianity is of faith, modesty, lowliness, subordination; but the spirit at work against it is one of latitudinarianism, indifferentism, republicanism, and schism, a spirit which tends to overthrow doctrine ... All parties seem to acknowledge that the stream of opinion is setting against the Church. I do believe it will ultimately be separated from the State, and at this prospect I look with apprehension ... Yet I do still think there is a promise of preservation to the Church, and, in its sacraments preceding and attending religious education, there are such means of heavenly grace, that I do not doubt it will live on in the most irreligious and atheistical times.
>
> And now I come to another phenomenon; the talent of the day is against the Church. The Church party, (visibly at least, for there may be latent talent, and great times give birth to great men,) is poor in mental endowments. It has not activity, shrewdness, dexterity, eloquence, practical powers. On what then does it depend? on prejudice and bigotry. This is hardly an exaggeration; yet I have good meaning and one honorable to the Church.[76]

Newman saw in Catholic emancipation a weakness in an older order passing away. He projected his concern onto what he detected as 'universal education': a means to promote a relativistic and rationalist

---

[75] Newman had been concerned with the rise of secular 'universal education' since his days at Oxford; see Arthur and Nichols (*John Henry Newman*, 20–2).
[76] *LD*, II, 129–30.

individualism over and against Church tradition. He also saw how stale Church tradition had become in terms of educating. For him, true education required intelligent and capable tutors, guided by reasoning and the vitality of ecclesial faith. The English Church was not closed to or shorn of new developments in knowledge, and yet had not cultivated the 'talent' to engage modern political and social developments and thus was slowly eclipsed. He saw the separation of Christian tradition and developments in knowledge as an emerging disaster for British society.

Both Newman and Peel saw the political outcome of Catholic emancipation in diverse ways: for Peel it was necessary to advance beyond religious differences and for Newman it marked a modern encroachment of the State over Church boundaries, especially in education. Their different views reverberated down to 1841.

Indeed, Peel never fully accepted the mantle as the defender of Church orthodoxy because he did not possess strong religious convictions. He tolerated the Ultras and the High Church for the sake of building a political coalition but privately he loathed their unbending religious and patrician beliefs. This attitude allowed him to reverse on emancipation despite Tory protest. However, 'Peel suffered for discounting their arguments. Peel was extremely able, but he was also proud, could be arrogant and found empathy with those of contrary view extremely difficult. A fatal flaw in his character was that, once convinced himself of the validity of an argument, he tended to regard it as proven and those who were not convinced as either mischievous or intellectually inferior.'[77] Peel had long since assented to a rationalist religion that, like the 'talent' of the day, saw faith as independent of the Church. Indeed, Peel's Tamworth speech of 1841 was one of the only public declarations of his religious views and they were consistent with what he had held as a young man. Norman Gash has summarized Peel's core religious beliefs:

> Because religion to him meant in effect duty and conduct, Peel also had faith in the progress of society and the spread of education and scientific knowledge. With so little dogmatic content to his own mind, he apprehended no danger to religion from the growth of secular knowledge. Indeed he welcomed it as a means of curing some of the

77 Evans, *Peel*, 26–7.

evils and bringing some of the divisions of his troubled contemporary society. In his speech when opening the Tamworth Reading Room in 1841 he asserted that there was nothing in knowledge which should harm religious belief. Only unwise men and fools formed unworthy conclusions of Divine nature and the Divine universe; and he expressed his conviction of the harmony of the Christian dispensation with all that reason assisted by revelation told them of the course and constitution of Nature. In religion as in politics Peel was essentially robust, optimistic, unmetaphysical and practical.[78]

When Peel put these religious convictions on display in his Tamworth address, Newman saw an opportunity to engage in an apology for faith arising from the heart of the Church, not a set of beliefs that did not necessarily depend on the Church.

The Reform Act and the Oxford Movement

Newman's fears in 1829 about the relationship of Church and State materialized in the 1830s. Peter Nockles notes: 'Oxford's repudiation of Peel in 1829 ... marks more accurately the true origin of the Oxford Movement than Keble's 1833 Assize Sermon ... For it was the campaign against Peel that first brought together the future Tractarian constellation on the basis of political discontent underpinned by moral principle.'[79] Although the Tractarians were concerned about ecclesiastical reform on the basis of principles drawn from the Apostolic Church, they were increasingly uneasy about the relationship that had developed between the Church and State. Education and Church governance became the arena in which they confronted the State.

In 1832, the Whigs sponsored the Reform Act, which, by granting broader political rights to the middle classes and consolidating 'rotten boroughs', overturned the political landscape. Although the Act was widely heralded—and feared by Britain's ruling class—it only brought

---

78 Gash, *Sir Robert Peel*, 186–7.
79 Peter Nockles, '"Church and King": Tractarian Politics Reappraised', in *From Oxford to the People*, ed. Paul Vaiss (Leominster: Fowler Wright Books, 1996), 96–7. Proponents of the Oxford Movement were also called 'Tractarians' after the *Tracts for the Times* (1833–41) which were written by different authors about the theology and aims of the movement; Newman wrote thirty of the ninety *Tracts*.

about modest changes. What was more important was what the Act signified and initiated: an age of social reform. The previous decade had been characterized by a return to fiscal stability, governmental reform, and a successful thwarting of radicalism. In contrast, the Reform Act brought with it calls for the transformation of many aspects of society.[80]

The Oxford Movement had its roots in the battles of 1829, but it began to blossom in 1833. In the wake of the Reform Act, members of the Movement, distinguishing themselves from the Ultras and High Churchmen, increasingly believed that an Erastian State[81] could no longer be a trusted ally for the Church. Their position was fraught with irony. The Oxford Movement arose and grew in reaction to what its participants saw as radical social reforms which increased the State's power. Yet the Movement's response was not reactionary; rather it conformed to the age by advocating reform—not, however, of the State but of the Church.

In December 1832, six months after the Reform Act passed, Newman began a Mediterranean voyage with his colleague, Hurrell Froude, and Froude's father. This was his first journey outside England.[82] On returning from his travels in the Mediterranean, Newman recognized the beginning of a protest movement at Oxford:

> The following Sunday, July 14th, Mr Keble preached the Assize Sermon in the university Pulpit. It was published under the title of 'National Apostasy'.[83] I have ever considered and kept the day, as the start of the religious movement of 1833.[84]

---

80 Evans, *Modern Britain*, 214–19.

81 A term associated with Thomas Erastus (1524–83), a Swiss Protestant theologian, in which the Church is subject to the State. M. L. Fell, 'Erastianism', *New Catholic Encyclopedia*, 2nd edn, vol. V (Detroit: Gale, 2003), 317–18. Newman wrote extensively on Erastianism in his *Certain Difficulties Felt by Anglicans in Catholic Teaching*, vol. I (London: Longman, Green, & Co., 1901).

82 See Mary Katherine Tillman, '"Realizing" the Classical Authors: Newman's Epic Journey in the Mediterranean', *Newman Studies Journal* 3/2 (Fall 2006), 60–77.

83 Newman, *Apologia*, 41, n. 1. Keble believed that the State usurped the rights of the Church, and reacted to the government's decision to suppress several Irish bishoprics.

84 Newman, *Apologia*, 41. David DeLaura (*Apologia*, 42, n.1) has remarked: 'The Oxford Movement began, practically speaking, in a series of meetings between July 25 and 29 at Rose's rectory at Hadleigh, Suffolk. Palmer, Froude, Perceval, and

'An aristocracy of exalted spirits'

Newman soon joined the Movement and, as Ian Ker has observed, began 'revealing himself as the master strategist'.[85] The ecclesiastical reforms which Newman and his allies proposed consisted in a return to the Church Fathers, a foray into 'red-hot Tractarianism' and the construction of the *via media*.[86]

Along with these intense efforts, Newman continued his pastoral ministry by preaching weekly at St. Mary's church in Oxford. His sermons complemented the *Tracts*, addressing the practical and spiritual dimensions of the Oxford Movement. Indeed, 'The whole range of activities, literary, homiletic, pastoral, and administrative were seen as part of the ministry'.[87]

Finally, because of his interest in the early Church and his efforts in the Movement, Newman felt compelled to reconsider his views about the Church. He eventually developed an ecclesiology that would occupy his attention throughout the 1830s—the *via media*. Newman's *via media* aimed to present the Anglican Church as the 'middle course' between Protestant Christianity and Roman Catholicism, which Avery Dulles has succinctly described:

> Fundamental to Anglo-Catholicism were the tenets that the Church of Christ must exist visibly in the world today, and that it must be both Catholic and apostolic. To defend these tenets against the objections coming respectively from the Protestant and Roman sides, Newman and his colleagues maintained that the Catholic Church had three branches: Orthodox, Roman, and Anglican, all of them stemming for the undivided Church of the first centuries. In relation to Roman Catholicism and Protestantism, Anglicanism represented a middle path, a *via media*, avoiding the errors of the two extremes. Protestants, with their biblicalism, fell short of recognizing the full content of faith as formulated in the creeds and dogmas of the early councils. Roman Catholics, by contrast, had overlaid the pure doctrine of the ancient Church with accretions that had no basis in Scripture or early tradition. Thus the Anglican communion, while not lacking Catholicity,

---

Rose agreed to unite in defending the doctrine of the Apostolic Succession and the Prayer Book.'
85 Ker, *Biography*, 81
86 Ibid., 90.
87 Tolhurst, 'Idea of the Church', 147.

could regard itself as the one in which the mark of apostolicity was most perfectly verified.[88]

Peel and the Conservative Ascendency

Peel's father died in 1830 and his baronetcy passed to his son. Now Sir Robert, Peel also succeeded his father as the MP for Tamworth, which had been his family home for decades. While Newman darted and dashed between Movement and ministry, Peel had gradually begun to rehabilitate his political standing.[89]

The Tories had resisted the Reform Act. Peel knew that he could not be seen as a Tory apostate again, and after the passage of the Reform Act, he saw an opening as a conservative reformer.[90] Peel had a threefold strategy to regain standing: 'first, to strengthen government and put 'public opinion' in its place; second to ensure so far was possible since he was out of office, that necessary changes strengthened, rather than weakened both the Constitution and Britain's governing elite; third to dispel the image of the Tory party as one of narrow reaction supported only by a small, unrepresentative proportion of the population.'[91] This third objective was crucial. Peel, the son of manufacturer, had never been part of the landed aristocracy and to some degree, he resented their parochial habits—in religion and in politics. Although never involved with the factory, he had observed that disruption of the agrarian order was essential to industrialization. His father's business had a lasting effect on how he thought and governed: acceptance of the landed gentry while promoting forward-looking policies, and adapting to what seemed to him the most rational course of action.

---

88 Avery Dulles, 'Newman: The Anatomy of a Conversion', in *Newman and Conversion*, ed. Ian Ker (Edinburgh: T. & T. Clark, 1997), 28; cf. Newman, *Apologia*, 64–5.

89 Evans, *Peel*, 28–9.

90 According to Evans (*Peel*, 42), Peel began a 'Conservative' faction within the Tory party in the early 1830s. The terms 'Tory' and 'Conservative', although distinct, were often used interchangeably. James J. Sack has traced how this label gained political currency: 'The Quarterly Review and the Baptism of the "Conservative Party"—A Conundrum Resolved', *Victorian Periodicals Review* 24/4 (Winter 1991): 170–2.

91 Evans, *Peel*, 33.

In 1834, a series of reforms such as the Poor Law were initiated in order to address the 'rapid changes being brought about by the industrial revolution'.[92] Peel was asked by William IV to serve as First Lord of the Treasury.[93] After a brief 'Hundred Days' ministry, Peel resigned because he did not believe that he had the support in the House of Commons to govern effectively. His only lasting accomplishment during his tenure was the establishment of an Ecclesiastical Commission.[94] The commission was to enact what Peel and other politicians saw as much-needed Church reform. For Newman and his Oxford conspirators this was but another insidious example of Erastianism.[95]

Peel also exploited his time in office to advance conservative solutions for reform. His 'Tamworth Manifesto' in 1834 was 'the logical outworking of the message of 1832'; although addressed his local constituency, the speech was intended for the national stage.[96] The Manifesto sought to maintain the unity of Church and State, while accepting moderate parliamentary reform, and to broaden the Tory middle-class base while rejecting democracy outright.[97]

By 1837, Peel had offered his outline of conservative political reforms and had begun to consolidate the party. For example, he actively cultivated a relationship with farming communities for political gains, supporting 'local agricultural societies and farmers' clubs'. These groups in turn formed political lobbies, generally in support of both parties; nonetheless, the agricultural sector drifted to the Conservative cause: 'In 1841 they provided a fundamental element in the party to whose victory at the polls he [Peel] owed his position as prime minister'.[98]

Peel also began to see that education was to become a battleground upon which Tories, Whigs, Radicals and the Church would meet. In

---

92 Evans, *Peel*, 31–2.
93 As Evans notes (*Peel*, 34), the First Lord of the Treasury was 'the senior official title of the prime minister'.
94 Ibid., 41.
95 *LD*, V, 24; 38.
96 Evans, *Peel*, 40.
97 Ibid., 41.
98 Norman Gash, *Aristocracy and the People: Britain 1815–1865* (Cambridge: Harvard University Press, 1979), 179–80.

November 1837, he wrote to his close friend John Wilson Crocker and reiterated his concern that direct State intervention in education would bring an end to religion. Peel expressed his belief that it was incumbent upon the Church to unite and to establish national education:

> Education is the great question to which the public attention should be called ...
>
> Two material points. First, if there is to be a national system of education, excluding the direct intervention of the National Church (at least only tolerating its intervention), there is an end of the Church, and probably an end of any religious feeling at all ultimately.
>
> But secondly, there is no ground on which the members of the Church, if united (lay and clerical), can so confidently and successfully defy agitation. They have it in their power to act independently of Sovereigns, Ministers, and Parliaments; to institute a system of education, based on instruction in the doctrines of the Church, which, if worked out with moderation and discretion, shall command much more of public confidence than any Government system founded on a different principle.
>
> It won't suffice to abuse the Government plan.
>
> There must be a cordial concert between the clergy and the laity, and a determination to undertake a duty which probably can only be well performed by voluntary exertions, unaided by Government.[99]

These opinions seemed in line with Peel's development of an expansive conservatism that began in 1834. In a speech at the Merchant Taylors' Hall in 1838, Peel provided a further refinement of his vision for reform conservatism:

> We feel deeply and intimately that in the union of the conservative party in the country is one of the best guarantees for internal tranquillity and the maintenance of our ancient institutions ... By that union we shall best be enabled to maintain the mild predominance of the Protestant faith in this country and in every part of the United Kingdom. By that union we shall be enabled and by that alone to promote what we call conservative principles. If you ask me what I mean by conservative principles ... I will, in conclusion, briefly state what I mean ...

---

99 Peel to Croker, 12 November 1837, in *The Croker Papers: The Correspondences and Diaries*, ed. Louis J. Jennings (London: John Murray, 1884), 323.

> By conservative principles I mean, that co-existent with equality of civil rights and privileges, there shall be an established religion and imperishable faith, and that that established religion shall maintain the doctrines of the Protestant Church. By conservative principles I mean, a steady resistance to every project which would divert church property from strictly spiritual uses. By conservative principles I mean, a maintenance of the settled institutions of church and state, and I mean also the maintenance, defence, and continuation of those laws, those institutions, that society, and those habits and manners which have contributed to mould and form the character of Englishmen ... and the enjoyment of a national and pure form of religion, which is at once the consolation of the virtuous man, and is also the best guarantee which human institutions can afford for civil and religious liberty.[100]

Although Peel had begun to gradually build consensus around his reform-minded ideas of conservatism, his achievements were beset by difficulties, notably in his dealings with Viscount Melbourne's administration, and the ascension of Melbourne's political protégé Queen Victoria. Indeed, through the maneuverings of Melbourne, the young queen involved Peel in a politically embarrassing situation. John Prest has explained what has since become regarded as the 'Bedchamber Crisis': 'In 1839, when the Whig majority fell to five ... and the ministry resigned, Peel was unable to take Melbourne's place because the queen would not grant him the expression of confidence for which he asked—the dismissal of some (the queen thought he demanded all) of the Whig ladies of the bedchamber. Peel could have forced the issue, but given his respect for royalty he preferred to yield and allow Melbourne to carry on.'[101] That same year Peel's opinions on the State, religion and education appeared subtly to change. His convictions again became tempered by political expedience. This shift can be detected in his views on education. In 1839, the Established Church and Ultra-Tories rallied to defeat a bill passed by Melbourne's government which would have laid the foundation for nationalized education. Peel did not side with

---

100 *The Peel Banquet: Speeches of the Rt. Hon. Sir Robert Peel, Bart., Lord Stanley, and Sir James Graham, Bart., at Merchant Taylors' Hall, May 12, 1838* (London: Robert Tyas; Edinburgh: J. Menzies, 1838); excerpt from: http://www.historyhome.co.uk/peel/politics/conprin2.htm.

101 John Prest, 'Sir Robert Peel' (1788–1850), in *DNB*.

the Ultras or the Church. He developed a nuanced position, which subtly shifted away from his prior pronouncements.[102] Peel opposed the Whigs' Committee of Council for education as essentially unconstitutional, but he felt that this did not exclude other ways in which a national policy might be implemented. Further, he sought only a modest concession for the Church to be involved in any future plan for education:[103]

> I disclaim, therefore, any intention to demand for the Church Establishment the right to interfere with the religion or the other institutions of those who are dissenters from its doctrines. This, however, I claim for the establishment, that no system of national education shall be founded, which studiously excludes from the superintendence and control of education, given to the children of the establishment, the dignitaries of the Established Church.[104]

Save for 1829, Peel believed that he had been a consistent proponent of conservative principles throughout his career. He altered course only where his notion of reason and prudence necessitated change. In spite of his repeated pledges to uphold the delicate balance of Church and State, over the course of the 1830s an explicit shift emerged in Peel's thinking. Whether this change came about through study, correspondence, or some combination thereof is unclear. His intolerance for the Ultras, and for what he perceived as religious zealotry, became more pronounced. Accordingly, he thought that from the Ecclesiastical Commission to educational policy, the Church should be increasingly subordinated to the aims of the secular ministrations of the State. This represented a tremendous move away from what he explained to Crocker in 1837. (Newman perceived this shift and exploited it in his letters to *The Times*.) Yet Peel saw no other way than the subordination of Church to State.[105] His desire was to transform the party and

---

102 Richard Aldrich, 'Peel, Politics and Education, 1839–46', *The Journal of Educational Administration and History* 13/1 (1981): 11–23, at 13.

103 According to Haly (*Opinions*, 210–13), Peel clearly had shifted his position on education with respect to Dissenters and other sectarian groups.

104 *The Speeches of the Late Right Honorable Sir Robert Peel, Bart.* (London: George Rutledge & Co., 1853), III, 645.

105 Similar to Evans, Boyd Hilton ('Peel: A Reappraisal', *The Historical Journal* 22/3 (September 1979): 585–614) claimed that once Peel became possessed of a

expand its base—and bigotry could not be a plank in the party platform. In many ways he was successful in achieving this goal, although there were some casualties.

These developmental shifts in principle and outlook provided the background to Peel's Tamworth address in 1841. His speech would reveal his wish for religion tempered and mediated by scientific knowledge and political reason while appealing to educational and economic improvements designed to reach a wide audience. For Peel, the contents of the Tamworth address seemed fitting and uncontroversial. Many, including Newman, did not share Peel's sanguine views.

Newman's *Experimentum Crucis*

Newman's work in the 1830s resulted in personal and religious development. Like Peel, Newman gradually and implicitly expanded or altered certain views. Several incidents and crises, however, would make these changes explicit. Between 1839 and 1841, Newman faced increasingly critical questions about his role in the Oxford Movement.[106] Also, suspicions that he was drifting from his native communion towards the Roman Catholic Church appeared in various letters and journals.[107] Such criticism weighed heavily upon Newman, who at times seemed not to know what or whom to believe.[108]

Newman continued to edit and write theological tracts that attempted to reassure the adherents of the Oxford Movement, while

---

conclusion he tended to be inflexible; Hilton's primary focus was on Peel's economic ideology; however, an analogue for his views about education and religion can be made.

106 For example, Newman wrote J. W. Bowden on 17 January 1840 that *The Record* had written something that was 'most *bitter* (that's the only word) against Keble, and me [Newman], and the new volumes of Froude. They are past *anger*; they say we are far worse than the unspiritual High Church of the last century, as sinning more against light—i.e. there was no "Record" then' (*LD*, VII, 216).

107 W. F. Mandel, 'Newman and his Audiences: 1825–1845', *Journal of Religious History* 24/2 (June 2000): 143–58.

108 See David Delio, 'A Multitude of Subtle Influences: Faith, Reason, and Conversion in Newman's Thirteenth Oxford University Sermon', *Newman Studies Journal* 5/1 (Spring 2008): 77–86.

simultaneously provoking the wrath of his critics.[109] Newman relished this role as a 'controversialist' mediating between the goals and aspirations of the Oxford Movement and those who would question his loyalty to the Anglican tradition. Indeed, he had reached his apogee of influence within the Movement; as he later reminisced in his *Apologia pro Vita Sua*: 'In the spring of 1839 my position in the Anglican Church was at its height. I had supreme confidence in my controversial *status*, and I had a great and still growing success, in recommending it to others.'[110]

However, Newman's exalted, 'controversial *status*' was tenuous. Twenty-five years later, he interpreted this period in his life as a 'great revolution of mind'—a period characterized by this poignant question: 'For who can know himself, and the multitude of subtle influences which act upon him?'[111] This question seemingly permeated his mind and work during this time, thus underscoring what he could not have known then:

> What will best describe my state of mind at the early part of 1839, is an Article in the British Critic for that April. I have looked over it now, for the first time since it was published; and have been struck by it for this reason:—it contains the last words which I ever spoke as an Anglican to Anglicans. It may now be read as my parting address and valediction, made to my friends. I little knew it at the time. It reviews the actual state of things, and it ends by looking towards the future.[112]

---

109 For example, Newman wrote to Mr. J. W. Bowden (*LD*, VII, 5), 'by the by have you observed that most grotesque of pieces of news in the *Christian Observer* of this month about me? One step alone is wanted—to say that I am the Pope *ipsissimus* in disguise'. Gerard Tracey (*ibid*), noted that apparently a 'correspondent' had speculated about a connection between Newman and Wiseman, who was the rector of the English College in Rome as well as a Professor of Oriental Languages; Wiseman's article on the Donatists in the *Dublin Review* in July 1839 made a great impression on Newman: 'In January, if I recollect aright, in order to meet the popular clamour against myself and others, and to satisfy the Bishop, I had collected into one all the strong things which they, and especially I, had said against the Church of Rome, in order to their insertion among the advertisements appended to our publications' (*Apologia*, 81).

110 Newman, *Apologia*, 81.
111 *Ibid*.
112 *Ibid.*, 82.

In the summer of 1839, Newman retreated for the 'Long Vacation' to study Patristic authors as well as the history of the Monophysite controversy of the fifth century. He was particularly 'absorbed in the doctrinal issue' raised by this crisis in the early Church and this was linked to his ongoing interest in the *via media*.[113] Towards the close of his vacation, Newman became alarmed by surge of doubt about 'the tenableness of Anglicanism':

> My stronghold was Antiquity; now here, in the middle of the fifth century, I found, as it seemed to me, Christendom of the sixteenth and the nineteenth centuries reflected. I saw my face in that mirror, and I was a Monophysite. The Church of the *Via Media* was in the position of the Oriental communion, Rome was, where she now is; and the Protestants were the Eutychians. Of all passages of history, since history has been, who would have thought of going to the sayings and doings of old Eutyches, that *delirus senex*, as (I think) Petavius calls him, and to the enormities of the unprincipled Dioscorus, in order to be converted to Rome![114]

The doctrinal issue in the Monophysite controversy that alarmed Newman centered upon the varying interpretations of Christ's natures. Newman discovered that both Eutyches and Dioscorus, radical successors of Cyril of Alexandria, had initiated a theological controversy at the council of Ephesus in 449.[115] Newman recognized the Christological excesses of 'of the Oriental communion'—most likely a reference to the Nestorians.[116] To his astonishment, these two extreme positions fell to either side of the arguments given by the Catholic 'Fathers of Chalcedon':[117] Pope Leo's 'Tome' and certain of Cyril's Christological formulations. In contrast to the 'heretical positions', Leo and Cyril

---

113 *Ibid.*, 64–5, 96.

114 *Ibid.*, 96; *delirus senex* may be translated: 'a senseless or wily old man'. Dionysius Petavius, the Latinized name of Denis Pétau, SJ (1583–1652).

115 Henry Chadwick, *The Early Church* (London: Penguin Books, 1993), 200–2. At this council, both Dioscorus and Eutyches sought to restore a previously condemned doctrine which asserted that Christ had 'one nature after union' (*monophysis*).

116 Chadwick, *Early Church*, 203.

117 Newman, *Apologia*, 97.

presented Christ as having two natures together in his divine person.[118] Newman's discovery found expression in an astonishing analogy:

> It was difficult to make out how the Eutychians or Monophysites were heretics, unless Protestants and Anglicans were heretics also ... The drama of religion, and the combat of truth and error, were ever one and the same. The principles and proceedings of the Church now, were those of the Church then; the principles and proceedings of heretics then, were those of Protestants now. I found it so,—almost fearfully; there was an awful similitude, more awful, because so silent and unimpassioned, between the dead records of the past and the feverish chronicle of the present.[119]

Following this analogy and its disquieting conclusion Newman experienced yet another occasion of doubt. In September, one of his friends, 'an anxiously religious man', pointed out some 'palmary words of St. Augustine' embedded within an article published in the *Dublin Review* by a prominent Roman Catholic clergyman, Nicholas Wiseman.[120] The article traded on a comparison between the Donatist controversies of Augustine's day and the current divide between Roman Catholics and Anglicans. At first, Newman 'did not see much' in the article, until his friend stressed Augustine's words, *securus judicat orbis terrarum* (the whole world judges with assurance).[121] With these words 'ringing in [his] ears'[122] Newman again perceived a profound analogy: the Roman Catholic Church—spread throughout the whole world—could make judgments about doctrinal matters with assurance in contrast to other Churches in schism. In dramatic fashion, Newman re-lived this profound moment in his *Apologia*:

> For a mere sentence, the words of St. Augustine struck me with a power which I never had felt from any words before ... they were like the 'Tolle, lege,—Tolle, lege,' of the child, which converted St. Augustine himself. 'Securus judicat orbis terrarum!' By those great words of the ancient Father, interpreting and summing up the long

---

118 Chadwick, *Early Church*, 204.
119 Newman, *Apologia*, 97.
120 Ibid., 98.
121 Ibid.
122 Ibid.

and varied course of ecclesiastical history, the theory of the *Via Media* was absolutely pulverized.[123]

These two occasions, or 'sudden visitations' of doubt, marked the gradual abeyance of his Anglican identity.[124] As he later recalled:

> After a while, I got calm, and at length the vivid impression upon my imagination faded away ... The heavens had opened and closed again. The thought for the moment had been, 'The Church of Rome will be found right after all;' and then it had vanished. My old convictions remained as before.[125]

Even with the reassurance of his 'old convictions', Newman would experience moments of uncertainty over the next few months, for example finding himself in prayer for ecclesiastical unity with Rome[126] and publishing a provocative exposition in January of 1840, 'On the Catholicity of the English Church'.[127] Yet, his correspondence and other writings during this tumultuous period revealed that he was still seeking to maintain some form of Anglican identity that would distance himself from what he thought were the excesses of the Roman Catholic Church.[128]

Newman's religious crises precipitated two significant events. First, he 'made arrangements for giving up [his editorship of] *The British Critic*, in the following July'.[129] Second, during the interval between winter and spring 1840, Newman began to consider leaving his residence at Oriel College in Oxford and retiring to Littlemore, between two and three miles distant from Oxford, where he had built a small church.[130] However, 'He had no intention of severing his connections with Oxford.

---

123 Ibid., 98–9.
124 See David Delio, 'Calculated to Undermine Things Established: Newman's Fourteenth Oxford University Sermon', *Newman Studies Journal* 5/2 (Fall 2008): 69–83.
125 Newman, *Apologia*, 99.
126 Ibid., 103.
127 Ibid., 107.
128 Ker, *Biography*, 193.
129 Newman, *Apologia*, 113.
130 Ibid., 109.

He could still take the Sunday afternoon service at St. Mary's.'[131] During these early spring months, Newman recognized that he would somehow have to justify his place in the Anglican Communion:

> This was in March, 1840, when I went up to Littlemore. As it was a matter of life and death with us [the Movement], all risks must be run to show it. When the attempt was actually made, I had got reconciled to the prospect of it, and had no apprehensions as to the experiment; but in 1840, while my purpose was honest, and my grounds of reason satisfactory, I did nevertheless recognize that I was engaged in an *experimentum crucis*. I have no doubt that then I acknowledged to myself that it would be a trial of the Anglican Church, which it had never undergone before.[132]

Amidst the swirl of his bold experiment, Littlemore provided a refuge where he could discern the interior dilemma that had become evident to himself and to others.[133]

Newman again considered resigning his post at St. Mary's church and retiring permanently to Littlemore in order to establish a contemplative Anglican community.[134] In October 1840, he sought the advice of his friend and mentor, John Keble, about this and other personal dilemmas.[135] Listing reasons why he was inclined towards resignation, he explained that among other things he believed that he had lost his standing among his parishioners.[136] More importantly, the Oxford

---

131 Ker, *Biography*, 195.
132 Newman, *Apologia*, 108.
133 According to Ker (*Biography*, 197–200), Newman, in his correspondence during this period and for the next seven months, revealed his crisis to others—in particular his exchange with Keble in the fall of 1840. As for Littlemore, it seems that Newman's dreams of a monastic community were slow to materialize since he had acquired a mere 'hovel such as St. Martin lived in or St. Basil' (*ibid.*, 197).
134 *LD*, VII, 416. In his *Apologia* (109), Newman noted that he had been contemplating a departure from St. Mary's since 1839. As vicar of St. Mary's (1828–43), Newman had pastoral responsibility for Littlemore, a village about three miles south of Oxford, where he supervised the construction of a church that was consecrated on 22 September 1836; the building, now enlarged, is still used as an Anglican church.
135 *LD*, VII, 416–18.
136 *LD*, VII, 417. Newman believed that he still held considerable sway over his Oxford students, although he felt that such influence was a distortion of his office as pastor of St. Mary's and feared that his position would soon turn into a

establishment had 'shown a dislike of [his] preaching' and some had begun to speak out against his views—even from his own pulpit! In spite of harassments and despite his own doubts, Newman averred:

> I cannot disguise from myself that my preaching is not calculated to defend that system of religion which has been received for 300 years, and of which the Heads of Houses are the legitimate maintainers in this place. They exclude me, as far as may be, from the University Pulpit; and, though I never have preached strong doctrine in it, they do so rightly, so far as this, that they understand that my sermons are calculated to undermine things established. I cannot disguise from myself that they are. No one will deny that most of my sermons are on moral subjects, not doctrinal; still I am leading my hearers to the Primitive Church, if you will, but not to the Church of England.[137]

Newman also explained to Keble that he believed certain topics in his tracts, articles, and sermons, as well as his activities in general, were disposing some Anglicans toward Rome.[138] Newman had received several letters which confirmed this conviction.[139]

Keble responded over a week later. While taking into account Newman's apprehensions, he advised him to remain at St. Mary's. Keble did not believe that Newman had actually lost touch with his parish or had incited any conversions to Rome. Although conversation about Newman at Oxford had been rather pointed, Keble believed that a precipitous break from St. Mary's would create more uproar than if

---

pseudo-university office. On the importance of personal influence for both his parishioners and his students, see John F. Crosby, 'Newman on the Personal', *First Things* 13/125 (August/September, 2002): 43–9.

137 *LD*, VII, 417.

138 There is no mention of the apostolic origins of the Orthodox Church in the letter; however, Newman believed that the Orthodox had a place in true apostolic succession; see Ker, *Biography*, 61–2; 353–4.

139 Newman corresponded with those who were intrigued by his writings on the Roman Church; for example, on 19 October 1840 (*LD*, VII, 407–8), he replied to several letters from Mary Holmes: 'As to your questions about the Church of Rome, they are most pertinent; there is nothing unfair or extravagant in them, and you have a right to an answer'. Holmes had Newman as a spiritual director, 'until her conversion to the Catholic Church in 1844'—the year prior to Newman's own conversion (*LD*, VII, 524).

he remained.¹⁴⁰ Newman agreed—for the time being; nevertheless, he resolved to minimize his role at St. Mary's, as well as to relinquish his editorship of *The British Critic*.¹⁴¹ Four months after sharing his concerns with Keble, Newman became entangled in the controversy with Peel over their competing ideas and commitments about the relationship between Church and State, religious belief and knowledge.

Newman and Peel: Idealists and Reformers

In the decades leading up to the Tamworth controversy both Peel and Newman were shaped by the opportunities and circumstances of their age, although they were more than the sum of their experiences. At their core both were idealists: Peel was driven by the idea of service to the Crown and country by means of expedient governance; Newman by God's fundamental relationship to persons and the Church as an oracle of divine truth. Neither wavered from their ideals. Each man was also a reformer advocating change: Peel sought economic, social, and educational reforms from a variety schools of thought; Newman desired a return to apostolic principles: holiness, faith, and the Church. Their core convictions and their quests for change transformed them and the effects of these transformations can be found in their oblique encounter of 1841.

In subsequent years, Peel's determination for efficient conservatism and hostility to the landed gentry ended in a disastrous splintering of the Tory party. He retired from political leadership and died unexpectedly in 1850.¹⁴² Newman's ideals—and his doubts about the *via media*—led him to the Roman Catholic Church. His conversion initiated a tumultuous yet successful vocation as an Oratorian priest up to his death in 1890.

---

140 *LD*, VII, 432.
141 Newman, *Apologia*, 111–12.
142 Evans, *Peel*, 78–80.

✣ 2 ✣

Adult Education and Peel's Tamworth Address

THE YEAR 1841 was a pivotal one for Sir Robert Peel. Having weathered Whig administrations throughout the 1830s and rehabilitated his image, he was poised to lead the Tories to victory in the coming months.[1] By the end of August, Peel swept into office as First Lord of the Treasury. In January of that year, however, he was still the leader of the opposition in the House of Commons. Along with his national political role, he was a Member of Parliament for Tamworth. In 1840–1, Peel decided to contribute money, time, and his stature to the community.[2] Whether his decision was politically motivated—for Peel sensed that the Tories would eventually come to power—or a genuine expression of patronage, is not clear, but it was probably some combination thereof. By January 1841, Peel had made a substantial financial donation and a commitment to serve as President of Tamworth's newly established library and reading room.

---

1 According to Evans (*Peel*, 46–52), by 1841 Peel had consolidated power and the Tory party really had no choice other than to follow him.

2 Gash (*Aristocracy and the People*, 182) described Tamworth's influence on Peel: 'Along with the basic themes of law, order, and defence of the great institutions of the country, including the established Churches of England and Scotland and the House of Lords, he [Peel] preached the Tamworth gospel of progressive improvement, the enlargement of the party's social base, and the improvement of party organization in the constituencies. To those who attached importance to social mobility and opportunities for wealth, talent and intelligence, he pointed to himself, the son of a cotton spinner, as proof that there was no natural barrier between the Conservative party and the middle classes of society'.

'An aristocracy of exalted spirits'
Britain's Adult-Education Movement

Institutions dedicated to reading, lectures, and research and open to all classes were not common in Peel's England.[3] For example, the Royal Society was the preserve of the landed or up-and-coming mercantile class.[4] Libraries were not government-sponsored nor did they command broad public support; they were not considered a public good and were either ignored or regarded by the landed and the learned as futile and even dangerous for the working classes. The occasional funding of libraries depended upon either private individuals or private societies which promoted education or learning, such as Henry Brougham's Society for the Diffusion of Useful Knowledge (SDUK).[5]

The Tamworth Library and Reading Room provided educational opportunity for the men and women in the Midlands. The institute was initiated and erected through private benefaction. Although designed and paid for by benefactors, the library's foundation was not arbitrary or isolated; rather, it participated in the emerging adult education movement which had developed steadily in England since the eighteenth century.

Two sources sparked this movement. First, in spite of Burke's protestations and Canning's fears of Jacobinism, Enlightenment ideals had spread from the Continent to England. These ideals, inspired in part by French political theory, the encyclopedias of the *philosophes*, and the application of scientific discovery to manufacturing, eventually 'led to a demand by the working classes for wider educational opportunities.'[6] The second source flowed from Scotland, which had developed a robust, independent, and coherent education system superior to that in England. The Scottish system included tradesmen as well as the landed. A religious, rational, and discursive approach to education was promoted, which in turn spread to all classes in society.[7]

---

3 Thomas Kelly, *A History of Adult Education in Great Britain* (Liverpool: Liverpool University Press, 1992), 112–17.

4 *Ibid.*, 113.

5 *Ibid.*, 165.

6 H. C. Barnard, *A Short History of English Education from 1760–1844* (London: University of London Press, 1961), 104.

7 Alasdair MacIntyre, 'The Idea of an Educated Public', in *Education and Values: The Richard Peters Lectures*, ed. Graham Haydon (London: Institute of Education,

Adult Education and Peel's Tamworth Address

The influence of the Continental and Scottish Enlightenments upon England soon became apparent. Lively conversation, lectures, and various print media circulated through coffee houses, Christian organizations, 'working men's libraries, book clubs, and mutual improvement societies.'[8] However, the core of the adult education movement took place in what were called mechanics' institutes. Their principal architect was George Birkbeck, a physician and professor of natural philosophy at the Anderson Institute in Glasgow. At the turn of the nineteenth century, Birkbeck decided to offer lecture courses and designed experiments for 'mechanics'. The 'mechanics', a term generally extended to refer to the British working class and the men with whom Birkbeck worked, were not simply machine operators, but skilled craftsmen.[9] According to Thomas Kelly, Birkbeck's decision to offer opportunities for these men had important consequences: 'Just as these institutes may be regarded as a downward extension of middle-class literary and philosophical societies, so also they may be regarded as an upward extension of the movement of the elementary education of children, which drew widespread support ... From yet another point of view they may be looked on as an educational reflection of the new political and economic aspirations of the working classes—aspirations which were repressed during the French wars but found an outlet once more, in the post-war years, in trade unionism, in the socialist and co-operative movements, and in demands for Parliamentary reform.'[10] Mechanics' institutes were aided by Brougham's tireless advocacy of utilitarian education, his SDUK, and 'penny' literature (cheap, digestible tracts on various scientific, political, and economic topics) aimed at spreading knowledge. The institutes, however, met with mixed success. Their initial and almost exclusive emphasis upon science, and affiliations with philosophic radicalism, presented two distinct challenges. First, most mechanics did not have the time to pursue extensive scientific research and study; nor did they want such a restrictive program. According to Kelly, 'The institutes suffered ... from their exclusive pre-occupation

1987), 18–21. See also Kelly, *History*, 124.
  8 Kelly, *History*, 64–98; 117.
  9 *Ibid.*, 119; 117.
 10 *Ibid.*, 116.

with scientific education. A great many people were not really interested in science: they were interested in literature, or in politics and economics, which were almost universally barred as controversial.'[11]

Second, 'The Tories and the Church either stood aside or were openly hostile' to the movement.[12] Indeed, the Church of England and Evangelical traditions, while active in educating their youth, did not offer much for working adults. Wealthy young adults attending college or university were exposed to classical and current trends in learning while also trying, more or less, to integrate these sorts of knowledge into their religious lives.[13] However, for the working class the High and Low Churches offered confessional and religious knowledge, but nothing of the new sciences that had quickly become popular. Save for developments in Scotland and some Christian organizations, there was no occasion for them to see the potential harmony between their faith and the new knowledge and thus many were left to seek edification outside their church communities.

Despite these difficulties, mechanics' institutes expanded in the 1830s to include literature, politics, and in some cases music and other arts. As a result they grew rapidly in popularity. By 1841, there were over 300 institutes in England alone.[14] Of all the varieties of adult education in England, the Tamworth Library and Reading Room resembled a revised and improved mechanics' institute.

Peel was a latecomer to the adult-education movement. His father had worked with Robert Owen (1771–1858) to improve conditions for factory workers, and this included education.[15] In contrast, the younger Peel had resisted the push for adult education, led in part by Brougham. However, his position evolved as he forged his way through political controversy and reform. Peel always knew that he must 'Deliberately [address] himself not only to the aristocracy but to the professional mercantile and industrial middle classes … It was evident, for example … in his Tamworth Reading Room speech of 1841, which brought

---

11   Ibid., 124.
12   Ibid., 123.
13   Ford, 'Newman's View of Education: The Oxford Background', 27–47.
14   Kelly, History, 125; 128.
15   Armytage, Four Hundred Years of English Education, 79.

down on him the attacks of Tories and High Anglicans for its secular and utilitarian outlook.'[16] His development in this direction was not necessarily strictly utilitarian, as Peel always saw himself serving Church and Crown; however, the inclusion of the rapidly expanding middle classes in the political future of Britain, pressed him to find innovative solutions. His solution was adult education, and this fateful choice engendered renewed opposition and resistance.

By late 1840–1, Peel's political design to extend knowledge and power into various classes and groups necessitated an expansion of his ideas. This was especially the case with education, which made some in his party and churchmen uneasy: 'The existence within Peel's party of an older Toryism and a new progressive Conservatism, divided on many issues among which education loomed very large, was of course a commonplace of the time'.[17] For representatives of this older Toryism, including many of the clergy and the country gentlemen, the diffusion of knowledge was associated with the suspect name of Brougham, with a philosophy of 'improvement' involving secularism and *laissez-faire* economics. Their fear of a secularized education is reflected in the widespread opposition to a State-aided national system, and the slowly dwindling distrust of mechanics' institutions.[18]

Peel's correspondence from January 1841 showed that he had been planning the main theme of his address: that one becomes better morally and materially through useful or technical knowledge independent of Church intervention. The ideas that would constitute his address were relatively new to his platform, and represented a dramatic shift away from his thinking in 1837 that the unity of the Church was essential for education.[19] However, the idea of knowledge independent of the Church was prevalent in mechanics' literature, and reflected Peel's current thoughts about politics, education, and the human condition. Sheridan Gilley asserted that Peel's address contained 'some unguarded expressions indicating the death of the old Tory philosophy of the

---

16 Gash, *Sir Robert Peel*, 236.
17 Burgis, *TRR*, 79. Burgis paraphrased Richard Leslie Hill, *From Toryism to the People* (London: Constable & Co., 1929), 142–54.
18 Burgis, *TRR*, 80.
19 Peel intended this for school children, but it did not necessarily exclude adults.

Anglican confessional state.'[20] Yet Peel's remarks were not unguarded, but rather voiced ideas that he had developed during the 1830s. And once convinced of a notion, he would defend it relentlessly without further considering alternative views. Peel's Tamworth address contained several of his newly formed and now unshakable ideals.[21]

Letters between Peel and his close friend, William Buckland, who had become a notable figure in the nascent science of geology, provide a window into his views.[22] A letter from 5 January 1841 disclosed that Peel and Buckland had been discussing ideas that might be included in the address. Peel seemed keen to demonstrate that through the acquisition of knowledge, a person could raise his station in life both socially and economically.[23] He believed with almost a religious faith that economics driven by technological progress would be society's great elixir.[24]

Buckland provided Peel with several examples of men who started from humble situations and rose through learning to some measure of fame:

---

20 Sheridan Gilley, *Newman and His Age* (Westminster, Maryland: Christian Classics, 1990), 195.

21 Contemporary newspapers which opposed Peel noted that several of his ideas about knowledge and education either contradicted his earlier positions or were simply imprudent for a man of his stature; see Burgis, *TRR*, 8.

22 Buckland was also professor at Christ Church College, Oxford. Newman attended his lectures starting in 1819 (*LD*, II, 65). On 8 June 1821, Newman (*LD*, II, 109) wrote to his sister Jemima: 'Buckland's lectures [on geology] I had intended to have taken down, as I did last term, but several things prevented me—the time it takes, and the very desultory way in which he imparts his information: for, to tell the truth, the science is so in its infancy that no regular system is formed. Hence the lectures are rather an enumeration of facts from which probabilities are deduced, than a consistent and luminous theory of certainties, illustrated by occasional examples. It is, however, most entertaining, and opens an amazing field to imagination and to poetry.'

23 Peel's desire that persons might rise through education was a common leitmotif in mechanics' institutes' literature; see Kelly, *History*, 123–4.

24 Gash, *Sir Robert Peel*, 186–7. According to Evans (*Peel*, 59), 'Peel's unequivocal belief was that the government's main concern with the 'social question' should be in helping to provide the economic conditions which would stimulate economic growth, create new jobs and enable ordinary folk to consume more.' Evans (*Peel*, 74) also stressed that after Peel's election as prime minister several months later, his 'objective was to provide conditions which would stimulate economic growth and prosperity sufficient to increase living standards for the population as a whole.'

Adult Education and Peel's Tamworth Address

> I forgot to mention yesterday [4 January], that Mr Grainger, the great architect ... began his career as a poor mason's boy, carrying a hod ... The late Mr Harvey ... three years ago a Professor at Woolwich, who published an excellent treatise on Meteorology in the *Encyclopaedia Metropolitana*, had worked for many years as a carpenter at the Dockyard at Plymouth, where he afterwards became a Teacher of Mathematics, and whence removed to the Professorship above mentioned. I will send you his treatise as I am sure it will interest you; and as there is in the first page a private letter from the author; which if to your purpose you are welcome to quote.[25]

On the back of the note, Peel jotted three points that he wished to include from Buckland's letter: 1. Grainger, the architect, 2. Harvey on Meteorology, 3. 'Quote the letter.' Peel included all three in his speech, making them the centerpiece of his lecture to the working classes. Buckland subsequently wrote to Peel on 9 January expressing his excitement about the library and his wish to contribute lectures and volumes to the new 'Institution at Tamworth.'[26]

Sir Robert Peel's Tamworth Address

On 19 January 1841, Peel gave the inaugural address for the new institution before a substantial crowd of Tamworth's citizens.[27] He did not seem to expect that his speech would go much further than his immediate audience.[28] The *Staffordshire Advertiser*, a small newspaper for the Midlands, had a reporter present for the address.[29] Whether Peel knew

25 Buckland to Peel, 5 January 1841, Peel Papers, 40429:2, British Library, London.
26 Buckland to Peel, 9 January 1841, Peel Papers, 40429:3, British Library, London.
27 The *Staffordshire Advertiser* of 23 January 1841 indicated a sizable crowd, with people from various classes of society, was on hand to listen. In his research of the Tamworth library, Harris ('Historical Forces', 201) could not find any records in the Peel collection or in Tamworth that indicated when the institution actually opened.
28 Burgis, TRR, 13; 19. *The Spectator* of 30 January 1841 implied that Peel had sought to reach a wider audience with his views although available evidence does not support this conclusion. See below, Chapter 6, 'Sir Robert Peel's Address and Catholicus', *The Times*, 10 March 1841, for a corroborating view that Peel did not think his address would be widely read.
29 A reporter for the *Staffordshire Advertiser* provided some initial remarks and a glimpse of the scene at the Tamworth town hall and also summarized some of

of the reporter's presence and had consented to the publication of his address cannot be determined. Nonetheless, this speech apparently was not intended to be a major policy statement designed to attract attention.[30] The *Staffordshire Advertiser* printed Peel's address on 23 January. The address also appeared the same day in the *Morning Post*, which provided a short summary and a favorable review. On the 25th, the conservative *Standard* printed the *Staffordshire Advertiser* version verbatim. The address eventually reached *The Times*—the country's largest-circulating newspaper. Peel's ideas were now guaranteed to attract national attention.

On Tuesday, 26 January 1841, *The Times* published the address under the heading: SIR ROBERT PEEL'S ADDRESS ON THE ESTABLISHMENT OF A LIBRARY AND READING-ROOM AT TAMWORTH.[31] A brief paragraph, originally inserted by the *Staffordshire Advertiser*, prefaced the address. Peel had 'come forward to liberally assist in the establishment of the library and reading-room for Tamworth and its neighbourhood'. He had given £100 for its establishment and offered to serve as its first president. The institution was founded on 'a comprehensive basis without reference to rank or to political and religious distinctions'.[32]

Peel opened his address by acknowledging institutions similar to the Tamworth Library—probably mechanics' institutes. He noted that his duty as president was to explain the goals and advantages of such an

---

Peel's extemporaneous remarks when he deviated from his written address.

30 This address has not been included in several of the anthologies of Peel's public speeches nor has it received sufficient attention by his biographers, for example, Gash, *Sir Robert Peel*, 236. Yet the address contained affinities with Peel's installation speech as rector of the University of Glasgow in 1837; see Haly, *Opinions*, 218–27. Indeed, Peel's Glasgow speech in many ways was a preamble to the notions and ideas laid down at the Tamworth reading room; see Gash, *Sir Robert Peel*, 151–5.

31 Multiple versions of the address exist. The most prominent was the revised pamphlet which Peel published with Bain. The edition of the address used here is from the *Staffordshire Advertiser/The Times*, which Newman mainly relied upon for his letters. The version which appeared in *The Times* has been reprinted in Newman's *Letters and Diaries* (LD, VIII, 525–33); these page references will be used (in parentheses) in the text.

32 This statement reflected not simply the intention of Peel and the Tamworth reading-room committee, but was typical of early mechanics' institutes; see Kelly, *History*, 121–4.

establishment 'in very simple and very perspicuous language'. Because Peel was addressing a popular audience, he struck an emotive, rather than formal, tone.[33] He 'felt' that regarding the 'extension of knowledge and intellectual improvement' it would be vain to employ 'novelty of argument or expression'. He wanted to avoid a 'parade of learning' but simply to express the benefits of scientific knowledge. There would be nothing controversial in the address; he was simply expounding truths 'very obvious and trite, so obvious as to not exercise a practical influence upon the conduct of men' (525). Yet, for a man who was poised to represent the Tory/Conservative party, his ideas about the utilitarian and recreational benefits of scientific knowledge were far from 'obvious and trite' truths to many in his class. Peel had co-opted tenets from the Whig and radical philosophical traditions within the last three years. And these ideas had become evident only from the middle of the 1820s.[34]

Peel offered a 'general summary' of the institute's by-laws which had been posted for the town. The reading room would be for the townspeople and would be open each day for members except 'holydays' and Sundays. Members would be able to borrow books, using them for their personal enjoyment or for their families. Peel repeated that library would be open to 'all persons of all descriptions, without reference to political opinions or religious creed' over fourteen years of age (526).

Peel further stipulated, in a radical/egalitarian vein, that men *and* women could become members: it would be a great injustice to the 'well-educated and virtuous women if we suppose them to be less capable of their husbands', etc. Women should also be allowed 'rational recreation and intellectual improvement'. Peel believed that men and women

---

33 This contrasted with the sober and smooth tone of some earlier speeches and the ensuing pamphlet. In particular, Peel's use of the first-person singular coupled with the word 'feel' or 'sanguine' tended to dominate the address. Harris ('Historical Forces', 197) claimed that Peel delivered a 'rather straightforward, low-keyed address'; this judgment is inaccurate, because Harris (and others) have focused on Peel's revised pamphlet and not the original version, whose tone especially concerned Newman (*LD*, VIII, 537).

34 For example, Kelly (*History*, 120) has noted that in 1825 notable figures such as Henry Brougham, James Mill, and Jeremy Bentham 'gave not only to the London Mechanics' Institute but to the whole mechanics' institute movement, a reputation for radicalism which took more than a quarter century to live down'.

should have equal power and influence in managing the reading room. As long as women maintained their virtue 'in whatever is sound and profitable in respect to knowledge' and manifested exemplary conduct they could hold office. Finally, Peel suggested that the committee extend the privileges beyond those who are 'not contemplated on paper' (526).[35]

Straying a little from his 'general summary', Peel declared that the new institution would lay the 'foundation of a great treasury of knowledge'. He felt that the library should have displays of minerals and works on mineralogy, because those were important industries developing in the Midlands. Moreover, if funds permitted there would be 'plain and popular lectures', which would be 'comprehensible by all'. They would include scientific subjects, industry, and agriculture which affected the borough of Tamworth: 'These are not', he proclaimed, 'over-sanguine expectations.'

Peel then introduced a central idea of the address: the 'acquisition of knowledge' is 'delightful path' for all. It opens those who follow to the 'gradual charms and temptations which will induce you to persevere' (526). He abruptly broke from this idea and returned to the 'immediate object' of presenting rules and regulations. Peel began to read directly from the committee's regulations about those who would 'constitute the society' of the library. They were not in his prepared remarks, for a third party (most likely the reporter) summarized what he stated. The committee would have clergy, aldermen, mechanics 'without distinction of party, political opinion, or religious profession'. Some persons would be excluded because of a limited amount of space, but nevertheless there would be a fair group assembled (526–7).

Peel next tackled the community's 'objections' about clergymen serving on the library's book committee. He took the objection 'head on'—shouts of 'Hear' and applause redounded when Peel declared that he did not 'feel the objection.'[36] The clergy were included because they were educated, conversant with literary works, and 'endowed by the state for

---

35 That the reading room would be open to men and women was an advance beyond many mechanics' institutes. Yet Peel's notion of including women from the upper echelon seemed incomplete: would working-class women be included? Was this what Peel meant by those not 'contemplated on paper'? His remarks about parity between the sexes contrasted with the list of the officers included in the speech, which did not include one woman. Newman would later exploit these discrepancies.

36 This seemed a stock phrase for Peel (for example, Haly, *Opinions*, 210).

Adult Education and Peel's Tamworth Address

the performance of the certain duties', chiefly the 'moral condition and improvement of the inhabitants' of Tamworth.[37]

Peel confidently claimed the importance of clergymen for the committee and the reporter's notes described the crowd as truly in favor of an ecclesial presence on the committee (527). However, Peel observed that some were 'jealous' of the clergy's influence. He felt that it was 'right to be jealous of all power held by [them]' and that he was perfectly willing to have a tempered conversation with those who had reservations. He assured members that there were to be checks on the clergy's power.[38]

Peel repeated that he would calmly mediate any objections; he acknowledged that clerical power is 'liable to be abused', and emphasized there would be checks or 'restrictions' on the clergy: they must 'accept their appointments and perform their duties [on the book committee] subject to this preliminary and fundamental rule that no works of controversial divinity shall enter into the library'.[39] Further, 'everything calculated to excite religious or political animosity shall be excluded'. The crowd approved Peel's temerity and continued to applaud him. The clergy also had to accept another rule: 'that no discussions on matters connected with religion, politics, and local party difference be permitted to take place' (527). This statement captured the essence of the Mechanics' Movement and now Peel's thought—partisan politics and religion were biased and caused dissention; science and reason did not.[40]

Peel continued to expound on the role for the clergy, declaring a third time that it was good for the 'objectors' to be 'jealous' of their power. He

---

37 See Evans, *Peel*, 41; 43–4. Peel increasingly viewed the Church of England not only as a bearer of social morality, but also as a functionary of the State.

38 Perhaps because of his aversion to fractious political parties and strong religious movements, especially the Ultras and the Tractarians, Peel felt the committee and the reading room should be above the factions vigorously vying for influence.

39 That Peel perceived himself to be above controversy—accompanied by what some perceive as intellectual arrogance—was considered by some contemporaries and some revisionist historians to be a serious character flaw. See for example, Hilton, 'Peel: A Reappraisal', 585–9.

40 However, stressing scientific knowledge to the exclusion of topics and ideas about which people cared deeply—politics and religion—had sapped the vitality of previous institutes; when such subjects were reinstated, the institutes thrived. See Kelly, *History*, 125; 128.

added that their power would be mitigated by the institution's regulations. The clergy would also be checked by the management of the institution which would be composed of lay persons. He appealed to members who 'by giving notice' could alter the regulations. Peel deemed that these checks were sufficient to prevent any abuse of power by the clergy. Thus, 'when this subject is calmly considered ... we avow that in giving knowledge we wish to take every security against that knowledge being perverted to evil or immoral purposes' (527–8).[41]

He concluded this rhetorical furrow with a question: 'We avow that as our great object; and that being so can any Dissenter from the establishment say that this is any interference with freedom of opinion, or ... that his religious scruples can be invaded or individually interfered with?' (528).[42]

Peel wanted to 'conciliate support' for the institution, by mitigating division and bringing people together from across the spectrum.[43] He noted that it was for 'rational amusement, recreation, and intellectual improvement' and believed himself able to 'moderate' extreme opinions (528). In accenting knowledge as recreation, Peel opted for a prevalent notion that in mechanics' institutes 'there must be relaxation ... [and] entertainment' along with science.[44] The library, again conforming to mechanics' institutes, did not inculcate simply abstract science but also practical knowledge. Peel instanced agriculture as one form of practical knowledge. He attempted to make the case that scientific agriculture should not be forced upon the experienced farmer—for he may know more in practical matters than an academic. However, he added,

---

41 This passage was excised from the pamphlet edition.

42 This passage was also excised from the pamphlet, in favor of the following: 'In advancing this Institution to its present state of maturity, I have had objections to contend with from opposite quarters, and of an opposite character'.

43 Harris ('Historical Forces', 204) has remarked: 'The widest possible support was needed to keep a subscription library going, especially in a small borough'.

44 Thomas Kelly, *George Birkbeck: Pioneer of Adult Education* (Liverpool: Liverpool University Press, 1957), 236. Benjamin Heywood, president of the Manchester Mechanics' Institute, articulated this goal in 1837: 'The great point, I am convinced is to combine more of what will be felt as relaxation and amusement without communication of knowledge. After a day of hard work a man wants refreshment and ease' (*ibid.*).

theoretical knowledge should be available to the working class. While affirming the experience and intelligence of the work-a-day farmer, who might distrust experimental science, he nevertheless stressed that most farmers were ignorant and that scientific knowledge would be useful. For Peel, a reasonable man would want such information (528–9).[45]

He then admonished the laboring classes in attendance—they would be at fault in not taking full advantage of science and literature:

> You will not be able to say 'chill penury' has 'frozen the genial current'[46] of your aspirations for knowledge and distinction. We tell you that here is access for you to that information which may at the same time facilitate your advance in your worldly occupations and lay the foundations of your mental improvement.[47]

In waxing poetic, Peel modeled a liberally educated mind for his listeners, while sticking to his point that with the resources available through the Tamworth library, the laboring poor could no longer blame their station on want of knowledge.

He cautioned farmers and all working adults, who were for the most part uneducated, not to be distracted by those who scoff at the acquisition of knowledge. To an outburst of laughter and applause, Peel wittily chided working people to make time for rational recreation. Industrious men work hard but must also work to acquire knowledge, which could improve their 'worldly pursuits.'[48] Knowledge was power:

---

45 The reporter summarized Peel's aside on the value of science for farmers.

46 He lifted the lines from *An Elegy Written in a Country Churchyard* by Thomas Gray (1716–71) (New York: Appleton & Co., 1854, 12): 'But knowledge to their eyes her ample page/ Rich with the spoils of time did ne'er unroll/ Chill Penury repressed their noble rage/ And froze the genial current of the soul'.

47 The fact that Peel regarded intellectual improvement for the laboring and working classes as desirable was problematic for the Ultras and for some of his political allies. For example, Charles Greville (*Greville Memoirs: A Journal of the Reign of Queen Victoria: 1837–1852* [London: Longman, Green, 1885], 35) noted the disdain many Tories had for Peel's 'liberal' positions.

48 Harris ('Historical Forces', 207) observed: 'Peel believed that the good in human nature required only to be nurtured. The improvement of material and intellectual circumstance would necessarily engender a higher spiritual life'. However, what Peel actually knew about the condition of the poor is another matter; for example, the editor from the American *Mechanics' Magazine* printed an excerpt

'Every steamboat, every railroad, all the facilities of intercourse, are operating as premiums upon skill and intelligence.'[49] If the working classes did not improve their minds they would be left behind by the march of economic progress (529).[50]

Peel cajoled his audience not to be afraid of scientific pursuits because of their lowly station. Here he employed ideas from Buckland's letter, offering a litany of accomplished scientists—Sir Humphry Davy, Michael Faraday, and others—who came from humble origins. He read excerpts of letters from persons who had risen above their station through knowledge and hard work. He lamented that if only these men had had access to the library, they could achieve more materially and scientifically. The good people of Tamworth should turn away from 'vulgar amusements', thus 'enabling [them] to walk in early life a

---

from Andrew Ure's work and connected Peel to it. In 'Ure's Philosophy of Manufactures', *Mechanics' Magazine* 9/1 (January 1837): 2–11, at 4, the Ure excerpt read: 'In the recent discussions concerning our factories, no circumstance is so deserving of remark, as the gross ignorance evinced by our leading legislators and economists ... relative to the nature of those stupendous manufactures which have so long provided the rulers of the kingdom with the resources of war, and a great body of the people with comfortable subsistence' ... The editor noted, [Even the eminent statesman lately selected by his Sovereign to wield the destinies of this commercial empire—Sir Robert Peel, who derives his family consequence from the cotton trade, seems to be but little conversant with its nature and condition]. Ure continued 'Till this ignorance be dispelled, no sound legislation need be expected on manufacturing subjects ... The blessings which physico-mechanical science has bestowed on society, and the means it has still in store for ameliorating the lot of mankind, have been too little dwelt upon; while, on the other hand, it has been accused of lending itself to the rich capitalists as an instrument for harassing the poor, and of exacting from the operative an accelerated rate of work ... Dr. Carbutt of Manchester says, "With regard to Sir Robert Peel's assertion a few evenings ago, that the hand-loom weavers are mostly small farmers, nothing can be a greater mistake; they live, or rather they just keep life together, in the most miserable manner, in the cellars and garrets of the town, working sixteen or eighteen hours for the merest pittance".'

49 Peel (Haly, *Opinions*, 223) made a strikingly similar claim in his Glasgow address. The difference was the audience—Glasgow embodied the best and brightest students in Scotland—in contrast to Tamworth, where Peel was addressing the entire community.

50 Peel's exhortations to the working poor to improve their lot were nevertheless genuine (Evans, *Peel*, 59).

path that leads to virtuous fame!' He pointed to numerous examples of people in the surrounding area who had risen above their station through knowledge (529–30).[51]

After lecturing the poor and working classes to garner more knowledge and to advance themselves, he turned to the wealthy. He solicited their financial contributions, but also their 'society' in the institution. He tried to allay their concerns that the library would injure 'the moral or religious character of the people'. On the contrary, knowledge—the great object of the library—united persons. Peel believed that the information, lectures, and so forth, provided a 'social connexion' between the landed and the virtuous mechanic and artificer, 'harmonizing the gradations of society, and binding them together'.[52] Progress through merit would be a fundamental tenet of Tamworth reading room and library. Peel offered the example of one of the members who though from humble origins was on the management committee (530–1).

Literature would also be included in the institute.[53] Peel did not think it would pose any 'risk to religious impressions and religious belief'.[54] In support of this contention, he referred to the much-admired inaugural address of the Bishop of London at King's College.[55] The Bishop had

---

51 Peel's examples of various persons resemble the type of literature made popular, for example, by George Lille Craik's *The Pursuit of Knowledge under Difficulties* (London: Charles Knight, 1830). Newman used this work in his critique of Peel.

52 Such acquired knowledge must be tied to financial improvement, as Evans (*Peel*, 56) observed: '[Peel] believed that the only route to social harmony was via economic progress, and he believed that the only route to economic progress was by treading the path of financial probity and rectitude'.

53 As previously noted, the almost exclusive focus upon physical science had contributed to the near demise of the institutions in the 1820s (Kelly, *Birkbeck*, 233–4). Peel and the Library's committee accommodated literature; however, Peel's correspondence with Buckland and the thrust of his address clearly show that he was intent on a program of partisan-free science.

54 In his original address, Peel averred: 'I cannot believe that there is any risk to religious impressions and religious belief by opening the avenues to literary acquirements' (531); this line was not included in the pamphlet, where Peel referred to the library and reading room as a 'Literary and Scientific Institution'.

55 Gerard Tracey (*LD*, VIII, 531) drew from *A Memoir of Charles James Blomfield*, ed. A. Blomfield (London: John Murray, 1863), I, 150–3, to explain the significance of King's College: 'The party who had been pressing forward the cause of Roman

maintained that God allowed people to inquire freely in any branch of knowledge and that 'the very constitution of man' is one of 'indefinite inquiry' and thus afforded sufficient reason that God intended people to be curious. Peel bolstered this idea with a comparison: an elephant's 'sagacity'[56] is constant in nature and does not develop whereas man's intelligence is 'sharpened and strengthened by exercise ... enlarged, and ... made the ground of future improvement'. He added that by philosophy or scientific research: 'Such studies removed the veil which to the ignorant or careless observer obscured the traces of God's glory in the works of his hands' (531).

Peel reviewed theological arguments from design to bolster his position: once one has learned scientific observation from the 'meanest weed ... to the magnificent structure of the heavens', one cannot fail to see 'proofs of a Divine intelligence'. When accustomed to such 'contemplations', he felt that a person obtains 'greater reverence for the name of the Almighty Creator of the Universe':

> We believe ... that the man accustomed to such contemplations will feel the moral dignity of his own nature exalted; and ... will yield more ready and hearty assent—yes assent of the heart and not of the understanding—to the pious exclamation, 'Oh, Lord how glorious are Thy works ...' It is the unwise man, and the fool, that form unworthy conceptions of the Divine Nature and the Divine Power. (531)

Peel provided lengthy quotations from Sir Isaac Newton and Sir Humphrey Davy as examples of those who have made 'the greatest (however imperfect) advances towards the understanding of it [the Divine

---

Catholic emancipation, had also been active in promoting secular, or, as it is called, non-sectarian education. With this object the London University had been founded, in 1827 by Mr. Brougham, Lord Landsdowne, and others of the same party. The exclusion of religion from this institution incited friends of the Church to make some corresponding effort on their own side.' One of the leaders of this group was C. J. Blomfield: 'A large meeting to further the object thus described was held in London, in June, 1828, with the Duke of Wellington in the chair; smaller meetings ... were held at the Bishop's own house; and with Joshua Watson, Bishop Lloyd, Dr. D'Oyley (who had written a pamphlet on the subject, under the name 'Catholicus'), and ... he took a leading part in giving shape and consistency to the plan. The result was the foundation of King's College, which however, was not opened till 1831.'

56 This odd comparison was eliminated from Peel's revised pamphlet.

Adult Education and Peel's Tamworth Address

Nature]'. He admired Davy, for on his deathbed he derived 'some pleasure and some consolation, when most other sources of consolation and pleasure were closed to him'. Davy believed that the scientific enquirer

> should always be awake to devotional feeling; and in contemplating the variety and beauty of the external world, and developing his scientific wonder, he will always refer to the Infinite Wisdom ... In becoming wiser he will become better; he will rise at once on the scale of intellectual and moral existence; his increased sagacity will become subservient to his exalted faith.[57] (531)

For Peel, an

> increased sagacity will administer to an exalted fame—that it will make men not merely believe in the cold doctrines of natural religion, but that it will so prepare and temper the spirit and understanding that they will be better qualified to comprehend the great scheme of human redemption.[58]

Those who cultivated this 'superior sagacity' would reject the current objections to revealed religion, and rather see the great harmony between reason and revelation (532).

He concluded by noting his 'views and hopes ... in the progress of knowledge' which had induced him to help establish the library. Before departing and 'engaging in the scene of warfare on the great arena of political contention', he hoped that he had

> laid the foundation stone of an edifice in which men of all political opinions and of all religious feelings may unite in the furtherance of knowledge without the asperities of party feeling—if ... there will be the means afforded of useful occupation and rational recreation—that men will prefer the pleasures of knowledge above the indulgence of sensual appetite—that there is a prospect of contributing to the intellectual and moral improvement of this town ... then I shall be repaid ... for any time I have spent [in] the formation of this institution. (532)

He then sat down to enthusiastic applause and was praised by one of

---

57 The words which Peel adopted were from Sir Humphry Davy's *Consolation in Travel* in *The Collected Works of Sir Humphry Davy*, ed. John Davy (London: Smith, Elder & Co., 1840), 9: 367.

58 Peel's last few remarks yielded loud applause.

the committee members 'for the kindness, good feeling and friendship, but above all, by that deeply religious feeling which he had instilled into all their hearts and minds' (532–3).

Press Reaction to the Address

Because of Peel's role as leader of the opposition party and because he had been on the public stage for well over twenty-five years, news of the speech filtered out into the British press. Eventually, his speech was published in several newspapers, receiving both scathing critique and favorable comment.[59] In contrast to his 'Tamworth Manifesto', evidence from Peel's letters and from newspaper accounts suggest that Peel had not designed his address to be covered beyond the local media or to spark a national debate. He envisioned himself expounding personal views about intellectual and economic improvement that were 'very obvious and trite, so obvious as not to exercise a practical influence upon the conduct of men' (525).

On 23 January, in concert with *The Staffordshire Advertiser*, the Tory-aligned *Morning Post* published a summary of the speech. The *Post* had received only an 'outline' of the address, 'Owing to peculiar causes we were not apprised of the meeting until too late to despatch one of our reporters.'[60] This admission confirmed that Peel had not expected much publicity for the speech. However, as Burgis makes clear, this was an oversight typical of Peel: 'If he [Peel] did not see that the Address could be made the subject of controversy then it was, as R. L. Hill has said, a striking example of Peel's lack of tact that when the Tories were protesting that "Brougham's" Mechanics' Institutes represented an ideal in education to which Tories were strangers and which Tories literally loathed, Peel must needs blunder into the Tamworth Reading Room to make a speech upon the glorious fruits of Useful Knowledge.'[61] The *Morning Post* praised Peel's 'inaugural address for the comprehensiveness of its views, and the noble spirit of liberality (rightly defined) which pervades it, surpasses anything of the kind which has previously

---

59 Relevant dates and a sample of newspapers are listed in Appendix III.
60 'Sir Peel at Tamworth—Important Meeting', *The Morning Post*, 23 January 1841.
61 Burgis, *TRR*, 19–20. See also, Hill, *Toryism and the People*, 62.

Adult Education and Peel's Tamworth Address

appeared'. A short summary followed, which highlighted the check on the clergy and the emphasis on useful knowledge for farmers. Also included was Peel's notion that knowledge adapts persons 'for the more adequate appreciation and comprehension of those blessings which Almighty Providence has thrown their way'.[62] Burgis summarized the modest media attention given to the address:

> The Ministerial *Globe*, which had not reported the Address, copied out the paragraph from the *Post*, adding the headline 'Sir Peel at Tamworth—First Appearance in a New Character'.[63] During the next week the Address was praised, but not reprinted in the Conservative *Morning Herald*, and gave rise to a certain amount of editorial comment in the Ministerial and Radical Press. The *Statesman* of 31 January reprinted the gibe of the *Staffordshire Examiner* that the diffusion of knowledge would be a death-blow to Peel and his party, and the *Sun* which reprinted the Address from the *Staffordshire Advertiser* on 29 January, hailed him as a late convert to liberal ideas.[64]

The most important critique of the speech appeared on 30 January in the independent, radical-leaning *Spectator*.[65] Under the sarcastic title, 'Sir Robert Peel's Debut as a Popular Lecturer', the anonymous author seemed intent on showing Peel's advocacy for radical positions while simultaneously debasing him: 'Not contented with rivaling the Whigs and Radicals in Parliamentary eloquence, he is determined to start against them in their own especial field—the Education of the People.'[66]

---

62 *The Morning Post*, 23 January 1841.

63 The *Preston Chronicle* did the same on 30 January—copying the piece from the *Post* while employing the *Globe*'s headline.

64 Burgis, *TRR*, 20.

65 'Sir Robert Peel's Debut as a Popular Lecturer', *The Spectator*, 30 January 1841. See also Burgis, *TRR*, 22.

66 This article adumbrated several themes that emerged in the Catholicus letters. There is no record that Newman saw *The Spectator* before composing his letters for *The Times* although the satire and other resemblances are striking. Had Newman seen *The Spectator*, perhaps he would have declined the offer to reply or taken his initial letters in a different direction. Newman's installments, however, were not strictly political, as so much of the newspaper coverage was, nor were they solely aimed at Peel.

Peel, crowned lecturer for the masses, was associated with Lord Henry Brougham[67] and was accused of being a sedulous reader of the publications of the Society for the Diffusion of Useful Knowledge; and what is more, that he has profited by their perusal—that his retentive memory has been abundantly stored from those repositories. The author inferred that Peel was 'guarded in his expression,'[68] lest he provoke Ultras. However, Peel had remarkably delivered a cascade of radical/liberal positions:

> Sir Robert Peel repudiated the notion that intellectual pursuits are incompatible with business ... He refuted with equal success the notion that increase of knowledge is unfavourable to morality and religion. Now let the reader dispassionately review the principles avowed and defended in these extracts. The condition of society rendering it impossible for any man to keep his ground who does not study; the importance of knowledge towards the formation of the moral man and the successful man of business ...; the vindication of the admission of the working classes, and even of females, to a share in the management; the pointing out the way to get quit of the clergymen when their countenance should no longer be wanted,—if all these things do not go up a rank Radical lecture, we do not know what does.

'In short', Peel had done 'everything in his power to sap and undermine the glorious structure of "Church and State".' The author concluded on a cynical note, one that had plagued Peel since Catholic emancipation. Peel was an opportunist, always ready to adopt a Whig/liberal policy once it had become politically mainstream:

> He is playing the same game now: the Whigs have been talking for years about elevating the working-classes; Sir Robert sees the time has come for admitting them to the full rights of citizenship, and is preparing to secure for himself the credit of performing that act of justice.

---

67 The article also mentioned a Mr. Buckingham; most probably the reference is to James Silk Buckingham (1786–1855), a popular lecturer and social reformer.

68 Gilley (*Newman and his Age*, 195) averred the opposite, interpreting Peel as delivering rather 'unguarded expressions'. Meriol Trevor (*Newman: The Pillar of the Cloud* [New York: Double Day, 1962], 239) had the same interpretation. The instincts of *The Spectator*, however, seemed to be more accurate in regard to Peel's intentions.

From Address to Pamphlet

The picture that emerged from this and other reviews fell along party lines. Conservative/Tory papers offered qualified praise; Whig/Radical papers either welcomed Peel to their camp or cast him as opportunistic. Beyond the initial reactions, Peel's address received scant notice; Britain's most important newspaper, *The Times*, merely reproduced the speech. However, while the press had been ridiculing or praising Peel's efforts, Henry Hooper of *Pall Mall* published an unauthorized pamphlet directly from the text of the *Staffordshire Advertiser*. Another pamphlet was published by James Bain of Haymarket.[69] Shortly after his January speech, Peel had planned to revise the address and issue a limited number of pamphlets.[70] According to Burgis, Bain's pamphlet contained several differences from the address and was the one authorized by Peel, who clearly attached some importance to the differences in the revised version.[71]

On 31 January, Lady Julia Peel wrote to their second son, Frederick, praising the speech and admonishing him to ignore Hooper's pamphlet and to wait for Bain's:[72]

---

69 According to Burgis (*TRR*, 13), the pamphlet 'was published in conjunction with J. Thompson, bookseller, of Tamworth, and Bain brought out a second "corrected" edition in March 1841—the revisions [for the second edition] are few and unimportant'.

70 *An Inaugural Address Delivered by the Right Hon. Sir Robert Peel, Bart. M.P., President of the Tamworth Library and Reading Room on Tuesday, 19th January, 1841* (London: James Bain, 1841).

71 Burgis, *TRR*, 13. Several authors who have studied *The Tamworth Reading Room* controversy have referred to the Bain pamphlet. For example, Harris ('Historical Forces', 190) justified his use of the pamphlet noting that Newman had referred 'to the differences between the speech as reported in *The Times* and its somewhat smoothed and tightened form in the pamphlet, but the differences are not major and Newman had both before him as he replied to *The Times* version'. However, there were substantial differences between the two versions and not simply in terms of style. Harris' comment also is inaccurate: Newman only received the pamphlet after he had finished his first letter; in addition, in the letters, Newman opted to quote from Peel's public address, rather than from the pamphlet; evidence does not indicate that Newman continued to consult both versions.

72 This correspondence suggested that the Bain pamphlet was released after 31 January but before 2 February when Peel received Buckland's letter of appreciation.

'An aristocracy of exalted spirits'

You shall certainly have your Papa's pamphlet of his beautiful speech, an address at Tamworth, as soon as it comes out. The one which you have seen advertised is not the true one.[73]

Two days later, Peel received a note of gratitude 'for the address' from Buckland—implying that he had received the Bain pamphlet.[74]

Looking Back and the Advent of Catholicus

From the vantage point of the present-day, many would see much to admire in Peel's vision as it is now the social imaginary[75] of Great Britain and also America and Europe: an egalitarian view of class and gender, the striving for democratic education, a distrust of ecclesial power, and a desire for moral and social order (if from a deity) shorn of Christian doctrine.[76] This last point is worthy of note. Many of the social elite (and even some religious) agreed with a core conviction found in Peel's address—although refracted along partisan lines, many liberal Tories, Whigs, and Radicals considered religion a matter of social morality or civic duty, and no more. Peel, himself, had never trusted what he deemed reactionary religion, nor could he abide the Oxford Movement. For him, conventional practice in the Church of England bounded by a Lockean reason was enough. This religion could be equated to the moral order; combining religion with orderly, scientific knowledge would have seemed only logical.

---

73 *The Private Letters of Sir Robert Peel*, 175.

74 Buckland to Peel, 2 February 1841, Peel Papers, 40429:54, British Library, London. On 29 January 1841, Peel received a note from Buckland, who did not mention the Tamworth speech. The letter from 2 February did not mention the pamphlet either; it is likely that the 'address' received was in pamphlet form. A few months later the Duke of Rutland wrote to Peel to thank him for the pamphlet (Rutland to Peel, 9 April 1841, Peel Papers, 40429:191, British Library, London).

75 Charles Taylor, *A Secular Age* (Cambridge, MA: Belknap Press, 2007), 146: the 'social imaginaryl is 'The way that [persons] collectively imagine [their] social life in the contemporary Western world'.

76 For a poignant account of this 'deism' in America see 'Summary Interpretation: Moralistic Therapeutic Deism', from Christian Smith with Melinda Lundquist Denton, *Soul Searching: The Religious and Spiritual Lives of American Teenagers* (Oxford: Oxford University Press, 2005), 162–71.

Adult Education and Peel's Tamworth Address

The notion of religion as reducible to morality and knowledge was clear throughout Peel's speech. Underlying this notion was a projection of an impersonal Creator/Providence upholding this moral order. This widespread belief derived from Christian apologetics and developed during the seventeenth and eighteenth centuries. Personal religion, which included worship and personal devotion to the God proclaimed in Christian faith, was desiccated. Now religion was simply following divine law and human law. No longer was religion about the 'saving action of Christ' or prayer and liturgy, but, as Charles Taylor has commented, a controlled morality:[77] 'apologetics, and indeed, much preaching, [was] less and less concerned with sin as a condition we need to be rescued from through some transformation of our being, and more and more with sin as wrong behavior which we can be persuaded, trained or disciplined to turn our backs on ... Religion was narrowed to moralism ... This morality in turn was cast in terms of the modern notion of order, one in which our purposes mesh to our mutual benefit. Self-love and social [sic] were ultimately at one.'[78] For those who would ratify Peel's views today, especially the equation of religion with morality, discerning the uncertainty and controversy generated by his speech among contemporaries proves difficult. The ideals he proclaimed seem a necessary triumph in the progress of human freedom against retrograde forces of ecclesial tradition.[79] Currently, it is difficult to picture how what radicals, utilitarians and later Peel urged was an attempt to exploit and circumvent the religious fractiousness of nineteenth-century Britain. That High and Low Churches, and the re-emergent Roman Catholic Church in England, could not agree on basic doctrines, but were united in suppressing democratic education, seems incredible at present. And yet because in part Churches could not agree on basic doctrines, they were inhibited from capitalizing on an

77 Charles Taylor, *A Secular Age*, 225.
78 Ibid., 225–6.
79 Alasdair MacIntyre, *Whose Justice? Which Rationality?* (Notre Dame: Notre Dame Press, 1988). For an analogous argument in the American tradition see, Stephen Prothero, *Why Liberals Win the Culture Wars (Even When They Lose Elections): The Battles That Define America from Jefferson's Heresies to Gay Marriage* (San Francisco: HarperOne, 2016).

apparent demand by the men and women swept into the industrial revolution.[80]

This demand had been escalating since the eighteenth century. And yet, a vision of progress in knowledge and education had not firmly taken root in the British imagination, and there were viable alternatives still to be considered. In Newman's mind these ideals were not inherent goods in themselves but could only come to fruition in relation to the venerable Church tradition. This problem of integrating the new and old had vexed Newman since his twenties right up to 1841.

Had Peel's subsequent pamphlets quietly filtered out—attracting, perhaps, another flurry of newspaper comment—the ideals set forth might have been quickly forgotten by the public as yet another oration by a man on the political make. However, in March 1841, Peel took the floor of Parliament to reiterate the views expressed in the address and to defend its underlying principles. What had seemed so clear and unobtrusive in his mind had in the course of a month become fodder for controversy. Why? In early February a letter appeared in *The Times* which critiqued the ideas which Peel believed to be unexceptional. This letter and the six others that followed did not merely make political jabs or seek to impugn his character as many editorials had. These epistles contained satire *and* substance, arguing for a robust understanding of faith and Church in concert with new knowledge and institutions. An immediate cacophony arose in the press and the political world, that examined and critiqued Peel's address as well as his anonymous assailant. Peel's vision regarding education, knowledge, and religion, a vision shared by the progressive intelligentsia of England, was challenged by the stinging letters of 'Catholicus'.

---

80 See Brad Gregory, *The Unintended Reformation: How a Religious Revolution Secularized Society* (Cambridge, MA: Belknap Press, 2012), especially chapter 2, 'Relativizing Doctrines' and chapter 6 'Secularizing Knowledge'.

☙ 3 ☙

The Background, Offer to Respond, and Letter 1

PEEL'S ADDRESS AT TAMWORTH initially seemed to have eluded Newman as he was immersed in several projects, correspondences, and events. Thus when *The Times* offered him the occasion to respond, he accepted reluctantly, perhaps after reading the address. The invitation and idea for a response to Peel's address originated with Newman's former student, John Walter III, a graduate of Oriel College, Oxford, in 1840, and the son of the proprietor of *The Times*. While at Oxford, Walter III had become an adherent of Tractarian ideals,[1] and his association with Newman and others in the Oxford Movement probably stirred the young and enthusiastic Walter to action. While working on his MA at Oxford and acting as a surrogate for *The Times*, Walter III learned of Peel's speech and subsequent pamphlet. His Tractarian views helped him to identify the potential catastrophe implicit in Peel's equation of religion with morality and the usurpations of scientific knowledge divorced from the Church.[2]

Walter III, however, did not officially work for *The Times*; his father, John Walter II, owned the paper.[3] Walter II knew Peel personally and

---

[1] Dilwyn Porter, 'John Walter III' (1818–94), in *DNB*.

[2] *LD*, VIII, 26. John Walter III (*The History of the Times: 'The Thunderer' in the Making, 1785–1841* [Nendeln, Liechtenstein: Kraus-Thompson, 1971], 446) may have also been influenced by Roundell Palmer, who had recently written for Newman in the January *British Critic*, and who had been on the staff of *The Times* since September 1840.

[3] Porter, 'Walter III', noted: 'The Puseyite sympathies which he [Walter III] had acquired at Oxford led to a disagreement with his father [Walter II] over the editorial line pursued by *The Times* on Church issues. This rift was sufficiently serious to prompt his temporary withdrawal from managerial duties, but appears

'An aristocracy of exalted spirits'

The Times had accorded him favorable coverage, especially of his opposition to the recent Melbourne administration.[4] However, through his son, Walter II had become sympathetic to some Tractarian positions and was thus critical of certain aspects of Peelite conservatism. The unadorned publication of Peel's Tamworth address on 26 January signaled a note of disapproval from *The Times*. Walter II was probably concerned with the radical educational ideas raised in the address and thus amenable to his son's petition to have Newman compose a series of controversial letters to the editor.[5]

Upon reading the Tamworth address, Newman knew that he had a riposte to Peel's vision: the theological 'idea' that the Church and its faith could be a companion to modern institutions and knowledge, not an adversary. Peel had been thinking explicitly of the notions and principles expressed in his Tamworth address for at least three years, but had touched upon general educational ideas as a young MP. Newman had been developing arguments and views contrary to those now espoused by Peel for fifteen years, and was well poised to accept the offer from *The Times*.[6] For example, in his 1832 parochial sermon, 'The Religion of the Day', Newman had already anticipated the core of Peel's address (and in the course of the sermon repudiated it):

> Moreover, to a cultivated mind, which recreates itself in the varieties of literature and knowledge, and is interested in the ever-accumulating discoveries of science, and the ever-fresh accessions of information, political or otherwise, from foreign countries, religion will commonly seem to be dull, from want of novelty. Hence excitements are eagerly sought out and rewarded. New objects in religion, new systems and plans, new doctrines, new preachers, are necessary to satisfy that craving which the so-called spread of knowledge has created. The mind becomes morbidly

to have been short-lived. After he returned *The Times* adopted a more open attitude to the Tractarians.'

4 *The Thunderer*, 351–7; 375.
5 *Ibid.*, 405.
6 Newman's first explicit treatment of the themes later found in Peel's address and his letters are found in 'The Philosophical Temper, first Enjoined by the Gospel' (2 July 1826) in *OUS*, 15–23 [1–16].

sensitive and fastidious; dissatisfied with things as they are, desirous of a change as such, as if alteration must of itself be a relief.[7]

However, his 'idea' of the Church, especially in relation to faith, had been a more recent development. Some of the themes that emerged in Newman's letters can be found in initiatives proximate to his letters to *The Times*. For example, between the summer of 1840 and early 1841 Newman served as the editor and a contributor to *The British Critic*. He was also working on a theological treatise, *Tract 90*, prior to and concurrently with the letters.[8] Most significantly, Newman preached a sermon, the 'Duty of Christian Educators', immediately after accepting the *The Times*' commission. This sermon disclosed how Newman conceived his 'idea' of the Church and how that should bear upon education. In turn, the 'Duty of Christian Educators' offered an interpretative key to understanding Newman's subsequent letters to *The Times*.

The British Critic

Although Newman had not written much for the popular press, he did have experience of printed media. He may have been inclined by the Walters' offer to expand his theological views to this contentious frontier. Newman had become the editor of *The British Critic* in January 1838.[9] Under his direction, the quarterly produced Tractarian-themed articles.[10] In the summer and fall of 1840 and in January 1841, several

---

7 PPS, I, 312–13.

8 Newman's *Remarks on Certain Passages in the Thirty-Nine Articles*, better known as *Tract 90* (1841), was the last and most controversial of the *Tracts for the Times* that were published by Newman and others from the Oxford Movement.

9 Ker, Biography, 158–9; 173. See Esther Rhoads Houghton, 'The British Critic and the Oxford Movement', Studies in Bibliography 16 (1963): 119–23. Skinner (*Tractarians*, 52; 54) characterized Newman as an 'aggressively dogmatic and prescriptive … editor' who envisioned a rigid Tractarian theology for the *Critic*; he was, however, 'patently disposed to sobriety in his editorial judgments'. Meriol Trevor (*The Pillar of the Cloud*, 212) provided a different view: 'Newman was a good editor, he allowed his contributors plenty of latitude, often publishing things he did not quite approve himself, rather than suppress anyone else's opinions'.

10 For a recent and complete account of Newman as editor of *The British Critic*, see Simon Skinner, *Tractarians and the 'Condition of England': The Social and Polit-*

articles appeared that addressed topics such as Utilitarianism, Christian charity, poverty among the working class, and education.[11] Most of these topics figured prominently in the letters to *The Times*.

During Newman's tenure as editor, philosophical, theological, and social questions received frequent and prominent attention. Newman not only was aware of these questions, but he actively cultivated them, especially among up-and-coming Tractarians.[12] In July 1840, Frederick Rogers, a former student of Newman's, penned 'Utilitarian Moral Philosophy'—a critique of Jeremy Bentham's recently published collected works.[13] Samuel Bosanquet published 'Pauperism and Almsgiving', a scabrous review of the State's involvement with the working poor.[14] In October, Thomas Mozley wrote 'Religion of the Manufacturing Poor', which detailed the relationship between poverty and worship in the swelling laboring classes.[15] Bosanquet contributed another essay

---

ical *Thought of the Oxford Movement* (Oxford: Clarendon Press, 2004), 31; 36–58. Unfortunately, Skinner's revisionist work used unnecessarily caustic language; for example, Newman was described as 'Machiavellian' in his 'abduction' of *The British Critic* (ibid., 14; 36); in spite of such defects, he has provided a usable description of Newman's editorship of *The British Critic*.

11 Newman had been sensitive to these issues for a long time; see, for example, *LD*, VII, 244–5, and especially his *Oxford University Sermons*. For a succinct although snarky review of some of these themes in *The British Critic*, see Simon Skinner, 'Liberalism and Mammon: Tractarian Reaction in the Age of Reform', *Journal of Victorian Culture* 4/2 (Autumn, 1999): 197–227.

12 Anne Mozley commented on Newman's editorship (*The Letters of Rev. J. B. Mozley, DD*, ed. Anne Mozley [London: Rivingtons, 1885], 71), 'One incidental use of the review was to furnish a field—a sort of practice-ground—for the younger members of the party'.

13 *The British Critic* 28 (July 1840): 93–125.

14 *Ibid.*, 195–257. He believed that Christian charity offered through the churches in contrast to the State established under the New Poor Law of 1834 was the most humane way encounter and hopefully to help the working poor.

15 *The British Critic* 28 (October 1840): 334–71. Newman complimented Mozley on his recent contributions (29 September 1840, *LD*, VII, 399): 'Your articles are capital—that on the Manufacturing Poor most miserably impressive'. In the spring of 1841, Newman made plans to hand his editorship to Mozley (*LD*, VII, 411; 424; 430; 473; 474). Mozley also had a keen interest in religion education, and his work may have influenced Newman's letters to *The Times*. Simon Skinner ('Mozley, Thomas' [1806–1893], *DNB*) has written, 'Mozley's first publication of

regarding poverty, politics, and Christian charity in 'Private Alms and Poor-Law Relief'.[16] Because Newman vetted these articles, he became acutely aware of the problems that Peel was seeking to redress with the emerging working classes. However, the Tractarian line, which saw a positive role for the Church and religion in the lives of the working class, was markedly different from either the conservative and unmoved High Church gentry or progressive utilitarians who urged separation of religion and knowledge.

The January 1841 issue of *The British Critic* also contained several articles which had some bearing on the Catholicus letters—the most important being Newman's review of Henry Hart Milman's *History of Christianity*.[17] A decade earlier Newman had read Milman's *The History of the Jews* and accepted many of his historical findings but rejected his rationalist presuppositions.[18] Newman regarded Milman's latest work as an attempt to be 'philosophical and above the world ... to show that a Clergyman could take an enlarged view of things, and yet be a firm believer'.[19] For Newman, reason and faith worked together; however, the type of rationalism at play in Milman's thought corroded faith. Writing to his friend Keble on 3 November 1840, Newman recalled Milman's views:

note was a pseudonymous pamphlet of November 1838, *A Dissection of the Queries on the Amount of Religious Instruction and Education*, which was addressed to Sir Robert Inglis, MP for Oxford University, and signed 'By a Clergyman of South Wilts'. It denounced the intrusion of the poor law commissioners into the Church's management of education, and their survey's susceptibility to exaggerated claims of nonconformist support. The polemical brio of the pamphlet alerted Newman to Mozley's potential as a reviewer for *The British Critic*, a High Church literary and theological quarterly for whose editorial control Newman had successfully maneuvered earlier that year'.

16 *The British Critic* 28 (October 1840): 441–70.

17 'Milman's *History of Christianity*', *The British Critic* 29 (January 1841): 71–113. H. H. Milman, *The History of Christianity: From the Birth of Christ to the Abolition of Paganism in the Roman Empire* (London: John Murray, 1840).

18 H. H. Milman, *The History of the Jews* (London: John Murray, 1829).

19 *LD*, II, 299. Ker (*Biography*, 204) has noted that Newman's assessment 'was a very early example of the carefully balanced approach to the problems for religious belief that were raised by scholarly and scientific research ... in sharp contradistinction to the polarized reactions of so many of his contemporaries'.

'An aristocracy of exalted spirits'

> Rationalism is the great evil of the day. May not I consider my post at St. Mary's as a place of protest against it? I am more certain that the Protestant [spirit], which I oppose, leads to infidelity, than that which I recommend, leads to Rome. Who knows what the state of the University may be, as regards Divinity Professors in a few years hence? Any how, a great battle may be coming on, of which Milman's book is a sort of earnest. The whole of *our* day may be a battle with this spirit. May we not leave to another age *its own* evil,—to settle the question of Romanism?[20]

Newman's critique of rationalism, a key notion in his letters to *The Times*, underpinned his 1841 article on Milman. His analysis and argument found that Milman's work derived in part from the first wave of German historical criticism and comparative religion.[21] As in his former work on the Jewish tradition, Milman concentrated on history only in its human aspect. He admitted that there could be a divine element in either the Jewish or Christian traditions but that was not a part of his narrative. Newman lamented this decision, while highlighting the sacramental nature of Christianity:

> The Christian history is 'an outward visible sign of an inward spiritual grace:' whether the sign can be satisfactorily treated separate from the thing signified is another matter; but it seems to be Mr. Milman's intention so to treat it, and he must be judged by that intention ... Christianity has an external aspect and an internal; it is human without, divine within. To attempt to touch the human element without handling also the divine, we may fairly deem unreal, extravagant, and sophistical; we may feel the two to be one integral whole, differing merely in aspect, not in fact.[22]

He also criticized Milman's detached, omniscient viewpoint as unreal:[23]

---

20 JHN to John Keble (Oriel, 6 November), *LD*, VII, 433–4. Newman reflected on the contents of this letter in his *Apologia* (111–12) noting that 'Such was about my state of mind, on the publication of Tract 90 in February 1841'.

21 Newman, 'Milman's *History of Christianity*', 87.

22 Ibid., 72.

23 Newman's critique of German historicism, here and elsewhere, resembled Hans Georg Gadamer's critique of 'romantic hermeneutics' in *Truth and Method* (New York: Continuum, 2004), 174–233. See also Thomas Karr, *Newman and Gadamer: Towards a Hermeneutics of Religious Knowledge* (New York: Oxford University Press, 1996).

The Background

> It is quite undeniable, and quite as astonishing, that he [Milman] thinks there is something high and admirable in the state of mind which can thus look down upon a Divine Dispensation. He imagines that it argues a large, liberal, enlightened understanding, to be able to generalize religions, and, without denying the divinity of Christianity, to resolve it into its family likeness to all others.[24]

Milman's work subtly down-played particular claims of Christian revelation. This omission, Newman believed, would lead many astray from seeing the divine element of the Church. Milman had failed to sufficiently account for Christian doctrines:

> He is, as he truly says, 'an historian rather than a religious instructor.' But still, when he is engaged in *specifying expressly* what the revealed doctrine consists in, and what the object of Christ's coming was, we consider it to be a very unhappy view of historical composition, which precludes him from mentioning what all members of the Church hold to be fundamental in that doctrine, and primary in that object.[25]

Milman's pursuit of the historical and comparative reduction of Christianity to an aspect of human culture led readers to a false conclusion: that Christian faith was merely one attempt among many for humans to posit and project the divine. Moreover, the Christian projection of God erected whole civilizations, but was ultimately based upon a mistaken notion of revelation:

> What tenet of Christianity will escape proscription, if the principle is once admitted, that a sufficient account is given of an opinion, and a sufficient ground for making light of it, as soon as it is historically referred to some human origin? What will be our Christianity? What shall we have to believe? What will be left to us? Will more remain than a *caput mortuum*, with no claim on our profession or devotion? Will the Gospel be a substance? Will Revelation have done more than introduce a *quality* into our moral life world, not anything that can be contemplated by itself, obeyed and perpetuated? This we do verily believe to be the end of the speculations, of which Mr. Milman's volumes at least serve as an illustration. If we indulge them, Christianity will melt away in our hands like snow; we shall be unbelievers before we at all suspect where we are … We shall look on Christianity,

24 Newman, 'Milman's *History of Christianity*', 86.
25 Ibid., 85.

not as a religion, but as a past event which exerted a great influence on the course of the world, when it happened, and gave a tone and direction to religion, government, philosophy, literature, manners; an idea which developed itself in various directions strongly, which was indeed from the first materialized into a system or a church, and is still upheld as such by numbers, but by an error; a great boon to the world, bestowed by the Giver of all good, as the discovery of printing may be, or the steam-engine, but as incapable of continuity, except in its effects, as the shock of an earthquake, or the impulsive force which commenced the motions of the planets.[26]

Newman concluded with a pithy sketch of how theory and method relate when dealing with religious traditions. He was concerned that Milman's theory did not sufficiently ground his correlational method. For Milman, Christianity was simply an amalgamation of religious rites and impulses found in the Near East and throughout the world. Newman, however, was able to twist his theoretical underpinnings, and use the same method to arrive at a radically different conclusion. For him, the Christian tradition united and fulfilled others' religious doctrines and practices that would otherwise be inchoately scattered throughout human history:

> A theory does not prove itself; it makes itself probable so far as it falls in with our preconceived notions, as it accounts for the phenomena it treats of, as it is internally consistent, and as it excels or excludes rival theories. We should leave Mr. Milman's [theory] undisturbed ... except that it might seem to be allowing to that theory, as it were, possession of the field, when, in truth, there is another far more Catholic philosophy ... Now, the phenomenon, admitted on all hands, is this:—that great portion of what is generally received as Christian truth, is in its rudiments or in its separate parts to be found in heathen philosophies and religions. For instance, the doctrine of a Trinity is found both in the East and in the West; so is the ceremony of washing; so is the rite of sacrifice. The doctrine of the Divine Word is Platonic; the doctrine of the Incarnation is Indian; of a divine kingdom is Judaic; of Angels and demons is Magian; the connexion of sin with the body is Gnostic; celibacy is known to Bonze and Talapoin; a sacerdotal order is Egyptian; the idea of a new birth is

26 Ibid., 108–9.

The Background

Chinese and Eleusinian; belief in sacramental virtue is Pythagorean; and honours to the dead are a polytheism. Such is the general nature of the fact before us; Mr. Milman argues from it,—'These things are in heathenism, therefore they are not Christian:' we, on the contrary, prefer to say, 'these things are in Christianity, therefore they are not heathen.' That is ... we think that Scripture bears us out in saying, that from the beginning the Moral Governor of the world has scattered the seeds of truth far and wide over its extent; that these have variously taken root, and grown up as in the wilderness ... and hence ... the philosophies and religions of men have their life in certain true ideas, though they are not divine.[27]

The alacrity with which Newman saw the error in Milman's rationalized method and its conclusions was striking.

This type of criticism was nascent and had not diffused throughout the culture as it has today. That Christianity is simply a relativized religious tradition, one that influenced civilizations, but is now passing away for something religiously syncretic or secular to emerge is assumed true without question for many *post-modern* men and women.[28] Yet in 1841, this was still an open argument and one which in principle Newman got the better part (although in practice eventually lost to the radical/utilitarian/Peelite vision). He would carry this line of attack against the relativizing of religion in his letters to *The Times*.

Two other articles in the January issue may have also influenced Newman's thought. Frederick Rogers provided a brief appraisal of William Sewell's text on moral theology and reprised his critique of Bentham and 'Utilitarian Moral Philosophy'. Rogers, contra Bentham, accented Sewell's argument that ethics, education, and Christian religion are intimately bound together.[29] In addition, Roundell Palmer detailed the on-going debate about public education and underscored the current fervor for a utilitarian education that would conform men

---

27 Ibid., 101.

28 For a contemporary argument that parallels Newman's, see Joseph Ratzinger, *Truth and Tolerance: Christian Belief and World Religions* (San Francisco, CA: Ignatius Press, 2005), 210–30.

29 'Sewell's *Christian Morals*/Utilitarian Moral Philosophy', *The British Critic* 29 (January 1841): 1–44, at 2–3.

to the developing industrial society:[30]

> Consistently with such conceptions of the useful and the good, the whole effect of a given system of intellectual training is estimated at the sum of its producible results; in other words, by the total amount of skill to do things, and knowledge of facts and opinions, with which it sends a man furnished into the world. And the marketable value of this skill and knowledge, is the criterion by which the merit of the system is assayed.[31]

However, Palmer insisted that a strictly utilitarian end could not furnish the same ends found in the long tradition of Christian education:

> We know how she [the Church] deems of the little ones, for whom her instruction is provided. Not as of future lawyers, or merchants, or members of parliament, but as of future *men*; heirs of immortality, the redeemed servants and sons of God. We know what she considers to be the uses of the intellect, regarding it as an instrument, first for apprehending the nature and ends of our being, our relations to the visible and invisible world, and to the Author of both; and, secondly, for improving our opportunities of intercourse with other men, to the service and honour of the same Heavenly Master. Assuredly it will be the design of the Church so to educate the intellect, as to make it fit for these, its highest and only real uses. She will not disregard the fact, that different men are intended to fill different stations in life; but she will attend to that fact rather for the purpose of estimating the extent to which the intellect will be concerned in executing the work of the man, and the proportional development which it may therefore require, than in order minutely to distinguish its ultimate functions.[32]

Newman's review of Milman's work, as well as other essays in *The British Critic*, anticipated several of the arguments which he made a month later in the Catholicus letters. He addressed topics that related to poverty, education, and utilitarianism, often exposing and inverting Peel's political and religious assumptions like he did Milman's theory. Indeed, the thrust of these articles that Newman selected and some-

---

30 'English Public Schools', *The British Critic* 29 (January 1841): 151–73. Newman (*LD*, VII, 442) had looked forward to Palmer's contribution: 'I shall receive your projected Paper with great pleasure, and thank you for the promise of it'.
31 *Ibid.*, 153.
32 *Ibid.*, 155.

times commissioned, as well as his review of Milman's work, revealed the extent to which he believed the Church still was a divine institution capable of being a powerful voice for the developing working classes. Unlike many High Churchmen, Catholics, and certain Evangelicals, Newman saw the Church as a participant in the shaping of modern institutions and people, not exclusionary because of ecclesial tradition nor to be strewn aside in the march of worldly progress.

Tract 90

During the winter of 1840–1, Newman focused intently[33] on a commentary that treated the Thirty-Nine Articles of the Church of England according to Catholic principles:[34] *Tracts for the Times, No. 90: Remarks on Certain Passages of the Thirty-Nine Articles*.[35] Newman hoped that *Tract 90*, an interpretative analysis capable of generating scholarly debate, would allay those who had started clamoring for defection to Rome and would bolster the Tractarian position on the catholicity of the English Church:[36]

33 On 22 January, Newman (*LD*, VIII, 21) recorded this humorous note in his diary (with a later emendation): 'went over to a large dinner party at Wilson's Woodperry. (At this time I was hard at Number 90. and went over to him forgetting to shave.)'

34 'Catholic' here denoted Tractarian usage for the universal Church. Newman's interpretations, however, included reference to certain doctrines of the Roman Catholic Church, especially those promulgated at the Council of Trent (1545–63).

35 See 'Thirty-Nine Articles', in *The Concise Oxford Dictionary of the Christian Church*, ed. E. A. Livingstone (Oxford: Oxford University Press, 2006): 'The set of doctrinal formulas finally accepted by the [Church of England]. The first text was issued by Convocation in 1563; they received their final form in 1571. They are not a statement of Christian doctrine in the form of a creed; rather they are short summaries of dogmatic tenets, each dealing with some point raised in contemporary controversy. Various interpretations have been put on some of them, and probably this licence was intended by their framers. Until 1865 the clergy were required to accept each and every one of them, but then a more general assent was substituted, and since 1975 the Articles have only to be accepted as one of the historic formularies of the Church of England which bear witness to the faith revealed in Scripture and set forth in the catholic creed.'

36 Newman (*Apologia*, 78) did not anticipate that *Tract 90* would create the 'sudden storm of indignation' that it did; however, he did anticipate that his inter-

> It is often urged, and sometimes felt and granted, that there are in the Articles propositions or terms inconsistent with the Catholic faith ... they are perplexed how best to reply to it, or how most simply to explain the passages on which it is made to rest. The following Tract is drawn up with the view of showing how groundless the objection is, and further of approximating towards the argumentative answer to it, of which most men have an implicit apprehension, though they may have nothing more. That there are real difficulties to a Catholic Christian in the Ecclesiastical position of our Church at this day, no one can deny; but the statements of the Articles are not in the number; and it may be right at the present moment to insist upon this.[37]

Since the late 1820s, Newman had contemplated a commentary on the Thirty-Nine Articles but other involvements, such as writing about the Fathers of the Church and for the Oxford Movement, had diverted his attention.[38] In 1838, with *Tract 85*, his concerns about ecclesiastical confessions and doctrines, and especially the Roman Church, shifted his focus from the Oxford Movement's recovery of the ancient Church to current questions of catholicity.[39] He came

---

pretations might provoke controversy: for example, in the conclusion of *Tract 90* (in *The Via Media of the Anglican Church* [London: Longman, Green, & Co., 1908], 345), he defended his Catholic interpretation: 'the Articles are evidently framed on the principle of leaving open large questions, on which the controversy hinges'. After 1839, Newman had wanted to remain peaceful concerning 'subjects of the day'; *Tract 90* and the letters to *The Times* were the two exceptions.

37 Newman, *Via Media*, 269.
38 Newman, *Apologia*, 71.
39 Ibid., 89–91. See especially his 'The Catholicity of the English Church', *The British Critic* 27 (January 1840): 40–88. In *Tract 85* (*DA*, 127), which considered the Protestant doctrine of *sola scriptura* compared to Apostolic tradition, Newman concluded: 'Either Christianity contains no definite message, creed, revelation, system, or whatever other name we give it, nothing which can be made the subject of belief at all; *or*, secondly, though there really is a true creed or system in Scripture, still it is not on the surface of Scripture, but is found latent and implicit within it, and to be maintained only by indirect arguments, by comparison of texts, by inferences from what is said plainly, and by overcoming or resigning oneself to difficulties;—or again, though there is a true creed or system revealed, it is not revealed in Scripture, but must be learned collaterally from other sources'. Ker (*Biography*, 60) observed that for Newman, "The second possibility is the Anglican, while the first and third positions are the Latitudarian and Roman Catholic points of view".

to believe that a commentary on the Articles would be important because of 'the restlessness, actual and prospective, of those who neither liked the *via media*, nor my strong judgment against Rome.'[40] Newman continued:

> The main thesis then of my Essay was this:—the Articles do not oppose Catholic teaching; they but partially oppose Roman dogma; they for the most part oppose the dominant errors of Rome. And the problem was ... to draw the line as to what they allowed and what they condemned.[41]

In order to achieve this end, Newman decided to accentuate what he saw as the 'catholic' principles disseminated in the Articles:

> Such being the object which I had in view, what were my prospects of widening and of defining their meaning? The prospect was encouraging; there was no doubt at all of the elasticity of the Articles ... I wanted to ascertain what was the limit of that elasticity in the direction of Roman dogma. But next, I had a way of inquiry of my own ... my method of inquiry was to leap *in medias res*. I wished to institute an inquiry how far, in critical fairness,[42] the text *could*, be opened; I was aiming far more at ascertaining what a man who subscribed it might hold than what he must ... I was making only 'a first approximation to the required solution,'—'a series of illustrations supplying hints for the removal' of a difficulty, and with full acknowledgment 'that in minor points, whether in question of fact or of judgment, there was room for difference or error of opinion,' and that I 'should not be ashamed to own a mistake, if it were proved against me, nor reluctant to bear the just blame of it.'[43]

Newman's reading of the Thirty-Nine Articles revealed his desire for ecclesial communion between Churches, for he believed both communities shared an underlying, fundamental faith.

---

40 Newman, *Apologia*, 71 (*via media*, ibid., 64–5).

41 Ibid., 72.

42 Joseph H. McKenna ('Honesty in Theology?', *Heythrop Journal* 62 [2001]: 49–60, at 50) has contended that Newman's *Tract 90* represents the first important modern attempt at 'revisionist theology'; McKenna's selection of Newman as 'modernity's' first 'dishonest' theologian was an 'ironic choice because Newman was a man unfriendly to the modernization of belief'.

43 Newman, *Apologia*, 72–3.

In purpose and method, *Tract 90* contrasted with his letters to *The Times*. So how did this work bear upon his letters? The tract was systematic, rigorously theological, in accord with some aims of the Oxford Movement and intended, in part, to assure Romeward-leaning Anglicans to remain in their native Church.[44] However, while Newman supported his arguments, his zeal for discovering a Catholic sense in the Articles led at times to some rather contorted interpretations. Newman thought that *Tract 90*'s method and inferred conclusions would generate vigorous discussions among scholars and clergy.

He had not intended the tract to be the final word on this subject:

> Whether it was prudent or not, whether it was sensible or not, any how I attempted only a first essay of a necessary work, an essay which, as I was quite prepared to find, would require revision and modification by means of the lights which I should gain from the criticism of others. I should have gladly withdrawn any statement, which could be proved to me to be erroneous; I considered my work to be faulty and open to objection in the same sense in which I now consider my Anglican interpretations of Scripture to be erroneous; but in no other sense.[45]

His letters to *The Times* differed in most of these aspects and were aimed at a different audience, the general public. Yet he may have hoped they, like the tract, would generate debate about the Church's role in English life. Moreover, questions in *Tract 90* concerned Christian unity and a shared faith in the English and Roman confessions and these provided the core nexus between the two disparate works. As his letters to *The Times* developed one could see Newman was sensitive to this notion of faith, as both Catholics and Protestants read *The Times*. Newman's *Tract 90* may have incidentally helped spur him to compose the letters, as a diversion:

> Tract XC and the Tamworth letters appeared in the very same month of 1841, in February. It is interesting to imagine Newman turning momentarily from the almost lawyer-like precisions and theological

---

44 Rune Imberg (*In Quest for Authority* [Sweden: Lund University Press, 1987], 130) described the method that Newman employed throughout the tract: 'he worked with a series of distinctions, stating what the Articles settled, and what they did not'.

45 Newman, *Apologia*, 83.

and ecclesiastical distinctions of his last and most fateful Tract, to those easy, idiomatic, epigrammatic letters to *The Times*.[46]

Elizabeth Jay supported this idea: '*The Times*' invitation to polemical journalism must have come as welcome relief from the writing of Tract No. XC where the onus of proof lay so heavily upon Newman.'[47]

'The Duty of Christian Educators'

The Church and unity of the faith weighed on Newman's mind as he explored a path to communion with Rome in *Tract 90*. He later reflected on this to Catherine Froude on 9 April 1844: 'At the time of the publication of Number 90, I was ... desirous of union with Rome, i.e. Church with Church.'[48] To achieve this end, however, unity was also required within the Church of England and among all Protestant traditions. In the tract, Newman urged faithful Christians to strive for communion:

> The present writer, for one, will be no party to the ordinary political methods by which professed reforms are carried or compassed in this day. We can do nothing well till we act 'with one accord;' we can have no accord in action till we agree together in heart; we cannot agree without a supernatural influence; we cannot have a supernatural influence unless we pray for it; we cannot pray acceptably without repentance and confession. Our Church's strength would be irresistible, humanly speaking, were it but at unity with itself: if it remains divided, part against part, we shall see the energy which was meant to subdue the world preying upon itself, according to our SAVIOUR's express assurance that such a house 'cannot stand.' Till we feel this, till we

---

46 Charles Frederick Harrold, 'Introduction' in John Henry Newman, *Essays and Sketches*, ed. Charles Frederick Harrold (London: Longman, Green, & Co., 1948), xiii–xiv.

47 *Evangelical and Oxford Movements*, ed. Elizabeth Jay (Cambridge: Cambridge University Press, 1983), 152.

48 JHN to Catherine Froude, 9 April 1844, *LD*, X, 203–4. Newman added three more points: '2. I was strongly opposed to the idea of *individual* moves. 3. I thought the *practical* system of Rome very corrupt—and thought those corruptions balanced our quasi-schism.' After the publication and public outcry against *Tract 90*, especially its rejection by many Anglican bishops, Newman commented: '4. I thought my occupation quite gone in the Anglican Church.'

seek one another as brethren, not lightly throwing aside our private opinions, which we seem to feel we have received from above, from an ill-regulated, untrue desire of unity, but returning to each other in heart, and coming together to GOD to do for us what we cannot do for ourselves, no change can be for the better. Till we, her children, are stirred up to this religious course, let the Church ... sit still; let her children be content to be in bondage; let us work in chains; let us submit to our imperfections as a punishment; let us go on teaching with the stammering lips of ambiguous formularies, and inconsistent precedents, and principles but partially developed.[49]

Tract 90 did not pursue or fully address Newman's aspirations for full ecclesial unity. However, he did articulate an outline for unity, the faith of the Apostolic and Catholic Church, in an untitled sermon delivered at St. Mary's, 31 January 1841.[50] This sermon, subsequently labeled 'The Duty of Christian Educators', was preached while he was composing *Tract 90* and one day after he had accepted the commission from Walter III to respond to Peel's address. In it Newman displayed his preponderant theological and personal apprehensions at that time. He presented the Apostolic and Catholic Church—his 'idea' of the Church which in turn permeated his letters to *The Times*. John Coulson has illuminated what Newman intended by his 'idea' of the Church:

> It was in this sense that the Church was an idea, and our acquaintance with it was not with a simply series of concepts or propositions, but with an object as indefinable, complex, and concrete as a living thing ... Since, therefore, our response is both to a whole and to its component parts, the Church cannot be confined to one mode of presence: it will be both as diverse as the human personality, and as unified.[51]

'The Duty of Christian Educators' delineated the 'idea' that then resurfaced throughout the letters: faith grounded in the idea of the Church.

---

49 Newman, *Via Media*, 270–1.

50 Newman, *Sermons 1824–1843*, ed. Placid Murray and Francis McGrath (Oxford: Clarendon Press, 2010), III, 399.

51 John Coulson, 'Newman on the Church—his final view, its origins and influence', in *The Rediscovery of Newman: An Oxford Symposium*, ed. John Coulson and A. M. Allchin (London and Melbourne: Sheed and Ward, 1967; London: SPCK, 1967), 127.

The Background

Newman preached the sermon 'for [the] Queen's letter for [the] National Society'.[52] Because he was preaching for the National Society, he concentrated upon education as administered by the Church of England. The tone and substance of this sermon shifted away from Newman's earlier thought about educating those from other ecclesial traditions.[53] Instead, 'The Duty of Christian Educators' developed notions of the Church and education referenced for example in his 1836 'Visible Church for the Sake of the Elect', an 1838 article that raised the question of faith within the Church, and dovetailed with the contents of his subsequent letters to *The Times*.

Newman commenced by noting that the congregation had just heard St. Paul's focus upon the 'strict and intimate connection of all its members with each other' (1 Co 12). To be in the body of Christ 'every part is necessary to the whole and all to each'. Unity was an imperative, 'Such is the contribution of the Church of Christ; not more certain is a human body of destruction if divided, not more incapable … those individual Christians of spiritual life, warmth, motion and action when separated from their brethren'.[54]

The need for community was not limited to the Church, but a fundamental principle of human life and culture:

> Man is not sufficient for himself. He needs informants, guides, patterns, associates, objects of love and admiration. He is a social, imitative, progressive being; he reaches around him and forwards. He is not born complete, entire, in[-]defective, mature. He cannot rest in self. He cannot live solitary; he cannot be content with what he is. He depends on others, and is able to help others—he has powers and he has needs. And his happiness and his work lies in supplying those needs and exercising those powers.[55]

---

52 *LD*, VIII, 25. The Queen's Letter was a tri-annual pecuniary grant given to the National Society.

53 Culler (*The Imperial Intellect*, 102) recounted that in 1834, on the heels of the Reform Act and the push to nationalize education, a petition was offered for 'mixed' education of Dissenters and Anglicans at Cambridge and Oxford. Newman (*LD*, IV, 208–9) opposed this petition, 'scribbling' a prophetic yet practical response to Hugh James Rose, then editor of the *British Magazine*.

54 *Sermons 1824–1843*, III, 399–400.

55 Ibid., III, 400.

Because people depended upon each other in community and because knowledge and experience were both relational and traditional, Newman regarded the formation of opinion or belief a first principle in education:

> And what is true of man in other respects, is quite as true as regards his opinions, moral and religious—He has to learn them. He is not born with them, he [is] not *able* to form them; he must receive them. And this is the use of education, in that point of view in which I am especially called today to consider it, it is the formation of opinion.[56]

There were prevalent approaches to the formation of opinion, especially religious opinion in British society. The first, which Newman perceived to be relatively limited, was that the young should be left to form their own opinions.[57] The second, which he considered widespread, was that because Christians were divided, a general notion of religion should be taught, 'but not Christian principles in their fullness.'[58] These flawed approaches were the result of a fractured Body of Christ, the Church:

> We Christians are all divided into sects and when we educate we seem to be giving, not the opinions of the body, but (as it were) the opinions of the separate hand, or foot, or eye … We seem to impart the belief not of the Church, but of our own sect.[59]

Newman affirmed the plausibility of segregated Christian education in the present age, but this fell short of the Christian 'idea' of the Church:

> It was not always this. Once there was in Christendom one Church Catholic, and one only, full of the notes of grace, uniform in teaching, various in gifts, rich in saints … When the truth by [sic] was quite plain, there is no doubt whether day is light or dark, or night dark or light. But when we come to the fine varied shades of colour, the case is different. Such is the case in these dreary times, in this cold melancholy anxious age, when all that is of this world abounds and thrives, when nations are great, and art has almost reached miracle, and science has well nigh revealed mysteries, and the riches of the

---

56 *Ibid.*

57 This contrasts with the West today in which children forming their own beliefs has become commonplace.

58 *Ibid.*, III, 400.

59 *Ibid.*

whole earth are becoming the property of each part of it, but alas in which religion to has become rank and grown into many unhealthy shapes and run into wild courses, and is weaker and weaker in proportion as it has become more various. Now no longer is it a choice between light and darkness, day and night, but between finer and paler shades of colour—and in which it is difficult to say which is good and which is bad, and this or that is to be chosen only because it is less far removed from that which certainly is not to be chosen.[60]

Newman returned to the generally held belief that Christian educators should refrain from teaching their own 'particular notions of Christianity'. He did 'not deny the reasonableness of the objection' but he denied that it applied to the 'English Church educating our children carefully and exactly in her faith'.[61]

Now if we look abroad all over the whole world and do not confine ourselves into this narrow corner of the earth in which we live, we shall find that Christians do every where agree in the main points of doctrine, in spite of their differences in lesser matters, and if so the objection will be found clearly not to apply to our teaching, so far as that teaching agrees with the teaching of the Catholic Church at large. The Church of Christ looked at in its width and breadth cannot err; for the promise is express to it ... If then we teach what all Christian Churches teach everywhere, we are following no private notions of our own, we are impressing on children committed to us nothing of a sectarian or private character ... but we are simply leading them to the voice of God and teaching them to listen <hear> and obey it.[62]

Newman appealed to the Scriptures to bolster this line of thought:

We have nothing to fear then while we teach after the pattern of that Church which the Apostles founded—and which has the promises—and while that Church is there is no manner of doubt at all—for there is but one such, and it lasts (as was foretold) to this day, and all over the earth too, as was also foretold ... Are not those words clearly in our Bibles? [Is] there any doubt when we look abroad into the world at large, what and where the Church is and what is her teaching every where? Is she not called the Church? does not the Scripture now

60 *Ibid.*, III, 401.
61 *Ibid.*
62 *Ibid.*, III, 402.

belong exclusively to one religious communion? ... *where can we be wrong if the Bible is right?*⁶³

Newman acknowledged the difficultly teaching a Catholic faith among the many Christian traditions as well as the 'fearful' responsibility—to God and fellow believers—that a Christian educator had in influencing the young. He believed, nevertheless, that this difficulty could be overcome, because the Spirit continued to inform the whole Body of Christ:

> We are not teaching private opinions while we teach doctrines which the Christian Church, (with whom are the promises), has ever taught, which it teaches now and everywhere in every part of the world ... For while we thus proceed, we discover and secure the teaching of that Spirit who lives in the whole body, and not in parts of the body except while they are its parts—in <by> whom the whole body of the Church is governed and sanctified, by whom we are baptized into the one body, and into whom we been all made to drink.⁶⁴

Despite of the 'most serious and melancholy differences' between ecclesial communities, Newman believed that essentially the English Church taught what the 'Catholic Church teaches'. He supported his claim by citing the Catechism of the Church of England as the 'rule of [their] teaching'. The Catechism essentially contained the 'fundamental faith': the doctrine of baptism, the Creed, Ten Commandments, and the Lord's Prayer, and concluded 'with a distinct account of the two sacraments [baptism and the Lord's Supper] necessary for salvation.'⁶⁵

> Here we have the teaching which all the Church has ever held,—everywhere and always. The Greek will recognize it and the Latin which [would] not dissent from it. The first age of Christians held it, and the present has not forsaken it. This is the faith of the Saints—the doctrine of the Blessed Trinity in Unity—the Incarnation of our Lord Jesus Christ—His immaculate conception—His birth, ministry, sufferings, death, atonement, resurrection, victory, Kingdom—the Mission of the Holy Ghost, the Holy Law, the privilege of prayer, the power of the Sacraments, the prerogatives of Holy Church, the unseen communion of all Saints, the

---

63 *Ibid.*, III, 403.
64 *Ibid.*, III, 404.
65 *Ibid.*, III, 404–5.

resurrection of the dead, the life everlasting, such I say is the faith of the Church throughout the whole world—In putting *it* forward therefore we hazard no private speculation. If Christianity itself be true, this faith is true too. The revelation and the faith have ever gone together—the one was never without the other. Revelation implies a thing revealed—*This* is that message; not a private idea of our own minds ... but a public notorious announcement ... If *this* is a sectarian doctrine, *Christianity* is sectarian.[66]

Newman reminded his listeners that those who diverged from this faith were truly sectarian. But those who adhered to the faith—which he adroitly summarized—are but 'fulfilling the divine command "Freely ye have received, freely give" [Mat 10:18]'.[67] Newman concluded with a nod to the Queen's patronage of the Church and the duty of all 'to teach what you have learned—to aid in continuing unto the end what has the promise of eternity'.[68]

'The Duty of Christian Educators' sketched in part a Church nostalgically pined for: 'Once there was in Christendom one Church Catholic, and one only, full of the notes of grace, uniform in teaching, various in gifts, rich in saints'.[69] This Church had, over time, disintegrated into various sects.[70] However, he saw that the Church(es) had a maintained a unified faith, however hidden among the currents of intra-communal strife and the slow secularization of Britain and Europe. In so far as various ecclesial communities proclaimed the Trinity, performed baptism, preached the Word, and so forth, they proclaimed 'the faith of the Church throughout the whole world ... If *Christianity* itself be true, this faith is true too.' This 'true faith' rising from the one Church fulfilled what Newman believed to be an essential mark of unity, the Vincentian canon: 'we have the teaching which all the Church has ever held,—everywhere and always'.[71] Thus, in this sermon Newman was

---

66 Ibid., III, 405.
67 Ibid., III, 405–6.
68 Ibid., III, 406.
69 Ibid., III, 401.
70 Ibid., III, 401–2.
71 Ibid., III, 405. Vincent of Lerins (d. 450) expressed the universality of the Church in the phrase: 'quod ubique, quod semper, quod ab omnibus creditum est'. Newman was extremely interested in Lerins's canon in *An Essay on the Development*

able to wed, in his own thought, the ancient, medieval, and now modern Church together in faith.

Although 'The Duty of Christian Educators' was unpublished and considered by Newman a perfunctory duty of his ministry, it provided a clear window into his ecclesiological concerns in 1841. This sermon presented a direct answer to Newman's own questions about where Christian faith was to be found, an answer that his published works, *Tract 90* and his letters to *The Times*, could only allude to. Perhaps the most important contribution of 'The Duty of Christian Educators' to understanding his letters to *The Times* was Newman's point that faith comes from the 'bosom of the Church'. He expressed the fundamental and shared faith laying upon the 'bosom of the Church' as *Christianity*. Indeed, Christianity denoted his 'idea' of the Church—not one particular sect or historical era but 'that Spirit who lives in the whole body [of Christ]'.[72] By identifying Christianity with the Church Newman did not create an abstract referent that encompassed all Christian sects. Rather, Christianity was the 'idea' that Coulson surmised in Newman's thought about the Church: a reality, 'indefinable, complex, and concrete as a living thing'. This 'living thing' or better 'living stones' (1 P 2:5) was the full (yet imperfect) expression of the Apostolic and Catholic Church.[73]

Avoiding Controversy

Newman preached 'The Duty of Christian Educators' knowing he would compose letters for *The Times*. He had prepared *Tract 90* knowing that his interpretation of the Thirty-Nine Articles might unsettle some people. Indeed in his *Apologia*, he recounted that 'there had been a smouldering, stern, energetic animosity, not at all unnat-

---

of Doctrine (1845). For a contemporary, although uneven discussion of Newman's use of Lerins see Thomas Guarino, *Vincent of Lerins and the Development of Christian Doctrine* (Grand Rapids, MI: Baker Academic, 2013), 43–80.

72 Newman previously made this identification in 'Evangelical Sanctity the Perfection of Natural Virtue' (6 March 1831), OUS, 37–47 [37–53]. He provided further explanation in *An Essay on Development of Christian Doctrine*, 33–41; 55–75.

73 For example, Newman, 'Milman's *History of Christianity*', 85–6.

ural, partly rational [feeling] against its author' for quite some time.[74] Although not fully aware of these sentiments at the dawn of 1841, Newman was reticent to agitate for the Tractarian cause beyond ecclesial settings or *Tract 90*. This attitude can be perceived in his gentle chiding of Frederick Rogers on 10 January about his views on Roman Catholic rituals: 'I declare I think it as rare a thing, candour in controversy, as to be a Saint'.[75] Two weeks later, he penned a remarkable and prescient response to a Robert Belaney on a similar theme and noted that, among other things, controversy may actually impede one's ability to perceive truth:

> I have great confidence in the maxim, Magna est veritas et praevalebit [Truth is great and will prevail], where the incipient flame is not blown out at once. The one thing I feared and deprecated years ago, when we began the Tracts for the Times, was the utter neglect of us on the part of the Church. I was not afraid of being misrepresented, censured or illtreated—and certainly hitherto it has done no harm. Every attack hitherto has turned to good, or at least is dying a natural death.[76] But *Controversy* does but delay the sure victory of truth by making people angry. When they find out they are wrong of *themselves*, a generous feeling rises in their minds towards the persons and things they have abused and resisted. Much of this reaction has already taken place. Controversy too is a waste of time—one has other things to do. Truth can fight its own battle. It has a reality in it, which shivers to pieces swords of earth. As far as we are not on the side of truth, we shall shiver to bits, and I am willing it should be so. The only cause of the prevalence of fallacies for the last 300 years has been the strong arm of the civil power countenancing them. This can hardly continue now. I see too that in the rising generation the most influential and stirring men in Church and State have in them a root of Catholic principles. All this is hopeful, that (whether any thing is to come of it or not) I do not think it can be made more hopeful by controversy. It is very painful certainly to find individual instances in which fallacious arguments have told with effect—but I doubt whether they can well be met for the benefit of such persons

---

74 Newman, *Apologia*, 85.
75 *LD*, VIII, 10–11.
76 Because of its controversial interpretations, *Tract 90* turned out to be the last of the *Tracts for the Times*.

'An aristocracy of exalted spirits'

except by those who are acquainted with them and know how best to influence and persuade them.⁷⁷

This note provided a window into Newman's state of mind in early 1841 as he was writing his letters: he detailed the Tractarian movement, his role in it, the problem of the Established Church, and his hope that (Catholic) truth would prevail. Newman had to be convinced to accept the commission from *The Times*, because he knew it invited controversy, and he was trying to do as he advised others. Thus in choosing to write the letters, he elected anonymity so as not to bring controversy directly upon him or jeopardize the Movement.

The Walters' Offer

John Walter III had written to Newman on 11 January and received a reply one week later. This correspondence preceded Peel's address. There was no indication in the exchange that Walter III asked Newman to write for *The Times*, although Newman may have had a standing offer.⁷⁸ However, on 30 January, Newman recorded in his diary, 'Walter came down *to Oxford* and called'. Newman later amended the entry with a parenthetical note: ('about letters of Catholicus in The Times'),⁷⁹ thereby indicating that Walter III served as the initial liaison between him and *The Times*.

On 2 February, after their face-to-face meeting, Walter III wrote to Newman to thank him for their meeting and to clarify what *The Times* expected. Walter also informed Newman that he would receive the Bain pamphlet of Peel's address:

8. Charing Cross Tuesday—Feb 2. [1841]

My dear Sir,

I write to thank you most sincerely on my own behalf and on my Father's for having so kindly undertaken the subject on which we were speaking the other day. I think the letters should be about a

---

77 JHN to Robert Belaney (25 January 1841), *LD*, VIII, 23–4.
78 Newman may have had such an offer from Walter III, who wanted to recruit Tractarians to write for *The Times* (*LD*, VII, 448).
79 *LD*, VIII, 25.

The Background

column and a half in length each, and with regard to the number of them, your own judgment will be your best guide.

My Father will send you down the Pamphlet this evening—and will be glad of the MS. as soon as you can conveniently prepare them.

Believe me sincerely Yr obliged friend J. Walter[80]

Several studies of *The Tamworth Reading Room* have interpreted Newman's recollection of 'Walter' as implying the senior Walter visiting him. However, the letter confirmed that it was Walter III and not his father who initially met with Newman at Oxford.[81] Walter III seemed buoyant about the 'subject on which [they] were speaking the other day'. His note set the initial parameters for how Newman's response would unfold—their approximate length and the number of letters to be written. That the number of letters was left up to Newman would soon become a point of contention between the parties.[82] It was Walter II that later sent Peel's pamphlet to Newman.

Newman already had three or four days to study the newspaper version of the address, as Newman received the pamphlet on 3 February, along with Walter's letter.[83] The discrepancy between the language and meaning in Peel's initial address and the later pamphlet concerned Newman—a concern that became evident in his letters.

Some time between the meeting on 30 January and 4 February, Newman finished the first letter. Burgis described a plausible explanation for its timing: 'the manuscript was in the printers' hands in time for it to be inserted on Friday, 5 February so that it must have been sent off almost as soon as Walter's [3 February] letter arrived. Possibly he had

---

80 John Walter III to JHN (8 Charing Cross, 2 February 1841), *LD*, VIII, 25.

81 See Ker, *Biography*, 206; Gilley, *Newman and his Age*, 195; *Letters and Diaries* (VIII, 25) and (XIV, 52). However, the letter of 2 February, along with Burgis's research (*TRR*, 24; 63), have corroborated that it was John Walter III who first called on Newman. Walter II may have also attended the meeting, although in his diary Newman only indicated that 'Walter' called on him. However, Walter II did meet with Newman at some point (*LD*, VIII, 31). This visit appeared to be corroborated in Newman's correspondence with Henry Wilberforce on 22 February (*LD*, VIII, 40), in which Walter II presumably was mentioned as visiting Newman. For more on this see Chapter 7, 'Correspondence between Newman and John Moore Capes'.

82 *LD*, VIII, 30–1.

83 *LD*, VIII, 25.

begun writing before he heard from Walter; from the first paragraph in the surviving MS it seems that when he began he had not seen the pamphlet which Walter said his father would send down "this evening", presumably the text of the Address published by Bain with its differences from the version given in *The Times*.[84]

The First Letter: An Anonymous Venture[85]

These activities and the offer culminated in Newman's first letter to the editor of *The Times*, which appeared on Friday, 5 February 1841. Newman dissected Peel's address and concentrated on three themes: human nature and its need for completion, knowledge in relation to human nature and to religion, and the assumption that secular knowledge produced societal unity.[86] This anonymous letter not only reacted to Peel but also correlated his thought to one of his political rivals, Henry Brougham, in order to show the two in unison regarding education detached from religion.

Newman had presumed that readers were familiar with Peel's address.[87] He opened his letter with the conventional 'Sir'. Because Peel was a political figure, Newman asserted his 'words and deeds' were 'public property'. Many who had read his address published some two to three weeks earlier in various papers must have found that it contained 'startling language'. Newman cast Peel—'this most excellent

---

84 Burgis, TRR, 64.

85 Burgis (*TRR*, 65) has noted that the first letter was unsigned but the following letters had the pseudonym 'Catholicus'. Accordingly, for the first letter Newman will be referred to as author; for the subsequent letters, Catholicus will be cited.

86 These themes roughly corresponded to Newman's title in 1872: 'Secular Knowledge in contrast with Religion' (*DA*, 254). The title seemed to indicate a clear contrast between 'secular knowledge' and 'religion'. However, such a contrast did not emerge. The term 'religion' was given brief and reference at the beginning and end of the letter, and its meaning implied. Perhaps Newman assumed his audience had a working knowledge of what 'religion' entailed. One can only surmise why he thought that this later title aided and clarified the letter—it would have been superfluous in the letter's initial appearance.

87 The version of the letters that will be used here first appeared in *The Times* in February 1841 and republished in Newman's *Letters and Diaries* (VIII, 536–61); references in the text will use these page numbers.

The Background

and distinguished man'—in sympathetic irony. He chided Peel's choice to revise and circulate his address as a pamphlet because it was 'not published in the fulness [sic] in which it was spoken'. Peel's status had compelled Newman

> to animadvert upon [the address] as it has appeared in your columns, since in that shape it will have the widest circulation. A public man must not claim to harangue the whole world in newspapers, and then to offer his second thoughts to such as choose to buy them at a bookseller's.[88] (534)

In comparing Peel's address in *The Times* to the pamphlet, Newman seemed to have received quite a shock. Some authors have maintained that in making the comparison, Newman was being needlessly provocative.[89] Yet, Newman's observation about Peel's revisions was both sardonic and yet addressed his concern about how language, ideas, and media influence opinion. Peel did 'harangue' the working class and even certain members of the Church in his address, but this was softened in the pamphlet. Newman's phrase 'the whole world' was hyperbole, yet the address had been circulated in one form or another in all the major newspapers, including *The Times*.[90]

Newman was concerned with more than the address in itself. Peel had been inspired by Buckland's letter to include scientists and men of industry who had achieved financial success through scientific

---

88 Burgis (*TRR*, 64) provided the context for this arresting line: 'In the MS of Letter 1 the first paragraph originally ended at "express act of its author". Before despatch Newman added a sentence ... and when the letter appeared in *The Times* the sentence had been expanded and altered ["A public man ..."]. In addition, the arrival of the pamphlet after the letter had been written would account for a difference between the MS and *The Times* in one of Newman's quotations from Peel.'

89 Coats ('Rhetorical Approaches', 175) maintained that Newman's depiction of Peel 'haranguing the whole world' was simply *ad hominem*. Jay (*Evangelical and Oxford Movements*, 152) found Newman's phrase disingenuous: 'Such revision between editions was the habitual practice of writers on controversial subjects and makes Newman's opening jibe at a politician exercising his immemorial right to emend between speech and pamphlet appear even more cavalier'.

90 Jay, *Evangelical and Oxford Movements*, 152. In certain spots Peel reverted to what must have been customary, although from today's perspective condescending if not scolding, tones toward the poor and working class in his address.

knowledge. Newman had no way of knowing about their correspondence, but he identified an intellectual tradition that undergirded and united both Peel and Buckland. He saw that Peel had derived certain of his ideas on knowledge, religion, and education from a philosophical tradition that ranged from ancient stoics to the vanguard of utilitarian and radical thought in Britain. This tradition in its current form targeted secular education for the working class but also for relatively new secular universities in England. Newman had recognized the modern incarnation of this tradition in 1829 in the wake of Catholic emancipation. In the letter to his mother he noted 'the spirit at work against [the Church] is one of latitudinarianism, indifferentism, republicanism, and schism, a spirit which tends to overthrow doctrine'. This tradition had formidable minds, 'the talent of the day', who made plausible secular education apart from the Church.[91] In a passage analogous to that of *The Spectator*, Newman drew a connection between the advent of the secular London University and the Tamworth reading room and library, both developments of this tradition:

> I shall surprise no one who has carefully read Sir Robert's Address ... that, did a person take it up without looking at the heading, he would to a certainty set it down as a production of the years 1827 and 1828,—the scene Gower Street, the speaker Mr. Brougham or Dr Lushington, and the occasion, the laying the first stone, or the inauguration, of the then-called London University.[92] (534)

Newman then set the course for his critique of Peel, on education but also on the epistemic and religious principles underpinning the address: 'Sir Robert [has given] expression to a theory of morals and religion, which of course, in a popular speech, was not put out in a very dogmatic form' (534). He gleaned from and expanded on these principles from Peel's remarks and examples. Newman then shaped and summarized Peel's convictions about human nature, the *function* of knowledge—and indirectly—religion:[93]

---

91 *LD*, II, 129–30.

92 The University of London was the first university in England to have no religious affiliation. Armytage (*Four Hundred Years*, 103) noted that the University of London was erected upon a 'disused rubbish dump in Gower Street'.

93 Newman (*LD*, VIII, 536) added a caveat, distinguishing Peel and Brougham,

> Human nature ... if left to itself, becomes sensual and degraded. Uneducated men live in the indulgence of their passions, or, if they are merely taught to read, they dissipate and debase their minds by trifling or vicious publications. Education is the cultivation of the intellect and heart, and useful knowledge is the great instrument of education. It is the parent of virtue, the nurse of religion; it exalts man to his highest perfection, and is the sufficient scope of his most earnest exertions. (534)

Newman highlighted one of the principal assumptions evident in Peel's address. Practical or useful knowledge, not wisdom or religious truth, elevated human nature, which was not marked by sin, but rather mere sensuality. Thus knowledge that could be put to some end, and move the person, was in a sense salvific. It brought humans to a worldly perfection that for Peel was laudable. Newman vehemently opposed such thinking, as both the diagnosis and cure were in error, and implied grace could heal sinful human beings. He expanded his sarcastic portrait of knowledge as salvific balm:

> Physical and moral science rouses, transports, exalts, enlarges, tranquillizes, and satisfies the mind.[94] Its attractiveness obtains a hold over us; the excitement attending it supersedes grosser excitements; it makes us know our duty, and thereby enables us to do it; by taking the mind off itself, it destroys anxiety; and by providing objects of admiration, it soothes and subdues us.
>
> And, in addition, it is a kind of neutral ground, on which men of every shade of politics and religion may meet together, disabuse each other of their prejudices, form intimacies, and secure cooperation. (534)

Had Newman simply confined his argument to adult and university education or to Peel's politics of expediency, then his letter would have been indistinguishable from several articles that had already appeared in print. However, Newman further critiqued Peel's ideas about human

with a tinge of satire: The only 'difference between the Gower Street and the Tamworth Exhibition' was that 'Sir Robert's personal religious feeling breaks out in his Address across his assumed philosophy. The author I say assumed; I might say affected—for I think too well of him to believe it genuine.'

94 Although Peel discussed physical science at length, he did not address morality or ethics thematically or directly; however, he certainly made many moral claims, for example, that investigations into physical science could exalt our moral nature.

nature. Peel, he implied albeit sardonically, believed religion to be important to discipline the populace and to uphold the Church–State alliance. However, because Peel equated religion with the moral order and thus did not consider other important theological doctrines, he apparently did not understand the nature–grace distinction. As a result, Peel believed that nature could be fulfilled by an increase in empirical knowledge, such as geology or political economy. Newman's jagged analysis plunged into these ideas, in many cases going beyond what Peel actually had allowed (or imagined) in his address.

Peel had tried to equate faith with reason and science with religion. However, in Newman's judgment, Peel had allowed faith and religion to be usurped by reason and science. He exploited Peel's position that a scientific education could become 'the parent of virtue and the nurse of religion'; or that such knowledge truly could satisfy, 'exalt, if not complete' the desires and lacunae inherent in human nature. Finally, Newman homed in on Peel's wish for knowledge to overcome the differences that existed among people. Peel had extolled the new sciences and morals and presumed that they wielded such power that they would produce a unity that neither politics nor religion had yet achieved.

Newman extended his portrayal of how useful knowledge—not grace—completed nature through a swift comparison between Peel and Brougham. To do so, he catalogued the affinities between the writings of Brougham and others in his school of thought and Peel's speech.[95]

---

95 John Walter III also noticed this mischievous marrying of minds; see his letter of 5 February (*LD*, VIII, 26). For Brougham's writings: Henry Brougham, *A Discourse of the Objects, Advantages, and Pleasures of Science* (London: Baldwin, Craddock, and Joy, 1827). Newman mistakenly attributed Craik's *Pursuit of Knowledge* to Brougham; Craik's work had been published anonymously through Brougham's SDUK. Newman most likely did not have a copy that attributed the work to Craik. Of the twenty three different quotations which Newman attributed to Brougham in the first letter, twelve came from Craik; however, many of Craik's ideas are similar if not identical to ideas in Brougham's writings. Newman seemed to have been familiar with both works, and used them simultaneously when composing the letter. What is surprising, if not disappointing, is that by 1872, Newman realized his error about Craik—or it had been pointed out to him. Newman emended this in a footnote (*DA*, 256): 'This latter work is wrongly ascribed to Lord Brougham in this passage. It is, however, of the Brougham school'. He chose not to attribute phrases to Craik which were found in his work, but continued to identify them with

The Background

Newman noted that Brougham's university address was wandering and 'expatiated' where Peel's approach showed a more 'characteristic moderation'. In bringing these two together, Newman knew that this was not an immediate or obvious comparison for his readers, considering they had been political rivals. However, according to Wendell Harris, around 1841 Brougham was generally held in disrepute and thus 'to cite and develop the parallel is of course a strategic choice; there was evident gain from directing an attack against the less popular figure while lamenting that Peel ... seemed to be following in his footsteps.'[96]

Newman began with an excerpt from Brougham and then followed with a word or phrase from Peel's address.[97] Indeed, seven consecutive paragraphs began with 'Mr. Brougham', and then 'Sir Robert'. Newman's decision to lead with Brougham was not simply chronological; Brougham had been a prominent figure in secular education. At this point, his figure eclipsed Peel's.[98]

That Peel had capitulated to radical or utilitarian ideas about education had already been noted in the *Sun* and in the *The Spectator*. Neither, however, had developed Newman's selective pairing. He flashed terms and ideas so that his readers could quickly apprehend the connections:

> Mr. Brougham pronounces that a man by 'learning truths wholly new to him,' and by 'satisfying himself of the grounds on which known truths rest,' 'will enjoy a *proud consciousness* of having, by his own exertions, become a *wiser*, and *therefore* a more *exalted* creature.' Sir Robert runs abreast of this great sentiment. He tells us, in words which he adopts as his own,[99] that a man 'in becoming *wiser* will

Brougham. Although rhetorically more effective to have one name counterposed to Peel's, it was rather disingenuous in its republication not to acknowledge Craik, whose importance in the letters in some sense outweighed Brougham's.

96 Wendell Harris, 'Historical Forces', 194.

97 Newman's excerpts from Craik and Brougham did not always conform to their original wording or, on occasion, to their original context. Some newspapers caught up in the ensuing controversy made much of this fact. Newman however did not betray either author's general sense.

98 Newman seemed to concede that Peel did not rely intentionally or explicitly on Brougham (*LD*, VIII, 537; 540).

99 Coats ('Rhetorical Approaches', 178) mistakenly accused Newman of claiming that Peel adopted Brougham's words 'as his own' and thus 'plagiarized' Brougham. Peel was actually quoting Sir Humphry Davy.

> become *better:* he will 'rise *at once* in the scale of intellectual and moral existence, and by being accustomed to such contemplations, he will feel the *moral dignity* of his nature *exalted.*' (536)

Such comparisons were meant to shock, amuse, and generate curiosity. Newman, however, also made a sober point about what he deemed a distortion of the purpose of scientific knowledge. For Peel, knowledge induced an 'aspiration for distinction' among the poor and placed 'premiums on skill and intelligence':

> At length [Peel] breaks out into almost conventicle eloquence, crying, 'Every newspaper *teems with notices* of publications written upon *popular principles*, detailing all the recent discoveries of science, and their connexion with improvements in arts and manufactures. *Let me earnestly entreat you* not to neglect the *opportunity* which we are now willing to afford you!'[100] (535–6)

Newman confronted Peel's advocacy for societal progress, especially through university and adult education. Some scholars have concluded that Newman's questioning of science and technology seemed a camouflaged form of antipathy towards the working class.[101] Coats believed that Newman harbored such a resentment:

> The opening of the reading room took on a particularly odious character when Newman considered the public targeted for improvement, namely men and women of all classes. The great danger here, he said, lay in allowing scientific instruction to take place prior to religious instruction.[102]

Coats conflated two separate issues: although Newman wanted religious instruction to have priority, the letters did not indicate a desire to impede education for all. Indeed, in several letters, especially the seventh, Newman agreed with Peel that all people should receive an education—the question for him was what constituted an education, which should include religious instruction, and from where, which

---

100 Newman then quoted the following lines of Peel's speech: '"*It will not be our fault* if the ample page of knowledge, rich with the spoils of time, is not unrolled to you! *We tell you*", etc., etc.' To Newman, Peel's 'harangue' seemed grandiose and out of touch with the working class.
101 See for example, Harris, 'Historical Forces', 205–6.
102 Coats, 'Rhetorical Approaches', 176.

The Background

should include the Church. Ultimately, Newman insisted that Peel's general view of education and its impact upon the working class was too narrow.[103]

Newman also provided an indirect critique of knowledge in relation to the university and to religion. Drawing from Brougham's inaugural address at the University of Glasgow,[104] Newman highlighted Brougham's view of religion in relation to knowledge. Brougham believed that knowledge, by 'putting to flight "the evil spirits of *tyranny and persecution*",[105] would no longer leave men to wander '*blindfold, in ignorance*'. Peel, in a similar vein, implied that those who are disposed to dogmatic or partisan 'religion' are prone to 'depress'[106] those trying to obtain knowledge (536).

Newman then abruptly shifted from the pairing of Brougham and Peel and turned the brunt of his critique toward Brougham:

> Mr. Brougham laid down at Glasgow the infidel principle, or, as he styles it, 'the great truth,' which 'has gone forth to all the ends of the earth, that man shall no more render account to man for his belief, over which he has himself no control.' (536)

These lines from Brougham's speech provide a crucial insight into Newman's argument about knowledge usurping religion. Knowledge could be learned and controlled by reason, religious belief was akin to an emotional response, over which humans have no control. In raising this point about Brougham, Newman returned to his initial difficulty

---

103 Recent articles in *The British Critic* may have inspired Newman's critique. See Chapter 8 for more on Newman's view on working-class education as an Oratorian.

104 'Inaugural Discourse of Henry Brougham, Esq., M. P., on being installed Lord Rector of the University of Glasgow' (Wednesday, 6 April 1825), in *Speeches of Henry Lord Brougham: upon Questions relating to Public Rights, Duties, and Interests with Historical Introductions* (Philadelphia: Lea and Blanchard, 1841), II, 114–29. Although Newman did not mention this address, he may have assumed his readers were aware of the fact that both Brougham and Peel served as rectors of the University of Glasgow.

105 By implication, these 'evil spirits' owed their life to religion (Brougham, *Speeches*, II, 128).

106 Newman equivocated here: Brougham used the word 'depress' to describe the philosopher Blaise Pascal (1623–62) in a way akin to psychological depression; Peel, however, used 'depressed' in the sense of actually keeping someone down.

'An aristocracy of exalted spirits'

with the secular university. His spare and subtle editing, however, did not provide the full context surrounding Brougham's infidel principle.[107] Yet, the principle was embedded in a past speech which some readers might have recalled. There Brougham disclosed many elements recapitulated in Peel's address that disconcerted Newman.

Brougham had distinguished between meritorious action and accidental opinion, his hope for the end of bigotry (implied in religious and political factions), and the unity formed by rational and scientific discourse. Newman combined these remarks with excerpts from Stephen Lushington's address at the opening of the University of London. Lushington was a colleague of Brougham and supported his efforts in education:

> And Dr. Lushington applied it [the infidel principle] ... by asking, 'Will any one argue for establishing a *monopoly* to be enjoyed by the few who are of one *denomination* of the Christian Church only?' And he went on to speak of 'the association and union of all *without exclusion or restriction* ... [thus] the softening of asperities which *ignorance and separation* have fostered'. (536)

Lushington had blended practical reasons for a secular university[108] with a desire to reduce confessional religious ties.[109] Newman objected to the view that secular knowledge necessarily softens bigotry and engenders societal cohesion and unity, although did not carry out the objection. Returning to the present, he showed Peel's ideas to be the unwitting progeny of the designs of Brougham, Lushington *et alii*—although not (yet) as daring. Nevertheless, the themes of unity through knowledge and of relaxing religious commitments were cemented in his mind:

---

107 Brougham, *Speeches*, II, 128. An excerpt of the text can be found in Appendix II.

108 In this speech, Lushington invoked a general Providence—a non-denominational God who has given man intellectual excellence as his greatest gift.

109 The broader swath of Lushington's speech possibly prompted Newman to include it in his portrait of Peel. For Lushington, progress to societal enlightenment required the severing of the University of London from Oxford and Cambridge, as indicated in the *Statement by the Council of the University of London, Explanatory of the Nature and Objects of the Institution*, ed. Thomas Coats (London: Richard Taylor, 1827), 52–4; see Appendix II.

The Background

> Long may it be before Sir Robert Peel professes the great principle itself! even though, as the following passages show, he is inconsistent enough to think highly of its application in the culture of the mind. He speaks, for instance, of 'this preliminary and fundamental rule, that no works of controversial divinity shall enter into the library'—of 'the institution being open to all persons of all descriptions, without reference to political opinions, or religious creed,'—and of 'an edifice in which men of all political opinions and all religious feelings may unite in the furtherance of knowledge, without the asperities of party feeling.' Now, that British society should consist of persons of different religions, is this a positive standing evil, to be endured at best as unavoidable, or a topic of exultation?[110] Of exultation, answers Sir Robert; the greater differences the better,[111] the more the merrier. So we must interpret his tone. (537)

Like *The Spectator*, Newman marveled at how Brougham's doctrines had infiltrated Peel's public thoughts and words. He saw that Brougham was 'leading in chains behind his chariot-wheels, a great captive, is a fact beyond question. Such is the reward in 1841 for unpopularity in 1827' (537). Behind this derisive image, however, was Newman's insight that the triumph of scientific knowledge in opposition to religious knowledge had moved to a powerful conservative leader in Peel.

Newman realized that comparisons to Brougham might be considered 'a slur upon the fair fame of Sir Robert Peel'; however, Brougham's influence on Peel's views (whether direct or indirect) required his critiques. Indeed, he hoped 'to be allowed an opportunity of assigning others'.

> It is, indeed, most melancholy to see so sober and experienced a man practising the antics of one of the wildest performers of this wild age; and taking off the tone, manner, and gestures of the versatile ex-Chancellor, with a versatility almost equal to his own. Yet let him be assured that the task of rivalling such a man is hopeless, as well as

---

110 In *Tract 90*, Newman made it clear that he desired unity between Catholics and Anglicans. The letter broached a different aspect of Christian unity, emphasizing that a fundamental faith united Churches in ways that human knowledge could not.

111 In regard to ecclesial schism, Newman earlier commented in his essay, 'The State of Religious Parties', *The British Critic* 25 (1839): 396–426, at 396: 'It is melancholy that there should be parties at all in a body which its Divine Founder intended to be one'.

unprofitable. No one can equal the great sophist. Lord Brougham is inimitable in his own line. (537)

Beyond the sharp critiques, Burgis captured Newman's sense of flippancy in all this: 'Two "humorous images" sum up his drift in the first Letter: Peel dragged at the wheels of Brougham's chariot, and Peel taking off Brougham's tone, manner and gestures, but both are lightly touched in and the effect is intellectual rather than pictorial; moreover Newman studiously preserves his own gravity, finding Peel's antics "most melancholy" not "most amusing".[112]

Newman concluded the letter with flair, and one can see that in comparison to his preaching, editorship, and labor on *Tract 90*, he enjoyed the anonymity and the wry dig at Brougham and Peel. And yet his tone was equally ominous, for it meant that Brougham had succeeded in convincing a powerful politician, and in a certain sense the Church had failed to do the same.

---

112 Burgis, TRR, 166.

✥ 4 ✥

The Catholicus Letters 2–4

O N THE DAY that his first letter was published Newman received a note of praise from *The Times*. The author of the note, however, was not John Walter III; rather, it was from his father. Newman's diary entries did not distinguish between authors. Nor did the notes themselves contain explicit evidence as to their author, they were signed 'J. Walter'. The editors of Newman's *Letters and Diaries* have attributed the notes which Newman received throughout February to Walter III's hand. Burgis and Henry Tristram have maintained that only the first note to Newman was written by Walter III. All subsequent correspondence was from Walter II.[1]

The position of Burgis and Tristram seems the most plausible for several reasons. First, a formal tone, absent in the first, can be detected in the second note. Next, the content of the letter indicated someone responsible for formatting and printing; Walter III's note indicated that his father would be the one who received Newman's manuscripts for publication. In addition, Walter III was not associated with the day-to-day operations of the paper, while his father was. Finally, the conventional closing of the second letter, 'Believe me my dear Sir yours most truly', differed from Walter III's more intimate closing, 'Believe me sincerely Yr obliged friend'. This closing remained a consistent feature in subsequent exchanges, as found in the letter from Walter II below:

> 8. Charing Cross Friday. Feb 5. [1841]
>
> My dear Sir,
>
> You will perceive by today[']s Paper, that no time has been lost in publishing your first letter, which is no less admirable as the most fitting introduction to the subject, than as presenting a striking instance of

---

1 Burgis, *TRR*, 63.

the similar effect produced on very different minds (if indeed they be different) by the false notions about education now so prevalent. I trust you will find it has been correctly printed, and that you will, ere long, favour us with your next.

Believe me my dear Sir yours most truly J. Walter[2]

Walter II suggested that the interest of *The Times* was to expose Peel's 'false notions about education'.[3] By requesting the next letter, Walter II reiterated his son's suggestion of 2 February that there would be a series.[4]

However, Newman may not have fully understood the Walters' offer. He included a cryptic remark at the conclusion of the first letter to the effect that he hoped to write more letters. His *hope* of continuing his critique of Peel suggested ambiguity about a series of letters.[5] This ambiguity presented two possibilities or some combination thereof: first, after writing his initial letter, Newman may have been uncertain of whether *The Times* would actually publish a series—especially one so sharp in critique and thick in satire. Newman was aware of the potentially unfavorable response that might have been precipitated, for example, by his graphic depiction of Peel as led 'in chains behind [Brougham's] chariot-wheels'. The other possibility was that Newman had already planned the series according to Walter III's directives, but made a rhetorical play to create a sense of anticipation for his audience.

Before his second letter appeared, Newman received another note from either Walter II or Walter III on 6 February, which was not preserved. Newman's reply on 8 February most probably included the manuscripts for the second and third letters.[6] *The Times* published

---

2 John Walter II to JHN (8 Charing Cross Friday, 5 February 1841), *LD*, VIII, 26.

3 The note also seemed to confirm Newman's statement in 1872 that the letters 'were written off as they were successively called for by the parties who paid the author the compliment of employing him' (*DA*, iii).

4 The 5 February letter had included the Roman numeral 'I' signaling *The Times*' intention.

5 This ambiguity was picked up by the Editorial in the *Morning Chronicle* on 8 February 1841, which commented on what 'promises to be a series' because it was titled 'Letter I', with others presumably to follow.

6 The letter of 6 February has not been preserved and its author remains unclear because Newman only recorded 'Walter' in his diary. He did not further communicate with *The Times* or Walter II until 11 February. However, the symmetry of the

the letters consecutively on 9 and 10 February, and they appeared as two movements in a single piece. The second letter, while continuing the critique of Peel and Brougham, also advanced some of Newman's ideas concerning human nature and morality. Theological allusions were situated throughout, for example, that human persons were disordered by original sin and that the Church—in contrast to secular institutions—was necessary for repentance and healing from sin. The third letter complemented the second by offering robust theological insights, including the importance of Christian faith, the Church, and the significance of grace, not knowledge, as completing and converting human nature. A few days later, the fourth letter, which bore close affinities to the second and third and probably was written in concert with them, made clear that faith and grace given through the Church were the true antecedents of moral improvement. These first four letters, and those that followed, were very much like Newman's sermons, meant to arouse ideas, challenge beliefs, and provoke assent to the living God.

Letters to the Editor and the 'Leading Article': from Anonymous to Catholicus

Newman referred to his contributions to *The Times* in 1841 as the 'letters of Catholicus'.[7] His first letter was anonymous; for the remaining letters, however, Newman decided on a pseudonym that could convey his meaning yet conceal his identity. In the case of his first letter, Burgis speculated that the omission of the pseudonym was an error on the part of the editor of *The Times*, Thomas Barnes. She observed that none of the manuscripts contained the word 'Catholicus'; it was 'only written on the wrapper' which contained the letters.[8] Another possible reason for the omission of this pseudonym was that Newman did not know whether he was going to contribute a full series of letters and so did not presume to create a name for himself. Walter II's note of 5

---

letters two and three and their consecutive printing suggest that they were included on 8 February.

   7 For example, *LD*, VIII, 56. See also, Newman, *Apologia pro Vita Sua* (London: Longman and Co, 1864), Appendix, 121.

   8 Burgis, *TRR*, 64. This label may have been affixed a decade later (*LD*, XV, 62).

February, prompting him to send more letters, may have encouraged him to adopt a name. Finally, the adoption of a pseudonym might have been suggested in the missing correspondence with Walter II between the 6th and the 8th of February.[9]

Newman's choice of 'Catholicus' revealed where his mind was in the winter of 1841. He was working on the 'Catholic' *Tract 90* and had given a sermon on the unity of the Church in December.[10] 'Catholicus' may have implied the power of the Church to unite people in contrast to Peel's dream of science 'harmonizing the gradations of society, and binding them together'.[11] Or Newman may have chosen the name because of what it evoked—disquiet for some and mystery for others. In 1855, reflecting on 'my Catholicus in the Times', he noted: 'The *mystery* [of the name] will make people begin to read'.[12]

Once Newman selected and finally employed this name it changed the trajectory and the potency of the ensuing letters. Burgis has nicely captured how this was so:

> The anonymity of the Letters allowed him to spice them with politics and he took advantage of the freedom it gave him in this and in other ways. The high spirits which characterise 'The Tamworth Reading Room' would have been unsuitable flippancy had they been signed, but hidden behind 'Catholicus' he could picture the 'sober and experienced' Peel 'practising the antics of one of the wildest performers of this wild age', soliciting the working classes like 'a street preacher, or the cad of an omnibus'; attribute his arguments for the spread of knowledge to muddled thinking ... and allow himself such delightful digressions as that on the implications of the admission of 'virtuous women only' to the Reading Room ... and the account of the incongruous juxtapositions of persons in the 'new Pantheon' of the *Pursuit of Knowledge*.[13]

---

9 On 8 February, Newman may have sent Walter II a list of *errata* found in the printed version. See below his letter of 10 February and *errata* on 11 February.

10 *LD*, X, 203–4. Newman, *Sermons 1824–1843*, III, 399.

11 Coats ('Rhetorical Approaches', 175) maintained that 'The pseudonym "Catholicus" was chosen not for its High Church ramifications, but for the universal, the catholic, need for religion in education'. Coats gratuitously added: 'Newman slanted his attack against science and secularism in every article'.

12 *LD*, XVII, 429.

13 Burgis, *TRR*, 156–7.

The Catholicus Letters 2–4

The Second Letter: Catholicus Appears

Newman's second letter, which appeared on page 6 of *The Times*, began with a critical observation: 'A distinguished Conservative statesman' held that the acquisition of scientific knowledge necessarily led to moral improvement. Catholicus then recounted Peel's rhetorical flourishes about knowledge and drew attention to his advocacy of 'well-educated and virtuous women' who could become members of the library. He surmised that 'It would be difficult to exhaust the reflections which rise in the mind on reading avowals of this nature' (538). Peel's claim that knowledge leads to moral or spiritual improvement prompted Catholicus to raise several questions: '*How* [are] these wonderful moral effects to be wrought under the instrumentality of the physical sciences?' Does scientific knowledge contain the means to perfect persons or does it 'act like a dose or a charm' to divert the mind? He continued: if 'you drench the popular mind with physics' could such knowledge impel religious and moral progress for society 'in spite of individual failures?' Mechanics' institutes, local libraries, and the University of London had grown in the past fifteen years; yet their results were inconclusive: 'Where has the experiment been tried on so large a scale as to justify such anticipations?'

Catholicus then used some literary images which had a Dickensian quality that captured 'the kind of obstinate depressing reality excluded from Peel's bland pronouncements':[14]

> To know is one thing, to do is another; the two things are altogether distinct.[15] A man knows he should get up in the morning,—he lies a-bed; he knows he should not lose his temper, yet he cannot keep it. A labouring man knows he should not go to the ale-house, and his wife knows she should not filch when she goes out charing; but, nevertheless, in these cases, the consciousness of a duty is not all one with the performance of it.[16]

---

14 Ibid., 190.

15 Jay (*Evangelical and Oxford Movements*, 153) commented that in this passage: 'Newman operates a particularly devious sleight of hand in his use of the verb "to know" in order to confirm his distinction between the acquisition of secular knowledge and the conscience through which alone God is revealed to man'.

16 This distinction seemed to echo Rm 7:19: 'For I do not do the good I want, but the evil I do not want is what I do'.

His vividly portrayed persons in concrete situations contrasted with Peel's, Brougham's, and Craik's abstract ideal of how persons should be. Catholicus's work-a-day persons had knowledge, and did not become morally better. What then did Peel (who directly relied on Buckland) and Brougham (and Craik) mean by knowledge improving a person?

An answer was elided and instead Catholicus introduced Jeremy Bentham into the fray. By 1841, Bentham had become identified with radical utilitarianism—in contrast, for example, to the Christian utilitarianism of William Paley—and a target of the Tractarians, for example, Rogers's articles in *The British Critic*. Bentham deeply influenced Brougham and, to a lesser extent, Peel. Newman's use of Bentham, although brief, was a distinctive feature in his letters, as Newman intended to show that Peel's address was influenced not by common knowledge but revolutionary sources.[17]

> [Bentham] would answer, that the knowledge which carries virtue along with it, is the knowledge how to take care of number one—a clear appreciation of what is pleasurable, what painful, and what promotes the one and prevents the other. An uneducated man is ever mistaking his own interest, and standing in the way of his own true enjoyments. Useful Knowledge is that which tends to make us more useful to ourselves—a most definite and intelligible account of the matter, and needing no explanation. (539)

While agreeing with Peel and Brougham about the utility of knowledge, Bentham differed from them in two ways. First, knowledge did not exalt human nature but turned it upon itself—a type of solipsism. Second, Bentham viewed language differently than Brougham's progeny. Catholicus noted that although Peel did '*obiter* talk of improved modes of draining, and the chemical properties of manure', both men tended to valorize knowledge and couch their ideas in decadent language. In contrast, Bentham

---

17 Coats ('Rhetorical Approaches', 174–5) attempted to show Newman's motives for including Bentham in the letters; however, Coats conjectured but provided no correlation between these two thinkers; he also used Bentham as a foil for casting Newman in a negative light.

had not a spark of poetry in him ... [For] Mr. Bentham ... fine language [wasn't] any better than a set of words representing nothing—flowers of rhetoric, which bloom, smell sweet, and die. (539)

Frederick Rogers had captured this sentiment in 'Utilitarian Moral Philosophy' a month earlier, and perhaps inspired Newman's line of attack:

[Bentham's] want of subtlety of mind (which has been observed by more friendly critics than we can pretend to be) leads often to a slovenliness and inaccuracy of thought and language most remarkable in a writer who professes to effect every thing, and does effect so much by a process requiring perhaps, beyond any other, the contrary excellences—exhaustive division. Most unusual definiteness, without any unusual precision—minute arrangement without subtle analysis—searchingness without depth—rough vigour joined to laboured technicality—are the curious characteristics of Bentham's moral inquiries. But it is yet a more serious obstacle to his pretensions, that he seems actually without all knowledge of one half of human nature, and that the better half. Poetry and refinement clearly are strangers to him.[18]

Catholicus believed that Peel's words and ideas, however superficial, were not meaningless rhetoric, although he did not elaborate further. He quickly moved to illustrate his basic idea of the human mind, which, interestingly, he and Peel shared:

Now, without using exact theological language, we may surely take it for granted, from the experience of facts, that the human mind is at best in a very unformed or disordered state; passions and conscience, likings and reason, conflicting, might against right, and the prospect of things getting worse.[19] (539)

However, for Peel, and the 'school of philosophy in which he has enrolled himself', the solution to the chaotic human mind was

---

18 Frederick Rogers, 'Utilitarian Moral Philosophy', 97.

19 Peel would have disagreed with Newman as to the prospects of human nature getting worse. Harris ('Historical Forces', 207) accurately captured Peel's view that the goodness in human nature simply needed to be nurtured. Although distorting Newman's view of original sin, Harris also provided a useful contrast.

> not a victory of the mind over itself ... not the education[20] of the rebels—not the unity of our complex nature—but the mere lulling of the passions to rest by turning the course of thought; not a change of character, but a mere removal of temptation. (539)

Catholicus opposed this school's doctrine, as it did not really improve a person but rather distracted with information. However, instead of refuting these ideas point by point, he countered in a rhetorically savvy way, inducing his readers to see the weakness knowledge by distraction with concrete, amusing, and psychologically astute examples:

> When a husband is gloomy, or an old woman peevish and fretful, those who are about them do all they can to keep dangerous topics and causes of offence out of the way, and think themselves lucky, if, by such skilful management, they get through the day without an outbreak. When a child cries, the nurserymaid dances it about ... or shows how ashamed poll parrot or poor puss must be of its tantarums. (539)

Human beings needed conversion, a turning around, not distraction for a few moments of blessed peace. Catholicus knew his readers would make the connection: those who are simply distracted were like children, but he hoped more for adults.

Adverting to the fact of original sin, Catholicus made a theological point to bolster his claim that the human mind, the whole of human nature, requires transformation not distraction. He despaired that Peel

> makes no pretence of subduing the giant nature, in which we were born, of smiting the loins of the domestic enemies of our peace, of overthrowing passion and fortifying reason, he does but offer to bribe the foe for the nonce with gifts which will avail for that purpose just so long as they *will* avail, and no longer. (539)

Catholicus then summoned another name—ancient and venerable—to his critique of Peel: Cicero. Behind his dramatic persona, Newman held Cicero in high regard as a rhetorician, and had extensive knowledge of his work.[21] He considered him 'the only master of

---

20 Newman wrote 'reduction' in the manuscript, but 'education' was erroneously printed by *The Times*; see Burgis, *TRR*, 67.

21 See Newman, 'Personal and Literary Character of Cicero', in *Encyclopaedia Metropolitana*, May 1824 (*Historical Sketches* I, 239–99).

style I have ever had (which is strange considering the differences of the languages)'.[22] Like Catholicus, however, the great Roman orator excelled in the art of using knowledge or philosophy to distract the mind.[23] This could not truly improve a person:[24] 'Cicero handed the recipe to Brougham, and Brougham has passed it on to Peel' (539–40). Brougham (and Craik) advocated this tradition, where knowledge functioned essentially as a distraction:

> If a man was in grief, he was to be amused; if disappointed, to be excited; if in a rage, to be soothed; if in love, to be roused to the pursuit of glory. No inward change was contemplated, but a change of external objects; as if we were all White Ladies[25] or Undines,[26] our moral life being one of impulse and emotion, not subjected to laws, not consisting in habits, not capable of growth. When Cicero was outwitted by Caesar, he solaced himself with Plato; when he lost his daughter, he wrote a treatise on Consolation. (540)

---

22 LD, XXIV, 241.

23 Cicero was included in the literature from which Newman drew in his critiques. For example, Craik (*Pursuit of Knowledge*, I, 106) observed: 'The cultivation of science and literature has often been united with the most active and successful pursuit of business, and with the duties of the most laborious professions. It has been said of Cicero, that "no man whose life had been wholly spent in study, ever left more numerous or more valuable fruits of his learning in every branch of science and the polite arts".'

24 Coats ('Rhetorical Approaches', 175) did not see Newman's argument as a critique of a philosophic tradition that could not accomplish what Christian faith could, but as a disingenuous pairing: 'The guilt by association which Newman laid at the feet of Peel [concerning Cicero] was that the latter's secularism was paganistic in its origin and, therefore, suspect in modern, Christian England'.

25 Possibly a reference to Sir Walter Scott's poems about the 'White Lady of Avenel', a soulless spirit who haunts river ways (*The Poetical Works of Sir Walter Scott: with a Memoir of the Author* [Boston: Little, Brown and Company, 1861], VII, 208–10). Also see the suggestion (in LD, VIII, 540, n. 2), that the reference may be to a French fairy also called the White Lady.

26 See LD, VIII, 540, n. 3: 'Undine was a water nymph who was born without a soul. By marrying a human she acquired a soul but also all the pains and trials of the human race. Undine was the subject of an enormously popular novel by F. H. de La Motte Fouqué [1777–1843]. A new translation by Thomas Tracy was published in 1840 and was reviewed in the October 1841 number of the *Bri. Crit.*'

'An aristocracy of exalted spirits'

Burgis provided some excellent insight into Newman's literary strategy in these passages: 'Often he [Catholicus] draws on commonplaces and on familiar objects and situations, calculated to come home to the widest readership and often, besides, providing the best comment on the oratory of Peel and Brougham. When he said that their morality, built on curiosity not conscience, was adapted for beings without souls like the White Lady and Undine, he knew that in 1841 he could count on almost as many readers knowing Scott and de la Motte Fouqué.'[27]

Catholicus returned to Peel, acknowledging, albeit satirically, that he may not have been consciously drawing from this tradition, although Peel knew his classics. Nevertheless, knowledge as distraction rather than an inquiry into what real conversion required was at stake:

> Whether Sir Robert Peel meant all this, which others have meant before him, it is impossible to say; but I will be bound, if he did not mean this, he meant nothing else, and his words will certainly insinuate this meaning. (540)

He underscored Peel's 'high authority' in advocating his view of knowledge. Peel was potentially the most important man in England at that time to advocate for an ancient tradition with a modern, utilitarian veneer. Catholicus stated that this tradition

> in one form or other is a chief error of the day, in very distinct schools of opinion,[28]—that our true excellence comes not from within, but from without; not wrought out through personal struggles and sufferings, but following upon a passive exposure to influences over which we have no control.[29] They will countenance the theory that diversion is the instrument of improvement, and excitement the condition of right action; and whereas diversions cease to be diversions if they are constant, and excitements by their very nature have a crisis and run through a course, they will tend to make novelty ever in request, and will set the great teachers of morals upon the incessant search after stimulants and sedatives, by which unruly nature may, *pro re natâ*, be kept in order. (541)

27 Burgis, *TRR*, 190.

28 Newman did not think that this tradition was exclusively confined to a distinct school of thought like Bentham's Utilitarianism.

29 Newman contrasted the utilitarian doctrine that the moral life was one of conditioning and consequence with his basic moral position: the Aristotelian/Christian doctrine of intrinsic virtue or excellence.

Newman knew this tradition intimately, that upheld knowledge as a distraction from the travails of life. He first noticed this form of diversion in Evangelical doctrines which insisted upon constant emotional stimulation for faith and worship. Thus this was not an attack on secular learning, *per se*, but rather a critique of where conversion begins—from within or without.

Turning to Brougham's 'philosophy of expedients', Catholicus employed a series of images that illustrated knowledge used as amusement. Using a sympathetic, world-wise idiom including the use of pharmaceuticals, he suggested that remedies for the drudgeries of life whether of the wealthy or the working class could not be secured by mere quantities of knowledge:

> Digestive pills half an hour before dinner, and a posset at bedtime at the best; and at the worst, dram-drinking and opium,—the very remedy against broken hearts, or remorse of conscience, which is in request among the many, in gin-palaces *not* intellectual ... Strong liquors, indeed, do for a time succeed in their object; but who was ever consoled in real trouble by the small beer of literature or science?

Burgis observed that these images contributed 'to the devaluation of the vague but splendid aspirations of the Address and Brougham's *Discourse*'.[30] Catholicus employed more literary images and caustic remarks to devalue Peel's address drawing from Craik's examples:

> Or who was made to do any secret act of self-denial, or was steeled against pain, or peril, by all the lore of the infidel La Place,[31] or those other 'mighty spirits' which Lord Brougham and Sir Robert eulogize? Or when was a choleric temperament ever brought under by a scientific King Canute[32] planting his professor's chair before the

---

30 Burgis, *TRR*, 191.

31 Laplace supposedly stated in his *Système du monde* that he 'had no need for the hypothesis' of God to explain the world. This statement and others led some in the nineteenth century to suspect that Laplace was agnostic or atheist; however, historical evidence for this suspicion is ambiguous at best. Brougham (*Discourse*, 47) had lavished praise upon Laplace and Newton, which may have led to Newman's characterization.

32 M. K. Lawson, 'Cnut' (d.1035), in *DNB*. Canute was king of England, Denmark, and Norway. A legendary tale, 'not recorded until the twelfth-century works of Henry of Huntingdon and Gaimar, [told] of how he attempted to turn back the waves [by planting his throne on the shore] and then used his failure to demonstrate

> rising waves? And as to the 'keen' and 'ecstatic' pleasures which Lord Brougham, not to say Sir Robert, ascribes to intellectual pursuit and conquest, I cannot help thinking that in that line they will find themselves outbid in the market by gratifications much closer at hand, and on a level with the meanest capacity. (541)

Catholicus cut away from this line of argument and imagery, and reprised his opening jibe about the admission of women to the Tamworth library and reading room:

> Sir Robert makes it a boast that women are to be members of his institution; it is hardly necessary to remind so accomplished a classic,[33] that Aspasia and other learned ladies in Greece are no very encouraging precedents in favour of the purifying effects of science. (541)

With that historical reference, Catholicus robbed Peel of his attempt at elevating the virtuous women. In nineteenth-century thought, Aspasia, often ridiculed for 'impiety' in Greek drama, was considered a prostitute and a brothel keeper. Newman was not slandering women but rather reminding readers that they were human too. Knowledge, for men or women, did not necessarily make them better, for example, Aspasia's intellectual virtue did not prevent her harlotry.[34]

Parting shots were fired at Peel's praise for Davy and his belief in 'the power, not of religion, but of scientific knowledge on a death bed'. Peel's new-found class-consciousness was rebuked as being detached from the actual lives of working people. Catholicus lamented that the glories of knowledge could not in themselves directly alleviate cold and hunger:[35]

> If anything were necessary *in cumulum* to complete the folly and nonsense of the whole affair, it is found in the circumstance[36] that

to his courtiers the weakness of his power compared with that of God'.

33 Newman (*LD*, I, 38) presumably knew that Peel had attained academic distinction in classics at Oxford.

34 See *LD*, VIII, 541, n. 2: 'Aspasia was the consort of Pericles from c. 445–29 B.C., and a woman of considerable intellectual talent, who taught rhetoric and [possibly] conversed with Socrates'. The historical Aspasia was not necessarily a harlot as popularly appeared in the nineteenth-century imagination.

35 Newman was alluding to the cold weather that had persisted through January and into February (*LD*, VIII, 3; 25).

36 This first clause was excised from the 1872 edition (*DA*, 268).

this new art of living, offered to the labouring classes—for instance, in a severe winter, snow on the ground, glass falling, bread rising, coal at 20d. the cwt., and no work. (541)

Finally, he summarized his central argument that the 'cultivation of knowledge' *cannot* effect moral or spiritual conversion:

> It does not require many words, then, to determine, that taking human nature as it is actually found, and assuming that there is an art of life, to say that it consists, or in any essential manner is placed, in the cultivation of knowledge—that the mind is changed by a discovery, or saved by a diversion, or amused into immortality—that grief, anger, cowardice, self-conceit, pride, or passion, can be subdued by an examination of shells or grasses, or inhaling of gases, or a chipping of rocks,[37] or observing the barometer, or calculating the longitude, is the veriest pretence which sophist or mountebank ever professed to a gaping auditory.[38] (542)

Catholicus then set the table for his theological response to this doctrine in his next letter. The Church—not the library or the reading room—was the true place of conversion: 'If virtue be a mastery over the mind, if its end be action, if its perfection be inward order, harmony, and peace, we must seek it in graver and holier places than in libraries and reading rooms' (542).

The 'E' Critique

Along with the second letter, *The Times* published a response to the first letter of 5 February. Burgis explained the motivation of *The Times* for publishing this letter:

---

[37] Newman reprised this image in *The Idea of a University* (110): 'Quarry the granite rock with razors, or moor the vessel with a thread of silk; then may you hope with such keen and delicate instruments as human knowledge and human reason to contend against those giants, the passion and the pride of man'.

[38] Harris ('Historical Forces', 192) considered this passage *the* hermeneutical key to the letters; although it was an important facet of his critique of the knowledge tradition, it was Newman's theological arguments, especially regarding the Church, that presented the real challenge to this tradition.

The ministerial and radical press had already seized on the appearance in *The Times* of an attack on the Tory leader and the insertion of E.'s letter may have been an attempt by the paper to satisfy Peel's supporters that they were being given a chance to reply and to draw some response from those who approved of 'Catholicus': whether it succeeded in this is not known; no letter in praise of 'Catholicus' appeared and none has been preserved by *The Times*.[39]

In a letter to the editor, 'E' expressed his reaction to the first letter; he felt 'exceedingly grieved that such a misrepresentation of the character of that address should have found so extensive a circulation as your paper has given it'.[40] Had the letter's anonymous author the 'charity which thinketh no evil', he would not have been so wrong in his conclusions or so hard on Peel. He was clearly mistaken to equate Tamworth with the University of London and had not read with enough care the details of the speech—the reading room was 'for all classes in Tamworth and its neighbourhood'. Moreover, 'E' felt that the author—Newman—had disparaged Peel's noble attempt to redress the wrongs in the education of children of Tamworth.[41] While most libraries were limited to 'religious books only, or ... in mechanics' institutions, they attempted to put religion out of their system', at Tamworth 'the desire has been to make science and knowledge the handmaids of religion'.[42] The anonymous author had not fully appreciated the role of the clergy at Tamworth and had made an 'unjust comparison' to the University of London 'over whose doors there seemed to be written, "Whereas we cannot agree what religion is, therefore we will have none at all"'.

'E' claimed that the letter had taken many of Peel's statements about knowledge, religion, and morals out of context. 'E' noted that the bulk of the address had been dedicated to mundane details about the institution.[43]

---

39 Burgis, *TRR*, 66.

40 One of the main reasons why Newman accepted the commission was *The Times*' extensive circulation.

41 An errant criticism in so far as the reading room excluded those under fourteen.

42 This statement was contrary to both the content of Peel's speech and Newman's critique.

43 Harris, 'Historical Forces', 193. Harris reprised this sentiment, noting that

'E' continued that the author of the letter did not fully understand that Peel's 'object is to encourage intellectual and scientific pursuits in preference to animal gratifications, *in all persons*, whether under the influence of religion or not'. He celebrated Peel's leading role in the institution and hoped that it would open 'the paths of sound knowledge and philosophy in all the parishes of our land'. The great success of Tamworth is that the 'ministers of our holy religion' would manage the institution. With his final jab that the anonymous author's letter was juvenile, 'E' declared:

> If these observations should induce the author of the letter and its admirers to suspend their judgments till they have more maturely considered the whole of the address, and the rules of the institution established at Tamworth, the object of the writer of these remarks will be answered.[44]

'E's' response was a careful reading of some of Newman's statements, even if he misapprehended or ignored Newman's satire. 'E' was able effectively to extrapolate certain themes which Newman had only implied. This may be an example, as Harris surmised, of the reading public's ability to understand Newman's critiques: 'Given the form of publication, Peel's contemporary status ... and the equally general awareness of the long struggle still taking place over the role of religious doctrine in education, the readers of *The Times* in 1841 would have had no difficulty [understanding Newman's letters]'.[45] However, Harris seemed to overstate his case about readers having no difficulty in understanding the letters. 'E', for example, seemingly did not understand that Newman was attacking philosophical first principles of a tradition, and not Peel's institution *per se*.

Newman did not mention any of the mundane details in Peel's address: 'Peel's initiative in founding the library was quite evidently being indirectly censured as well as his comments on the value of scientific education'. Newman, in fact, mentioned mundane details in the second letter and did not censure scientific education.

44 *The Times*, 9 February 1841. All quotations are from this day.
45 Harris, 'Historical Forces', 192.

The Third Letter: Grace and the Church

The following day—Wednesday, 10 February 1841—*The Times* published Catholicus's third installment. He had begun to move beyond the initial philosophical critiques and theological allusions in his first two letters. Although playful satire and irony punctuated the third letter, Catholicus made several theological claims which were cast for a wide audience and presented without technical precision. However imprecise the terms, a formal contrast between his vision of the Church and the views of Bentham, Brougham, and Peel emerged.[46]

Catholicus recalled the distinction he made in the second letter between the empiricist/solipsistic tradition of Bentham and the rationalist/stoic tradition of Brougham and Peel:

> There are two schools of philosophy, in high esteem, at this day, as at other times, neither of them accepting Christian principles as the guide of life, yet both of them unhappily patronized by many whom it would be the worst and most cruel uncharitableness to suspect of unbelief. Mr. Bentham is the master of the one; and Sir Robert Peel is a disciple of the other. (543)

This had been Newman's strategy all along, not simply to take on Peel, but as he recognized in 1829, to reveal the 'bodies and principles', i.e., traditions, behind his thinking.[47] Bentham contributed the importance of utility, but ultimately remained distinct from the glories of knowledge promoted by Brougham. Furthermore, this coy but grave implication of unbelief bound both traditions together, and therefore distinct from Christianity. Catholicus may have included this because the mechanics' movement was notorious for attracting subversive and radical views of politics and religion. Coats interpreted Newman's sleight of hand about atheism as his most egregious attack against Bentham and Brougham.[48]

---

46 The 1872 title (*DA*, 269)—'Secular Knowledge not a direct Means of Moral Improvement'—mirrored that of the second letter. Newman seemed to be marking out continuity and progression in his letters. However, the content of the third letter was preponderantly theological, yet the title did not indicate religion, doctrine, etc. Implied in the terms—'Means of Moral Improvement'—were Newman's notions of Christian morality found in grace and in the Gospel.

47 *LD*, II, 130.

48 Coats, 'Rhetorical Approaches', 179.

However, James E. Crimmins has vindicated Newman's suspicion of Bentham: 'Around 1815 Bentham set about elaborating systematically the materialist, nominalist, and linguistic principles that had informed his social science from the outset of his philosophic career ... On the religious front, however, Bentham's critique took on a far more urgent character. [He] conducted an attack on religion with the declared aim of extirpating religious beliefs, even the idea of religion itself, from the minds of men.'[49] According to Michael Lobban, Brougham was at best a liberal Anglican and more plausibly an agnostic.[50] However, the religious beliefs of Bentham, Brougham, or Peel were not the immediate concern; rather, Catholicus wanted to spell out the core of Bentham's thought for his readers:

> Mr. Bentham's system has nothing ideal about it; he is a stern realist, and he limits his realism to things which he can see, hear, taste, touch, and handle. He does not acknowledge the existence of anything which he cannot ascertain for himself. Exist it may nevertheless, but, till it makes itself felt, to him it exists not; till it comes down to him, and he is very short-sighted, it is not recognized by him, as having a co-existence with himself ... With him a being out of sight is a being out of mind; nay, he allows not the traces or glimpses of facts to have any claim on his regard, but with him to have a little and not much, is to have nothing at all. With him to speak truth is to be ready with a definition, and to imagine, to guess, to doubt, or to falter, is much the same as to lie. (543)

Bentham was 'such an iron thinker' that he would not accept Cicero's or Brougham's and Peel's 'airy nothings' about the glories of knowledge. Ian

---

49 James E. Crimmins, 'Religion, Utility, and Politics: Bentham versus Paley', in *Religion, Secularization, and Political Thought: Thomas Hobbes to J. S. Mill*, ed. James E. Crimmins (London: Routledge, 1990), 140.

50 Michael Lobban, 'Henry Brougham' (1778–1868), in *DNB*. Newman's doubt about the sincerity of Brougham's faith was echoed by Leslie Stephen (*The English Utilitarians* [London: Duckworth & Co., 1900], II, 269): 'The Whigs were inclined to Shaftesbury's doctrine that sensible men had all one religion, and that sensible men never said what it was. Those who had a more definite and avowable creed were content to follow Stewart's amiable philosophising. Brougham professed, let us hope, sincerely, to be an orthodox theist, and explained the argument from design in a commentary upon Paley.'

Ker has detected an element of praise in Newman's view of Bentham: 'As a great proponent of realism himself, Newman has a certain reluctant respect for that "stern realist" Jeremy Bentham.'[51] Ker also noted Newman's critique of Bentham's strictures about sensate knowledge. Yet, the above passage does not seem to indicate that Newman really did respect Bentham's 'realism', especially in stating how 'short-sighted' Bentham was. While Newman agreed about the importance of sense knowledge, his view of Bentham's 'realism' was ultimately that it was unreal—sense knowledge simply could not account for all that humans can know, in terms of love, friendship, and spiritual matters; moreover, Newman recognized the importance of transcendence (which was absent from Bentham's philosophy).

Ultimately, Catholicus acknowledged the benefits of science and literature, yet agreed with neither 'school' as a legitimate end:

> Their misfortune [was], not that they look for an excellence above the beaten path of life, but that whereas Christianity has told us what that excellence is, Cicero lived before it was given to the world, and Lord Brougham and Sir Robert Peel prefer his involuntary error to their own inherited truth. (543)

These schools of philosophy recapitulated ancient philosophical traditions within modern knowledge and developments. In contrast, Catholicus asserted that the Church offered excellence, by which he may have meant Christian virtue. However, he may have alluded to Paul's 'more excellent way' of love in his First Letter to the Corinthians (12:31–13:13). That 'way' was the grace-filled love from God and given through Jesus Christ. His readers may have been aware of these alternate, yet complementary, meanings.

By contrasting Christian excellence—the way of love—to the ancient and modern exaltation of knowledge, Catholicus indicated how Christianity made a difference in people's lives. For him, the way of love cannot derive from knowledge or philosophical virtue, but from the Gospel proclaimed by the Church:

> Surely, there is something unearthly and superhuman in spite of Bentham; but it is not glory, or knowledge, or any abstract idea of virtue, but

---

51 Ker, *Biography*, 201.

great and good tidings which need not here be particularly mentioned, and the pity is, that these Christian statesmen cannot be content with what is divine without hankering after what was heathen. (543)

The principal difference between what the 'philosophical school' and the faith of the Christian Church lay in what was offered and effected. Through Christ's grace, the Church could offer healing, forgiveness, and confidence in ultimate things. Philosophy properly could inform, but did not have the living power of faith and grace:

> Now, independent of all other considerations, the great difference, in a practical light, between the object of Christianity and of heathen belief, is this—that glory, science, knowledge, and whatever other fine names we use, never healed a wounded heart, nor changed a sinful one; but Christ's word is with power.[52] The ideas which Christianity brings before us are in themselves full of influence ... in order to meet the special exigencies of our nature. (543)

Catholicus deepened this contrast by pairing Brougham's claims, which had co-opted and distorted Bacon's *scientia potestas est* (knowledge is power), with the Christian understanding of grace. Kelly has documented that 'Knowledge is Power' became the motto of the *Mechanics' Magazine* in 1823. This enlightened axiom, a clarion call for the London Mechanics' Institute, became synonymous with the adult education movement spearheaded by reformers such as J. C. Robertson, Thomas Hodgskin and Birkbeck. Hodgskin triumphantly declared in the October 1823 issue of *Mechanics' Magazine*: '"KNOWLEDGE", says one of the wisest men, Lord Bacon, "IS POWER"; and the first step, probably, towards the mechanics of this great empire obtaining power to raise themselves to their proper station in society, is to acquire knowledge.'[53]

The use of this phrase was ironic: Bacon originally intended to describe God's attributes, knowledge being principle, against those who claimed to limit God's power.[54] The phrase was now used exclusively

---

52 A possible gloss from Hebrews 4:12. In the 1872 revision (*DA*, 270), Newman substituted the 'Divine Word' for 'Christ's word'.

53 Kelly, *History*, 78–9; 96–7.

54 In 'De Haeresibus' (*Meditationes Sacrae*, in *The Works of Francis Bacon: Minor Latin Works*, ed. Basil Montague [London: William Pickering, 1829], XI, 373), Bacon argued: 'Tertius gradus est eorum, qui arctant et restringunt opinionem priorem

for human agency—to empower those who obtain modern scientific knowledge. Although knowledge did enable people to accomplish tasks and see things and people in different ways, it could not fundamentally transform the person for his or her ultimate end. Grace through Christ the Word generated conversion, which elevated persons to the communion of saints. Further juxtaposed to libraries or reading rooms, grace not only transformed individuals but allowed for the creation of a new society—the Church:

> Knowledge is not 'power,' nor is glory 'the first and only fair;'[55] but 'grace,' or 'the word,' by whichever name we call it, has been from the first a quickening, renovating, organizing principle. It has new-created the individual, and diffused and knit him into a social body, composed of members each similarly created. It has cleansed man of his moral diseases, raised him to hope and energy … :—it introduced a new force into the world, and the impulse which it gave continues in its original vigour down to this day. (543–4)

By referring to the Church as a 'social body … of members each similarly created', Catholicus deftly transposed St. Paul's metaphor of the Body of Christ (for example, 1 Co 12:12–14) for the British public. He continued on this line by depicting the Church's tradition as 'light' which defeats death, unites people in a living bond of love, and heals. Knowledge, by itself or its transmission, cannot attain these ends:

tantum ad actiones humanas, quae participant ex peccato, quas volunt substantive, absque nexu aliquo causarum, ex interna voluntate et arbitrio humano pendere, statuuntque latiores terminos scientiae Dei quam potestatis, vel potius ejus partis potestatis Dei (nam et ipsa scientia potestas est), qua scit, quam ejus, qua movet et agit: ut praesciat quaedam otiose, quae non praedestinet et praeordinet.' ('The third degree is, of those who abridge and restrain the former opinion only to those human actions which partake of sin, which actions they will have to depend substantively and originally, and without any sequel or subordination of causes upon the will, and make and set down and appoint larger limits of the knowledge of God than of his power, or rather of that part of God's power, (for knowledge itself is a power whereby he knoweth,) than of that by which he moveth and worketh, making him foreknow some things idle, and as a looker on, which he doth not predestinate nor ordain', *The Works of Francis Bacon*, 1 [New York: Worthington, 1884], 71.)

55 Eventually Brougham's SDUK adopted the motto; Newman directly attacked a statement in Craik's *Pursuit of Knowledge* (II, 2): 'Knowledge is, essentially and directly, power; but it is also, indirectly, virtue'.

> Each one of us has lit his lamp from his neighbour, or received it from his fathers, and the lights thus transmitted are at this time as strong and as clear as if 1800 years had not passed since the kindling of the sacred flame. What has glory or knowledge been able to do like this? Can it raise the dead? can it create a polity? can it do more than testify man's need and typify God's remedy? (544)

Grace could change 'the whole man', and elevate communities, nations, and empires. Readers could see Catholicus's theological prowess. Peel and Brougham, who were principally politicians, could only offer something outside their own expertise—science or literature—as diversions. Unlike Peel's address and Brougham's *Discourse*, which put a premium on physical scientists, Catholicus limited his critique not to scientists but to social reformers and politicians such as Bentham, Brougham, and Peel. Brougham had done some amateur scientific work, and was a member of the Royal Society, but eventually turned to law and politics. Scientists and others were cited in the text, but none, save possibly for Davy, received the wrath directed towards Brougham or Peel. Newman focused his attack on these figures who extolled science without really understanding its practice; he was not against scientists or science, but the naïve views of science by those who had little or no experience of the field.

Because these men advocated science, but were not themselves scientists, Catholicus lamented that 'the great orators and statesmen are busy, forsooth, with their heathen charms and nostrums, their sedatives, correctives, or restoratives' (544). He used these 'humorous images' to convey a serious critique of Peel's view of knowledge:

> The image of the quack doctor runs through the second [letter] without being made explicit [and is explicit in the third]: Newman asks whether the production of moral effects by the physical sciences is like a dose or a charm which comes into general use empirically' (Using 'empirically' here in the sense of 'through an empiric or quack doctor') and whether it is only necessary to drench (that is forcibly to administer a dose) the popular mind with physics for moral and religious advancement to follow; he speaks of Peel's 'prescription' for 'the good people of Tamworth'.[56]

---

56 Burgis, *TRR*, 165–7.

Not only was the knowledge tradition filled with 'quacks', but they were retrograde in their prescriptions: just as ancient scientific knowledge did not hold sway in the present, neither should pagan philosophy and morality substitute for Christianity. Such an idea was preposterous—'as if we were to build our men of war [warships], or conduct our iron works, on the principles approved in Cicero's day'. Brougham's[57] and Peel's view of knowledge as amusement, curiosity, and distraction was more than what Bentham's offered, although not enough to satiate human longing for transcendence:

> I will not assert that Lord Brougham, and certainly not that Sir Robert Peel, denies any higher kind of morality, yet when he rises above Benthamism, in which he often indulges, into what may be called *Broughamism proper*, he commonly grasps at nothing more real and substantial than these Ciceronian ethics. (545)

Catholicus's argument continued to degrade the paradigms of enlightenment proposed by Bentham and Brougham (and to an extent Peel). He goaded his readers to see that these men represented a tradition that held orthodox Christianity as a form of darkness and ignorance. However, for Catholicus Christian faith had vivified the world with worship of the true God and a moral vision elevated by grace. Turning their argument on its head, he believed that to return to a pagan past would be to return to obscurity. Catholicus succinctly and ironically named this tradition 'The Knowledge School':

> In morals, as in physics, the [stream][58] cannot rise higher than its source. Christianity raises men from earth, for it comes from Heaven; but human morality creeps, struts, or frets upon the earth's level, without wings to rise. The Knowledge School does not contemplate raising man above himself; it merely aims at disposing of his existing powers and tastes, as is most convenient or practicable under circumstances.

---

57 Newman provided a lengthy quotation from Brougham's *Discourse* on literary knowledge—a 'degrading waste of precious time'—in contrast to scientific knowledge—a 'pure delight'. In 1872, Newman (*DA*, 271–2) altered the quotation, making it more appropriate to his overall argument.

58 In the published article, the word 'spring' had appeared instead of 'stream'; it is not clear who made the mistake—Newman or Barnes.

It finds him, like the victims of the French Tyrant,[59] doubled up in a cage in which he can neither lie, stand, sit, nor kneel, and its highest desire is to find an attitude in which his unrest may be least.[60] (545)

The images of human beings stooped to a crawl or imprisoned in a cage cut through the haughty metaphors offered by the Knowledge School. Catholicus did not lament new knowledge and its genuine effects, but rather circumscribed what it could actually do. Only Christian grace could raise one out of often uncomfortable paradoxes and moral ambiguities of living. Catholicus turned from these impressionistic metaphors to the actual social reality: the poor and laboring classes. Drawing from his own pastoral experience with and concern for the poor,[61] he criticized Peel's obliviousness to their plight:

> The poor indulge in low pleasures; they use bad language, swear loudly and profanely, laugh at coarse jests, and are rude and boorish.[62] Sir Robert would open on them a wider range of thought and more intellectual objects, by teaching them science; but what warrant will

---

59 According to *LD*, VIII, 545, n. 1, this was, 'almost certainly Louis XI (1461–83) who features prominently in Scott's *Quentin Dunward*'.

60 This image was reprised to hilarious effect in Newman's *Certain Difficulties Felt by Anglicans in Catholic Teaching Considered*, I, 167. Here the metaphor was not related to the Knowledge School but to the Church of England: 'If, however, on the contrary, you find that the more those great principles which you have imbibed from St. Athanasius and St. Augustine, and which have become the life and the form of your moral and intellectual being, vegetate and expand within you, the more awkward and unnatural you find your position in the Establishment, and the more difficult its explanation; if there is no lying, or standing, or sitting, or kneeling, or stooping there, in any possible attitude; if, as in the tyrant's cage, when you would rest your head, your legs are forced out between the Articles, and when you would relieve your back, your head strikes against the Prayer Book; when, place yourselves as you will, on the right side or the left, and try to keep as still as you can, your flesh is ever being punctured and probed by the stings of Bishops, laity, and nine-tenths of the Clergy buzzing about you; is it not as plain as day that the Establishment is not your place, since it is no place for your principles?'

61 As a young curate at St. Clement's in Oxford (4 July 1824 to 21 February 1826), Newman often worked with the poor in the community (Ker, *Biography*, 25).

62 In this passage, one cannot know if Catholicus was playing to his audience's presumptions, or reflecting Newman's own prejudice, or a combination of both. Harris ('Historical Forces', 202, 205) implied that Newman held antipathy towards the poor, but this passage and others do not necessarily warrant that inference.

be given us that, if his object could be achieved, what they would gain in decency they would not lose in natural humility and faith? If so, he has exchanged a gross fault for a more subtle one.' Temperance topics' stop drinking; let us suppose it; but will much be gained, if those who give up spirits take to opium? *Naturam expellas furcâ, tamen usque recurret*,⁶³ is a heathen truth though a Christian fable, and universities and libraries which recur to heathenism may reclaim it from the heathen for their motto. (545)

Human nature, 'hardly or partially Christianized' remained under 'the heathen law' which Catholicus had already identified as goodness beset by sin, decay, and ignorance. Even 'where Christianity has power, the venom of the old Adam is not subdued' (545). Catholicus provided an example of the 'old Adam', not in the poor or working class, but in privileged university students:

> external discipline may change the fashionable excess, but cannot allay the principle of sinning. Stop cigars, they will take to drinking parties; stop drinking, they gamble; stop gambling, and a worse license follows.⁶⁴ You do not get rid of vice by human expedients ... You must go to a higher source for renovation of the heart and will.

However, 'human expedients' do have their place and should not be forsaken. Calling to mind both Bacon (and Aristotle) regarding the proper place of science and its methods, Catholicus averred:⁶⁵

---

63 'You may drive nature out with a pitchfork, but she will return every time' (Horace, *Epistles*, 1.10.24).

64 Newman ruefully observed his peers' drunken revelry as an undergraduate at Oxford (*LD*, I, 66) and as a tutor (*AW*, 207).

65 Jane Rupert ('Newman and Bacon', *The Downside Review* 118 [2000]: 45–70, at 46) noted: 'Newman shared Bacon's appreciation of the importance of method. From his vantage point in mid-nineteenth century, he recognized that the [inductive] method proposed by Bacon had come to dominate the processes of thought, to be accepted as the sole rational instrument ... Newman agreed with Bacon's clear distinction between the divine and the natural; but, while he admired Bacon, he deplored the Baconian successors who recognized only a single method and applied it to all subject matters. Newman observed that although this favoured method had enjoyed dazzling success in the physical sciences, if applied to other subject matters such as theology or ethics, it led to distortions through omission'. She also observed that Newman and Bacon 'shared common ground with Aristotle', who recognized the importance of a variety of methods in relation to a given subject (49).

> I say, you must use human methods *in [their] place*, and there they are useful; but they are worse than useless out of their place. I have no fanatical wish to deny to any whatever subject of thought or method of reason a place altogether, if it chooses to claim it, in the cultivation of the mind ... The great and true maxim is to sacrifice none—to combine, and therefore to adjust all. (545)

Because science or its methods could not restore humanity, Catholicus once again had to pose a Christian alternative. The heart of the third letter was laid bare—Christian faith and grace through the Church must be *the* priority for redeeming humanity. Catholicus implied that Christianity should be the first principle in education because it was able to acculturate and develop a range of knowledge without obscuring its origin and end. The letter's concluding summary unified the disparate allusions, images, and arguments from his previous letters and set the course for those to follow:

> Here then it is that the Knowledge Society, Gower-street College, Tamworth Reading-room, Lord Brougham, and Sir Robert Peel, are all so deplorably mistaken. Christianity, and nothing short of it, must be made the element and principle of all education. Where it has been laid as the first stone, and acknowledged as the governing spirit, it will take up into itself, assimilate, and give a character to literature and science. Where revealed truth has given the aim and direction to knowledge, knowledge of all kinds will minister to revealed truth. The evidences of religion, natural theology, metaphysics,—or, again, poetry, history, and the classics,—or physics and mathematics, may all be grafted into the mind of a Christian ... But if in education we begin with nature before grace, with evidences before faith,[66] with science before conscience, with poetry before practice, we shall be doing much the same as if we were to indulge the appetites and passions and turn a deaf ear to the reason. In each case we misplace what in its place is a divine gift. If we attempt to effect a moral improvement by means of poetry, we shall but mature into a mawkish, frivolous, and fastidious sentimentalism—if by means of argument, into a dry, unamiable longheadedness—if by good society, into a polished outside, with hollowness within, in which

---

66 The reference is to the 'evidence school' of William Paley. See Charles R. Amico, *The Natural Knowability of God according to John Henry Newman with Special Reference to the Argument from Design to the Universe* (Rome: Urbaniana University Press, 1986), 45–65.

vice has lost its grossness, and perhaps increased its malignity[67]—if by experimental science, into an uppish supercilious temper, much inclined to scepticism. But reverse the order of things; put faith first and knowledge second; let the university minister to the church, and then classical poetry becomes the type of gospel truth, and physical science a comment on Genesis or Job, and Aristotle changes into Butler, and Arcesilas into Berkeley.[68] (545–6)

However, Brougham and Peel could not abide such an ordering of knowledge to Christian faith, 'Far from recognizing this principle, the teachers of the Knowledge School would educate from natural theology up to Christianity, and would amend the heart through literature and philosophy' (546). Recognizing this, Catholicus concluded the piece with a doleful question: 'Can the nineteenth century produce no more robust and creative philosophy than this?' (546).

A Note of Panic from Walter II

Walter II sent an anxious note to Newman on the day in which his third letter appeared. The 'E' letter had apparently not satisfied Tory/conservative readers; rather it was the Whig and Radical press that had delighted in Newman's letters. These developments plus political pressure apparently jarred Walter II and Barnes. Walter II wrote to Newman, rescinding *The Times*' offer:[69]

> 8. Charing Cross Wednesday. [10 Feb. 1841]
>
> My dear Sir,
>
> I am sorry your note has not arrived in time to admit of the wrong expressions you mention being corrected, but they shall be mentioned as 'Errata' in tomorrow's paper.

---

67 Here Newman specifically countered the claims of the wealthy or elite. Although seemingly harsh with the poor, he gave no quarter to the rich.

68 Jay (*Evangelical and Oxford Movements*, 213–14) claimed that Newman's thought was truly affected by Berkeley, but Edward Sillem (*The Philosophical Notebook of John Henry Newman* [Louvain: Nauwelaerts, 1969], I, 25), is more convincing in concluding that Berkeley was but a minor influence upon Newman.

69 No direct evidence of political pressure has been found; however, Walter II's letters, the leading article of 12 February, and comment in *The Spectator* on 13 February provide indirect evidence that pressure had been applied on *The Times*.

The Catholicus Letters 2–4

Nothing can possibly be more convincing and satisfactory than the letters themselves, and I know they have made a great impression on many of the literati, but unfortunately we are so situated with reference to the political world, that [it] is thought dangerous to raise a question about the principles of the leader whose party we are supporting, even on the most independent subject, and people cannot be persuaded that the condemnation of certain principles when adopted by such a person does not imply an attack on his character, and a desertion of his cause. I am thus explicit with you my dear Sir, because I wish you fully to understand, that all here whose opinions I am bound to respect are perfectly satisfied themselves with the opinions you have expressed on Sir R. P.'s conduct, but yet think it would hardly be *discreet* to pursue the subject at present, when a change in the Government is contemplated as likely, and Conservatives however much they may disapprove of Sir R. P. for this and many reasons, have yet no one else to look to as a leader.[70] If however you should have finished a fourth letter, we shall doubtless be able to make use of it, if you please, in some other way.

The three other papers shall be forwarded to you, but I am not aware of anything worth sending you from any other.

Believe me my dear Sir Yours most truly J. Walter[71]

P. S. I hear the Chronicle has been attacking your letters. It shall be sent with the rest.

Newman's 'Incendiary' Response

Walter II's letter arrived on 11 February and Newman immediately replied. He mirrored the flat praise from Walter II and agreed to end the series. Newman closed with the suggestion to 'burn' the letter—a suggestion perhaps intended to shame Walter II, rather than propose how it should be used:

---

70 Walter II acknowledged what many Tories and Conservatives had come to think about Peel; see for example, Evans, *Peel*, 41.

71 John Walter II to JHN (8 Charing Cross, 10 February 1841), *LD*, VIII, 30.

'An aristocracy of exalted spirits'

My dear W

I had your kind note this morning and thank you for it. I quite acquiesce in it and enter into your reasons, and am content with such opportunity as I have had of putting out views which I think important through so influential a medium—though of course I should not have begun unless I had expected to finish. Do what you will with No. 4—perhaps you had better burn it.[72]

Yrs very truly JHN

Newman's reply provided further evidence that he was writing to Walter II. His greeting, 'My dear W', seemed to imply a familiarity and friendship which he shared with Walter III rather than with Walter II; however, his use of 'dear' and the ingratiating tone of the note suggested annoyance rather than friendship. Such conjecture can be corroborated from Newman's abrupt line to 'burn' the fourth letter. Walter II also was the one who had received the manuscripts and this letter indicated that one was enclosed. Although Newman's note signaled disgust, it also showed his desire not to press controversy. The note also provided a good window into his motivation for his initial acceptance of the Walters' commission. Newman had a certain number of letters in mind because he wanted to develop an idea. He may have assented to writing a series of letters because he realized that he would have 'so influential a medium'—*The Times*—to develop popular theological arguments for Christianity. Contrary to what Walter II, many of the *literati*, and some contemporary scholars believed, Newman did not hope simply to score political or religious points against Peel.[73] Nor did Newman desire to

---

72 JHN to John Walter II (11 February 1841), *LD*, VIII, 31. Newman's *Letters and Diaries* did not indicate whether this letter was a copy of Newman's letter to *The Times* or if, as Burgis noted (*TRR*, 68), it was Newman's draft that he wrote on Walter's note. The latter alternative seems more plausible, since this is the only extant letter from Newman to the Walters. Burgis nevertheless transcribed the draft note. *The Times*, and especially Walter II (*The Thunderer*, viii) had the practice of destroying correspondence 'so that the public men of his day were safe' from later, and possibly scandalous, revelations.

73 Walter's note seemed to indicate that Newman was only writing about education. The wider press and the leading article of *The Times* on 12 February construed the letters as mainly political. Harris ('Historical Forces', 201) and Coats

The Catholicus Letters 2–4

exact revenge for Catholic emancipation in 1829 or the Ecclesiastical Commission which Peel established in 1835.[74]

Though these events may have factored into Newman's decision to write the letters, his principal motive was to use Peel's address as a foil to put forth an evocative and popular ecclesiology to the widest possible readership. He availed himself of the opportunity in *The Times* to broadcast certain of his ideas throughout all of England.[75] Peel had happened to be a very prominent messenger for what Newman considered a subversive ideology. Newman hoped both to expose the limits of Peel and the Knowledge School and to promulgate his own vision of the Church's role in modern developments.

'Errata' in the Second and Third Letters

Walter II's note of 10 February suggested that Newman sent *The Times* a list of several mistakes in the second and third letters.[76] On Thursday, 11 February, page 4 of *The Times* published the corrections which Walter III mentioned:

> Errata.—In yesterday's paper, the 3d letter of 'Catholicus,' first column, 17th line from the bottom, for 'spring' read 'stream;' and in the second letter, published Tuesday, 43d line from the bottom of the 1st column, for 'education of the rebels' read 'reduction of the rebels.'[77]

('Rhetorical Approaches', 175) caricatured Newman as an Ultra-Tory Churchman. These interpretations do not correspond with the content in or Newman's idea for the letters.

74 Gilley, *Newman and his Age*, 195.
75 Not only his note to Walter II but also a letter to Henry Wilberforce later that month (*LD*, VIII, 41) indicated Newman's desire to cast Tractarian thought far and wide.
76 Newman did not record this list in his diary; the last entry which indicated correspondence with Walter was on 8 February.
77 *The Times*, 11 February 1841.

'An aristocracy of exalted spirits'

The Leading Article: Praise for Peel

The following day, Friday, 12 February, *The Times*' leading article on page 4, presumably written by Barnes, took note of the Catholicus controversy and offered reluctant support for Peel:

> We insert one more letter from our correspondent 'Catholicus.' It is necessary to use some caution upon this subject. We find an idea gradually creeping forth—probably only among very hasty reasoners—that our attachment to Sir ROBERT PEEL is sustaining some diminution. A morning paper also,[78] the organ of Government, throws out hints to that effect, and casts an imputation upon us of being influenced by a bigoted party—acting under the highest impulses of Toryism. Now the answer to such an imputation is, to men of taste and judgment, easily found in the letters themselves. Was it fit that such letters should be suppressed or rejected? Sir R. PEEL himself, we are convinced, as a man of learning and knowledge, would answer that question in the negative. The attention which the letters have excited concur also in that decision. We know not whether it be our misfortune or not, but certainly the fact is—and we refer to the past history of this journal for the confirmation of it—that we have judged of public men, have adhered to or rejected them, without any reference whatever to their political position: whether they were in or out of office has made no difference with us; and Sir ROBERT PEEL's obvious approach to HER MAJESTY's councils, from the incapacity of those who now direct them, does in no degree tend to make us think or speak more highly of his talents than we have hitherto done. He is beyond all doubt a great and able statesman—virtuous and disinterested—much more capable of directing the councils of the SOVEREIGN than those by whom HER MAJESTY is at present surrounded; but still not infallible: and it is right that he himself should know what great and able men think of him. He will have his own natural and acquired talents to conduct him; but he is not placed beyond availing himself of the advantages which may be derived from attending to those opinions which others entertain of his separate acts and proceedings. The speech at Tamworth we think not a wise one. What man is wise at all times? Its errors and blemishes are ably exposed in those letters which we have published: Sir ROBERT, we are convinced, will be the better for them; at least in one respect—he will be more cautious in

---

78 *The Morning Chronicle*, 8 February 1841.

future; and the country will gain also by any improvement which he may derive from the suggestions of others.[79]

The editorial offered oblique praise of the Catholicus letters,[80] for only 'hasty reasoners' would judge the letters as bigoted and of the Ultra Tory faction. It also acknowledged Peel as an important leader who was susceptible to rash claims.[81] The suggestion that Peel would see the wisdom in Catholicus's response appeared to be an attempt to appease critics who tried to suppress the series.[82]

Barnes and Walter II knew that Newman had accomplished something important. His letters were unequivocal that Peel had explicitly adopted a philosophical tradition that was opposed to Christianity, and yet inferior to it. This insight, which had in many ways moved beyond the parameters of the address, was striking a chord across British society. Although Newman used satire, amusing images, and sleights of hand, his were not the typical slanderous fodder in the dailies. His letters had a permanence and gravity, a way of framing the rivalry between the Church and the Knowledge School that had escaped others. Perhaps that is why it became impossible for *The Times* to ultimately suppress the fourth letter.

The Fourth Letter: Rising from the Ashes

Newman did not know whether his fourth manuscript would go to press, and was peeved at their dithering. Fortunately, Walter II did not follow Newman's advice—the letter did not go up in flames. Rather, it appeared on Friday, 12 February 1841, and recapitulated his argument that Christianity provided the true good for improving the human condition in contrast to the utilitarian tradition or the Knowledge School.

---

79 *The Times*, 12 February 1841.

80 Harris ('Historical Forces', 193) considered the letter a 'brief defense' of Catholicus. The contents of the letter do not bear this interpretation.

81 That Peel had been careless represented a Tory/Conservative wish; Peel had held these convictions for some time.

82 It remains unclear who was pressuring *The Times* to end the Catholicus series. Likely, some of Peel's supporters, and possibly Peel, made the request. See for example remarks from *The Spectator*, 13 February 1841 in Chapter 4. *The Times* also miscalculated Peel's magnanimity: Peel rebuked the letters in Parliament in March and recalled them in an address to the Tamworth library in 1849.

Catholicus began with a claim: that human nature needed to be 'recast' (alluding to the need for grace in the third letter); in contrast, Brougham's solution was to 'tinker' with but not seek the means to fundamentally transform it. He avoided any mention of Peel; instead he compared those who believed knowledge to be equal to or superior to faith—Brougham to Bentham:

> [Brougham] understands that something more is necessary for man's happiness than self-love; he feels that man has affections and aspirations which Bentham does not take account of, and he looks about for their legitimate objects. Christianity has provided these; but, unhappily, he passes them by. He libels them with the name of dogmatism, and conjures up instead the phantoms of Glory and Knowledge; *idola theatri*, as his famous predecessor [Bacon] calls them.[83] (547)

A passage from Bacon's *Novum Organon* followed which explained what the Idols of the Theater were.[84] By citing Bacon and criticizing Brougham, Newman highlighted the ascendency of scientific knowledge over Christian faith which was increasingly characteristic in his era. Bacon had critiqued various philosophies, showing that their theories of knowledge were more or less certain. Brougham and the mechanics' movement had disregarded this analysis in part, and applied a glorious certainty to the scientific aspect of philosophy. Whereas faith, although the 'evidence of things not seen' (He 11:1), was unwavering and a grace-filled 'aspiration', the situation had changed: according to Brougham faith equaled uncertain opinion fortified only by 'dogmatism'; science corresponded to positive truth. However, using Bacon's excerpt, Catholicus imputed to the Knowledge School that their theories were born in myth (unlike the rutted but real history of the Church),

---

83 Although utilitarianism has been synonymous with Bentham (and his disciple J. S. Mill), Newman labeled Bacon the prophet of utility in *The Idea of a University* (118): 'His mission was the increase of physical enjoyment and social comfort; and most wonderfully, most awfully has he fulfilled his conception and his design'. Rupert (51) has pointed out that 'Bacon's affirmation of the limitations of human reason, of the role of 'the word and oracle of God' in the experience of moral and religious life, is on a different plane from the shift in perspective evident in Bacon's followers who moved towards utilitarian ethics and natural theology'.

84 *Novum Organum*, 2.7; 3.1, in *The Works of Francis Bacon* (London: M. Jones, 1815), IV, 16; 30–1.

of kin to those that in great variety formerly flourished among the Greeks. And these theatrical fables have this in common with dramatic pieces, that the fictitious narrative is neater, more elegant and pleasing, than the true history. (547)

Catholicus then acknowledged that at present physical science seemed more interesting 'than the study of the New Testament' and added that Brougham fixed 'upon such science as the great desideratum of human nature, and puts aside faith under the nickname of opinion'. He wished that 'Sir Robert Peel had not fallen into the snare, insulting doctrine by giving it the name of "controversial divinity"'. Peel, however, differed from Brougham—his address celebrated science as leading to Christianity. To support this claim, Peel had drawn out a 'long and complicated sentence', which 'sets before us a process and deduction'. Here, Catholicus was alluding to Peel's use of William Paley's popular natural theology, which sought to prove the existence of God from scientific facts.[85] He did not believe that natural theology could substitute for the doctrine of God found in Scripture and the Church's tradition. Indeed, scientific induction did not guarantee Christianity as the conclusion.[86]

> The way is long, and there are not a few half-way houses ... along it; and who is to warrant that the members of the Reading-room and Library will go steadily on to the goal he would set before them? And when at length they come to 'Christianity,' pray how do the roads lay between it and 'controversial divinity'? Or, grant the Tamworth readers to *begin* with 'Christianity' as well as science, the same question suggests itself, What *is* Christianity? Universal benevolence? Exalted morality? Supremacy of law? Conservatism? An age of light? An age of reason?—Which of them all? (548)

These questions recapitulated themes from his previous letters and set the path for Catholicus to answer. He did not answer directly, leaving

---

85 For Newman's critique of natural theology, see Patrick J. Fletcher, 'Newman and Natural Theology', *Newman Studies Journal* 5/2 (Fall 2008): 26–42.

86 Frank Turner (*John Henry Newman: The Challenge to Evangelical Religion* [New Haven: Yale University Press, 2002], 331) has suggested that through these letters 'Newman short-circuited the entire debate over natural theology that was to erupt throughout the British scientific community from the mid-1840s through the 1870s'. Turner did not substantiate this claim, nor has evidence been found linking *The Tamworth Reading Room* to such an exaggerated conclusion.

'An aristocracy of exalted spirits'

his readers to wonder. However, he eliminated the possibility that the doctrines of the Church could be discovered simply by empirical investigation. Moreover, the doctrines, history, and faith of the Church would have to be known prior to her pairing with science.

Catholicus pushed on with his argument. He denied any insinuation that Peel had 'any intention at all to put aside Religion', nonetheless his words could 'mean something very irreligious'. Peel's exhortation for the laboring classes to study and learn science after a hard day's work, was troubling. He had offered an impractical ideal for workers and, along with Brougham, had effectively 'taken from Christianity what he [gave] to Science'. Catholicus countered these ideals with 'common sense and practical experience':

> The multitude of men have neither time nor capacity for attending to many subjects. If they attend to one, they will not attend to the other; if they give their leisure and curiosity to this world, they will have none left for the next. We cannot be everything; as the poet says, '*non omnia possumus omnes*.'[87] We must make up our minds to be ignorant of much, if we would know anything. And we must make our choice between risking Science, and risking Religion. (548)

Although it seemed that Catholicus forced a decision between choosing either reason or religion, he rather was stating what was true for all people—the scarcity of time. With this in mind, it was a reminder of ordering knowledge to faith, a dominant theme of the third letter.

Catholicus then declared he would make a 'fair' offer to Peel and Brougham, one that radiated mockery: if Peel would ensure that Tamworth's inhabitants earn 'a ticket' granted by 'public ministers of religion'[88] that attested to their 'proficiency in Christian knowledge' then 'they shall have a *carte blanche* from me to teach anything or everything else second'. Thus, he teased, 'We will have no "controversial divinity" [doctrine] in the Library, but a little out of it.'[89] In high tones and with

---

87 Virgil, *Ecologues*, 8.63.

88 Peel considered the clergy 'public' servants—a standard Tory view of the alliance between Church and State; Newman considered this position opposed to the principle of ecclesial independence. See Nockles, 'Church and King', 106–7.

89 Jay (*Evangelical and Oxford Movements*, 152) has claimed that this paragraph was only added later in the pamphlet version; however, she confused this paragraph

great affect, Catholicus reiterated the priority of faith to knowledge without disparaging the latter:

> Not a word has been uttered or intended in these letters against science; I would treat it, as they do not treat 'controversial divinity,' with respect and gratitude. They caricature doctrine under the name of controversy. I do not nickname science infidelity. I call it by their own name, 'useful and entertaining knowledge;' and I call doctrine 'Christian knowledge;' and, as thinking Christianity something more than useful and entertaining, I want faith to come first, and utility and amusement to follow. (548–9)

Several scholars have taken issue with Catholicus's assessment of faith and science, a theme prominent in this letter. Coats claimed that 'Peel and Brougham had reason and logic on their side', thereby implying that Newman rejected them for 'dogmatic expressions'.[90] Harris asserted that Peel 'looked to the logical/scientific model of thought', while Newman 'insisted on the inviolability of dogmatic principles' garnered through converging probabilities.[91] Jay alleged that Newman was 'anxious only to deny any connection between reason and faith'.[92] However, in this passage and elsewhere, Newman consistently argued that neither Peel nor Brougham were 'logical' or 'scientific'; rather they acted as rhetoricians seeking *to convince* people of the sciences with which they (especially Peel) were little or no longer acquainted. Newman did not seek to belittle scientific knowledge; rather he maintained a priority of faith in relation to scientific knowledge. This priority did not denigrate scientific knowledge, but rather allowed each its proper place for they were not equal in their origins or ends.

Further, Catholicus was no enemy to education. Unlike the Ultra-Tories, he did not prescribe who could and could not learn. He saw education was attainable by all classes and both sexes. He therefore subtly questioned Peel's 'enlightened' but rather arbitrary prescriptions against age and religious affiliation:

---

for the two paragraphs omitted in the fifth letter and later added to the pamphlet. Newman's 'offer' paragraph was originally published in the fourth letter to *The Times*.

90 Coats, 'Rhetorical Approaches', 179.
91 Harris, 'Historical Forces', 206.
92 Jay, *Evangelical and Oxford Movements*, 153.

> That persons indeed are found in all classes, high and low, busy and idle, capable of proceeding from sacred to profane knowledge, is undeniable; and it is desirable they should do so. It is desirable that talent for particular departments in literature and science should be fostered and turned to account, wherever it is found. But what has this to do with this general canvass of '*all* persons of all descriptions without reference to religious creed, who shall have attained *the age of fourteen?*' (549)

Calling to mind recent articles from *The British Critic* on the laboring classes, Catholicus queried Peel's seemingly haughty calls to working people:

> Why solicit 'the working classes, without distinction of party, political opinion, or religious profession;' that is, whether they have heard of a God or no? Whence these cries rising on our ears, of 'Let me entreat you!' 'Neglect not the opportunity!' 'It will not be our fault!' 'Here is an access for you!' very like the tones of a street preacher, or the cad of an omnibus—little worthy of a great statesman and a religious philosopher? (549)

By comparing him to a 'cad of an omnibus', Catholicus would either have inflamed Peel's supporters or had his opponents doubled over in laughter. By 1841, the 'cad' had become notorious in Victorian England: 'It was [George] Shillibeer who introduced the omnibus to London ... Their lower fares, regular service, and speediness made the new omnibus hugely popular. Conductors were initially treated with enormous respect, hired only if there were fluent in French and English, and dressed in smart military-style uniforms to enhance their authority. However, they soon became infamous for swindling foreigners, mistreating passengers, drunkenness, and other rude behavior. The popular term for them was "cad."'[93] Burgis commented that the image was the 'least dignified of the comparisons [Newman] finds for Peel and was carefully worked over as the MS shows. Like the other images (the imitation of Brougham's antics and the quack doctor), it is justified because it conveys with such force Newman's criticism of a 'great statesman'

---

93 Jessica Lang and Jennifer Speake, 'Buses and Coaches', in *Literature of Travel and Exploration: An Encyclopedia*, ed. Jennifer Speake, vol. I (New York: Taylor and Francis Group, 2003), 152.

treating neither reader nor subject with the respect and seriousness they deserve from him'.[94] She also noted the use of humorous images in the letters, such as 'cad', was not intended to terminate in their subject (for example, Peel or Brougham) but to awaken readers to the gravity of his argument: 'The subject matter and the anonymity of the Letters allowed greater freedom to the controversialist and he certainly justified his treatment of Peel and Brougham by "humorous images", "satirical nicknames, epigrammatic hits" calculated to excite attention and to "diffuse light" over his subject; but to make the verses an epigraph to the pamphlet would have been an unnecessarily cruel stroke ... and one likely to direct the reader to the humour at Peel's expense to the exclusion of the ideas for which it was a vehicle.'[95]

The manifest of comical images, pointed questions and critiques that concluded the letter climaxed in Catholicus's repeated gibe at the library's policy on women and virtue: 'A very emphatic silence is maintained about women not virtuous. What does this mean? Does it mean to exclude them, while bad *men* are admitted?' (549). Exploiting what he saw as hypocrisy, Catholicus wondered if knowledge would make the vicious virtuous, then why exclude the former at the outset? If knowledge could do what religion could not, then why have any barriers?

> Alas, that bigotry should have left the mark of its hoof in the great 'fundamental principle of the Tamworth Institution!' Sir Robert Peel is bound in consistency to attempt its obliteration. But if that is impossible, as many will anticipate, why, O why, while he is about it, why will he not give us just a little more of it? *Cannot* we prevail on him to modify his principle, and to admit into his library none but 'well-educated and virtuous' men? (549)

The Times' Volte-Face

That the leading article was published along with the fourth letter of Catholicus signaled a reversal by *The Times*. Newman was not notified of this change in course until after his letter was published. Walter II sent a note which feebly explained the *volte-face*; he indicated that the

---

94 Burgis, *TRR*, 167–8.
95 Ibid., 166.

political pressure on *The Times* had subsided. Possibly the editorial affirming *The Times*' support of Peel was the crucial element allowing Newman to complete his series of letters. Yet Burgis commented: 'Walter was in a very difficult position: he [and his son] had offered Newman a free hand and the brilliance of the *Catholicus* letters was beyond question. At the same time, he and his editor Barnes may well have had strong objections to the publication of any further letters. Their doubts about the wisdom of allowing 'Catholicus' to continue [were] unlikely to have been removed by Letter 4—where Peel [was] compared to "a street preacher" or the "cad of an omnibus"'.[96] Walter II apologized to Newman and asked him to finish his letters. He recognized their virtuosity—hoping to publish them as a pamphlet—while recommending how the letters should end.

8. Charing Cross Feb. 12 [1841]

My dear Sir,

You will perceive that your fourth letter has been inserted in today's paper, and also that some remarks have been made on the former ones in the leading Article, which it is hoped will have the effect of satisfying people's minds that they were not intended to serve political purposes, nor to create any personal animosity towards the subject of them.

I should be sorry indeed, that any difficulties on our part should prevent you from completing the task you have so kindly undertaken or defeat the good ends that we all anticipate from it; but the materials we have to deal with are so various that it is difficult, as you may suppose, to please all. I am very glad however to find that persons who were alarmed, on the grounds I have mentioned, at the first two letters are now becoming wiser, and we therefore hope that if you can sum up in one or perhaps two letters more what you have to say you will let us have them, and they shall appear immediately. We then propose, with your leave, to publish the whole series in a pamphlet, and if you will state anything you may have omitted, or may wish to add, in the form of a preface, it shall be published in the Paper likewise. I hope to be in Oxford next Wednesday and to have the opportunity of explaining personally what cannot be so well stated in a letter.

Believe me my dear Sir Yours most truly J. Walter[97]

---

96 *Ibid.*, 70.
97 John Walter II to JHN (8 Charing Cross, 12 February 1841), *LD*, VIII, 31.

This letter from Walter II to Newman was the last that has been preserved in their correspondences. Unlike his ebullient son, who had left the number of letters up to Newman, Walter II knew that this series must come to a close quickly, lest there be further backlash. Newman must have become aware of this and agreed to end the letters.

Hiatus between Letters Four and Five

Walter II's note of 10 February, Newman's response, and Walter's retraction and then the publication of the fourth letter on 12 February must have given Newman pause. Thus Newman did not have a new letter ready for publication, as he had the first four. Burgis provided a hypothetical account of what might have transpired during the eight-day interim between the fourth and fifth letters:

> Walter said that *The Times* was willing to publish one or two more letters and any prefatory matter Newman thought necessary, that the letters should be published immediately, and that he would arrange for their publication in pamphlet form. Three more letters in fact appeared but no preface, and the letters did not appear immediately ... The eight days between 4 and 5, the longest interval in the series, may be accounted for in at least three ways. *The Times*, in spite of Walter's assurances, may have been responsible; or Newman may not have been able to complete another letter before that date—he was probably engaged in seeing Tract 90 through the press. Another explanation that suggests itself is that, having completed four letters, Newman could see his way clear to the end and knowing that he needed three more letters was reluctant to continue until he had a more certain undertaking than Walter's agreement to insert 'one or perhaps two letters more.'[98]

Further, Newman may have temporarily abandoned the letters because he was put off by Walter II's previous letter and *The Times*' editorial. He may have decided to finish the series as a result of negotiations with Walter II later in the week: 'The fifth letter did not appear until after Wednesday, 17 February, the day when Walter hoped to call on Newman and give him a personal explanation of his treatment of

---

98 Burgis, *TRR*, 71.

his distinguished contributor. There is no record of the interview in Newman's diary but he wrote to Walter accepting his suggestions on 18 February.'99 Although no record of their meeting remains, apparently Newman did meet Walter II, or, as he recounted in 1850, 'Old Walter'.100 Henry Tristram's claim that Newman wrote a letter to Walter II on 18 February and his exchange with Henry Wilberforce on 22 February, in which he mentioned Walter as visiting Oxford, provide corroborating evidence of the meeting.101 Moreover, the fact that Newman wrote three more letters rather than a concluding letter and a preface which Walter II had requested suggests that a *modus procedendi* had been achieved in their personal meeting. This meeting may also explain why Newman recalled that he had been 'pressed several times' by 'Old Walter' before he consented to write against Peel.102

Newman had met Walter III initially on 30 January and it seems only on one occasion; however, he subsequently met 'Old Walter' on 17 February 1841. In his later recollections, Newman may have conflated these meetings. Newman had to be convinced initially to write against Peel—he apparently needed more encouragement to finish the series of letters.

Coats's study of *The Tamworth Reading Room* has posed an alternate explanation for the hiatus and the formation of the Catholicus letters. He believed that as a series they lacked any coherent theme or idea.103 Newman had simply followed the convention of the time—his letters were occasional and thus conceived independently of one another.104

99 Ibid., 72. Burgis's source for the 18 February letter was Henry Tristram's unpublished article, 'Newman and *The Times*', where Tristram noted that Newman had 'accepted' Walter's suggestions. Unfortunately, this letter was most probably destroyed by *The Times*. Like Newman's reply of 12 February, Newman probably composed a rough draft on a piece of paper, which has since been lost.

100 *LD*, XIV, 52

101 Ibid., VIII, 40.

102 Ibid., XIV, 52.

103 Coats, 'Rhetorical Approaches', 177.

104 This observation has merit. Reflecting on his Catholicus letters in 1855, Newman understood that most readers would only peruse a letter or two. Accordingly, Newman thought that each letter had to stand on its own so that it would create a lasting impression on the reader (*LD*, XVII, 428–9). However, Tracey (*LD*, VIII, 525) has noted that, 'the extant manuscript working drafts show that, while

However, Coats asserted that the first three did resemble one another although their bond was extrinsic—these letters merely shared Newman's conservative political and religious agenda filtered through attacks *ad hominem* against Peel, Brougham, and Bentham.

Coats refined this claim regarding the final four letters: in light of the 'E' critique and commentaries in other papers, Newman had softened his tone and mitigated his attacks on Peel and Brougham. This softer tone accounted for another form of extrinsic unity. According to Coats, Newman was forced to adjust the form and substance of his letters because he was chastened by the press:

> In this and in similar letters in the columns of other periodicals, Newman perceived a challenge which he answered by altering the rhetoric of his final four offerings to *The Times*. All *ad hominem* efforts were abandoned. Moreover, Newman separated Peel from Brougham and in a serious tone offered refutation for their ideas. The references to Cicero and Bentham are entirely absent as Newman concentrated on the more recent antagonists. Throughout the seventh letter, Peel is described as being 'a religious man' whose only fault rests in his misunderstanding that science does not directly lead man to God ... Brougham, whose earlier speech is more clearly anti-religious, is no longer scoffed at. He is handled with a new sense of sadness ... Unlike the first article which had Brougham actively perverting his nation, Newman's last description of the older statesman lamented that the latter spent his time 'in preserving the mean, not in aiming at the high.'
>
> Newman's altered rhetoric compromised an advantageous response to his critics in the press. By dropping the personal attacks against Peel and Brougham (especially the charge of atheism leveled at Peel), he relieved himself from similar *ad hominem* attack and focused on issues of dogma which historically were his strength in argument. In forgiving Peel the grievous association with Brougham and praying for the latter's soul, Newman took on a mantle of magnanimity and demonstrated the hope of new life offered by his theological principles. By no longer trivializing the opposing arguments, he did not so much

not conceived as a single unit, they [the Catholicus letters] were not composed as individual letters'. As will be shown below, Newman revisited certain themes throughout the letters, sharpening their intent and allowing the idea of the Church to develop and connect each letter.

dignify his antagonists as he dignified his own statements. After all, Peel and Brougham had reason and logic on their side.[105]

Unfortunately, Coats's study had several unforced errors. First, Newman continued *ad hominem* images for literary effect,[106] mentioned Bentham in the fourth and sixth letters, and maintained a consistent view of Peel and Brougham, a mixture of sardonic comment, goading, and compliment. Coats's article also lacked evidence of going through Newman's personal correspondences in order to support his claims. Had Coats done so, he presumably would have noticed that Newman relished the attention he received in the press.[107] In addition, although Coats believed that it was the reaction in the press that caused Newman to shift the tone and content of his letters, he offered no evidence of having read other critiques outside *The Times*, for example the *Chronicle* of 10 February. Had he done so, he might have concluded otherwise.

Coats misinterpreted the causes and timing of Newman's change in rhetorical strategy. Coats believed that because of the attacks in the press, Newman shifted his tone and method between the third and fourth letters. The exchange between Walter II and Newman between 10 and 11 February, however, revealed that Newman had not yet read other press critiques prior to his fourth letter. This exchange also showed that Newman had composed most, or all, of the fourth letter before receiving newspapers from Walter II. Thus, whatever changes Newman made occurred after the fourth letter and during the week during which he did not publish for *The Times*. Coats rightly perceived a change in the letters. Newman did adjust his rhetorical approach, but not from circumstances such as Coats described. Rather, he explicitly

---

105 Coats's assessment ('Rhetorical Approaches', 179) unwittingly resurrected many of the same arguments found in the Whig press in 1841. This is ironic in so far as his work showed little or no familiarity with the contemporary press other than *The Times*. His conclusions also seem influenced by various historical and hermeneutical errors in his research. Harris, 'Historical Forces', 193; 200–1, also seemed to advocate what the Whig press argued against Newman in 1841.

106 The letters show plainly that *ad hominem* attacks, for example, the 'cad', were used in the fourth letter; they continued in the fifth, sixth, and seventh letters, although abated.

107 Burgis (*TRR*, 92) arrived at a similar conclusion.

unveiled his 'idea' of the Church which unified the letters and which effected a change in rhetoric.

Newman had conceived this shift in the tone and content of the letters prior to and independent of outside critiques. His exchange with Walter II on 11 February indicated that he wanted to compose more letters in order to develop the idea that had gradually emerged in the first four. His fifth letter clearly expressed the idea of the series—that unity of faith through the Church, which was distinguished from the often disordered knowledge of the world, could engage and prosper modernity. The fifth letter denoted the real change in his approach, for it laid bare the 'idea' of the Church that in turn showed the coherence of the letters.

✟ 5 ✟

The Catholicus Letters 5–7

NEWMAN USED THE TIME between the fourth and fifth letters to hone his 'idea'. He did not directly follow the threads of letters two, three, and four; rather, he returned to a theme in the first letter: unity and difference. This theme, which undergirded the first four letters, became fully manifest as an idea in the fifth: the Church cleansed the disordered mind, helped to purify human nature, and united Christians. Scientific knowledge or political agendas, on the contrary, could not intrinsically unify society and tended to veil qualitative differences. In presenting this idea, Newman as Catholicus tempered his playful approach to Peel and Brougham's Knowledge School. Instead he desired to show the Church distinct from, yet able to edify, the growth in modern knowledge and institutions.

The Fifth Letter: 'Christianity is Faith'

In his fifth letter to *The Times*, published on Saturday, 20 February 1841, Catholicus began by recalling the egalitarian nature of the Tamworth library and reading room: it would be open to all 'without with reference to political opinions or to religious creed'.[1] Peel wanted all members on the book committee—especially the Anglican ministers—subject to the rule that there would be no debate over religious or political differences at the institution.[2] Rather, members should unite 'in furtherance of

---

[1] Peel had noted the exception would be for those under fourteen years of age; however, families would be able to use library materials. Were women who were not well educated and virtuous excluded?

[2] Many of the lines in this opening foray were quoted from the newspaper address. Peel either excised or radically altered them in the Bain pamphlet. The pamphlet muted the comparison between political and religious difference and primarily censured the latter.

knowledge.'³ Catholicus emphasized that Peel had equated religious difference with the problems of political and class faction:

> are religious principles to be put upon a level even with political? Is it as bad to be a republican as an unbeliever? ... To a statesman, indeed, like Sir Robert, to abandon one's party is a far greater sacrifice than to unparliamentary persons; and it would be uncandid to doubt that he is rather magnifying politics than degrading religion in throwing them together; but still, when he advocates concessions in theology *and* politics, he must be plainly told to make presents of things that belong to him, not seek to be generous with other people's substance. (550)

Catholicus reminded his readers Peel's politics is human invention, but religious principles have a divine origin, for 'Another made theology'. This final sentence set up the distinction to be explored through a question previously asked. Catholicus implicitly returned to a query in his fourth letter: 'What *is* Christianity?' His answer pierced Peel's conflation of politics, the principles of the Knowledge School, and faith of the Church. Catholicus believed that there must be a distinction between human activity in politics or science and the divine gift of faith in the Church. That distinction was marked by doctrine, or 'Christian Knowledge', which developed through the faith of the Church (550).

Peel declared that scientific, inductive knowledge could easily lead to and secure Christian faith. But for Catholicus this could not be, because faith assumed God's initiative which human reason did not control. To answer 'What Christianity is (and does)' was to know from whom it originated, which Peel did not justly acknowledge, but he and most of Christian Britain implicitly understood this. Although Catholicus did not explicitly state the origins of Christianity—that Christ, God and man, had been sent by the Father and in turn sent the Holy Spirit to guide the Church in truth (Jn 16:13)—he knew that many of his readers held these to be so. These doctrinal truths, implied throughout the third and fourth letters, created a difference for the Christian Church and reinforced the priority of faith over

---

3 This line also was removed from the Bain pamphlet. The revision resembled the original proposition but did not have the clear meaning which Catholicus derided. These excerpts reintroduced the themes unity and difference introduced in the first letter.

knowledge. Such a priority, however, carried a burden, for although it unified believers, it created a distinction from the world of politics, science, and economy. In a passage reminiscent of the 'Duty of Christian Educators', Newman framed his 'idea' of the Church by identifying faith with Christianity:

> Christianity is faith, faith implies a doctrine; a doctrine propositions; propositions yes or no, yes or no differences. Differences, then, are the natural attendants on Christianity, and you cannot have Christianity, and not have differences. (550)

The equation of Christianity with faith represented an innovation in Newman's thinking. Faith and the Church intricately entwined marked out the difference from the 'intellectual pantheon'. Catholicus did not intend to say that Christianity, the faith of the Church, stood apart from the world as a walled-off city. However, the origin and purpose of the Church was distinct from human politics, science, art, or commerce. The difference that faith made actually freed the Church to engage the world in an extraordinary way. This passage had an almost identical cadence to a refrain from one of Newman's sermons. The refrain complemented and mirrored what he declared Christianity to be in a sermon preached during this time: 'Christianity is religion, and something more; and the spirit of love is faith, and something more. *Christian* faith is faith developed into love, it lives in love, and love is greater than faith, because it is its Gospel perfection.'[4]

Christian faith, in Newman's mind, flowered into love and that love was enveloped in doctrine. Faith, love, and doctrine could only properly flow from the heart of the Church, which embraced the world while maintaining its divinity. Indeed, in speaking of the 'yes and no' differences of Christianity, Newman seemed to have improvised upon 2 Co 1:18–21:

> But as God is true, our word toward you was not yea and nay. For the Son of God, Jesus Christ, who was preached among you by us … was not yea and nay, but in him was yea. For all the promises of God in

---

4 Newman, *PPS*, VI, 185. On 21 February, one day after this letter was published, Newman preached 'Judaism of the Present Day' (*PPS*, VI, 174–89). Although his diaries do not indicate when Newman worked on the fifth letter or the sermon, it is reasonable to conclude both were composed during the same interval.

him are yea, and in him Amen, unto the glory of God by us. Now he which stablisheth us with you in Christ, and hath anointed us, is God.

Gilley has rightly commented that this statement 'Christianity is faith' 'was the heart of the matter' for the Catholicus letters. He drew this conclusion that Newman made this declaration because by 1841 the Church of England's power had eroded. This erosion 'led a realistic politician like Peel to edge towards a Christian ecumenism away from Anglican confessionalism'.[5] Although correctly interpreting Peel's religious situation, as well as the centrality of the faith of the Church, Gilley's identification of Newman with the Tory High Church tradition was not accurate. Newman was less concerned about preserving Anglican trappings of power than with his desire for the renewal of faith in what he termed the Church Catholic.[6] Only this Church, present in his deepest longings and also concrete reality, could accomplish what Peel desired politically with the education of the working classes.

The themes of 'unity and difference' further unfolded as the letter progressed. Catholicus brooked no truck with Peel's desire to collapse all things, especially religious, into politics. This produced a false unity. He also resisted the relativizing of truth claims in the name of tolerance. Holding all 'opinions' equal resolved eventually into political manipulation and endless struggle for power. Thus, Catholicus suggested that Peel, 'so cautious, so correct', obliterated the difference that Christianity made because he thought not primarily as a Christian politician but as minister of the Crown:

> His great aim is the peace and good order of the community, and the easy working of the national machine. With this in view, any price is cheap, everything is marketable; all impediments are a nuisance ... It is a mistake, too, to say that he considers all differences of opinion as equal in importance; no, they are only equally in the way. He only compares them together where they are comparable in their common inconvenience to a minister of State. They may be as little homogeneous as chalk is to cheese, or Macedon to Monmouth, but they agree in interfering with social harmony; and, since that harmony is the first of goods and the end of life, what is

---

5 Gilley, *Newman and his Age*, 197.
6 Delio, 'Calculated to Undermine Things Established', 71–80.

left us but to discard all that disunites us, and to cultivate all that may amalgamate? (550–1).

Peel had given himself over to his political foe, Brougham, by cultivating the latter's philosophical tradition and rejecting faith as the 'fulcrum of society'. Instead he rested society 'upon knowledge' that purportedly would 'harmonize' the working and wealthy classes and provide a new bond of unity (551).

> The old and ordinary bond, he seems to say, was religion;[7] Lord Brougham's ... is knowledge. Faith, once the soul of social union, is now but the spirit of division. Not a single doctrine but is 'controversial divinity;' not an abstraction can be imagined (could abstractions constrain), not a comprehension projected (could comprehensions connect), but will leave out one or other portion or element of the social fabric. We must abandon religion, if we aspire to be statesmen. Once, indeed, it was a living power, kindling hearts, leavening them with one idea, moulding them on one model, developing them into one polity. Ere now it has been the life of morality; it has given birth to heroes, it has wielded empire. But another age has come in, and faith is effete; let us submit to what we cannot change; let us not hang over our dead, but bury it out of sight. Seek we out some young and vigorous principle, rich in sap, and fierce in life, to give form to elements which are fast resolving into their inorganic chaos; and where shall we find such a principle but in knowledge?[8] (551)

7 Newman seemed to have associated Peel's notion of a 'bond' with the common etymology of religion—*religare*: to rebind. On 14 February 1841, Newman preached an untitled sermon on 'faith, baptism, and regeneration' (*Sermons 1824–1843*, III, 272) that clarified his notion of religion, and possibly shaped his meaning in the letter: 'By religion is meant the relations between man and God ... It consists of the means of approaching him [God], the means of pleasing Him—viewed externally it consists of doctrines, ordinances, precepts, a polity, and a course of action—viewed internally it consists of faith, obedience, worship, and the like.'

8 In Newman's manuscript was an ensuing paragraph not included by *The Times* (*LD*, VIII, 551–2). The editors made an unfortunate omission, although this paragraph was reinserted when his pamphlet was published in March. Newman had chastised Peel's concession that Anglican clergy would be on the book committee as they were functionaries of the State. In circumscribing their roles as moralists, as *literati*, and as able to be removed by popular demand, Peel and the library committee had ensured that ministers could not unify members through faith. Rather all would have to submit to political strictures. The paragraph indirectly revealed a

'An aristocracy of exalted spirits'

Catholicus provided a melancholy but serious comment upon his day. Faith, issuing from the unity of God and the harmony of the three persons, would provide the image of unity and harmony for the faithful in the Church and by extension society. This was once, at least here in his stylized nostalgia, Christendom, bound together by the faith of the Church. The Church in relation to society was not necessarily an oppressive unity, a 'tyranny and persecution', as Brougham and the philosophes before him asserted. Christendom was not the City of God, for it contained the City of Man beset by sin, but nevertheless it had a center—faith. But 'another age has come' and a unified faith in the wake of the Reformation, the rise of Enlightenment agnosticism, and political and economic upheaval had for those on the vanguard of modernity become a principle for division. However, enlightened knowledge could not do what faith had done, so what vital resource was on offer? This was a troubling question for Catholicus.

Brougham had laid the foundation that 'knowledge can do for society what has hitherto been supposed the prerogative of faith'. He had 'complimented ... faith and its preachers', by characterizing them as the 'evil spirits of tyranny and persecution'. His infidel principle 'borrowed from the records of faith (for after parsons no men quote Scripture more familiarly than Liberals and Whigs)' the notion that Christian faith or belief was but an opinion (552).

> And then he proceeds to his new *Vitæ Sanctorum*, or, as he calls it, 'Illustrations of the Pursuit of Knowledge;'[9] and, whereas the badge of Christian saintliness is conflict, he writes of the 'pursuit of knowledge *under difficulties;*' and, whereas this knowledge is to stand in the place of religion, he assumes a hortatory tone, a species of eloquence in which decidedly he has no rival but Sir Robert. (552)

Catholicus reprised his critique of the mechanics' motto that knowledge equates to happiness and power[10] and that knowledge teaches

---

central piece of Newman's developing ecclesiology: the Church must be independent of the State. See Appendix I.

9 This does not appear to be an exact quotation from Craik or Brougham, but rather Newman's encapsulation of the contents of Craik's volumes which sketched individual after individual pursing knowledge.

10 Craik, *Pursuit of Knowledge*, I, 418.

its 'children' virtues such a as patience, heroism, etc.¹¹ In response to the idea that knowledge could substitute for faith, and could create alternate 'Lives of the Saints', Catholicus demurred. He persisted as in past letters, though with new vigor and clarity, with the argument that God's grace, which effected faith and conversion, united the community of believers as the Church:

> Faith, viewed in its history through past ages, presents us with the fulfilment of one great idea in particular—that, namely, of an aristocracy of exalted spirits, drawn together out of all countries, ranks, and ages, raised above the condition of humanity, specimens of the capabilities of our race, incentives to rivalry and patterns for imitation. (552)

Here Catholicus showed the intimate bond between faith and the Church. Faith was the 'fulfilment' of the 'idea' of the Church, 'an aristocracy of exalted spirits'. Readers may have wondered what Catholicus meant by an 'aristocracy' metaphorically representing the Church. Was it identified with the hierarchy? Or did he intend the original meaning of aristocracy—rule by the best? If so, what did 'best' mean? Catholicus signaled the original meaning of the word in describing the 'best' as those drawn not from nobility but from all of humanity. He implied that God ruled and 'exalted' believers by divine grace. Who were the 'spirits' inhabiting this aristocracy? Did Newman denigrate the *body* of Christ with this euphemism? In selecting that word, Newman touched on what was highest in humanity, but what was also ordered to the body in order to be exalted. The Church as an 'aristocracy of exalted spirits' further illustrated how it differed from the elite in the political order.

Catholicus then compared this ecclesial 'aristocracy' to the Knowledge School. Brougham *et alii* had 'borrowed' the notion of Church's unity through faith and elevation in grace and applied these doctrines to the tradition of intellectual progress. What was characterized as an independent, rival, and superior tradition actually had Christian roots.

> [Brougham's] new pantheon, which is equally various in all attributes and appendages of mind, [has] this one characteristic in all its specimens—the pursuit of knowledge. Some of his worthies are low born, others of high degree; some are in Europe, others in the

11 *Ibid.*, I, 2.

Antipodes; some in the dark ages, others in the ages of light; some exercise a voluntary, others an involuntary toil; some give up riches, and others gain them; some are fixtures, and others adventure much; some are profligate, and others ascetic; and some are believers, and others are infidels. (552–3)[12]

In the new pantheon none were truly unified or converted. From Franklin to Lady Jane Grey, 'human beings who agreed in nothing but in their humanity and in their love of knowledge are all admitted by Lord Brougham[13] to one beatification, in proof of the Catholic character of his substitute for faith' (553).[14] Catholicus stated that in Brougham and Craik's pantheon, 'saints and sinners' had been 'torn from their proper homes and recklessly thrown together under the category of knowledge'. Catholicus had been drawing from Craik's work, which had become fodder for his volley of derision. Indeed, the opening passage from Craik's second volume summarized much of what he chose to critique and framed the content of the arguments:

> We remarked, at the close of our former volume, that the moral habits which the Pursuit of Knowledge has a tendency to create and foster, form one of its chief recommendations. Knowledge is, essentially and directly, power; but it is also, indirectly, virtue. And this it is in two ways. It can hardly be acquired without the exertion of several moral qualities of high value; and, having been acquired, it nurtures tastes,

---

12 Newman listed names found in the two volumes of Craik's work, for example, from Protagoras to Newton, and from Democritus to Pascal. He was concerned because some of these characters were amoral save for their pursuit of knowledge. For example, Craik (*Pursuit of Knowledge*, II, 8–9) described Julian the Apostate:'The emperor Julian ... does not exhibit to us quite so beautiful a picture of philosophy on a throne. He had neither the simplicity, sincerity, and perfect truthfulness of his predecessor's moral character ..., nor the unimpassioned sagacity and clearness of vision which distinguished his understanding; and is chargeable indeed with acting in many respects in a spirit of affectation and blind prejudice, anything but creditable to a philosopher.'

13 Newman meant Craik and in 1872 substituted for Brougham: 'this writer' (*DA*, 289).

14 A paragraph which listed more luminaries in the pantheon of knowledge was originally in the manuscript, but omitted from *The Times*, and restored to the pamphlet (*LD*, VIII, 553); see Appendix I. Jay (*Evangelical and Oxford Movements*, 213) identified most of the persons mentioned in this passage.

and supplies sources of enjoyment, admirably adapted to withdraw the mind from unprofitable and corrupting pleasures. Some distinguished scholars, no doubt, have been bad men; but we do not know how much worse they might have been, but for their love of learning, which, to the extent it did operate upon their characters, could not have been otherwise than beneficial. A genuine relish for intellectual enjoyments is naturally as inconsistent with a devotion to the coarser gratifications of sense, as the habit of assiduous study is with that dissipation of time, of thought, and of faculty, which a life of vicious pleasure implies.[15]

Catholicus drew the letter to a close, noting ironically that unlike Christianity they had excluded angels from their 'intellectual temple' (553). He lifted a few lines from Milton's *Paradise Lost* to make his point.[16] The conclusion returned readers to the essential contrast between the limited power of knowledge and the excellence of faith:

> Such is the oratory which has fascinated Sir Robert; yet we must recollect that in the year 1832, even the venerable Society for Promoting Christian Knowledge herself, catching its sound, and hearing something about sublimity,[17] and universality, and brotherhood, and effort, and felicity, was beguiled into an admission of this singularly irreligious work into the list of publications which she had delegated to a Committee to select *in usum laicorum*.[18] That a Venerable Society

---

15 Craik, *Pursuit of Knowledge*, II, 1–2.

16 In support of his biting remark Newman lifted a few lines from Milton's *Paradise Lost*, 1:558–9; 564–5.

17 Charles Taylor (*A Secular Age*, 339–43) has offered an interesting discussion of the notion of the sublime. This notion developed in the eighteenth century as a vague form of the transcendent and functioned as a romantic alternative to the 'shallow' anthropocentrism evinced by Enlightenment rationalists; however, this notion was also devoid of the doctrinal depth of the Christian tradition. Newman seemed to imply that the Society for Promoting Christian Knowledge (SPCK) had opted for this romantic alternative (Brougham's or Craik's intellectual pantheon) instead of doctrinal Christianity.

18 Newman had been in a controversy with the SPCK over Craik's book seven years earlier. On 4 June 1834 (*LD*, II, 265), Newman's friend John William Bowden informed him that the SPCK had Craik's *Pursuit of Knowledge* in their catalogue and asked Newman to 'furnish me with whatever information you can respecting the crimes and misdemeanors of the Committee in question'. Newman replied on 5 June: 'As to the Education Committee I have already talked to my friends here and

should be caught by the vision of a Church Catholic[19] is not wonderful; but what could possess philosophers and statesmen to dazzle her with it, but man's need of some such support, and the divine excellence and sovereign virtue of that which faith once created? (554)

The Sixth Letter:
Heart Knowledge and Scientific Reasoning

Newman's Catholicus letters had extended over almost the entire month of February and caused quite a stir in the Tory, Whig, and Radical press. His critiques of Peel and the Knowledge School were dissected, applauded, or derided almost each day.[20] Newman's awareness that the press had construed his message mostly along political lines may have influenced the content and method of the sixth letter. He may have realized that in attempting to clarify the idea of the Church in the fifth letter, he could not continue to thrust and parry with Peel and the Knowledge School.

This was the most distinctive letter of the series. Unlike the previous five, it contained few of Peel's or Brougham's words; rather, the letter presented a didactic argument combing through the distinctions between believing and reasoning. His philosophy and theology of mind elucidated the difference that Christian belief, or faith nurtured in the Church, offered to the welter of knowledge that increasingly characterized modern society. Thomas Vargish observed that Newman's view of how and what humans know was decisive for understanding and evaluating the world around them: 'Newman based his criticism of society, including his reaction to the romantics and to the utilitarians, upon his philosophy of the mind. In *The Tamworth Reading Room*... his views on the scope and limitations of knowledge led him not only to a complex

---

will with others. The Pursuit of Knowledge is on the Supplemental Catalogue I believe—a worse place, but nothing to the Education Committee ... I hope to send you a budget of criticisms before the time' (of the next meeting).

19 Here, Newman referred neither to Rome nor to the Tractarian notion of the Church; rather, he was playing with the false 'catholic' pantheon which Brougham, Craik, *et alii* had attempted to portray as one in the pursuit of knowledge.
20 *The Thunderer*, 406–7.

of qualifications about the aims and limits of education but to a direct attack on what he ironically termed his "civilized age".[21] J. H. L. Rowlands augmented Vargish's point that Newman's philosophy of mind was capable of critiquing society. Rowlands pointed out that his philosophy of mind was not grounded in an isolated individual but was communal and relational. Newman was able to critique society, because, 'In the act of pure living, the heart, the passions, the senses, the emotions as well as the mind were involved. Newman's concern was to gather all things into one, in the totality of the Holy, Catholic and Apostolic Church and in the unique individuality of each human personality.'[22]

In the sixth letter to *The Times*, published on Monday, 22 February 1841,[23] Newman transposed his idea of the Church to theological and philosophical questions of faith and knowledge. He provided epistemological warrant for the Church, extending it to an intimate level—between the ecclesial faith and experiential knowledge of each person in relation to their social world. Newman saw these two levels as distinct but unified.

Catholicus opened the letter by deftly reacting to the critques his letters were receiving. He reminded his readers that the purpose of his letters was to offer religious resistance to the 'pretence' of utilitarian thought. He did so by revisiting the question of Christendom past, as in 'The Duty of Christian Educators', contrasted with the present. This passage challenged the assumptions of the Knowledge School: if the faith of the Church could not unite and exalt humanity, how then could purely human resources do so?

> People say to me, that it is but a dream to suppose that Christianity should regain the organic power in human society which once it possessed. I cannot help that; I never said it could. I am not a politician; I am proposing no measures, but exposing a fallacy, and resisting a pretence. Let Benthamism reign, if men have no aspirations; but do not tell them to be romantic, and then solace them with glory; do not attempt by philosophy what once was done by religion. The

---

21 Thomas Vargish, *Newman: The Contemplation of Mind* (Oxford: Clarendon Press, 1970), 72.

22 Rowlands, *Church, State, and Society*, 171.

23 There is no record of when Newman sent this letter to Walter II; he either sent it with the fifth on 18 February or did not record having done so.

ascendancy of faith may be impracticable, but the reign of knowledge is impossible.[24] The problem for statesmen of this age is how to educate the masses, and literature and science cannot give the solution. (555)

Catholicus made a capital point, embedded within this contrast. The 'reign of knowledge [was] impossible' because it had already been tried prior to the advent of the Church. Although new ideas about education and politics had emerged, as well as advances in science, it did not follow that these advances could do better than the old in raising humanity from its wounded condition. A tautology emerged. Knowledge of the world, new and old, came from the world, so how could it possibly unite and exalt people to a transcendent future as Peel, Brougham, *et alii* promised? Although Catholicus saw the present Church as a society of faith in decline, it nevertheless laid claim to a divine origin and was therefore always on offer as a means for human redemption.

Catholicus recalled Peel's 'sanguine' view that science transcended the 'cold doctrines of Natural Religion' and would necessarily lead to Christian faith. Peel was 'wrong', and Catholicus explained why:

> Science gives us the grounds or premises from which religious truths are to be inferred; but it does not set about inferring them, much less does it reach the inference—that is not its province. It brings before us phenomena, and it leaves us, if we will, to call them works of design, wisdom, or benevolence; and further still, if we will, to proceed to confess an Intelligent Creator. We have to take its facts, and to give them a meaning, and to draw our own conclusions from them. First comes knowledge, then a view, then reasoning, and then belief. This is why science has so little of a religious tendency; deductions have no power of persuasion. (555)

This passage was a recapitulation of an article which he composed almost twenty years earlier. In 1822, Newman helped Richard Whately to compose an article on 'Logic' for the *Encyclopaedia Metropolitana*.[25]

---

24 In 1872 (*DA*, 292) Newman replaced 'impossible' with the more fitting 'incomprehensible'.

25 'Logic', in *Encyclopaedia Metropolitana*, ed. Edward Smedly *et al.* (London: B. Fellowes and J. Rivington, 1845), I, 202: 'Three operations of the mind which are concerned in argument: 1st. Simple Apprehension; 2d. Judgment; 3d. Discourse or

He represented Whatley's system in less technical language for *The Times*' readers. Whatley's logic used the terms 'simple apprehension, judgment, and reasoning', which Newman modified to 'knowledge, view, reasoning'. His addition of the term 'belief' in this sequence seemed a logical consequence of the preceding terms. Belief, here, did not have the sense of a conviction received by the imagination; rather it is synonymous with a conclusion or opinion reached at the end of an inferential investigation.

Newman believed that an inferential argument had its own form of validity, and yet both premises and conclusions required interpretation and decision. A logical method could not, in itself, disclose the truths of religion, but only aid and clarify. This was why scientific logic could not persuade as poetry could for love, or the Scriptures for God. Catholicus's argument also turned his readers to the Aristotelian notion that different sets of knowledge are disclosed according to their objects, principles, and methods.

He continued to tutor his readers on the distinction between inferential knowledge (science) and personal religious knowledge:

> The heart is commonly reached, not through the reason, but through the imagination, by means of direct impressions, by the testimony of facts and events, by history, by description. Persons influence us, voices melt us, looks subdue us, deeds inflame us. Many a man will live and die upon a dogma; no man will be a martyr for a conclusion. A conclusion is but an opinion; it is not a thing which *is*, but which *we are certain* about; and it has often been observed, that we never say we are certain without implying that we doubt. To say that a thing *must* be, is to admit that *it may not* be. No one, I say, will die for his own calculations; he dies for realities. This is why a literary religion is so little to be depended upon; it looks well in fair weather; but its doctrines are opinions, and, when

---

Reasoning. 1st. Simple apprehension is the notion (or conception) of any object in the mind, analogous to the perception of the senses. 2d. Judgment is the comparing together in the mind two of the notions, (or ideas) whether complex or incomplex, which are the objects of apprehension, and pronouncing that they *agree* or *disagree*, with each other; (or that one of them belongs or does not belong to the other. Judgment therefore is either affirmative or negative. 3d. Reasoning (or discourse) is the act of proceeding from one judgment, to another founded upon it, (or the result of it).'

> called to suffer for them, it slips them between its folios, or burns them at its hearth ... Now Sir Robert thinks better of natural history, chemistry, and astronomy, than of such ethics; but they too, what are they more than divinity *in posse*? He protests against 'controversial divinity:' is *inferential* much better? (555–6)

In this segment Catholicus, although making a technical distinction, revealed his rhetorical strategy for the letters. 'Impressions, testimony, and description' were the engine of his letters, for they were meant to persuade his readers. He knew that the verbal pictures he painted of the working class, virtuous women, and the Knowledge School would rouse or inflame his readers one way or another. He stated explicitly his rhetorical approach, and the ensuing reaction in the press and in Parliament proved his point.

However, Catholicus was not solely making a rhetorical point. Rather, this passage was principally concerned with contrasting two distinct powers of the mind: the heart, or *nous*, and calculative or scientific reasoning. He had maintained this contrast since his studies of Aristotle's *Nichomachean Ethics* as a student at Oxford for his whole life. When in 1884 he concluded a public controversy over faith and reason with the Protestant theologian, A. M. Fairbairn, he provided clear account of this distinction:

> There is a faculty in the mind which acts as a complement to reasoning, and as having truth for its direct object thereby secures its use for rightful purposes. This faculty, viewed in its relation to religion, is, as I have before said, the moral sense; but it has a wider subject-matter than religion, and a more comprehensive office and scope, as being 'the apprehension of first principles,' and Aristotle has taught me to call it [*nous*], or the *noetic* faculty.[26]

The core of the mind, *nous*, apprehended the truths for reason to then draw out or explore. The term 'reason', as he used it, may have been familiar to some but not all of his readers. For Catholicus, 'reason' in this context denoted the method of scientific investigation. This form of reasoning commenced with doubt, questioned facts, and arrived at conclusions which tended toward certainty. In turn,

---

26 John Henry Newman, *Stray Essays on Controversial Points Variously Illustrated* (Privately printed, 1890), 97.

these virtual certitudes could be further questioned. Scientific reasoning may pause in a conclusion, but did not necessarily end. His allusion to the heart/*nous* provided a difference: beliefs/assents, apprehended in the 'heart', begin with trust in concrete realities or first principles and are immediate and complete. This noetic or 'heart knowledge' needed reason to help elucidate. Yet 'heart knowledge' differed from reason, as not something to be simply tested and pondered, but which spurred people to action like sacrificing for one another in the name of justice, love, or Christ.

This picture of the heart and the reason indicated how religion might be unreal in the hands of those who trade solely in inferential knowledge:

> I have no confidence, then, in philosophers who cannot help having religion, and are Christian by implication. They sit at home, and reach forward to distances which astonish us; but they hit without grasping, and are sometimes as confident about shadows as about realities. They have worked out by a calculation the lie of a country which they never saw, and mapped it by means of a gazetteer;[27] and like blind men, though they can put a stranger on his way, they cannot walk straight themselves, and do not feel it quite their business to walk at all. (556)[28]

Catholicus wanted his readers to recognize the difference between the Knowledge School's pronouncements about inferential knowledge and the knowledge that grounds personal relationships and religious belief. He pointed out what he knew from experience: people had little time to spend working out religious inferences in a logical way; this in no way invalidated personal knowledge or true belief:

---

27 Newman reformulated this example in GA, in order to explain how a person can believe something without fully understanding the subject: 'We are all absolutely certain, beyond the possibility of doubt, that Great Britain is an island ... Our reasons for believing that we are circumnavigable are such as these:—first, we have been so taught in our childhood, and it is so in all the maps; next, we have never heard it contradicted or questioned; on the contrary, every one whom we have heard speak on the subject of Great Britain, imply it in one way or another' (234).

28 In regard to these paragraphs, Ker (*Biography*, 211) has remarked that Newman was at the 'height of his literary powers. He would certainly write as well again, but hardly with greater force than in these passages where the aphoristic, the colloquial, and the ironic come together in a dazzling display of imagery.'

> Logic makes but a sorry rhetoric with the multitude; first shoot round corners,[29] and you may not despair of converting by a syllogism. Tell men to gain notions of a Creator from His works, and if they were to set about it (which nobody does), they would be jaded and wearied by the labyrinth they were tracing. Their minds would be gorged and surfeited by the logical operation. Logicians are more set on concluding rightly than on drawing right conclusions. They cannot see the end for the process. Few men have that power of mind which may hold fast and firmly a variety of thoughts. We ridicule 'men of one idea;' but a great many of us are born to be such, and we should be happier if we knew it. To most men argument makes the point in hand only more doubtful, and considerably less impressive. (556)

'The man of one idea' contrasted with the popular definition of the rationalist who doubted all and inferred everything. Catholicus believed the human person transcended endless questions or a calculative habit of mind:

> After all, man is not a reasoning animal; he is a seeing, feeling, contemplating, acting animal. He is influenced by what is direct and precise. It is very well to freshen our impressions and convictions from physics, but to create them we must go elsewhere. (556)

Here, Newman was playing with the classical Aristotelian definition of man, although developed through Christian and empiricist philosophy. He had studied Aristotle's *Organon* and *Nichomachean Ethics*, and knew 'animal' denoted that which had a sensitive soul and included seeing, feeling, and acting. Humans believe, reason, and contemplate (in religious or philosophical ways) and this last most differentiated them from other animals.[30] Although reason was a distinctive trait in

---

29 This arresting and perplexing phrase denoted the idea of impossibility. Ian Ker (e-mail to author, 15 December 2010) has also suggested that 'Newman ... is surely thinking of trains going round corners and the dangers of that in the early railways'. This is a plausible interpretation, as Newman was apprehensive of rail travel (*LD*, VII, 392). On 16 September 1840, he wrote to his sister Jemima, 'I would propose to come to you for some days after the 29th, but that these numerous railroad accidents frighten one'.

30 Regarding the attribution to Aristotle that 'man is a rational animal' Hannah Arendt (*The Human Condition* [Chicago: University of Chicago Press, 1998], 27),

human persons, Newman departed from the arid empiricist notion of reason that had developed. He elevated Aristotle's notion of contemplation, as the activity of *nous*, and married it to belief. Belief, or *doxa*, was not simply opinion, but trust and commitment (analogous to faith) and this led to action. Contemplation in action was definitive of the human person.

Returning to Peel's address, Catholicus presented another instance of inferential versus personal knowledge. Peel had argued that science would lead to 'a higher reverence for His name'; yet Catholicus observed, 'If he speaks of religious minds, he perpetrates a truism; if of irreligious, he insinuates a paradox'. He wanted his readers to recall that one finds God in the world because one first assents to God in faith through the Church, and not the other way around. Consistent with his previous letters, in which faith must precede knowledge, *nous* (the natural power that receives truth, divine and human) contrasts with reason (the natural process of knowing), he declared:

> Life is not long enough for a religion of inferences; we shall never have done beginning, if we determine to begin with proof. We shall ever be laying our foundations; we shall turn theology into evidences, and divines into textuaries. We shall never get at our first principles. Resolve to believe nothing, and you must prove your proofs and analyse your elements, sinking further and further, and finding 'in the lowest depth a lower deep,'[31] till you come to the broad bosom of scepticism. I would rather be bound to defend the reasonableness of assuming that Christianity is true, than to prove a moral governance from the physical world. Life is for action. If we insist on proofs for everything, we shall never come to action: to act you must assume, and that assumption is faith. (556)

The idioms, examples, and arguments that Catholicus used to paint the contrast between the two forms of knowing culminated in his teaching that faith/belief/assent lead to action; reasoning leads to more

observed, 'Aristotle meant neither to define man in general nor to indicate man's highest capacity [for example, in the *Politics*, 1253a:4; 10: ἄνθρωπος φύσει πολιτικὸν ζῷον or λόγον δὲ μόνον ἄνθρωπος ἔχει τῶν ζῴων], which to him was not *logos*, that is, not speech or reason, but *nous*, the capacity of contemplation, whose chief characteristic is that its content cannot be rendered in speech'.

31 Milton, *Paradise Lost*, 4:76.

reasoning. One form allowed for faith and action, the other simply more understanding.

> Let no one suppose that in saying this I am maintaining that all proofs are equally difficult, and all propositions equally debatable. Some assumptions are greater than others, and some doctrines involve postulates larger than others, and more numerous. I only say that impressions lead to action, and that reasonings lead from it. Knowledge of premises, and inferences upon them,—this is not to *live*. It is very well as a matter of liberal curiosity and of philosophy to analyse our modes of thought; but let this come second, and when there is leisure for it, and then our examinations will in many ways even be subservient to action. But if we commence with scientific knowledge and argumentative proof, or lay any great stress upon it as the basis of personal Christianity, or attempt to make man moral and religious by libraries and museums, let us in consistency take chemists for our cooks, and mineralogists for our masons.
>
> Now I wish to state all this as matter of fact, to be judged by the candid testimony of any persons whatever. Why we are so constituted that Faith, not Knowledge or Argument, is our principle of action, is a question with which I have nothing to do; but I think it is a fact, and if it be such, we must resign ourselves to it as best we may, unless we take refuge in the intolerable paradox, that the mass of men are created for nothing, and are meant to leave life as they entered it. (556–7)

Catholicus could not provide an *a priori* argument as to why faith/belief preceded reasoning. Yet *a posteriori* he asserted this to be true. Both forms of knowing were complementary, but one could not substitute for the other. The former allowed for the reception of God's grace, or philosophical first principles, or simply trusting one's mother.[32] The latter aided in understanding faith, love, or the natural world, but if allowed to dominate, paralyzed the person in its own operations.

He concluded by daring his readers to ask themselves whether they acted upon a question or a belief in matters of everyday life. If they acknowledged the latter then they could accept Catholicus's climactic analogy for religious commitment. Religion, like many ways of human living, originates in a command, not in a question. This fact has been embraced from age to age and he laid bare the absurdity that the nine-

---

32 On this latter point see Newman's discussion in GA, 33–4.

teenth century should be the exception:

> So well has this practically been understood in all ages of the world, that no religion has yet been a religion of physics or of philosophy.[33] It has ever been synonymous with revelation. It never has been a deduction from what we know: it has ever been an assertion of something to be believed. It has never lived in a conclusion; it has ever been a message, or a history, or a vision. No legislator or priest ever dreamed of educating our moral nature by science or by argument. There is no difference here between true religions and pretended.[34] Moses was instructed, not to reason from the creation, but to work miracles. Christianity is a history supernatural, and almost scenic; it tells us what its Author is, by telling us what He has done. (557)

A nuanced comparison followed to illustrate further the difference between religious faith and inferential knowledge. Instead of pitting scientists and politicians against believers, Catholicus contrasted two Christian traditions: Protestant Dissenters[35] and the Church Catholic. For Catholicus, the preaching and theology of Dissenters was the closest thing to a 'religion of inferences'.[36] Unlike a sacramental faith which allowed for direct impressions and real assent, their 'religion of inferences'

> came to nothing—that it was dissipated in thoughts which had no point, and inquiries which converged to no centre, that it ended as it began, and sent away its hearers as it found them. Whereas, the

---

33 The case could be made that during Newman's lifetime and certainly afterwards, there had been a cult or religion of 'science', for example, Darwinism. This would of course depend upon how one used the term 'religion'; for Newman the term denoted some form of supernatural revelation and relationship with the divine and so a religion of 'science' was impossible.

34 Here and throughout the letter, Newman attacked the tenets of Paleyan Natural Theology. To further see how Newman approached Paley, see Amico, *The Natural Knowability of God*, 43–57.

35 Dissenters, for example Baptists or Methodists, not in the Established Church

36 In this passage, Newman averred that he did not intend to disparage Dissenters, although there may have been hint of irony in this admission. Newman had long believed that dissenting theology depended essentially upon private judgment, a form of religious rationalism. That Newman included Dissenters in his critique of secular knowledge may have seemed odd to readers; however, he did not have the opportunity to explicate his position that dissenting religion could easily tend toward skepticism.

instruction in the church, with all its defects and mistakes, came to some end, for it started from some beginning.[37] (557)

Catholicus did not further elaborate, but it was significant that he returned to an ecclesiological comparison. He then concluded with an abrupt return to Brougham/Craik. He noted that orators like Brougham did not present their 'philosophical religion' in strictly logical arguments; rather, they used words and figures which played upon the human imagination. Thus the Knowledge School was not strictly 'logical' or 'scientific'; rather, it had its own form of affective rhetoric, thus proving his argument that 'The heart is commonly reached, not through the reason, but through the imagination, by means of direct impressions, by the testimony of facts and events, by history, by description' (555). Peel's emotive speech and Brougham's and Craik's 'glories of science' used 'direct impressions' and testimony to convince people of science's power and worth. Their arguments themselves, however, were not scientific, and this because they could not persuade or 'inflame' their readers to *believe* them:[38]

> Why should he depict a great republic of letters, and an intellectual Pantheon, but that he feels that instances and patterns, not logical reasonings, are the living conclusions which alone have a hold over the affections, or can form the character? (557)

It is relevant to note that Catholicus's letters three through six concluded with a question, while the first, second and the seventh concluded with an assertion. The concluding questions seemed to indicate that another letter would follow in part as an answer. These questions also created a sense of anticipation for his readers. The fact that Newman did not conclude the first letter with a question may indicate that he was unsure if he would actually write a series, letters two and three seemed to be one letter divided, and the absence of a question at the end of the seventh letter signaled an end to the letters.

---

37 In 1872 (*DA*, 297), Newman added a line to clarify this passage: 'Such is the difference between the dogmatism of faith and the speculations of logic'.

38 This holds true today to even atheistic scientists and *literati* who write for popular audiences, from Stephen Hawking to Sam Harris or Richard Hitchens.

Letter to Henry Wilberforce: The Identity of Catholicus

The same day that the sixth letter appeared, Newman wrote to his close friend Henry Wilberforce[39] about the Catholicus letters, among other matters:

> I fear I shall be, or am, found out in that matter [Catholicus]. London people say they come from Oxford—and Ryder saw Walter coming into and going out of Oxford in the course of a few hours, and knew that I saw him. And then comes internal evidence.
>
> The Article in the M Chr. [*Morning Chronicle*] was not at all in Carlile's [*sic*] style. I thought of Macaulay.
>
> You should have seen a late article in the Globe, silently alluding to Catholicus. It seems as if hitherto they had thought of Puseyism a thing of copes and lighted tapers. Geese, they never read a word, till the fist is shaken in their face.[40]

The note disclosed three important facts about what Newman was thinking about his own letters. First, he was concerned to keep a low profile; he had only waded into this controversy on the promise of anonymity; he also confirmed a visit, presumably, from Walter II.[41] Second, Newman was interested in the reaction to his letters in the press; at least two of the papers he listed were sent to him by Walter II on or around 10 February. Third, Newman's exclamation—'Geese, they never read a word, till the fist is shaken in their face'—underlined his motives for writing the letters.

---

39 JHN to Henry Wilberforce (Oriel, 22 February 1841), *The Correspondence of John Henry Newman with John Keble and Others* (London: Longman, Green, 1917), 142; the editors mistakenly commented: 'Even Newman's friends did not know who Catholicus was'; this mistake was repeated by Harris ('Historical Forces', 193). This letter indicated that Wilberforce and Newman had already had some discussion about the letters, even though Newman was concerned that his identity should not be discovered.

40 *LD*, VIII, 40–1. This letter included several topics; only portions relevant to the Catholicus letters are included here.

41 The editorial notes in Newman's *Letters and Diaries* add to the ambiguity of who actually visited Newman by vacillating between Walter II and Walter III. This letter seemed to confirm that Walter II recently had visited him and had been seen by Newman's acquaintances. A visit by Walter III, who at that time was at Oxford, would not have given rise to suspicion; this letter also seemed to validate Newman's recollection that 'Old Walter' (*LD*, XIV, 52) had visited him.

'An aristocracy of exalted spirits'

As he indicated to Walter II on 12 February, *The Times* had provided him with an extraordinary venue for reminding England that Christianity was faith, and that fact made all the difference. Yet Newman seemed peeved at what the press and the general populace thought of 'Puseyism' in contrast to what he believed to be the 'idea' of the Church. Finally, Newman's image of the 'fist shaken in their face' revealed that he understood the power of his letters.

The Seventh Letter:
The Perils of Knowing God, and Summary

Five days after his exchange with Wilberforce, *The Times* published the seventh and final letter on 27 February 1841.[42] (*Tract 90* circulated that same day, and within a few weeks caused Newman's life to descend into unforeseen chaos.) This letter may have been what Walter II had in mind when he requested a summary on 12 February. It was, however, more than a concession to that request.[43] Newman considered his seventh installment necessary for his overall project. The first half reprised arguments in the fourth letter regarding his understanding of the human discovery of the divine (natural theology) in relation to the God proclaimed in Christian faith (revealed theology). He had continued his sixth letter's sketch about scientific and personal truth, and in the seventh raised the question of the divine ends of science *and* religion. Undergirding these arguments was the shadow of atheism that threatened the delicate balance of conscience, faith, and scientific knowledge. The end of the letter united many strands which ran through the previous six, including a return to Catholicus's wicked satire. This was the *coda* for his score.

The letter opened with Catholicus reminding his readers that Peel was not a scientist but a politician and, at times, an orator. Thus, Peel's claim that 'physical science must lead to religion' was deemed 'unreal'. As he had observed in the previous letters, Peel (and by implication the Knowledge School) had distorted the priority of faith and the processes

---

[42] There is no record in Newman's diaries of when he sent the letter to Walter II.

[43] When Walter II and Newman met on 17 February, there must have been some negotiations about letters five and six.

of scientific knowing. Most importantly, he carried over a theme from the sixth letter that what seemed like bold, new arguments for science leading to God actually contained latent Christian presuppositions, and thus were neither bold nor new. If one found the God of Christian faith at the end of an investigation, one already had the faith to begin with. And yet Catholicus noted that 'it is not easy to decide at this day whether science creates faith, or only confirms it'. Scientific knowledge could lead to different gods (for example, the Aristotelian, the Stoic, or Deist) or possibly no god at all. To accentuate this line of argument, Catholicus recalled pre-Christian science:

> Now, considering that we are all of us educated as Christians from infancy, it is not easy to decide at this day whether science creates faith, or only confirms it; but we have this remarkable fact in the history of heathen Greece against the former supposition, that her most eminent empirical philosophers were atheists, and that it was their atheism which was the cause of their eminence.[44] (558)

To bolster his argument, Catholicus cited Bacon's account of the Greek atomists, like Democritus, 'who [allowed] no God or mind in the frame of things', for all was reduced to the arbitrary combination of matter. Bacon believed that their physics was superior to the physics of Plato and Aristotle because the latter viewed the natural world in terms of final causes which implied divine beginnings (558). This cautionary example served to show that science does not necessarily lead to divinity and in its modern variant more often does the opposite.

Turning to the present, Catholicus again pressed the idea whether science could 'create' faith or confirm it. He rightly pointed out that physicists, according to their own methods, could not discover the 'why' behind the universe, but only 'how' it worked. When they overstepped their limited discipline by positing 'why' they moved from science to theology, which was not their competency. In so doing, they tended 'to make a system a substitute for a God'. Catholicus then smartly moved from scientists to various professions, showing that the knowledge and experience persons gained from their career was no guarantee for a holy or moral life. Knowledge could not elevate and save a person, no matter how talented:

---

44 'Of the Advancement of Learning' in *The Works of Francis Bacon* (London: W. Baynes and Son, 1824), I, 106.

> Each pursuit or calling has its own dangers, and each numbers among its professors men who rise superior to them. As the soldier is tempted to dissipation, and the merchant to acquisitiveness, and the lawyer to the sophistical, and the statesman to the expedient, and the country clergyman to ease and comfort, yet there are good clergymen, statesmen, lawyers, merchants, and soldiers, notwithstanding; so there are religious experimentalists, though physics, taken by themselves, tend to infidelity; but to have recourse to physics to *make* men religious is like recommending a canonry as a cure for the gout, or giving a youngster a commission as a penance for irregularities. (558)

Hidden within this paragraph was one of Catholicus's critiques of the Anglican clergy, presumably those who had assented to the strictures at the Tamworth library and reading room. These men had not been coopted by Peel, but rather were willing partners in denying religious topics at the institute. In these biting lines Catholicus was implicitly goading his fellow priests to recall their ordination and calling, which did not include substituting knowledge for faith or living a life of 'ease and comfort'.

Catholicus then offered an extended argument contrasting science, natural theology, and Christian faith. Newman briefly wanted to show that natural theology, along the lines inscribed by Plato and Aristotle, could conclude in affirming the divine. But these pagan philosophies differed from the natural theology of his day, which combined Christian presuppositions with atheistic atomism, a grievous concoction. This combination could eventually end in knowledge of God, but equally in unbelief:

> The whole framework of Nature is confessedly a tissue of antecedents and consequents; we may refer all things forwards to design, or backwards on a physical cause. La Place is said to have considered he had a formula which solved all the motions of the solar system;[45] shall we say that those motions came from this formula or from a divine fiat? Shall we have recourse for our theory to physics or to theology? Shall we assume matter and its necessary properties to be eternal, or mind with its divine attributes? Does the sun shine to warm the earth, or is the earth warmed because the sun shines? The one hypothesis will solve the phenomena as well as the other. Say not it is but a puzzle in

---

45 *Traité de Mécanique Céleste* (1799).

argument, and that no one ever felt it in fact. So far from it, I believe that the study of nature, when religious feeling is away,[46] leads the mind, rightly or wrongly, to acquiesce in the atheistic theory, as the simplest and easiest. It is but parallel to that tendency in anatomical studies, which no one will deny, to [re]solve all the phenomena of the human frame into material elements and powers, and to dispense with the soul. To those who are conscious of matter, but not conscious of mind, it seems more rational to refer all things to one origin, such as they know, than to assume the existence of a second origin such as they know not. It is religion, then, which suggests to science its true conclusions; the facts come from knowledge, but the principles come of faith.[47] (558–9)

This last statement vexed his contemporaries as well as later interpreters.[48] Here Catholicus seemed to commit the same error Peel did by conflating faith with science, although with faith usurping science. If this was so, Catholicus had contradicted himself. He had stated again and again in the preceding letters that each discipline had its own methods and ends. Religion, denoted here as faith and worship of the true God, clearly had different ends from natural theology or modern science. In 1872, Newman must have seen the ambiguity in this last line, as he clarified it. He commented in a endnote that 'This is too absolute, if it is to be taken to mean that the legitimate, and what may be called the objective, conclusion from the fact of Nature viewed in the concrete is not in favour of the being and providence of God'. Newman's later emendation reflected what he had maintained in the letters. Human reasoning could admit, with certainty, to a god inferred from nature, but not the God revealed in faith. With the complement of faith given through the Church and its Scriptures, the god of reason eventually could be identified as God revealed in Christ.

46 Newman was not appealing here to romantic notions of feeling versus reason; rather, 'Religious feeling' here connoted faith as a cognitive principle of belief.
47 Newman (*DA*, 304) amended this statement in 1872: 'This is too absolute, if it is to be taken to mean that the legitimate, and what may be called the objective, conclusion from the fact of Nature viewed in the concrete is not in favour of the being and providence of God.—Vide "Essay on Assent", 336, 345, 369, and "Univ. Serm." 194'. Newman's later emendation reflected his view, edified as a Roman Catholic, which maintained that human reasoning could admit, with certainty, to the divine inferred from nature.
48 See Chapter 6 below and for example Gilley, *Newman and his Age*, 198.

Catholicus resumed his exploration of natural theology, stating that the world could be thus read in two ways: 'as a machine and as a work'. If by faith the world was assumed to be a creation, then 'we shall study it with awe; if assuming it to be a system, with mere curiosity'. Peel did not 'make this distinction' (559). Rather he, believed that 'greater insight into nature will lead a man to say, "How great and wise is the Creator, who has done this!"' However, he did not consider 'that his thoughts may take the form of "How clever is the creature who has discovered it!" and self-conceit may stand proxy for adoration'. To the Knowledge School's claim that physical science could elevate human nature, Catholicus retorted:

> So, this is the religion we are to gain from the study of nature; how miserable! The god we attain is our own mind; our veneration is even professedly the worship of self.
>
> The truth is that the system of nature is just as much connected with religion, where minds are not religious, as a watch or a steam-carriage. The material world, indeed, is infinitely more wonderful than any human contrivance; but wonder is not religion, or we should be worshipping our railroads.[49] What the physical creation presents to us in itself is a piece of machinery, and when men speak of a Divine Intelligence as its author, this God of theirs is not the living and True, unless the spring is the god of a watch, or steam the creator of the engine. Their idol, taken at advantage (though it is *not* an idol, for they do not worship it), is the animating principle of a vast and complicated system; it is subjected to laws, and it is connatural and coextensive with matter. Well does Lord Brougham call it 'the great architect of nature;' it is an instinct, or a soul of the world, or a vital power; it is not the Almighty God. (559–60)

For Catholicus, Peel's or Brougham's Knowledge School philosophy did not allow for a relationship with a personal God. For them, the cosmos may inspire a sense of awe in a shadow of divinity, but not necessarily gratitude toward a personal Creator. There was no personal connection, and without that one could just as easily slip into unbelief. If one held

---

49 Charles Frederick Harrold (*John Henry Newman: An Expository and Critical Study of His Mind, Thought and Art* [London: Longman, Green, & Co., 1945], 172), observed: 'At a time when Carlyle was declaring wonder to be the essence of religion, Newman tersely reminds his readers that "Wonder is not religion ..."'

the premise that there was not necessarily a personal Creator then it was logical to conclude that there was only an impersonal 'system of nature' that superseded God. 'Why', Catholicus pondered, 'persist in calling the study of [nature] religious, when it can be treated, and is treated, thus atheistically?' In response to the ideas of science advanced by Peel and the Knowledge School, Catholicus proposed a view of religion founded in conscience. One's conscience was the interior meeting of God, proclaimed in the faith of the Church, and the person. It was where all persons could connect to God. For Newman that constituted religious experience.

> The essence of religion is the idea of a Moral Governor;[50] now let me ask, is the doctrine of moral governance conveyed to us through the physical sciences at all?[51] Would they be physical sciences if they treated of morals? Can physics teach moral matters without ceasing to be physics? But are not virtue and vice, and responsibility, and reward and punishment, nothing else than moral matters, and are *they* not of the essence of religion? In what department, then, of physics are they to be found?

Catholicus then provided his own answer to this question.

> What we seek is what concerns us, the traces of a Moral Governor; even religious minds cannot discern these in the physical sciences; astronomy witnesses divine power, and physics divine skill; and all of them divine beneficence; but which teaches of divine holiness, truth, justice, or mercy? Is that much of a religion which is silent about duty, sin, and its remedies? Was there ever a religion which was without the idea of an expiation? (560)

Here, and throughout the letter, the notion of 'religion' was used to contrast the glories of knowledge. Catholicus used religion in a general sense, in which all persons had 'religion' through conscience. But he also implied another sense of religion in this letter much as he did in a prior sermon. No mention was made of the Church in this sermon, and yet

---

50 The term 'Moral Governor' was one title that Newman gave to conscience; see, for example, 'A Letter Addressed to the Duke of Norfolk on Occasion of Mr. Gladstone's Recent Expostulation', in *Certain Difficulties Felt by Anglicans in Catholic Teaching Considered*, II (London: Longman, Green, & Co., 1900), 250.

51 Newman later added 'and a particular Providence' to this sentence (*DA*, 303).

a 'religion' that 'teaches of divine holiness, truth, justice, or mercy' could only be born of the Church.

Returning to Peel's address, Catholicus again noted Peel's admiration of Davy, who as he lay dying, derived a modicum of consolation pondering physical science:

> Now, if we are on trial in this life, and if death be the time when our account is gathered in, is it at all real or serious to be talking of 'consoling' ourselves at such a time with scientific subjects? Are these topics to suggest to us the thought of the Creator or not? If not, are they better than story books, to beguile the mind from what lies before it? But, if they are to speak of Him, can a dying man find rest in the mere notion of his Creator, when he knows Him also so awfully as His Moral Governor and his Judge?[52] (560–1)

Desiring to move beyond this 'most painful portion of Sir Robert's address', Catholicus attempted to 'sum up in a few words' the meaning of his letters:

> I consider, then, that intrinsically excellent and noble as are scientific pursuits, and worthy of a place in a liberal education, and fruitful in temporal benefits to the community; still they are not, and cannot be, the instrument of education;[53] that physics do not supply a basis, but only materials for religious feeling; that knowledge does but occupy, instead of forming the mind; that faith[54] is the only known principle capable of subduing moral evil, educating the multitude, and organizing society; and that whereas man is born for action, action flows not from inferences, but from impressions; not from reasonings, but from faith. (561)

Catholicus concluded by suspending his satirical treatment of Peel. He returned to his opening letter's concerns about Peel. He knew that Peel wielded considerable political power, power to truly affect society. A critical and conciliatory plea was made for Peel to return to the first principles of faith in the Church which truly united society:

---

52 Newman included this sharp refrain in 1872 (*DA*, 304): 'Meditate indeed on the wonders of Nature on a death-bed! Rather stay your hunger with corn grown in Jupiter, and warm yourself by the Moon'.
53 Newman replaced 'education' with 'an ethical training' in 1872 (*DA*, 304).
54 Newman substituted 'apprehension of the unseen' for 'faith' in 1872 (*ibid.*).

That Sir Robert would deny these propositions I am far from contending. I do not even contend that he has asserted the contrary at Tamworth. It matters little to me whether he spoke boldly and intelligibly, as the newspapers represent, or guarded his strong sayings with the contradictory matter with which they are intercalated in his own report. In either case the drift and the effect of his address are the same. He has given his respected name to a sophistical school, and condescended to mimic the gestures and tones of Lord Brougham. How melancholy is it that a man of such exemplary life, such cultivated tastes, such political distinction, such Parliamentary tact, and such varied experience, should have so little confidence in himself, so little faith in his own principles, so little hope of sympathy in others, so little heart for a great venture, so little of romantic aspiration, and of firm resolve, and stern dutifulness to the Unseen! How sad that he who might have had the affections of many, should have thought, in a day like this, that a Statesman's praise lay in preserving the mean, not in aiming at the high; that to be safe was his first merit, and to kindle enthusiasm his most disgraceful blunder! How pitiable that such a man should not have understood that a body without a soul has no life, and a political party without an idea, no unity! (561)

Catholicus' final plea was to spur Peel to action, to a change of heart; this was his last opportunity to engage him in the pages of *The Times*.[55]

Peel's address assumed that impartial scientific knowledge administered in settings such as the Tamworth reading room and library were requisite for individual and societal progress. Such knowledge would purportedly improve the moral character of persons with the added benefit of securing a path to religious truth without the burden of ecclesiastical tradition. From Britain's Areopagus, *The Times*, Newman contested Peel and the Knowledge School, for he believed that, 'intrinsically excellent and noble as are scientific pursuits, and worthy of a place in a liberal education, and fruitful in temporal benefits to the community; still they are not, and cannot be, the instrument of education'. Newman responded to these ideas in an informal tone and

---

55 Harrold ('Introduction', xiv) claimed that because of the Catholicus letters, *The Times* offered Newman a staff position, which he declined. No evidence exists for this offer—neither in Newman's *Letters and Diaries* nor in the archives of *The Times*. Harrold may have confused the offer that *The Times* made in 1844 to Thomas Mozley, who was Newman's brother-in-law ('Tom Mozley', *DNB*).

'An aristocracy of exalted spirits'

style, similar to that of his *Parochial and Plain Sermons*, in order to reach a wide audience. His informally crafted responses to Peel and the Knowledge School flowed from a coherent 'idea' of the Church.

Newman would never again write for *The Times*.[56] *Tract 90* immediately embroiled Newman in a far-reaching controversy which consumed him for the rest of 1841. Newman's absence, however, did not stop the wider press, or Peel, from commenting upon and keeping the Catholicus letters alive in the Victorian mind throughout the spring and summer.

---

56 Newman, however, wrote a letter—'Rome and the St. Bartholomew Massacre'—to *The Times* on 13 September 1872, concerning Pope Gregory XIII's alleged role in the massacre and the doctrine of infallibility.

✢ 6 ✢

The Reception of the Catholicus Letters

NEWMAN'S LETTERS, a mixture of political satire, literary imagery, and philosophical argument, coalesced in his theological vision. They were like a series of popular sermons, which did not reflect upon biblical passages and apply them to everyday concerns, but started with human life, politics, and history juxtaposed to divine truths. Newman preached to a national congregation, proclaiming how the Church united persons of faith which altered their relation to modern institutions and arrangements. Like his sermons at St. Mary's, the Catholicus letters challenged all variety of classes and peoples and had an instant and widespread impact in Britain's press and public.

Because Newman's letters advocated the faith of the Church as distinct from the goals of the Knowledge School, and because they involved a popular politician, the press instinctively knew they had a controversy to sell. Many editorials and articles were published for and against the Catholicus letters in 1841, and this generated political backlash. Newman did not come out from anonymity, perhaps because of the *Tract 90* conflagration, to further engage the debate. Thus his letters did not have a visible, lasting effect on developments in Victorian society.

The Areopagus: 'The wise men of Athens heard the Apostle and despised him'[1]

The Catholicus letters have a biblical-historical analogue: St. Paul debating at the Areopagus (Ac 17:16–34).[2] Like Paul, who was carried

---

1 'Righteousness not of us, but in us' (19 January 1840), *PPS*, V, 128.
2 The complete passage from the King James Version is found in Appendix II.

up the Hill of Ares to explain his views against popular philosophers (Ac 17:19), Newman was 'pressed' by the Walters to write against Peel (and *de facto* the Knowledge School). Both men chose to engage the curious and the philosophically proud in order to advocate for the faith of the Church. Both were mocked for their faith, and yet also attracted votaries to their cause.

Paul's evangelization at the Areopagus was an occasional, yet significant, theme in Newman's theology.[3] Newman's Catholicus letters resembled Paul's speech in ancient Athens, in so far as they reflected the Pauline desire to correlate the Gospel message with contemporary philosophy and popular thought. In his fifth Catholicus letter, Newman explicitly referred to Paul at the Areopagus in contrast to Brougham's and Craik's intellectual pantheon:

> The persecuting Marcus is a 'good and enlightened emperor,' and a 'delightful' spectacle, when 'mixing in the religious processions and ceremonies' of Athens, 're-building and re-endowing the schools,' whence St. Paul was driven in derision.[4] (553)

Newman saw in historical Athens a place for philosophy but also the challenge of the Gospel, and this fitted perfectly with his letters. However, he may have also seen in the contrast between a philosopher king, Marcus Aurelius, a victor, and Paul, the vanquished. This contrast may have paralleled how he saw Peel, the 'enlightened' politician, and Catholicus, who had already become the subject of ridicule in the press.

In 1836, Newman commented on the ecclesial significance of Paul's evangelization at Athens in 'The Visible Church for the Sake of the Elect'. Paul illustrated the consequences of preaching the Church's faith. Newman's reflection upon the Areopagus anticipated his character Catholicus and the argument for the Church in the letters to *The Times*. Catholicus represented Paul in preaching and debating: he was not there to 'civilize the world' but 'for the sake of the elect' or

---

3 Newman also mentioned the Areopagus in 'Jacobson's *Apostolical Fathers*', in *The British Critic* 25:49 (January 1839): 49–76, and in 'Righteousness not of us, but in us' (19 January 1840), *PPS* V, 128.

4 This sentence, which was in the original manuscript, was not included in *The Times* on 20 February 1841; it was, however, reinstated in the pamphlet published in March and in the 1872 revision.

the Church. This distinction also revealed a contrast. Peel had hoped the Tamworth library would 'smooth the face' of his community, while Newman's letters were really a call to faith for the elect. Because the motive of his letters mirrored Paul's at Athens, his final comment on how Paul was both mocked by some and followed by others was a striking parallel to the press's varied reaction to his letters.

> If we were asked what was the object of Christian preaching, teaching, and instruction, what the office of the Church, considered as the dispenser of the word of God, I suppose we should not all return the same answer ... It may be useful then to consider with what end, with what expectation, we preach, teach, instruct, discuss, bear witness, praise, and blame; what fruit the Church is right in anticipating as the result of her ministerial labours.
>
> Paul gives us a reason ... different from any of those which I have mentioned. He laboured more than all the Apostles; and why? not to civilize the world, not to smooth the face of society, not to facilitate the movements of civil government, not to spread abroad knowledge, not to cultivate the reason, not for any great worldly object, but 'for the elect's sake.' This is instanced of him and the other Apostles in the book of Acts. Thus, when St. Peter first preached the Gospel, on the day of Pentecost, 'they were all amazed,' some 'mocked,' but 'they that gladly received the word were baptized.' ... When St. Paul preached at 'Athens, 'some mocked,' others said, 'We will hear thee again,' but 'certain men clave unto him.'[5]

He had used the Areopagus narrative at various times during the 1830s,[6] and often the image of the Areopagus in sermons illustrated notions of conscience and divine economy, faith and reason, notions that propelled letters.[7]

---

5 'The Visible Church for the Sake of the Elect' (20 November 1836), *PPS*, IV, 150.

6 See for example: 'Obedience to God the Way to Faith in Christ', 31 October 1830, *PPS*, VIII, 207–8; *OUS*, 69–70 [87–8]; *Arians of the Fourth Century*, 65–6: hereafter cited; *Arians*. Newman did not seem to make much use of this narrative before 1830; it is not found earlier in his published *PPS* or *OUS* sermons. Prior to 1841, there are no direct references to Paul at Athens in his *Letters and Diaries*, though there is a possible indirect reference (*LD*, I, 108).

7 Newman made use of this narrative in relation to his conversion to the Roman Catholic Church in 1845; references to Paul at Athens can be found in his *Idea of a University* and in his *Essay in Aid of a Grammar of Assent*. To list and explain the

'An aristocracy of exalted spirits'

Paul debated with his cultured despisers at the Areopagus and won some of them over; Newman directed his letters toward the politicians and intelligentsia who sponsored institutions like the Tamworth reading room and library. The Catholicus letters consistently called attention to certain members of the political and philanthropic classes as practicing an idolatry analogous to that of first-century Athenians.

Newman opposed those in nineteenth-century England who had reduced God to 'a representation by the art and imagination of man' (Ac 17:29); however, this manufactured God was no longer simply enshrined in statues and temples. Rather, Newman accused certain presumably enlightened people of replacing God with modern technological science and enlightened self-centeredness. As Paul had done for the early Church, Newman summarized the religious errors of his day in his seventh letter:

> So, this is the religion we are to gain from the study of nature; how miserable! The god we attain is our own mind; our veneration is even professedly the worship of self.[8]

Newman's view of knowledge mirrored Paul's, who did not remonstrate against Athenian philosophers and poets, but praised what the wise men of the day held in high esteem: 'Not a word has been uttered or intended in these letters against science; I would treat it ... with respect and gratitude' (548). Some recent interpreters have not accepted this statement *prima facie*, but rather ascribed to it an ironical antipathy

---

ways in which Newman used the narrative in his later career would be a study in itself; one example, however, suffices. One of Newman's most insightful uses of the narrative occurred in 1847, in his 'Rough Draft of Matter for Preface to French Translation of Univ. Sermons, Afterwards Written for Dalgairns in Latin', where he attempted to elucidate *evidentia credibilitatis* as applied 'to the case of faith': 'For instance, the probability itself prior to any proof that God will give a revelation appears faint to one man, strong to another ... To such a one ... might have sufficient *evidentia credibilitatis* for his coversion ... as we know it was enough in the case of those converted by St. Paul at Athens. On the contrary, had St. Paul been directed to work a miracle, it would have done far more towards making his divine mission evident, but would have tended to reduce the proof to a *scientific* instead of *personal* character, and, as it were, to force spectators to believe, instead of giving opportunity for their respective characters to display themselves' (OUS, 'Appendix B', 243).

8 *LD*, VIII, 559.

to science.⁹ However, Newman as Catholicus was sincere in this profession, so long as the priority of faith over scientific reasoning was acknowledged. Newman, however, did not wholly adopt Paul's conciliatory style to explain these notions; rather, his letters contained barbs of invective and sinews of satire, absent from Paul's plaintive tone.¹⁰ Yet in asserting the priority of faith over knowledge or science, Newman, like Paul, appealed to people's fundamental but forgotten 'sense of religion [and] inward convictions',¹¹ which was distinct from knowledge attained from method and material progress. For example, Newman had previously explored this point in his 1830 Oxford University Sermon, 'The Influence of Natural and Revealed Religion Respectively':

> When St. Paul came to Athens, and found the altar dedicated to the Unknown God, he professed his purpose of declaring to the Heathen world Him 'whom they ignorantly worshipped.' He proceeded to condemn their polytheistic and anthropomorphic errors, to disengage the notion of a Deity from the base earthly attributes in which Heathen religion had enveloped it, and to appeal to their own literature in behalf of the true nature of Him in whom 'we live, and move, and have our being.' But, after thus acknowledging the abstract correctness of the philosophical system, as far as it went, he preaches unto them Jesus and the Resurrection; that is, he embodies the moral character of the Deity in those historical notices of it which have been made the medium of the Christian manifestation of His attributes.¹²

Finally, like Paul at the Areopagus, proclaiming God 'will judge the world in righteousness by that man whom he hath ordained', Catholicus

---

9 Coats, 'Rhetorical Approaches', 175.

10 This also was Luke's narration of the Areopagus event, and was molded into Luke's softer narrative tone and style. Paul himself used all forms of rhetoric—including barbs!—in his Apostolic letters.

11 *OUS*, 129–30 [180–1]. The manuscript of this sermon indicates that Newman originally penned a more profound insight into Paul's motives and actions: 'St Paul's preaching at Athens: Then he was among the disputers of this world. Did he merely tell them that they reasoned badly, captiously, dishonestly, profanely? No—he does not appeal to their reason at all. He appeals to quite a different principle—their existing sense of religion—to their inward convictions' (*OUS*, n. 130, 358).

12 'The Influence Natural and Revealed Religion Respectively', 13 April 1830, *OUS*, 29 [24–5].

'An aristocracy of exalted spirits'

called for an acceptance of Christ's righteous grace:

> Now, independent of all other considerations, the great difference, in a practical light, between the object of Christianity and of heathen belief, is this—that glory, science, knowledge, and whatever other fine names we use, never healed a wounded heart, nor changed a sinful one; but Christ's word is with power. The ideas which Christianity brings before us are in themselves full of influence... in order to meet the special exigencies of our nature. (543)

However, Newman's 'preaching' in the Catholicus letters differed from Paul's in many ways, and one in particular. The Apostle preached for those who did not know the Gospel. Newman had a more complicated task—he was writing to a culture formed by the Gospel and by the Church, however fractured. In his eyes, many had either forgotten the message or had begun to adopt 'enlightened' alternatives to Christianity. In his eleventh University sermon, 'The Nature of Faith in Relation to Reason,' Newman commented upon how Paul did this, and in a sense his Catholicus letters did the same:

> Thus to take the instance of St. Paul preaching at Athens: he told his hearers that he came as a messenger from that God whom they worshipped already, though ignorantly, and of whom their poets spoke. He appealed to the conviction that was lodged within them of the spiritual nature and the unity of God; and he exhorted them to turn to Him who had appointed One to judge the whole world hereafter.[13]

His Catholicus letters were not intended merely to bludgeon Peel and Brougham or inundate readers with High Church doctrine or Tory platitudes. Although his arguments and aphorisms contained Tractarian elements, they developed from his early experiences of God, of Oxford, and of his parish work. The idea for the letters originated in his desire to remind the *The Times*' readers of Christian first principles found in the 'Church Catholic'. Although the letters seemed intent on disparaging a politician, educational reformers, and others, the Apostolic and Catholic Church was the luminous idea in Newman's mind in 1841 and this idea, more than anything, propelled him to discourse in the *The Times*, Britain's Areopagus.

---

13 OUS, 144–5 [203–4].

The Reception of the Catholicus Letters

Press Reaction to the Catholicus Letters

Newman noted on several occasions that Paul's preaching at the Areopagus resulted in accusations and ridicule. Yet Paul's witness also won converts, for 'certain men [and women] clave unto him and believed' (Ac 17:34). Where Paul preached 'strange notions' about the Christian God to philosophers and pagans upon the Hill of Ares, Newman's Areopagus was *The Times* of London. The Catholicus letters were meant to reawaken readers to the Gospel of Christ and His Church. Was Newman successful? How was his apology for the Church and faith in English life received by the public?[14]

Newman's letter to Walter II on 11 February 1841 indicated that he was 'content with such opportunity ... of putting out views which [he thought] important through so influential a medium'.[15] Newman was aware of *The Times*' immense influence. It was 'a towering Everest[16] of a newspaper with sales ten times those of any other daily, combining leadership in circulation, in new services ... in advertisement revenue, commercial profit and political influence to an extent no other newspaper anywhere in the world has ever done before or since'.[17] The format of *The Times* was conducive to propagating his ideas. The paper 'consisted of eight pages, four of which were usually filled with advertisements; on the average only one letter was published per issue. Any letter to *The Times* thus had high visibility'.[18] Leading articles or prominent letters published by *The Times* were in either larger, leaded type—which indicated importance—or small, unleaded type. Peel's speech was published in the latter; Newman's letters in the former.[19]

---

14 Portions of this chapter rely on the excellent scholarship of Nina Burgis, who traced the British newspaper reaction to the Catholicus letters (*TRR*, 75–124); although her work merits reading, there are some lacunae which this chapter attempts to fill.

15 *LD*, VIII, 31.

16 This is an apt although anachronistic description of the paper in 1841; Mount Everest was so named by the Royal Geographic Society in 1865.

17 Francis Williams, *Dangerous Estate: The Anatomy of Newspapers* (New York: MacMillan, 1958), 100.

18 Harris, 'Historical Forces', 193.

19 Ibid. Harris implied that Peel's speech may have been printed in smaller type because *The Times*' did not agree with its content. While *The Times* did not condone

Newman did not stand before Britain as an evangelist preaching a new Christian doctrine. He intended to proclaim what seemed old as new. As the mysterious Catholicus he used bold arguments and subtle allusions; authorial anonymity was essential for Newman and for *The Times* to communicate the message. Newman chose the pseudonym 'Catholicus' primarily to avoid controversy, to elicit a reaction from readers, and to signal his ecclesial desires.

His intentions aligned with Thomas Barnes, editor of *The Times* from 1817 to 1841. Barnes 'made *The Times* the most obstinately anonymous newspaper in the world. Power he loved, but it was sweeter to him for its secrecy.'[20] Although Walter III was the initial liaison and Walter II the subsequent contact, Newman's letters were addressed to Barnes, who decided on their placement and most probably had a hand in some final editing.

That Barnes agreed to accept these letters, critical of Peel and Brougham, revealed the editorial philosophy of *The Times*. A decade earlier, Barnes had been under the sway of Whig-liberals, especially Brougham. By 1834, after a public 'war' with the Lord Chancellor, he somewhat shifted his allegiance to Peel's up-and-coming Conservative party.[21] Barnes tried to remain politically neutral, although *The Times* was widely regarded as sympathetic to Tory principles. He 'consulted, first, public interest, and secondly, public opinion. *The Times*, not being tied to a party, could afford to vary its expressions in accordance with the ebb and flow of public sentiment. It could direct and it could indicate public opinion.'[22]

Newman's anonymous letters fit perfectly into Barnes's philosophy:

---

the address, the length of his remarks—over 6500 words—also may have been a factor in the choice of type.
20 *The Thunderer*, 205.
21 Ibid., 209.
22 Ibid., 207.

The Reception of the Catholicus Letters

Whereas newspaper readers had been accustomed since the days of 'Junius'[23] to devote their attention to 'Decius'[24] or 'Vetus'[25] or some similarly signed communication addressed 'To the Editor,' Barnes brought them to regard the leading article as the *vital part of the paper* [emphasis added]. He addressed not a governing class but all classes. He was eager to be read by all who could read ... he accustomed the whole country to ask 'What does *The Times* say?'[26]

Newman's Catholicus letters were in a vein very similar to 'Junius', and he availed himself of *The Times'* influence. He knew that he had a 'towering' peak upon which he could proclaim his message and may have shared Barnes's idea that:

> Newspaper writing is a thing *sui generis*; it is in literature what brandy is in beverages. John Bull, whose understanding is rather sluggish—I speak for the majority of readers—, requires a strong stimulus. He consumes his beef and cannot digest it without a drain; he dozes composedly over his prejudices which his conceit call opinions; and you must fire ten-pounders at his densely compacted intellect before you can make it comprehend your meaning or care one farthing for your efforts.[27]

---

23 Francesco Cordasco, 'Junius' (1768–73), in *DNB*. 'Junius was the pseudonym adopted by the author (or possibly authors) of a series of letters which appeared once or twice monthly (sometimes more often) in the *Public Advertiser* ... between 21 January 1769 and 21 January 1772. In this series Junius—named after the popular republican hero Lucius Junius Brutus—opposed the policies of George III and the administrations of the serving prime ministers ... Now a classic of English political commentary, the correspondence owes its influence to three interrelated factors: the high whig philosophy espoused to attack tory policies and celebrated political personalities; the literary power of the letters, one of the most effective uses of slanderous polemic ever employed in English political controversy; and, finally, the uncertainty surrounding their authorship.'

24 'Decius' was an anonymous correspondent to *The Times* who in 1808 wrote letters to the editor 'on the causes of late military disasters' (Walter II, *The Thunderer*, 149).

25 'Vetus' composed a series of letters to *The Times* in 1812. These letters became quite popular and 'came to be identified with a certain strident patriotism' as well as attacks on certain political leaders (*The Thunderer*, 150–1).

26 Ibid., 391–2.

27 Ibid., 210–11.

'An aristocracy of exalted spirits'

The power of *The Times* and the principle of anonymity hurtled Newman's letters like ten-pounders toward Peel and the Knowledge School as well as torpid or confused Christians who did not or could not imagine the Church's spiritual potential for the working classes and its capacity for assimilating the onrush of scientific knowledge. Newman, as he said to Henry Wilberforce, was 'shaking a fist' in the face of his readers.

The Times did not offer cover for Peel but set up his easy alliance of scientific knowledge and Christian faith to be knocked down: Peel's name had been prominently tied to the address, yet the address itself was diminished by small, unleaded type. Neither Barnes nor Walter II supported Peel's ideas.[28] The Catholicus letters had the full support of *The Times*—at least initially. They incited a new surge of reaction, swift and fierce, from readers of *The Times* and the wider press.[29]

On 8 February, three days after Newman's first letter to *The Times*, two London-based Whig papers, *The Morning Chronicle* and *The Globe* published reactions. Newman's first letter, concerned mainly with the relationship of knowledge to human nature and societal unity, were immediately translated by the papers into politics. *The Chronicle* pounced upon the status given to the letter. The commentary interpreted the letter as signaling the offense of 'old Tories' at Peel's promotion of learning for the 'industrious classes'.[30] *The Globe* had an article on the special election in Monmouth[31] yet made an indirect comment on Peel's desire to avoid controversial divinity and Newman's critique of his position.[32]

The following day, 9 February, *The Times* published the 'E' critique. *The Sun*[33] and *The Morning Herald* published articles on the Catholicus

---

28   This policy changed in reaction to Newman's success.

29   In contrast, comment about Peel's address was left to lesser, more partisan newspapers. The string of January editorials about Peel's address faded quickly.

30   Burgis, *TRR*, 77.

31   There was special election in Monmouthshire in February 1841 because an MP resigned due to illness; see Philip Salmon, *Electoral Reform at Work: Local Politics and National Parties, 1832–1841* (Rochester, NY: Boydell and Brewer, 2002), 93.

32   Burgis, *TRR*, 78.

33   Walter II's letter to Newman on 10 February mentioned that he was sending four newspapers to Newman—three of them unnamed in addition to *The Morning Chronicle*. Newman seemed to want to know how his letters were being received and

letters on 10 and 11 February. In an attempt to tamp down mounting criticism of Newman's letters, the pusillanimous leading article from *The Times* by Walter II or—most likely—Barnes appeared on 12 February. That same day new articles from *The Globe* and *The Morning Chronicle* appeared in which 'neither paper quoted from the letters, or indeed showed any interest in the way Newman's argument was developing';[34] rather, they mostly interpreted the letters along the lines of political and ecclesiastical conflict.[35] Newman did not mind that the contents of his letters were being dissected. Rather, he relished the attention his letters were garnering—particularly their religious and ecclesial themes.

Newman especially savored the *Chronicle*'s critique—he speculated that it was written by Macaulay.[36] He copied by hand the entirety of the article and later included it in his manuscripts labeled, 'Movement towards Rome. 1841'.[37] The editorial showed that Newman had an intellectual peer who had theological insight into his letters—it was one of only two articles which he mentioned in his correspondence:

> The growing spirit of Puseyism in the Church appears thus far to have worked tolerably well in harness with Toryism. But the symptoms of restiveness are beginning to show themselves, which plainly indicate that such will not be the case long. Nor is it difficult to foresee that

Walter II obliged. Burgis (*TRR*, 76) identified two of the three of unnamed papers: *The Globe* and *The Sun*. She could not locate the fourth paper and speculated that it might have been a 'provincial' paper or one of the papers that had written about Peel's address in January. It may have been that one of the unnamed papers was a copy of *The Times* which included the 'E' critique.

34 Burgis, *TRR*, 81.

35 Interestingly, Coats's assessment unwittingly resurrected many of the same arguments found in the Whig press in 1841. This is ironic insofar as his work showed little or no familiarity with the contemporary press other than *The Times*. Harris, 'Historical Forces', 193; 200–1, also seemed to advocate what the Whig press argued against Newman in 1841, thus not substantially providing scholarly insight into Newman's actual positions.

36 JHN to Henry Wilberforce (Oriel, 22 February 1841), *LD*, VIII, 40–1, at 40. Newman's speculation may have been correct, because others, for example, Newman's friend, R. W. Church writing to Frederic Rogers on 14 March 1841, independently reached the same conclusion (*LD*, VIII, 108–11, at 108).

37 Burgis, *TRR*, 81.

eventually this Popish heresy in a Protestant Establishment will split the Tory faction into fragments incapable of any further re-union.

With the Toryism of two centuries ago, Puseyism might have permanently amalgamated. But it has come too late into the world. Modern Toryism is quite a different affair from the absolutism and Jacobitism to which it has succeeded. The vitality of principle is gone; and the carcass is only animated by the demon of expediency. The professed attachment of Toryism to national institutions never regards the idea and final cause of those institutions, but some sinister class interest which, in them, it would conserve ... It is a thing of shreds and patches.

Not so Puseyism. That is earnest and uncompromising. It disclaims and disdains expediency ... The one duty of its education is obedience; first to the parent, then to the State; above all to the Church.

The columns of the *Times* itself are thrown open to this sect for attacks upon Sir ROBERT PEEL. We do not say the attacks are not well founded. His sincerity of speech is impeached in the form of a compliment to his understanding. His philosophy is shown to be superficial. The low-toned character of his morality is exposed. His shiftings, turnings, and inconsistencies, to catch this or that class, are laid bare unmercifully. The conviction of his thorough want of mental honesty is enforced ... The Puseyites work out their morality into politics and practice. They do not play at religion and righteousness according to the good old conventional ways of the Church. They are all for realities. We like their spirit. But it will never do with the Tories ...

[We] are mistaken in the Puseyites if they will either put up with a rebuff or consent to a compromise. With the exception of their dishonest participation in the moneys of the National Church—and they, doubtless, make that out, somehow, to their own consciences—they have all the marks of the most right-down earnestness that the world has seen, in religion, since the times of the Puritans and the Reformers.[38]

The author of the *Chronicle* article made several astute observations. First, he noted that the three letters were composed by a Tractarian or Puseyite—not simply a Tory Partisan or a High Churchman. The power behind the Catholicus letters flowed from an adherent to the Oxford Movement—that since 1833 had increasingly distanced itself

---

38 *The Morning Chronicle*, 12 February 1841; see the full text in Appendix III.

from the High Church and elements of the Tory party.[39] Although certain of these ideals undergirded the letters, there was a philosophy and theology that went beyond Tractarian positions by alluding to it as a 'Popish heresy'.

The editorialist's insight into the transformation of the Tory party and its alliance with the High Church was also significant. Newman's letters were not primarily political. That they were treated as merely political or as rantings by a reactionary High Churchman revealed less about the letters and more about the aims and intentions of the Whig and Tory press. The author of the *Chronicle* article knew that there was a difference in the form and substance of the letters. The letters were articulating something beyond convention, something bold:

> The Puseyites work out their morality into politics and practice. They do not play at religion and righteousness according to the good old conventional ways of the Church. They are all for realities. We like their spirit. But it will never do with the Tories.

The *Chronicle* editorial was an exception to the common Whig reaction to the letters. Burgis's survey found two main lines of approach in the Whig press:

> The [Catholicus] letters then were treated as evidence of Tory hostility to the intellectual advancement of the masses, and of the religious intolerance of a powerful 'priest-party' within it. Their appearance in *The Times* [sic] could be made to show either that the Tamworth Address was no more than a liberal mask on the same old Tory face, or that Peel, if he was not a hypocrite, was the leader of a divided party and his own liberalism doomed to defeat by reactionary ultra-Tories and churchmen.[40]

Catholicus was also attacked by Tory and Conservative editorials, as evidenced by the 'E' critique in *The Times* and by *The Standard* on 2 March. *The Standard* came to the defense of Peel's ideals and lamented the bigoted critique of Catholicus:

> We have read those strictures [of Catholicus] with pain, and with compassion for one who, possessing so many accomplishments as the

---

39 Nockles, 'Church and King', 95.
40 Burgis, *TRR*, 79.

writer, and evidently meaning so well, could still allow his mind to be compressed within the narrow limits by which it is too plainly confined.[41]

The weeklong hiatus between Newman's fourth and fifth letters did not quell the press: between 13 and 20 February, at least five more critiques of the letters were published, with one or more coming from Ireland.[42] The most incisive of these articles appeared in *The Spectator*. The author recapitulated the paper's January derision of Peel, indicated the widespread comment on the letters, and offered a sharp appraisal of Peel and of *The Times*' pathetic leading article. The author also indicated that Peel had been in contact with *The Times* about the letters:

> Sir Robert Peel's début as a diffuser of useful knowledge, at Tamworth, has made a commotion among both the parties of which he may be reckoned a leader, Tories and Whigs. The Whigs exhibit a sort of hesitating desire to welcome him as their own, as if still doubtful whether too open advances might not be spurned. The Tories are quite shocked at his having committed himself so far; and three or four clever letters have been published in the *Times* in large type, by way of timely check. They started from nearly the same ground that *The Spectator* occupied the week before last; and afterwards laughed and scolded by turns, to bring the scapegrace back to his duty. These letters have given rise to much remark; and the *Times* hints that its correspondent is some great man, or the Coryphaeus of 'great and able men.' The Leading Journal seems to fear, however, lest the severe correction might render the offender desperate; and yesterday it had a grave talk with Sir Robert upon the subject, winding up with an imposing air of forgiveness.[43]

The Spectator and the other papers seemed to expect that more letters were forthcoming. During this time Newman had reconsidered finishing the letters because *The Times* had wavered. However, the widespread press may have impelled him to complete the series and to clarify the unifying idea which animated each letter in its own way: the 'idea' of the Church as bearer of 'Christian Knowledge' and the visible means of God's grace.

41 *The Standard*, 3 March 1841.
42 'Peel's Tamworth Speech', *Dublin Freeman's Journal*, 15 February 1841.
43 *The Spectator*, 13 February 1841.

Newman's View of the Controversy

After Newman had published his fifth and sixth letters, he revealed his identity to Henry Wilberforce. Newman savored the treatment that his letters received. He marveled at how this 'popular medium' combatted certain prejudices against Tractarians and displayed their prophetic impetus behind the movement—a call for a return to the faith of the Church.

Newman seemed cheerfully annoyed at the article of *The Globe and Traveller* of 22 February, which was a direct assault on Puseyism:

> We leave to more expert theologians the task of deciding whether the Puseyites are heretics or schismatics, and take the humbler course of occasionally directing public attention to their doctrines, and the effect produced upon their followers ... The age is unfavourable to clerical assumption ...
>
> A procession round the church with 'bell, book, and candle,' splendid dresses and a goodly train of choristers may produce reverence; but a man in a simple surplice, folding his arms, and making unusual bows and genuflections, is likely to produce tedium or ridicule.
>
> Though Puseyism may have made progress in the clergy, we do not hear that it has taken root in the congregations. When, however, it does get hold of a layman, we [see] its symptoms in increased dogmatism and intolerance ... LAY PUSEYISM—that fine assertion of infallibility and scorn of public opinion.[44]

The Globe's contrived fear of 'LAY PUSEYISM' may have been the veiled reference to which Newman referred when he quipped about 'shaking his fists'.

During this time, Newman wrote to Wilberforce with his plans concerning the letters.[45] He was already thinking ahead to their pamphlet form:

> Tell me if this be common or coarse as a motto to my letters to Sir R P [Peel] which are to be published separate
>
> > Away went Gilpin neck or nought,
> > Away went hat and wig

---

44 *LD*, VIII, 41.
45 The date of this letter was uncertain (*LD*, VIII, 46–7).

'An aristocracy of exalted spirits'

> He little thought when he set out
> Of running such a rig[46]

> I want a second *opinion*—and *quick*[47]

Wilberforce eventually replied:

> Given, that the letters [of Catholicus] are to be published—and that it is intended to hit Peel hard;—I think the Gilpin verses will make a capital motto[.]
>
> But you know you never asked me anything about it till you had resolved to write and had written the first 2 letters. Else I confess I should have hesitated whether it is politic to pull Peel[']s tail at all. Won[']t it prevent Pusey being a Bishop perhaps. Also, I never thought of any one dreaming that you wrote anything in the Times. So that I never thought what the effect might be if it were discovered.
>
> However all this is only to the point of your publishing the letters at all for certainly they must be regarded as an attack on Peel. Now if they are to be so published I don't see that the motto is much worse than the letters (or indeed so bad) and it [is] certainly capital.

Wilberforce's reply revealed a certain ambivalence and surprise that Newman would be so bold in lampooning a political figure in of all places *The Times*. This was a move away from the tracts or *The British Critic*. However, Newman seemed to know this, and calculated that he could best 'undermine things established'[48] by bringing his theological concerns to the most powerful paper in England. Wilberforce's reply was much more concerned with political fallout, than with the theological ideas which Newman salted throughout the letters. Depending on when Newman saw Wilberforce's note, however, he may have softened his tone for the final letter regarding Peel. His central question, about the motto, was never brought to fruition even though the letters were published in pamphlet form.

---

46 Tracey (*LD*, VIII, 47) linked this verse to William Cowper, 'The Diverting History of John Gilpin; showing how he went farther than he intended, and came safe home again', in *The Poetical Works of William Cowper*, ed. Rev. George Gilfillan, I (Edinburgh, 1854).

47 Newman, *LD*, VIII, 47.

48 *LD*, VII, 417.

The Reception of the Catholicus Letters

Four more articles and a cartoon depicting Peel as Brougham's lackey appeared before Newman's final letter on 27 February.[49] *Tract 90* was published on the same day as his final letter; however, the press did not immediately seize upon this tract nor did they discover any connection between the letter and the tract. Newspapers continued to probe and critique Catholicus. On 28 February, the *Weekly Chronicle* published an article concerning the letters. Eleven more articles were written about Peel's address and the series between 1 and 10 March.[50] Newman had achieved his goal of bringing theological ideas in a novel way into the public square.

Looking at this media controversy Coats claimed that *The Times* 'printed an editorial [on 6 March] meant to conclude its part in the ensuing debate' (about the Catholicus letters).[51] However, the leading article of 6 March responded to criticism of an unrelated editorial published by the paper two days earlier. On 4 March, *The Times* discussed a recent parliamentary debate, which centered on public funding for the Maynooth Seminary in Ireland, and within the course of debate curiously took a swipe at the recently published *Tract 90* and

---

49 Harris, 'Historical Forces', 197. Burgis (*TRR*, 93) observed: 'This sign of controversial success was conferred on the "Catholicus" letters on 25 February when there was published "Nicholas Nickleby's Introduction to Squeers", no. 672 of the current series of caricatures by the famous H. B. (John Doyle) whose satire on political subjects and public men, prolific in comic ideas and noted for faithful likenesses and lack of exaggeration, had been delighting a wide audiences since 1829'.

50 Burgis (*TRR*, 96–7) noted that during this time one particularly able critic from the *Morning Chronicle* wrote under the names 'Tamworth' and 'Protestans'. The form of his critiques mirrored Newman's : 'Letter I of "Protestans" is clearly intended to be an answer to "Catholicus" using his own approach. Just as Peel was reproached with imitation of Brougham, "Catholicus" was said to be 'reviving the arguments of Mr. Collins, and other free thinkers and Atheists' of the eighteenth century, in opposing physical science and faith. Just as "Catholicus" had absolved Peel of intending an attack on religion, so "Protestans" declared, "I do not, of course, presume to charge you with joining in the views of such persons; you seem, on the contrary, to have sincere objects of religion at heart", although what "Catholicus" had written was reminiscent of dilemmas often pronounced between Popery and Atheism' (*TRR*, 96). 'Protestans' also raised questions about Newman's probity in selecting quotations from Peel's address.

51 Coats, 'Rhetorical Approaches', 179.

the 'Puseyites'. The author of the editorial (likely Barnes) questioned this oblique condemnation in Parliament. The subsequent article of 6 March was written to counter accusations that had arisen about *The Times*' supposed 'defense' of Puseyism. The editorial offered a brief history of Puseyism and a fair reading of the Oxford Movement.[52] It is unclear whether or not the article was also intended as an indirect defense of the Tractarian elements embedded in the Catholicus letters.[53]

While *The Times* sought to justify and to clarify its position on Puseyism, opposition to *Tract 90* was gaining momentum. Newman was aware of this, yet not overtly concerned about the burgeoning controversy; he still had to finish his work for *The Times*. On 4 March Walter II paid Newman for his letters.[54] Newman wrote to him the following day; he also wrote to Wilberforce on 5 March, wryly observing the vain searching in the press for the identity of Catholicus:[55]

> The Globe says that the letters of Catholicus are written by an Oxford Dignitary—Faussett? it is a fit occasion for such a Malleus Hæreticorum.[56]

Newman implied with irony that Faussett was a 'Hammer of the Heretics', but the glee with which he wrote this line signaled that this title was better reserved for Catholicus himself!

On 6 March, Walter II sent him the printed letters to be revised for the upcoming pamphlet. Newman sent out 'a parcel' to Walter II that

---

52 The thoughts and sentiments in *The Times*' leading article were echoed and expanded in a private letter from R. W. Church to Frederick Rogers (*LD*, VIII, 108–11).

53 Coats misinterpreted this letter as a direct critique of the Catholicus letters. He also claimed that no other mention of the letters was given in *The Times*; however, on 10 March, *The Times* published a rebuttal to Catholicus which was signed by an anonymous MP (which will be discussed below). On 26 March, the pamphlet, *The Tamworth Reading Room*, was advertised in *The Times*. Finally, a recapitulation of the letters was given in Newman's obituary on 12 August 1890.

54 In his diary for 4 March (*LD*, VIII, 54) Newman recorded that Walter II had sent him '½ notes'; for the sake of security in sending currency through the mail, Victorians cut banknotes in half and sent the halves in separate letters.

55 Burgis (*TRR*, 105–22) analyzed at length the press's preoccupation with the identity of Catholicus.

56 JHN to Henry Wilberforce (Littlemore, 5 March 1841), *LD*, VIII, 56.

same day.⁵⁷ Jay has suggested that Newman's consent to publish a pamphlet included a small measure of hypocrisy.⁵⁸ Newman had ridiculed Peel's revised pamphlet: 'A public man must not claim to harangue the whole world in newspapers, and then to offer his second thoughts to such as choose to buy them at a bookseller's' (534). However, unlike Peel's, Newman's pamphlet changed very little in tone or style. He did add two paragraphs to the fifth letter which were originally in his manuscript and were excised, most likely because the letter exceeded the requisite column length. Neither addition in the pamphlet altered his argument or the tone of the letters.⁵⁹ Newman also had little time to revise his letters, as the controversy over *Tract 90* increased from the beginning of March.

Peel's Counter-attack

10 March marked a new turn in the drama surrounding the Catholicus letters. *The Times* published a letter to the editor that brazenly supported Peel and commended the principles embedded in his address. Strong words and sharp questions were directed at Catholicus. This was the second letter published by *The Times* to mollify Peel's supporters. For all their efforts in printing Newman's letters—anonymously and in bold type—*The Times* offered little outward and no direct support for them. Walter II neglected to warn Newman about the decision to print the second letter to the editor, SIR ROBERT PEEL'S ADDRESS AND CATHOLICUS:

> Sir,—I cannot regret that the letters of 'Catholicus' have come to a conclusion. I do not know, that in giving them so prominent a position in your columns, you have overrated their literary value or incidental importance, but I think you can hardly have calculated the effect they were likely to produce on your readers.
>
> Perhaps the exact sense and precise intention of an author is never perfectly apprehended by any readers but those whose minds are not

---

57 *Ibid.* Newman also received a 'packet' (presumably his letters) from Walter II.
58 Jay, *Evangelical and Oxford Movements*, 152.
59 Newman revised and republished the pamphlet as a part of his uniform collected works in 1872; in contrast, Peel's speech, except in reference to Newman, has faded into obscurity.

> only analogous to, but nearly on the same level with his own; and thus I am by no means prepared to accuse this writer of a desire to leave an unjust impression on the general reader; indeed, he has positively disclaimed any such result, but it is none the less certain that persons not conversant with the metaphysics of theology, and not familiar with philosophical distinctions, have risen from the perusal of these letters with a vague notion that Sir Robert Peel has promulgated doctrines of an irreligious tendency, and that he has avowed himself an adherent of a school of philosophy which ostentatiously excludes religion from its consideration ...
>
> In all this [Peel's speech] there was nothing extraordinary, nothing perhaps not common-place—nothing that looked for any wider fame than the county newspaper ...'Catholicus' has surely shown himself somewhat deficient, in taking this simple and customary incident as the text for an elaborate discussion of the most solemn questions which are agitating the heart of Christendom, and fixing on Sir Robert Peel as his hero and his victim.[60]

This letter was significant in two ways. The author, 'a Member of Parliament', shrewdly underscored the theology and philosophy interlaced throughout the letters, and although presumably a politician, departed from the usual political accusations. He also correctly noted that Newman had taken a seemingly innocuous address and raised some 'of the most solemn questions which are at the heart of Christendom'. Catholicus himself could not have stated more succinctly the aims and goals of the letters. However, what made this letter important was not simply its contents. Rather, its timing and authorship also raised important questions: Why did *The Times* publish the letter two weeks after Catholicus's final installment? Why was the author identified, not in name, but as an MP?

The answers to these questions materialized the next day in Parliament. On 11 March, Peel took the floor and delivered an impassioned denunciation of the Catholicus letters. The MP's letter and Peel's speech appeared to be more than a coincidence but rather a coordinated counter-attack against Catholicus.[61] *The Times* had played both sides in this controversy.

---

60 'Sir Robert Peel's Address and Catholicus', *The Times*, 10 March 1841. The letter was signed: A MEMBER OF PARLIAMENT.

61 No evidence exists, however, that explicitly relates their connection.

The Reception of the Catholicus Letters

The attack indicated that Peel had kept abreast of the Catholicus letters and had not forgotten their sting. He mocked the letters during a debate about public funding for mechanics' institutes. He took the occasion to push beyond the private patronage set out in his Tamworth address and sought public funding for secular institutes. In the course of his remarks he pivoted to confront a more pressing, personal concern:

> I hope public money will only be required as a stimulus to local exertion; I hope the affluent who are connected with the great seats of manufacture, who have derived and are deriving their wealth from the manufacturing industry of the country; that they will insist upon reserving to themselves the gratifying duty of promoting the social improvement of the working classes, and providing for them the means of rational amusement and recreation.
>
> It may be well to ridicule all this; it may be well to see with perfect indifference countless thousands of rational beings immersed in ignorance and low degrading vices, and to insinuate the charges of irreligion and infidelity against those who would tell a working man of the pleasures or advantages of knowledge; and who would think of substituting some relaxation from labour, connected with mental improvement, for drunkenness and quarrelling, and mere sensual indulgence. I for one look down with scorn on such insinuations. My consolatory belief is, that by refining the tastes, and improving the habits and manners of those who subsist by the sweat of the brow, you are advancing the cause of morality, advancing the cause of true religion. As Mr. Hope observes, we be not foolish enough or wicked enough to suggest these means of improvement, as superseding religious instruction; but we hope and believe, that they are aids to religious instruction; and that you cannot reclaim men from indolence and vice, without softening their minds, and subjecting them to the higher and purer influence of religious impressions.
>
> There is one material consideration that must not be overlooked. Great efforts have been made by public authorities, and by individuals, for the education of youth. Every year releases from the restraints of school, thousands and tens of thousands of intelligent boys, into whose hands we thus put the keys of knowledge. We can impose by law no restraint upon the subsequent uses to which those keys may be applied; they give free access to good and evil, and there are many temptations to select that which is evil; if there be no effort made to supply that which is good. But if that effort be made; if there be the

ready access to useful knowledge and rational amusement, there is that in the human mind which will secure a preference for the good, and the instruction that has been given to the child, instead of being perverted to evil purposes, will be made subservient to the improvement and the happiness of the man. I do what I can within my own narrow circle, to found education on a religious basis. I insist in every school to which I contribute, on conformity to the doctrines, and attendance on the worship, of the Church, and shall I be told, that I am defeating the purpose for which this early training of the mind was intended, if I extend my care beyond the age of thirteen or fourteen, and endeavour to provide salutary food to satisfy the appetite which I have created?[62]

The preemptive *Times* letter and Peel's speech signaled a *coup de grâce*. Peel had the last word and Catholicus would be vanquished. However, Peel did not grasp Catholicus's core idea. He was not saying perfunctory church attendance and memorizing of doctrines were the requisite compliments for modern institutions educating youth or adults. Rather, he proclaimed what the Church was—divine, a means of grace, a healer, and the inspiration for faith in action. It complemented modern establishments and movements, but not in a passive way. Seeing the Church Catholic, as healer and guide distinct in origin and purpose, required new eyes and a desire to be an active member of the body of Christ. Peel had failed to appreciate this idea.

Moreover, Burgis detailed how Peel's speech did not shore up his position, but yielded the opposite effect: 'Predictably this public reply to the letters revived the dying controversy; it was followed by comment from the Ministerial *Globe*, *Chronicle*, *Sun*, *Spectator*, and *Weekly Dispatch*, and from the Conservative *Post*, *Standard*, *Britannia*, and *Conservative Journal*. The *Globe* and *The Chronicle* made much of the alleged discomfort of Peel's own party in the House. The *Globe* of 12 March described him as repeating the part of "Juvenile Whig" played at Tamworth, and said that if he kept moving at that rate, he would 'come to be considered as a "perfect Young Rabid"; though his performance did not seem to have been "a cure for the heartache" to his party.'[63]

---

62 *Hansard's Parliamentary Debates*, 11 March 1841, 125–6, available at: http://hansard.millbanksystems.com/commons/1841/mar/11/education-of-the-working-classes.

63 Burgis, *TRR*, 102–3.

The Reception of the Catholicus Letters

Peel's speech not only raised concerns in the press. Privately, people were commenting. On 14 March, the politically connected socialite Charles Greville recorded in his diary:

> The other night Peel, who has been a good deal nettled by the attacks on him in a series of letters, signed 'Catholicus' in the 'Times,' made a very striking speech upon the education and recreation of the people, which was enthusiastically cheered by the Whigs, but received in silence by the Tories. He made a sort of reply in this speech to the charges of irreligion insinuated in these letters, and took the opportunity of expressing those liberal sentiments which mark his own identification with the progress of society, and which render him, from their liberality and wisdom, the object of such suspicion, fear, and dislike with the Tory democracy who reluctantly own him for their leader.[64]

That same day, 14 March, Newman's close friend, R. W. Church, began a letter to fellow Tractarian Frederick Rogers, providing him with details about two recent articles in *The Times* and the emerging crisis surrounding *Tract 90*. Church provided astute commentary on the events that surrounded the letters, citing *The Times*' double dealings with Catholicus and Peel.

> I quite dread to begin a letter to you, not from lack, but from abundance, of matter. Don't, however, prick up your ears too high, else you may be disappointed: people on the spot can scarcely tell what is great and what little; yet I think that curious things have happened since I wrote last. I think I told you that the 'Times' had been letting in letters signed 'Catholicus' against Sir R. Peel, criticising an address delivered by him in the Tamworth Reading Room, in which he took Lord Brougham's scientific natural-theology line; and not only had let them in, but puffed them in its leading article, without however giving up Peel. These said letters, signed 'Catholicus,' with one or two others of the same sort on duelling, &c., were thought to smack strongly of Puseyism, and brought out furious attacks on the said Puseyites in the 'Globe,' expostulations and remonstrances on political and theological grounds from the 'Standard,' and a triumphant Macaulayism in the

---

64 Charles C. F. Greville, *The Greville Memoirs: A Journal of the Reigns of King George IV, King William IV, and Queen Victoria, 1837–1852*, ed. Henry Reeve, IV (London: Longman, Green, 1902), 398.

'An aristocracy of exalted spirits'

'Morning Chronicle,' in which the writer, with great cleverness, drew a picture of alliance between effete plausible, hollow Toryism with Puseyism, which he described as a principle which for earnestness and strength had had no parallel since the Reformers and Puritans, and rejoiced greatly over the prospect that Puseyism must soon blow Toryism to shivers. And the 'Globe' admitted that people were most egregiously out in supposing that this same Puseyism was an affair of vestments and ceremonies: that it was, on the contrary, something far deeper and more dangerous. Such was the state of things out of doors last month.[65]

This letter, found in Newman's archives, must have been kept because of its insight into this tumultuous period. Church had started the letter on the 14th and finished it on the 21st. He sent Newman a copy of the letter for comment and Newman then forwarded it to Rogers. Anne Mozley recorded that on the flap of the letter dated 21 March, Newman wrote a personal note to Rogers about the controversy over *Tract 90*.[66] Newman chose not to comment on the Catholicus controversy, or reveal his identity to either of his compatriots—possibly because of the storm surrounding *Tract 90*.

Newman quietly concluded his business with *The Times* in March. He did not rise to Peel's direct challenge. He wrote to Walter on the 9th, 16th, and 22nd, presumably to put the finishing touches to the pamphlet. The last explicit reference to the Catholicus[67] letters in *The Times* occurred on 26 March on page 7 within the advertisement columns. The advertisement included a boisterous line from the first letter:

---

65 R. W. Church to Frederick Rogers, *LD*, VIII, 108–11, at 108; the remainder of the letter concerned *Tract 90*. Church finished with a postscript: 'P.S.—H.B. [possibly Hablot Knight Browne, a caricaturist] has brought out a caricature: Nicholas Nickleby (Sir R.P. [Peel]) coming to Mr. Squeers (Lord Br. [Brougham]), and asking, "Do you want an assistant?"' (*LD*, VIII, 111).
66 Anne Mozley, *Letters and Correspondence of John Henry Newman to 1845*, II, 298–9.
67 *Oxonius-Catholicus* and *Anglo-Catholicus* were pseudonyms used at different times in 1841, in addressing a range of issues including *Tract 90*, the Jerusalem bishopric, and greater tolerance of Roman Catholics.

Sir Robert Peel and his Address at the Tamworth Reading Room.—Revised and corrected by the Author, price 2s.

THE LETTERS OF CATHOLICUS. 'It is, indeed, most melancholy to see so sober and experienced a man practising the antics of one of the wildest performers of this wild age, and taking off the tone, manner, and gestures of the versatile ex-Chancellor, with a versatility almost equal to his own.'—Catholicus. London, John Mortimer, 21, Wigmore-street, Cavendish-square.[68]

The press did not comment on the newly minted *Tamworth Reading Room* pamphlet. The politics of the High Church and *Tract 90* had become a story and consumed Newman's personal life. However, a trickle of speculation ran through the newspapers concerning the author of the letters.[69] They had become quite well known and such speculation added to their notoriety.[70] Some papers continued to reference the letters as a pretense to critique Peel. Monthlies and quarterlies commented on the Catholicus letters and some eventually reflected on Newman's *Tamworth* pamphlet into June.[71]

The Tamworth Reading Room in The British Critic

The fading controversy briefly resuscitated during the summer. In June 1841, the Melbourne government collapsed. Following the elections in

---

68 *The Times*, 26 March 1841. Although the advertisement announced the publication as 'The Letters of Catholicus', the pamphlet was titled *The Tamworth Reading Room*. Newman often referred to these letters as 'Catholicus'; however, the title, *The Tamworth Reading Room*, was retained in 1872. On 2 October, the *Morning Chronicle* also printed an advertisement for the pamphlet following closely, but not exactly, the format of *The Times*. Although unclear, it may have been announcing a second edition; however, the title, *The Tamworth Reading Room*, was still not used; apparently, the 'Letters of Catholicus' still remained the popular reference.

69 On 23 March Newman's friend, J. F. Christie, wrote to him (*LD*, VIII, 117–18), commenting on the *Tract 90* controversy; he concluded his letter with a line that may indicate that he knew of the identity of Catholicus: 'I have seen one or two of the newspaper Articles—a very good one in the Times of a fortnight or three weeks back' (*LD*, VIII, 118).

70 Burgis, *TRR*, 111.

71 Ibid., 103–8.

June and July, Peel became Prime Minister.[72] The change in his political fortunes increased the media's scrutiny of him. Concurrently, a caustic fifty-three-page article on 'The Tamworth Reading Room' was published by Thomas Mozley in the July issue of *The British Critic*.[73]

Newman had turned over the editorship of the *Critic* to Mozley during the spring and encouraged him to continue writing for the quarterly. In late May and early June, they discussed Mozley's first issue that would be published in July.[74] Mozley informed Newman of his plans to contribute an article about mechanics' institutes.[75] Newman raised some questions about the article, but because Mozley had written on this topic in prior installments and no explicit mention was made of Peel's Tamworth institute, he did not press further. Newman may have suspected it would include his Catholicus letters, but he did not disclose his identity as Catholicus to Mozley.[76]

In his autobiographical *Reminiscences Chiefly of Oriel and the Oxford Movement* (1882), Mozley recounted this event:

> [There was] an article on an Address delivered by Sir R. Peel, on the establishment of a reading-room at Tamworth, and on letters written thereupon by 'Catholicus,' in the 'Times.' I had utterly forgotten the article and the address for a whole generation, till just now reminded by opening the number of the Review. I did not at the time know, though I half suspected, that Newman was 'Catholicus,' but was informed of the fact some years after by one who could not but know, and who could hardly understand my ignorance on the point.

---

72 Gash, *Sir Robert Peel*, 265–70.
73 'The Tamworth Reading Room', *The British Critic* 30 (July 1841): 46–99.
74 LD, VIII, 150–1; 156; 164.
75 LD, VIII, 200–1.
76 In late July, Mozley ran into some trouble with his first issue, especially regarding his criticism of a prominent Anglican and Peel; Mozley acknowledged this to Newman in a letter on 24 July: 'My dear Newman, I do not think that for the next two numbers of the B. C. there is any reason to fear excessive sharpness or satire. It is true I said the same beforehand of the last No but at that time I did not contemplate either of my subjects. They were both accidental and as it happened I had always felt strongly about Peel, and also about F. [Faussett] whenever he crossed my thoughts. Concerning Peel, I said exactly the same to Christie.' Newman's response four days later did not acknowledge his identity as Catholicus even though Mozley clearly indicated his authorship of the article.

The Reception of the Catholicus Letters

But I have always made it a rule to avoid secrets. I cannot keep them, except by immediately forgetting them; and the communicators of secrets never intend them to be kept, thus putting the persons confided with them into false position. The article labours under the incurable disadvantage of being a comment upon a comment, the weak echo of a vigorous original. However, I introduced 'Catholicus' to speak for himself.[77]

Mozley's reminiscence was peculiar. He did not know the identity of Catholicus in 1841, even though his later account mischievously and incorrectly hinted that he might have. However, he provided insight into his aim for the article—a commentary on Peel via the Catholicus letters. Although Catholicus needed no further introduction, Mozley's article expanded on some ideas that could only be briefly touched upon in *The Times*.

Because he was close to Newman and to the Oxford Movement, Mozley's commentary was important. He clearly saw the Tractarian elements in the letters[78] and ably expanded on some of them. Mozley gathered that Catholicus was not simply engaging in political satire, but exposing the principles of the Knowledge School which undergirded Peel's address. He recognized one of Newman's core objectives—to provide philosophical and theological arguments against Peel's prescriptions which could be understood by the populace:

> We cannot suppose that so flimsy and unoriginal a thing as the Tamworth Address is really likely to draw any right-minded person into burning incense to the Baal of our day, the God of nature and natural science, to the manifest contempt of revealed truth. Surely, though the writer be 'the leader of the Conservative party in the House,' and has great weight in questions of malt, registration, and sugar,—surely by this time his name is a nullity in any question in the smallest degree connected with religion. We are therefore quite content that the

---

77 Thomas Mozley, *Reminiscences Chiefly of Oriel and the Oxford Movement* (London: Longman, Green, 1882), 243–4. Newman did not think highly of Mozley's *Reminiscences*. Writing to his brother Frank on 13 June 1882, shortly after receiving a copy from Mozley, Newman complained: 'I could show, by letters which I have kept, as well as from personal memory that what he says or implies is untrue' (*LD*, XXX, 99).

78 In his article, Mozley used the pamphlet, rather than the letters in *The Times*.

> Address should have been delivered for the sake of one of the most noble confutations, not of it (for it needed none), but of its pernicious principles, which has appeared of late years ...
>
> Whoever this [Catholicus] may be, he has done his work well, and written a series of letters worthy of any subject or any occasion; deep, yet brilliant; philosophical, yet popular; fit to be read at the breakfast-table, perused again in the study, and honourably installed on the shelf for future reference.[79]

Mozley's piece did not have much of a theological or philosophical accent. Nor did Mozley employ Newman's delicate satire and irony; rather, he directly skewered Peel:

> Sir Robert is small with nations, petty with a constitution of ages, and (we say it sadly and seriously) unfaithful to the everlasting Catholic Church. He wishes to know nothing beyond the House of Commons.[80]

Long and meandering, the article flashed at times with brilliance. Mozley often thematically combined and categorized passages from Catholicus's letters rather than offering a chronological commentary. He also showed his own experience and interest in social and political topics. He developed many of the political consequences either asserted or implied in the Catholicus letters:[81]

> The Conservative leader, however, as Catholicus most strikingly points out, is merely following the lead. His party has been stigmatized as bigoted, as hostile to social improvement, as preferring orthodoxy and legitimacy to general knowledge. He is therefore anxious to rescue 'himself and his party' from an imputation so grievously in his way, and suddenly obtrudes himself on the public as the patron and founder of a Mechanics' Institute. He would probably have been the last person in the kingdom to originate the project; but finding it existing as a popular idea, however unpractical, he takes it up.[82]

Mozley recognized that Peel's and Brougham's prescriptions for science as an elixir did not really address the problems of the working poor.

---

79 Mozley, 'The Tamworth Reading Room', 47.
80 Ibid., 59.
81 Burgis (*TRR*, 112) arrived at similar conclusions; she also provided an account of Mozley's article (110–17).
82 Mozley, 'The Tamworth Reading Room', 60–1.

The Reception of the Catholicus Letters

Mozley offered an opposing view of the working classes to Peel, who believed that persons such as mechanics needed recreation and knowledge. However, Mozley accurately portrayed their perilous existence, in which survival and ruin pressed upon their minds. Echoing Catholicus, he noted that if they were to reflect upon their condition, they would not terminate in scientific knowledge, but in the mystery of God:

> The artisan is exhausted with toil, chained to his post by the pressure of poverty, dispirited by the all but impossibility of rising, with pauperism ever gaping beneath his feet; the strength of his days is broken by labour, his moments of leisure spoilt by anxiety; he sees above him a class whose prosperity he little shares, whose reverses he must often feel; his position is the focus of grievances, which may perhaps bear equally upon all, yet press palpably on him, for he is at the very paying point of taxation, and his scanty income is the very gauge of fiscal pressure and mercantile vicissitude. Meanwhile he is one of the multitude, and it is in the mid sea of human affairs that he is tossed to and fro. He is surrounded by distresses which he cannot remedy, systems which he cannot comprehend, anomalies which he cannot explain, projects and projectors whose prudence and justice he cannot weigh; yet still everything about him is human: abstraction, seclusion, speculation, are the luxuries of pampered ease and cultivated mind, not of incessant manual toil. The mechanic sees man and human motives in every circumstance of his condition; and when he rises above what he sees, it is not so much to general laws as to their Almighty Author.[83]

Mozley pointed out that the artificial restrictions of religion or politics at Tamworth bucked the general trend of most institutes. Peel's decision to exclude 'controversial divinity' had more to do with his own predilections rather than what had developed in the adult-education movement:

> In the majority of [mechanics'] institutes, we believe, there is no longer any attempt to exclude either politics or 'controversial' divinity, if there ever was. They receive any books that are given to them; and in some cases we know have so received and now retain what we should call professedly infidel works, though not of the most flagitious sort. These ... are not aimed at by the ban against controversy; for in point of fact now ... a man who professes himself to hold any

---

83 Ibid., 57.

positive opinion in theology which he might lawfully not have held, is thought a much greater enemy to society, than he who professes himself to hold positively nothing.[84]

Finally, Mozley understood the import of Catholicus's emphasis on 'Christian Knowledge', which contradicted the relativistic narrative spun by the Knowledge School and Britain's most powerful political figure:

> Little as we think Sir Robert is accustomed to look beyond the present emergency, yet he cannot be so blind as to facts, as to think the institutions he is abstractedly contemplating and recommending, to be really possible. There is no such thing, and there cannot be such a thing, as a society utterly excluding political opinions or religious creeds. Such a pretence of neutrality and indifference to differences is seldom made but with a smile at its own utter insincerity. The thousand and one religious societies in London, not to speak of their provincial offspring, which pretend to comprehend all Christians, without distinction, &c, no longer attempt to keep their countenance at the farce they are exhibiting. A few years ago perhaps they laughed at it in the committee room, but were serious on the platform. They now think they can afford to be honest, and avow that they include all opinions but one, and that is Catholic truth as such ... A universal peace, not based on justice, is merely the prelude of universal war.[85]

Mozley then questioned whether the presumed neutrality of Peel's Tamworth institute was really possible, in a sense challenging the modern ideal of tolerance:

> If it were possible for a Mechanics' Institution open to all creeds to be really neutral,—as really neutral as a grocer's shop, i. e. neutral, without expressly laying down the principle of neutrality, which, in the matter of religion, is no neutrality at all,—that would be a very

---

84 *Ibid.*, 93. Mozley's belief has been confirmed by Kelly's *History* (125; 128) of the Mechanics' institutes movement. Harris (205), in his zeal to show Newman's (and Mozley's) supposed hostility to science, claimed the opposite: 'The program of education in basic scientific knowledge advocated by Brougham and others early in the century was evidently still persuasive when the Tamworth library was founded in 1841.' In light of Mozley's contemporary view and to Kelly's scholarly work, which showed mechanics' institutes eschewing strictly scientific paradigms, this seems an incredible conclusion.

85 Mozley, 'The Tamworth Reading Room', 54.

different thing from the Tamworth Reading Room, as Sir Robert has made it ... The Tamworth Reading Room excludes all who think it wrong to covenant not to confess Christ before men;—in other words, all good and honest Christians. Many good sort of people doubtless are content to be silent for a time, in hope to purchase thereby future influence; Jesuitry? It doubtless is right not to obtrude the most awful doctrines on all kinds of people, but it does not follow that it is allowable to enter into covenant with those people not to do so.[86]

The most significant outcome of Mozley's article was its ability to reignite reactions from the press and from people like Peel and Greville. Although *The British Critic*'s readers benefited from Mozley's nuanced discussions of the mechanics' movement, newspapers did not return to those winter and spring debates about Catholicus's letters. Rather, many leading articles opportunistically made use of Mozley's acerbic lines to attack Peel. Burgis observed that the politics of the moment concerned Peel's ascendency:

For many readers of the *British Critic* the article may have done the useful service of emphasizing that reading rooms were not hotbeds of sedition and irreligion and that the real importance of the 'Tamworth Reading Room' lay in Newman's exposing the false ideas about education which had found expression in Peel's Address in such a diluted and muddled form. For the Whig-Liberal press, on the other hand, its appearance at just that time provided welcome material for leading articles which did not fail to quote from the personal criticism of Peel, while omitting any reference to the discussion of institutes and reading rooms.[87]

Peel's letters indicate that he had read Mozley's article. On 26 July, Peel received a letter from Lord Ashley, admonishing him that the people had elected him to be 'an instrument in the hands of Almighty God for the advancement and glory of His Church the welfare of His people, and all of Mankind'. Ashley implored Peel to avoid 'false and liberal shoals' and rather keep his eye fixed on the Lord.[88] Peel did not respond directly to Ashley's admonishments, but rather offered a rather pointed

---

86 *Ibid.*, 54–5.
87 Burgis, *TRR*, 117.
88 Ashley to Peel 26 July 1841, *Sir Robert Peel: From his Private Papers*, 474.

comment about Mozley's article and added a general statement on the status of the Church:

> If you will read a late article in the 'British Critic' you will find that I do not stand very high in the estimation of the Puseyites.
>
> I have no doubt you state correctly both the extent and the bitterness of the feud which is raging in the Church. It is fit and right that men should adhere steadfastly to sincere religious opinions, and should enforce and maintain them with all the ability and strength of argument they can command. But it frequently happens that these zealous controversialists on religious matters leave on the minds of their readers one conviction stronger than any other, namely, that Christian charity is consumed in their burning zeal for their own opinions.[89]

On 1 September, two days after Peel took office as Prime Minister, Charles Greville summarized what many sympathizers thought of Peel's January address. As he did in March, Greville also provided insight in the controversy that surrounded Peel's speech. He hoped that Peel had repudiated many of the ideas of his Tamworth speech:

> It is impossible for Peel to have begun more auspiciously than he has done. I expected that he would act with vigour and decision, and he has not disappointed my expectations ... Those liberal views, which terrified or exasperated High Tories, High Churchmen, and bigots of various persuasions; those expressed or supposed opinions and intentions which elicited the invectives of the 'British Critic,' or the impertinences of 'Catholicus' were to me a satisfactory earnest that, whenever he might arrive at the height of power, he was resolved to stretch his wings out and fly in the right direction.[90]

By the fall of 1841 only a few references to the Catholicus letters or *The Tamworth Reading Room* were made.[91] In a letter on 14 September to John Keble, Newman acknowledged one possible fallout from the nine months of press and parliamentary debates—the Tractarians would have no place in Peel's new government:

---

89 Peel to Lord Ashley, 1 August 1841, *ibid.*, 475.

90 *The Greville Memoirs: A Journal of the Reign of Queen Victoria: 1837–1852*, I (New York: Appleton & Co., 1885), 371.

91 Burgis (*TRR*, 119–21) examined a pamphlet by an anonymous 'Verus' that attacked Mozley and Catholicus and defended Peel.

Again, (entre nous) from what we hear, though of course we must expect heterogeneous proceedings, it is not at all certain that Sir R. P.[Peel] will not be taking men called Puseyites, as thinking them more suited for certain places.[92]

As the year came to a close, the controversy faded—save for a cryptic reference that appeared in the *Morning Chronicle* on 2 December. Mixed in the middle of several advertisements for theater events appeared this sentence: '"Catholicus" *should give us his name*'.[93] It is not clear whether the reference was to Newman and the controversy that had lingered throughout the year, since Catholicus was a pseudonym used by others.[94] Even if the *Morning Chronicle* was not looking for Catholicus of *The Times*, that name consumed much of 1841 and became a symbol for Peel and Newman. Peel desired a more 'catholic', that is universal, access to science and learning for his town and really for the nation. Newman was in search of and argued in the pages of the British Areopagus for a robust 'catholic' Church. Both achieved their desires, albeit in unexpected ways.

---

92 Newman to Keble, 14 September 1841, *LD*, VIII, 274.
93 *Morning Chronicle*, 2 December 1841.
94 For example, a letter to *The Times* published on 14 September in *The Times* was signed by 'Anglo-Catholicus'.

☩ 7 ☩

The Legacy of Newman's Letters and Tamworth Pamphlet

THE CATHOLICUS CONTROVERSY was essentially finished by late summer 1841. In subsequent years, Peel did not modify the ideas which he articulated in his address and later defended on the floor of Parliament; indeed, the Whig-radical movements in education which he had once repudiated were now embraced and expanded throughout Britain. Similarly, the theological principles and arguments that Newman put forth in his Catholicus letters resurfaced again in his final Anglican works, his later correspondence, and in his Roman Catholic works.

The 1842 Tamworth Report

The first to reflect on the 1841 controversy was Peel. On 20 January 1842, a year and a day after Peel's Tamworth address, the new Prime Minister received a letter from R. C. Savage, the vicar of Tamworth. Savage, a member of the Book Committee, had sent the institute's annual report for Peel's approval and also commented on the harsh criticism leveled against the institution. Although there had been negative press, the reading room was thriving.[1] Peel responded that the success of the reading room was

> the best answer that can be given to the gross misrepresentations which have been published in respect of the Constitution and objects of our Society—The best answer also, to the calumnies with which I have been assailed for having attempted to substitute for idleness

---

1 Savage to Peel (20 January 1842), Peel Papers, 40608:74–5, British Library, London. Burgis, *TRR*, 122–3.

and dissipation (under conditions and regulations that appeared to me calculated to preclude the Risk of their abuse or perversion to any evil purpose), the means of rational recreation—and intellectual and moral improvement.

You can bear witness that in the district in which this Institution has been established the higher Interests connected with the religious education of the Young—and with the means of attendance on the services of the Church have not been disregarded.[2]

The report was in large part a justification for excluding religious books from the institute's inventory—a reaction to the critiques of Catholicus and Mozley:

> it would be unwise in the formation of an institution like this, designed for the benefit of a population constituted as our own is, to declare by the name we give it, or the principles on which we found it that ... there was any chance of making our young men indifferent about the attainment of religious knowledge still less that it could produce opposition to religious truth—or that such advantages for intellectual improvement, could have any other than a beneficial influence on their moral and religious conduct.[3]

Peel was still clearly nettled by the letters and generally disdainful of the Tractarian movement.[4] He felt chagrin that Catholicus had disagreed with what he believed to be the most rational and humane solution to religious and political conflict.

---

2 Peel Papers, 40608:78, British Library, London.
3 Burgis, *TRR*, 123–4.
4 Tracey (*LD*, VIII, 437) noted that Peel made a controversial ecclesial recommendation which was related to the Catholicus letters: 'A. T. Gilbert had been nominated to the vacant see of Chichester by the Duke of Wellington on 22 Jan. (*DNB* says 24 Jan.), and was consecrated Bishop on 27 Feb. The idea had come from Peel, who was said to be distressed at the alarming spread of Tractarian doctrines, and had admired Gilbert's tenacious opposition to I[ssac] Williams in the contest for the Poetry Professorship. Woodgate wrote on 30 May: "Peel is known, (or presumed) to be hostile to the Puseyites, on account of the article on Catholicus letters in the B. C."'

The Trajectory of Catholicus

Newman did not directly acknowledge the Catholicus letters after March 1841. The *Tract 90* controversy had enveloped him. As Coats surmised: 'Newman quickly left the Tamworth Articles and the public debate they stirred. With the publication of *Tract 90* [sic], he had new public and private battles of faith to wage ... Years later, he must have felt the letters to be of little importance as he did not mention them at all in the *Apologia*. Instead he indeed remarked that 'since the summer of 1839 I have written little or nothing on modern controversy.'[5] Coats's conclusion, while true in part—especially regarding Newman's desire to avoid controversy—unfortunately exhibits several errors. In the years following 1841, Newman at times forgot about the letters and was possibly embarrassed by them. This could be because they were associated with the painful *Tract 90* controversy which precipitated his alienation from the English Church and the Tractarian *via media*.

However, Newman commented on the Catholicus letters in his correspondence and diary entries in the 1840s and 1850s. He also included several lines from the letters in his *Discourses on the Nature and Scope of University Education* in 1852. Newman listed the letters of Catholicus in an appendix of his *Apologia* (1864). He employed the letters in his *Grammar of Assent* and included them in a collection of his works with the title *Discussions and Arguments*. The Catholicus letters, in one form or another, followed Newman throughout his life.

---

5 Coats, 'Rhetorical Approaches', 179; cited in *Apologia*, 172. The context of the reference in the *Apologia* was the poignant correspondence of 25 October with Henry Manning (*LD*, IX, 584–6). In the letter, Newman began to retrace his movement away from the Anglican Church beginning in 1839; he mentioned a certain reticence toward public controversy; he clearly was not looking to wage an open battle with Peel. The letters did not originate from his own initiative but from the Walters' insistence and the pseudonym 'Catholicus' effectually kept him clear of a direct public battle.

'An aristocracy of exalted spirits'

Correspondence with the Froudes 1844;
The Oratory at Birmingham 1847

In April 1844, Newman began a lengthy correspondence with William Froude, one of his former pupils and the brother of his departed friend Hurrell, and his wife Catherine.[6] At the time, Froude, a promising young engineer who eventually became a leading naval architect in Victorian England, was beginning to experience doubts about his faith. He was also perplexed by Newman's now palpable drift towards the Church of Rome. How could Newman, once so vigorous a defender of Church of England, really consider such a move? What would such a move mean for Froude's own understanding of truth and of certainty? Newman for a time evaded Froude's (and his wife's) questions about these matters, but eventually decided to respond.[7]

Newman planned to share with the Froudes his own changing ecclesial opinions that had raised questions about where truth is to be found and what to do about doubt.[8] In a pastoral way, he also wanted to address the problems of 'scepticism and unsettlement about truth and falsehood generally'.[9] Although Newman briefly discussed the problem of doubt *vis-à-vis* truth and falsehood—especially how change may actually *reveal* the objectivity of truth—his letters to the Froudes also

---

6 On 8 July 1859, Newman recorded in his diary: 'Mrs. Froude has lent me the Letters which I sent her in 1844. I am going to transcribe them, before returning them to her. I have not seen them, from the day I wrote them, till now that I transcribe them. J H N' (*LD*, X, 183).

7 JHN to William and Catherine Froude, 2 April 1844, *LD*, X, 183.

8 JHN to William and Catherine Froude, 3 April 1844, *LD*, X, 185. Newman addressed all but the first letter to Catherine, for William was 'working as an engineer on the Exeter-Barnstaple railway ... and was frequently away from home. Hence Newman's reason for addressing the rest of the correspondence to Mrs. Froude, on the understanding that the correspondence was a three-sided one.' Eventually, Mrs. Froude and her children entered the Roman Catholic Church under Newman's guidance; William Froude remained skeptical towards religion and became increasingly agnostic later in life; however, these and later exchanges with Newman, especially after he became a Roman Catholic, became part of the impetus for *An Essay in Aid of a Grammar of Assent*.

9 Ibid.

provided Newman an opportunity reflect on his own life.[10]

Newman began by recounting how he had earlier thrown himself into the Anglican tradition through the Oxford Movement, but by the mid-1830s had wanted to surrender his 'heart to the authority of the Church of Rome'. However, he had been repulsed by certain Roman Catholic doctrines and practices, such as the supposed worship of Mary and so could not conceive of converting.[11] Because of his revulsion at certain aspects of the Roman practice, he set about to further the *via media* as the Anglican ecclesial position. He also admitted that his belief in the *via media* began to unravel in 1839, first with his reading about the Monophysite controversies surrounding the Council of Chalcedon and then by carefully reading Nicholas Wiseman's article in the *Dublin Review*, 'The Anglican Claim of Apostolical Succession'.[12]

Newman emphasized that while he had started to entertain serious doubts, 'I set about ... to keep myself in my own place' (the Church of England). Yet, because of the shock that he had received, he began to make some practical changes in his life; in particular, he had ceased writing about controversial topics or 'subjects of the Day':

> Except [Tract] Number 90, I have not (as far as I remember) written anything on subjects of the Day since 1838, six years—I have always excepted Sermons. (I suppose you will say certain Letters in the Times in the beginning of 1841 are exceptions. I was *pressed* to write them).[13]

There are several striking features about this parenthetical mention of the Catholicus letters: first, Newman apparently considered his Catholicus letters an exception to his desire to avoid conflict.[14] Second, he had indicated that by 1844, his identity as Catholicus had become

---

10 Twenty years later, these letters figured prominently in Newman's *Apologia pro Vita Sua* (1864); Newman, some months earlier (25 October 1843; *LD*, IX, 584–5) rehearsed several themes found in his letters to then Archdeacon Henry Manning. What was important in the Manning and Froude exchanges and eventually in his *Apologia* was Newman's insistence on avoiding controversy after 1838–9. At that time, Newman's ideal theological position (*via media*) fell apart and so he proceeded to act cautiously, rather than controversially, in his capacity as an Anglican minister.

11 *LD*, X, 187.

12 *The Dublin Review* 7 (August 1839): 139–80.

13 JHN to William and Catherine Froude, 9 April 1844, *LD*, X, 202.

14 *LD*, VIII, 10–11; 23.

common knowledge, at least among his friends, for he did not have to further elaborate what he meant. Finally, Newman implied that he had felt compelled to produce the letters. Unlike other 'subjects of the day', the impetus for the letters which became the 'Tamworth Reading Room' did not derive directly from his ministerial duty (sermons) or his involvement in the Oxford Movement (*Tract 90*).[15]

This brief and guarded avowal was the only explicit reference to his letters that Newman provided for the rest of the 1840s. However, after his entrance into the Roman Catholic Church in 1845 and his ordination in Rome, Newman indirectly referred to a key element of the controversy—mechanics' institutes—during several correspondences in early 1847. In a letter to John Dalgairns in January he explained his desire to establish an oratory in Birmingham. He conceived of the oratory's outreach to the community to be similar to a mechanics' institute, although one that allowed for open and honest discussion of Christian topics.[16] Newman had never disparaged the mechanics' movement, even Peel's Tamworth library, but consistent with his letters maintained the priority of faith to scientific and literary knowledge. Here he had the potential to put the vision which he asserted in the Catholicus letters into action.

The following February, Newman addressed the notion of mechanics' institutes in Birmingham. He composed a letter to Cardinal Franzoni, explaining the spiritual situation of England and his plans for an Oratorian ministry. He noted that Birmingham's Catholic population had come under the sway of the mechanics' movement, and specifically cited Brougham's desire to replace religious knowledge with science. The themes and problems raised in the Catholicus letters, still haunted him even though he did not directly acknowledge the controversy of 1841.[17]

---

15 In his *Autobiographical Writings*, ed. Henry Tristram (New York: Sheed and Ward, 1957), 272, Newman noted: 'What I have written has been for the most part what may be called official, works done in some office I held or engagement I had made ... or has been from some especial call, or invitation, or necessity or emergency'.
16 *LD*, XII, 17.
17 *LD*, XII, 38.

The Legacy of Newman's Letters and Tamworth Pamphlet

Peel at Tamworth in 1849

Peel, however, had not forgotten. He had 'presumed' the Tractarians, whom he opposed, were behind the letters against him then,[18] and was glad that the movement had died down with Newman's overtures and then departure to Rome in 1845.[19] Although Peel still did not know that Newman was behind the letters, his residual bitterness was publicly manifest in 1849. Almost eight years to the day that his Tamworth address was published in *The Times*, Peel gave another speech at the library and reading room. He had experienced a brutal political defeat in 1846 and his career was on the wane; however, he had neither forgiven nor forgotten the controversy; as *The Times* reported on 27 January 1849, in an article with the heading, SIR ROBERT PEEL AND MIDDLE-CLASS EDUCATION:

> This morning a meeting of the subscribers to the public library in this town, instated several years ago under the auspices of Sir Robert Peel, was held at the rooms of the institution, Lichfield-street. The right hon. Baronet took the chair, and was supported by the clergy, magistrates, and leading inhabitants of the town. The report for the past year described the operation of the society as most successful. Several resolutions of a formal character having been adopted, thanks were voted by acclamation to the President for his kindness in attending the meeting, and his able conduct in the chair. In acknowledging the compliment, Sir R. PEEL said,—I am very much gratified by the kind feeling which has induced you so cordially to acquiesce in the resolution ... Although there has been no call for any great ability on my part in presiding on the present occasion, I watch the progress of this institution with very great interest. I dare say some of you recollect the objections made to its first establishment. It was said it would utterly fail,—that, on account of its disconnexion with religion, there was reason to apprehend infidelity would take root in Tamworth. I felt confident that the reverse would be the case; I knew that animosities, political and personal, would here be assuaged, that the class now most exposed to temptation would here find new sources of amuse-

---

18 *LD*, VIII, 437.
19 Peel to Reverend T. Henderson, 18 November 1845, Peel Papers, 40578:345, British Library, London.

> ment,—that we should improve their morality, and strengthen the foundation of religion, by the means we took to insure the progress of knowledge. To those who objected to the course I took in promoting this institution I deem this statement in the report a sufficient answer,—'The number of the volumes issued is 5009 and discussed circulation numbers.' That, I think, is a conclusive proof that the interests of morality have not been injured by the establishment of the Tamworth Library and Reading-room (Cheers.) Now, the great object we should have in view is to increase the number of those who derive benefit from it.[20]

This was the last public mention of the controversy from Peel. There was no further commentary on this speech in *The Times*. Unlike in 1841, when the British press buzzed about his views of education in connection to his rise to power, his political fortunes had faded. In July 1850, a little over a year and a half after this address, Peel died tragically from an equestrian accident.

Correspondence between Newman and Frederick Faber

That same year, *The Tamworth Reading Room* resurfaced in Newman's life through a series of letters exchanged between 21–3 August, with his fellow Oratorian, Frederick Faber. Faber had decided to compile various pamphlets which Newman had written as an Anglican and present them to Archbishop Nicholas Wiseman in Rome.[21] Newman had several pamphlets, such as *Tract 90*, to give. He also recalled the Catholicus letters:

> As to the Pamphlets, I can't tell till I rummage about at St. W's [Wilfred's],[22] what I can give you. But I should like you to try to get them in London—If the price asked is above the original price (and I don't suggest it would be for Suffragans and Catholicus[23] *if* they can

---

20 'Sir Robert Peel and Middle-Class Education', *The Times*, Saturday, 27 January 1849.
21 LD, XIV, 47.
22 A religious community established by Faber in rural North Staffordshire.
23 In his correspondence, as well as in labeling his manuscripts, Newman referred to the 'letters of *Catholicus*'. The title 'The Tamworth Reading Room' may have been suggested by *The Times* when the pamphlet was published in March 1841.

be got *at all*) I won't offer them you, supposing I have them—but if the price is raised, then I will.[24]

Newman's letter suggested that he still considered certain works valuable—his Catholicus letters apparently were not among them.

Correspondence between Newman and John Moore Capes

One week later, on 28 August, Newman revisited his letters to *The Times*. John Moore Capes, editor of the lay Catholic journal, *The Rambler*, had been working on a three-part series, 'The Rise, Progress and Results of Puseyism'.[25] He had made several inquiries to Newman regarding the Oxford Movement. Newman provided Capes with a list of important dates, events, and explanations regarding this period of his life. In the course of his recollections, he answered what appeared to be a series of questions about the Catholicus letters:

> Old Walter called on me at Oriel, and pressed me several times to write against Peel's address, before I consented. It was just when the *Times* took us up, and just as the publication of Number 90 (the *same month*) took us down. It was a false step in the *Times*—had it waited a month, it would not have made it.[26]

Capes's piece was heavily shaped by Newman's terse remarks. Unfortunately Newman's recollections were not quite accurate and Capes did not corroborate the information from other sources (although this would have been difficult, since Capes was the first to write about the history of the Catholicus letters in the context of Puseyism). For example, Newman use of 'old Walter' seemed a false memory. He could have referred to Walter III as an 'old' acquaintance or in a colloquial way: 'In familiar or affectionate forms of address, usually with no connotation of age, as in 'old boy or old chap'.[27] However, this rendering of 'old' is not likely for two reasons. First, in his diaries Newman consistently

---

24 LD, XIV, 49.
25 The requests from Capes were in regard to the second part, published in 1851; see Appendix II for an extended excerpt of Capes's article.
26 LD, XIV, 52. N
27 'Old', *Oxford English Dictionary*.

referred to Walter III as 'Walter' or 'younger Walter'.[28] Second, Newman used the phrase 'old Walter' twice in his correspondence, referring directly to Walter II.[29]

Furthermore, in this passage, Newman used the word 'pressed' as he had in his 1844 letters to the Froudes. Although the correspondence between Newman and Walter III in 1841 did not show any duress in his decision to write the letters, it may have been that he conflated his meeting with Walter II later in February. Nevertheless, Walter III was very persistent and an exchange between Frederick Rogers and his sister in July 1840 seemed to corroborate how Newman felt 'pressed' by Walter III.[30] Finally Newman retrospectively viewed the letters as a 'false step' which he would have avoided had he foreseen the furor that was later triggered by *Tract 90*.[31]

Capes, however, was impressed by the letters. He believed that 1841 was a pivotal year for the Oxford Movement. He seemed to reaffirm Newman's earlier view that the Catholicus letters were as 'fists shaken in the face' of politicians, academics, clergy, and the people. In January 1851, Capes provided the first account of the letters and the first public acknowledgment that Newman was Catholicus. Burgis has provided background information and a critique of Capes's account:

---

28 For example, *LD*, VII, 28; 188; 239; 457.

29 *LD*, XIV, 52: Prior to mentioning 'Old Walter' in connection with the Catholicus letters, he noted the 'Surplice Row': 'It was the occasion old Walter took of ratting round in the Times'. An editorial note added that although Walter II been sympathetic to the Tractarians in 1841, 'He seized the opportunity of the Surplice Riots at Exeter in 1844 to revert to his attitude of opposition'.

30 Rogers (*LD*, VII, 448) indeed used similar language to Newman in accenting that it was the 'younger' Walter who was apt to 'press' fellow Tractarians into writing for *The Times*. Rogers outlined the basic agreement between Newman and Walter III for the Catholicus letters: 'I have had young Walter with me again pressing me to write for his father even if I cannot edit ... I almost think I shall try my hand. No one will know anything about the matter except my own private friends and I can do just as much and as little as I please.'

31 In his remarks, Newman mentioned nothing of his critique of Peel as a public figure. This was an issue at the time, raised by the Walters and by his friend Henry Wilberforce. Twenty years later in his *An Essay in Aid of a Grammar of Assent*, 91, Newman recalled Peel as holding a 'dangerous doctrine. He seemed, in hindsight, to have altered his view about his letters to *The Times* being a 'false step'.

their occasion was the publication of Newman's *Anglican Difficulties*. Capes's thesis [was] that the movement was bound to carry men to Rome if its truths were taken to their logical conclusions and he singles out Tract 90 as the occasion of the movement showing itself before the world 'in its true colours'. Walter's commissioning of the [Catholicus] Letters was 'a singular step taken in its regard by a no less acute observer than the proprietor of *The Times* newspaper' which proved 'how strange and unexpected had been its [i.e. the Movement's] progress up to 1841'. Capes, who had some of his information from Newman, makes no mention of young John Walter's part in the affair and only alludes to his continuing espousal of the Tractarian cause in an amusing account of his father's part in the 'surplice' controversy, the occasion John Walter senior took, in Newman's words, 'of ratting round in the Times'. The omission of any reference to John Walter III or to the articles of Roundell Palmer which had been appearing since October 1840, makes the commissioning of the Letters sound a far more 'singular step' even than it was.[32]

The Idea of a University

Media reaction to Capes's identification of Newman as Catholicus was minimal or non-existent.[33] The controversy of 1841, and all the political issues surrounding it, had passed: Peel was dead, education had increasingly become secularized, and Newman was now a prominent Catholic. However, he had not forgotten the theological themes and ideas raised in the letters. In the spring of 1852 Newman revisited the contents of his Catholicus letters for the first time since 1841 and labeled the manuscripts.[34] According to Dwight Culler:

> During the early months of 1852 the Oratorians were engaged in moving from their house in Alcester Street to the new building in Edgbaston ... It was on April 3 that he 'finished getting in all my

---

32 Burgis, *TRR*, 124.

33 Burgis (*TRR*, 126) has pointed out that in 1859, William Gresely's second volume of *Bernard Leslie* contained a scathing review of the Catholicus letters and their treatment of Peel. Along with Capes article, Gresely's book was the second history of the Movement that included the letters.

34 Burgis (*TRR*, 64) noted that the manuscripts were rolled in a wrapper labeled 'Catholicus'.

books and papers into my room at Edgbaston'... He put his papers in their places and felt how much of his past life they contained ... He sorted them out not merely as one does who is moving but also (he wrote to Mrs. Bowden) 'as if I were dying.' He tied them up in packets and labeled them, he wrote comments on them for some future biographer or literary executor and all the time he did this he was simultaneously composing the first three discourses of the *Idea of a University*.[35]

During this move and reorganization, Newman consulted the letters, and many of the ideas they suggested were explored at length in his development of his 'University Discourses', the foundations of the *Idea of a University*. Ironically, his 'Discourses' responded to a major policy decision in Peel's second administration. In 1845, Peel's government founded the 'Queen's Colleges' in Ireland. These colleges were modeled on the Knowledge School platform at the University of London and Peel's suggestions in 1815 and 1841—secular knowledge would be primary in order to reduce religious strife.[36] In 1847 and in 1849, Rome issued rescripts against the Colleges. The foundation of a Catholic university in Ireland was also urged. Newman was invited by Archbishop Cullen in 1851 to offer lectures on Catholic university education, in opposition to the Queen's Colleges. These discourses were a prelude to his appointment as the first rector of the Catholic University of Ireland and eventually were included in his *The Idea of a University*.

Newman's aim was to present the university as 'the place of teaching universal knowledge'[37]—which would include Catholic theology and religious formation. His ideal university was a direct rebuke to Brougham's University of London and Peel's Queen's Colleges. Although Newman did not directly mention the Catholicus letters in his *Idea*, he recapitulated themes and passages from them. For example, he reprised his critique of Brougham's infidel principle.[38] He also devoted an entire discourse to the notion that knowledge was not confined to the secular

---

35 Culler, *The Imperial Intellect*, 141; *LD*, XV, 62.

36 Fergal McGrath, *Newman's University: Idea and Reality* (London: Longman, Green, 1951), 43–61.

37 Newman, *The Idea of a University*, ed. Martin J. Svaglic (Notre Dame, IN: University of Notre Dame Press, 1982), xxxvii.

38 *Ibid.*, 22–3.

sciences.[39] Newman modified and expanded on his view in the fourth letter that 'religious doctrine is [also] knowledge'.[40] Fergal McGrath has pointed out the intrinsic connection between *The Tamworth Reading Room* and *The Idea*: 'Again and again in his *Discourses on the Idea of a University* and in his correspondences concerning the Catholic University the main themes of his letters to the *Times*, [concerning] the proper relations between secular and religious knowledge [recur]'.[41] Implicitly, Newman had redressed Peel and the Knowledge School—this time as a Roman Catholic.

Catholicus in the *Catholic Standard*

In the spring of 1855, Newman wrote a series of letters for the *Catholic Standard* about England's involvement in the Crimean War. These letters were eventually republished in 1872 as 'Who's to Blame' in his *Discussions and Arguments*, the same volume that included his *Tamworth Reading Room*. The appearance of both series of letters in the same anthology seems appropriate in so far as both were concerned with 'subjects of the day': *The Tamworth Reading Room* concerned the Church's relation to knowledge and education, while 'Who's to Blame' directly engaged British politics. In addition, 'Who's to Blame' was the only other work in which Newman used the pseudonym 'Catholicus'.

Writing to Henry Wilberforce, his confidant during the controversy in 1841, now the editor of the *Standard* and a recent convert to the Roman Catholic Church, Newman explained the advantages of the pseudonym Catholicus:

> As to my Letters [(signed Catholicus, 'Who's to blame?')] I think altogether your wish is *not to be entertained*.
> 1. If they are known as mine, you separate them off from the Standard. What you should aim at is that people should say 'Really there was a very good letter in the Standard on such and such a subject.'

---

39 Thomas Vargish (*Newman: The Contemplation of Mind* [Oxford: Clarendon Press, 1970], 129) has compared these two works.
40 Newman, *Idea of a University*, 31.
41 Fergal McGrath, *The Consecration of Learning* (New York: Fordham University Press, 1962), 90–1.

'An aristocracy of exalted spirits'

2. Next ... People may not read the 1st 2nd or 3rd—but some one or other will read the 4th—he won't read 5th or 6th—but he will take up the 7th. Then it will come to him, 'well, really there is a good deal in these letters—whose can they be?' My Catholicus in the Times [February 1841] was ascribed to Phillpotts.⁴² The *mystery* will make people begin to read. But even supposing they are but half read by any one, by the end of them the idea is created and grown up. 'There are clever writers in the C. [Catholic] Standard.' People won't recollect what was cleverly done—but there will be a general feeling—'I recollect reading one or two very good letters', etc.⁴³

Here Newman provided a window into why he chose the pseudonym 'Catholicus' in 1841, as well as his approach to writing the letters. Newman chose the name so as to spark interest in his readers—he knew that the popular medium and its audience needed to be drawn into the letters. However, his choice of that particular word, Catholicus, also had something to do with his state of mind in 1841, groping toward a catholic idea of the Church. His insight into how he composed the letters was also important. He knew that he might only have one chance with his readers to persuade them. Thus each letter had to have a strong and clear message that could influence his readers—a technique honed from his copious sermons. However, as he knew there would be a series of letters, he used various means, such as vivid satire and lingering questions to bring readers back to see how he would develop his core idea of the Church that ran through the letters.

The *Apologia pro Vita Sua*

Newman's first public admission that he was the author of the Catholicus letters occurred in an appendix of the 1864 edition of his *Apologia*

---

42 Henry Phillpotts was the bishop of Exeter and a staunch High Church Tory. In March of 1841, *The Patriot* and *The Examiner* speculated that Phillpotts was the author of the Catholicus letters. Burgis (*TRR*, 86) noted: 'Those who identified "Catholicus" with Phillpotts must have done so only because he was a High Church "pamphleteering Bishop". Phillpotts, by the way, issued no denial, and newspapers of July 1841 show that five months later he was still being given the credit (or blame) for the letters, in some quarters at least.'

43 *LD*, XVI, 428–9.

pro Vita Sua, which he wrote to vindicate his 'religious opinions' in response to the charges of dishonesty made by the popular Victorian author, Charles Kingsley.[44] In his response to Kingsley, Newman stated: 'The request has been made to me from various quarters for a list of my writings. This I now give, omitting several pamphlets and articles in Reviews &c. of minor importance.'[45] Newman then included 'the Letters of Catholicus' under the heading 'Pamphlets', thereby suggesting the letters had attained significance; indeed, he may have reviewed them while writing his *Apologia*. Also, in his note on 'Liberalism' in the *Apologia*, Newman 'denounced and abjured' eighteen tenets of 'Liberalism'; the last one clearly echoed the language of Peel's address and ideas the Catholicus letters sought to redress:

> 18. Virtue is the child of knowledge, and vice of ignorance. Therefore, e.g. education, periodical literature, railroad travelling, ventilation, drainage, and the arts of life, when fully carried out, serve to make a population moral and happy.[46]

An Essay in Aid of a Grammar of Assent

Six years after his *Apologia*, Newman published *An Essay in Aid of a Grammar of Assent* (1870),[47] which was an innovative and sustained effort to navigate between the exigencies of faith/assent and experiential knowledge.[48] The roots of his *Grammar* included his correspondence

---

44 Newman, *Apologia*, 1–4. Newman used the occasion to recount his dramatic conversion as a young man, his involvement in the Oxford Movement, and his reasons for entering the Roman Catholic Church.

45 *Apologia* (1864), Appendix, 121. Newman also included the list in the Appendix of subsequent editions of the *Apologia*. In the first and second editions of 1864 and 1865, Newman used the label 'Letters of Catholicus'; in the third edition (1875), the title was changed to 'The Tamworth Reading Room' and the material was no longer in the section under pamphlets, but cited in the uniform edition of his works under *Discussions and Arguments*.

46 Newman, *Apologia*, 224.

47 Newman, GA, 25–7.

48 See Nicholas Lash, 'Introduction', GA, 12. To view the *Grammar* strictly as a strictly formal written composition would be to overlook the fact that it grew out of sermons, conversations, letters, etc. In a letter dated 12 June 1853, Newman

with his brother Charles; his reflections on the relationship between faith and reason in the *University Sermons*; his spirited exchange of letters with William Froude;[49] as well as his justification for converting to the Roman Catholic Church detailed in his *Apologia pro Vita Sua*.[50] Newman believed the *Grammar* was a definitive achievement; as he commented to Richard Hutton shortly after its completion:

> For twenty years I have begun and left off an inquiry again and again ... I began in my Oxford University Sermons; I tried it in 1850—and at several later dates, in 1859, in 1861 ... but, though my fundamental ideas were ever the same, I could not carry them out. Now at last I have done all that I can do according to my measure—I finished it yesterday.[51]

In this work Newman worked out the activities of the mind: notional and real apprehension/assent; simple and complex assent; certainty and certitude; formal, informal, and natural inference. He also advanced an epistemological innovation—*the illative sense*—which described how the mind really interacts with and judges events, persons, and the divine in the world.[52] He conceived his *Grammar* as a personal and apologetic argument about the multifoliate activity that is human knowing: knowing could not be reduced merely to verified sensible realities; nor could knowing consist solely of relative, indeterminate perspectives; finally, knowing did not resolve into a fideistic view of the world. Rather, knowing included the personal dimensions of both reason (empirical/perspectival) and belief/faith. Belief equated to assent: an unconditional reception of truth. Indeed this marked a refreshing difference from most modern theories of knowledge that began in doubt, or only allowed for tentative assents. For Newman belief/assent could

---

acknowledged: 'How could I syllogize either in the pulpit of St. Mary's ... Nearly every thing I have published of an argumentative nature, has been spoken' (*LD*, XV, 381).

49 *LD*, XXI, 541.

50 Robert A. Colby, 'The Structure of Newman's *Apologia pro Vita Sua* in Relation to his Theory of Assent', *The Dublin Review* (Summer 1953): 140–56.

51 *LD*, XXV, 29.

52 For a brief discussion of each of these categories, see William R. Fey, *Faith and Doubt: the Unfolding of Newman's Thought on Certainty* (Shepherdstown, WV: Patmos Press, 1976), 145–55.

be to ideas, concrete realities, or divine truth/experiences, and this act, rather than questions or inferences, was the core of all real knowledge. Belief in God, or faith, was crucial to Newman's argument—for faith was both divine gift and human act. Faith involved an assent to divine truth without necessarily having a full complement of formal evidence.

While working on the *Grammar*, Newman explicitly revisited the letters of Catholicus, as he knew that letter six in particular had anticipated important themes in the book. For example, in the sixth letter he declared 'The heart is commonly reached, not through the reason, but through the imagination, by means of direct impressions, by the testimony of facts and events, by history, by description' (555). He expressed the same idea in more direct language in the Grammar, 'Experiences and their images strike and occupy the mind, as abstractions and their combinations do not'.[53] Within his discussion of 'Real and Notional Assents', for the first and only time, Newman commented on the letters as a whole. He first acknowledged the letters, obliquely, in his analysis of inference and assent, noting that he

> insisted on this marked distinction between Beliefs on the one hand, and Notional Assents and Inferences on the other, many years ago in words which it will be to my purpose to use now. I quote them, because, over and above their appositeness in this place, they present the doctrine on which I have been insisting, from a second point of view, and with a freshness and force which I cannot now command, and, moreover, (though they are my own, nevertheless, from the length of time which has elapsed since their publication), almost with the cogency of an independent testimony.[54]

Newman had new eyes upon his Catholicus letters. He had reviewed them in 1851, 1864, and now for the *Grammar*. In them he saw himself as a different man, and yet still maintained a consistent position. The confident Newman of 1870 truly differed from his searching self of 1841. He then commented on his impetus for writing the Catholicus letters, something he had only touched on before:

> They [the letters] occur in a protest which I had occasion to write in February, 1841, against a dangerous doctrine maintained, as I

---

53 *GA*, 50.
54 *GA*, 91.

> considered, by two very eminent men of that day, now no more—Lord Brougham and Sir Robert Peel. That doctrine was to the effect that the claims of religion could be secured and sustained in the mass of men, and in particular in the lower classes of society, by acquaintance with literature and physical science, and through the instrumentality of Mechanics' Institutes and Reading Rooms, to the serious disparagement, as it seemed to me, of direct Christian instruction. In the course of my remarks is found the passage which I shall here quote, and which, with whatever differences in terminology, and hardihood of assertion, befitting the circumstances of its publication, nay, as far as words go, inaccuracy of theological statement, suitably illustrates the subject here under discussion.[55]

His comment offered considerable insight not only into his central concern for the letters, but into the compositions themselves. As was clear from his letters, Newman believed that the Church, who offered 'direct Christian instruction' was a necessary compliment to literature and science found in mechanics' institutes, and that the latter could not usurp the former. He also implied that the letters were principally theological, although because of their medium (and therefore space allotted and audience) were incomplete in argument, rhetorically oriented, and definite in their claims rather than tentatively concluded. Following this comment, he included almost the entirety of his sixth Catholicus letter without any substantial change.

Discussions and Arguments

Newman's final statement about the Catholicus letters appeared two years later in his *Discussions and Arguments* (1872), a compilation which was intended as 'a fresh contribution...towards a uniform Edition of his publications'. *The Tamworth Reading Room* was included with this preface:

> [It] was written for the *Times* newspaper, and appeared in its columns in February 1841, being afterwards published as a pamphlet. The letters, of which it consists, were written off as they were successively called for by the parties who paid the author the compliment of employing him, and are necessarily immethodical as compositions.[56]

55 GA, 91–2.
56 DA, iii.

The Legacy of Newman's Letters and Tamworth Pamphlet

Although Newman stated that the letters were composed one at a time in response to *The Times*, his correspondence of 1841 indicated that the exchange did not happen so smoothly. In fact, Newman composed several of the letters in rapid sequence and he had envisioned an ideal number of them apart from what *The Times* proposed.

The most interesting comment in this preface was Newman's claim that his letters were 'immethodical'. His manuscripts, subsequent correspondences, and his reflection in the *Grammar* indicated that Newman did have a guiding idea which unified each letter and the series as a whole. However, unlike the rigorous reasoning in *Tract 90*, or the explicit connections between the final six *Oxford Sermons*, the Catholicus letters were not programmatic and explicitly connected as they would have been for a scholarly audience. Peel's address, the column length allotted by *The Times*, and the uncertainty of how many letters would be written were factors in Newman's rhetorical and unsystematic approach to these letters. Despite lacking a coherent method, the letters did have an underlying idea that unified them, the Church distinct and yet complementary to the modern world.

In addition to his brief preface, Newman provided another indirect hermeneutic, often overlooked by later commentators—the titles assigned to each letter. When the Catholicus letters were originally drafted, they did not have titles, but were simply numbered. His 1841 pamphlet simply retained the number; however, for the 1872 republication, Newman attached headings to each of the letters.

1. *Secular Knowledge in contrast with Religion*
2. *Secular Knowledge Not the Principle of Moral Improvement*
3. *Secular Knowledge Not a direct Means of Moral Improvement*
4. *Secular Knowledge Not the Antecedent of Moral Improvement*
5. *Secular Knowledge Not a Principle of Social Unity*
6. *Secular Knowledge Not a Principle of Action*
7. *Secular Knowledge without personal Religion, a Temptation to Unbelief*

While these headings may have been inserted to provide a formal structure to the letters, they did not provide a sufficient portal into the letters' contents. Although these headings do elicit one or another theme in each letter and so reveal something of what Newman wanted to communicate—morality, religion, and the limits of secular knowledge—

the headings also muted and constrained some of the more dynamic theological ideas within each letter.

Burgis noted that following the publication of *Discussions and Arguments* there were several specific comments in the press about *The Tamworth Reading Room*:

> Most of the periodicals which noticed it made special mention of the 'famous' letters, whether they welcomed them as particularly relevant, 'now that we have to face a secular system of National Education with Huxley for its prophet', or saw them as an illustration of the 'antagonism which a large body of clergy, Protestant as well as Roman Catholic, maintains towards all who are earnestly striving to promote the secular education of the people.'[57]

The Tamworth Reading Room provoked some strong reactions in the press;[58] for example, Sidney Colvin in the *Fortnightly Review* simultaneously loathed and marveled at the letters a generation removed:

> How dexterously he anon deserves assent in order that he may anon command it without deserving; how he mixes up the preposterous with the obvious, the just with the unjust, and hits the real blots in our mechanical ideas of progress, our ampullated self-congratulations over sterile gain, at the same moment as he reverses all order of history and all hope of human nature. How delightedly he strikes and smiles when he gets at his real butts and aversions—over the body of Sir Robert Peel at Bentham, and at Lord Brougham.[59]

Burgis concluded that 'Colvin's review shows why the letters were more than a brilliant response to a particular occasion; even for a man to whom Newman's first principles were incomprehensible, the work of 1841 hit the real blots in the ideas of progress of 1872'.[60] Indeed, by the time he wrote the *Grammar*, Newman had come to understand the concrete yet timeless quality of the letters. The ideas contained within not only redressed the Knowledge School in his day, but continued to chasten its progeny.

The timeless feature of the letters, containing ideas that challenge all moments of antiquity and modernity, was recognized by Newman

---

57 Burgis, TRR, 127–30.
58 Ibid., 199.
59 1 May 1872. Cited by Burgis, TRR, 129.
60 Ibid.

not only in where he placed and included the letters as a Catholic, but how he did so. Burgis found that the Catholicus letters, unlike many of Newman's early controversial works, were not extensively amended or altered for *Discussions and Arguments*. Most of the ideas in this work continued into his new ecclesial home. This stood in stark contrast, for example, to his lengthy revision of *Via Media* (1877) and *Essay on the Development of Christian Doctrine* (1878): 'When he revised the Letters for *Discussions and Arguments* he found necessary only a single modification of the views he had expressed in 1841 ... The 'Tamworth Reading Room' did not need the corrective as [his other] works of Anglican controversy did.'[61] As Burgis beautifully observed:

> The piece of writing which he found worth all this care, weaves together many different strands and makes of them something colourful and sparkling. The issues it raises he explored more fully elsewhere, but their combination in this playfully ironic context is everywhere a delight, and rewards the reader with insights into 'our complex nature'.[62]

The Times' Obituary and Conclusion

The final press reaction in the nineteenth century to the Catholicus letters occurred the day after Newman's death. On 12 August 1890, *The Times* published a lengthy obituary which recounted the facts of his death and a narrative of his life and work. Within the piece, the author (unnamed) offered a stirring passage:

> The present generation, that knows of the Cardinal chiefly in the comparatively quiet retreat of the Oratory and in the continual ovation everywhere and by almost all people accorded to his pre-eminent character, can be little aware of the inexhaustible energy and indefatigable industry with which he fought, what no doubt he believed the fight of faith. It would be exceeding the limits of our space to do common justice to his manifold labours. He was incessant in correspondence; he was always accessible to visitors; he kept journals and wrote 'memoirs justificatives:' he read, translated, analysed, and abstracted; he wrote and delivered sermons of the most intense originality; he lectured, he kept account of his army of followers. Before the publication of

---

61 Ibid., 199–200.
62 Ibid., 206.

the Tracts, he wrote letters to the *Record* newspaper, which he had helped to start, and which inserted his letters till he had taxed to the utmost its forbearance and its space. Some years afterwards, upon the occasion of Sir R. Peel's delivery of a 'march of mind' address on the opening of Tamworth Reading Room, he wrote, with the signature of Catholicus, a series of letters in this journal, read with eager interest by many who never guessed the author, still less that he would one day be a member of the 'Sacred College.'[63]

The Times' obituary appeared to be the only one which mentioned Newman's Catholicus letters. Following Newman's death, the letters were briefly treated in Dean Church's *The Oxford Movement* (1890). However, other biographical portraits, for example, Richard Hutton's *Cardinal Newman* (1891), Wilfrid Meynell's *Cardinal Newman* (1907), and Wilfred Ward's magisterial biography, *The Life of Cardinal Newman* (1912) did not cite the event. Not until Ward's *Genius of Newman* (1914) did the letters receive scholarly attention. Newman biographies subsequently discussed *The Tamworth Reading Room* as a significant but isolated event, eclipsed by *Tract 90*.[64]

The Catholicus letters, however, were more than an isolated event. They formed a portion of Newman's Christian witness and proclamation. His ideas were cast amid the torrents of politics, science, industry, and religion in the nineteenth century yet remain perennial—like St. Paul's impassioned soliloquy on the Areopagus.

---

63 'The Death of Cardinal Newman', *The Times*, 12 August 1890.
64 For example, Gilley, *Newman and his Age*, 195.

✣ 8 ✣

The 'Idea' of the Church: From Tamworth to Rome

SIR ROBERT PEEL desired the Tamworth reading room and library to be free of bias and 'without reference to rank or to political and religious distinctions.'[1] His inaugural address assumed that scientific and literary knowledge administered in the new institute were requisite to individual growth, societal unity and national progress. Such knowledge would improve the moral character of persons, increase their economic fortunes, and secure religious truth without the burden of ecclesiastical tradition. He delineated the usefulness and 'glories' of the new sciences for both the laboring classes and the gentry, which would become a new foundation for society:

> I cannot help thinking that by bringing together, in an institution of this kind, intelligent men of all classes and all conditions in life, by uniting together, as we have united, in the committee of this institution the gentleman of ancient family and great landed possessions with the skilful mechanic and artificer of good character.—I cannot help thinking that we are all establishing a bond of social connexion that will derive more than common strength from the pure motives that influence us, and from the cause in which we are engaged. (Applause.) I cannot help believing that we are harmonizing the gradations of society, and binding men together by a new bond, which, as I said before, will have more than ordinary strength on account of the object which unites us. (Loud applause).[2]

From Britain's Areopagus, *The Times*, John Henry Newman's shadowy Catholicus contested Peel's ideas. Catholicus sketched the range of

---

1 LD, VIII, 525.
2 LD, VIII, 531.

assumptions and limits to human knowledge, identifying a knowledge tradition stretching back to Cicero and the Atomists. The modern form of this tradition arose in part with Bacon, developed through Bentham's utilitarian doctrines and culminated in the mechanics' movement, which included Brougham and subsequently Peel.[3] This tradition was what Newman termed the Knowledge School. By 1841 this tradition was palpable, one with which he and his co-religionists had to contend. Peel and the Knowledge School advocated for faith bounded by reason, divorced from the Church.[4] Yet this faith could not accomplish what Christian faith could. For Christian faith, 'matured into a determinate character by the gracious influences of the Holy Ghost', was real and effective through the Church.[5]

Newman's response revolved around his vision for education, especially ecclesial faith preceding, yet not effacing, knowledge. In his seventh letter, Newman indicated that the faith of the Church was the anecdote to the 'charms and nostrums' of knowledge prescribed by Peel, Brougham, *et alii*:

> I consider, then, that intrinsically excellent and noble as are scientific pursuits, and worthy of a place in a liberal education, and fruitful in temporal benefits to the community; still they are not, and cannot be, the instrument of education ... that faith is the only known principle capable of subduing moral evil, educating the multitude, and organizing society; and that whereas man is born for action, action flows not from inferences, but from impressions; not from reasonings, but from faith.[6]

---

3 For example, 'Cicero handed the recipe to Brougham, and Brougham has passed it on to Peel' (*LD*, VIII, 539–40). Newman's historical sketch was cursory.

4 Newman rejected this type of faith succinctly in his eleventh Oxford University sermon, 'The Nature of Faith in Relation to Reason': 'It is usual at this day to speak as if Faith were simply of a moral nature, and depended and followed upon a distinct act of Reason beforehand,—Reason warranting, on the ground of evidence, both ample and carefully examined, that the Gospel comes from God, and *then* Faith embracing it' (*OUS*, 143 [202]). Such faith, for Newman, was not an ecclesial faith, but a distortion thereof.

5 See for example Newman, 'Evangelical Sanctity the Perfection of Natural Virtue', *OUS*, 40–1 [43].

6 *LD*, VIII, 561.

The 'Idea' of the Church

Newman recapitulated this passage almost thirty years later in his *Grammar of Assent*. He described his Catholicus letters as a 'protest' against a 'dangerous doctrine' espoused by Peel and Brougham. They had believed 'that the claims of religion could be secured and sustained in the mass of men, and in particular in the lower classes of society, by acquaintance with literature and physical science'.[7] This 'dangerous doctrine' in turn supplanted 'direct Christian instruction'.[8]

However, in 1841 and 1870, Newman was not focused principally on science or education, but with *what* was being taught directly to the wealthy, working classes, and the poor alike. Newman as Catholicus presented a substantive 'counter-offer' to the Knowledge School: ecclesial faith or 'the claims of religion' had to be at the core of any educational project.[9] His *Grammar* further elucidated his intentions, implying not just *what* was important for Newman, but *from where*. His desire for 'direct Christian instruction' flowed from the Church, which taught the faith, offered grace, absorbed and elevated science and culture, and united peoples from around the world. Peel's vision of a merely human institution dedicated to knowledge could not accomplish these ends.[10]

From Anglican 'Fundamentals' to Faith 'in the Bosom of the Church'

As a young minister at Oxford, Newman recognized the importance of belonging to a visible Church that communicated the rites and doctrines of Christian faith.[11] Through the course of the 1830s he had constructed a paper Church—The *via media*. This Church did not exist, his 'theory of the *via media* was absolutely pulverized', and by 1839 he felt intuitively that this meant he could no longer be an Anglican.

---

7 GA, 91–2.
8 *Ibid.*
9 LD, VIII, 548.
10 LD, VIII, 560.
11 Newman's lifelong belief in doctrine and the necessity of an ecclesial community, embedded within his Anglican sermons, were as seeds that grew and developed in Newman and grounded his later thought as a Roman Catholic. See James Tolhurst, *The Church ... A Communion in the Preaching and Thought of John Henry Newman* (Leominster: Fowler Wright Books, 1988), ix–xiii.

Although he began a slow migration from his ecclesial home, he did not see clearly where his journey would take him. Newman's search for an 'idea' of the Church, as Coulson suggested, could no longer be a projection; it had to be as 'concrete as a living thing'—sinners and saints gathered and renewed in their worship of the Holy Trinity.[12] This was difficult for him, because the 'idea' of the Church had to correlate to the actual divine–human communion moving through the world.[13] From at least 1835, Newman desired to see the Church as it appeared in society and history, glorious and fallen, not how he wanted it to be. His research and personal quest eventually led to an assent: that there truly was an Apostolic *and* Catholic Church, which for a time seemed only a theory.

One of his key insights in moving from a theory to an 'idea' was that Christian faith had to originate from the Head of the Church and spread throughout the Body. The Church and its faith had to be an integral whole. After a decade of reading, reflecting, and preaching, Newman recognized that since the Reformation a theological error had developed in his own communion and in other Protestant traditions—the idea that faith could exist apart from the Church. Newman wrestled with this error in his *Apologia*. He personally and theologically had to contend with the question of the relation of faith to the Church:[14]

> [At] the end of 1835 or beginning of 1836, I had the whole state of the question before me, on which, to my mind, the decision between the Churches depended ... [In] my view the controversy ... turned upon the Faith and the Church. This was my issue of the controversy from the beginning to the end. There was a contrariety of claims between the Roman and Anglican religions, and the history of my conversion is simply the process of working it out to a solution. In 1838 ... [I said that] the peculiarity of the Anglican theology was this,—that it 'supposed the Truth to be entirely objective and detached, not' (as

---

12 Vin Boa Luu Quang, 'Newman's Theology of the Immanent Trinity in his *Parochial and Plain Sermons* 1829–1834', *Newman Studies Journal* 7/1 (Spring 2010): 73–97.

13 *OUS*, 222 [330].

14 See Ian Ker, '"Mere Christianity" and Catholicism', in *C. S. Lewis and the Church: Essays in Honor of Walter Hooper*, ed. Judith E. Wolfe and Brendan N. Wolfe (London: T & T Clarke, 1988), 129–34.

The 'Idea' of the Church

the Roman) 'lying hid in the bosom of the Church as if one with her, clinging to and (as it were) lost her embrace, but as being sole and unapproachable, as on the Cross or at the Resurrection, with the Church close by, but in the background.' As I viewed the controversy in 1836 and 1838, I viewed it in 1840 and 1841.[15]

Newman's search for faith in 'the bosom of the Church' clarified 'the underlying difference ... between Protestantism generally and Catholicism'.[16] This disparity lay in the Protestant belief that 'the faith is separate from the Church and comes before the Church, whereas on the Catholic view, the faith is inseparable from the Church, which comes first as the source of faith'.[17]

The relation of faith to the Church vexed Newman. He queried this relationship, in 1838, analyzing the 'fundamental' Anglican doctrine of faith and the Church:

> The received notion in the English school seems to be, as has already been observed, that the faith which the Apostles delivered, has ever existed in the Church whole and entire, ever recognized as the faith, ascertainable as such, and separable (to speak generally) from the mass of opinions, which with it have obtained a footing among Christians. It is considered definite in its outline, though its details admit of more or less perfection; and in consequence it is the property of each individual, so that he may battle for it in his day, how great so ever the party attacking it; nay, as not receiving it simply from the Church of the day, but through other sources besides, historical and scriptural, he may defend it, if needs be, against the Church, should the Church depart from it; the faith being the foundation of the Church as well as of the individual, and the individual being bound to obey the Church, only so far as the Church holds to the faith. This is the doctrine of Fundamentals, and its peculiarity is this; that it supposes the Truth to be entirely objective and detached, not lying hid in the bosom of the Church as if one with her, clinging to her and (as it were) lost in her embrace, but as being sole and unapproachable as on the Cross or at the Resurrection, with the Church close by, but in the background.[18]

15 Newman, *Apologia*, 94–5.
16 Ker, '"Mere Christianity" and Catholicism', 133.
17 Ibid.
18 Newman, 'Palmer's *Treatise on the Church of Christ*', *The British Critic* 24 (1838): 347–72, at 367.

As a youth Newman saw faith as separate from the Church. Through his work with Hawkins and over the course of the Tractarian revival, however, he increasingly understood that a strict separation of faith and the Church was as heretical as Christ having two distinct persons.[19] Such a separation could not in the end mirror the unity of God or the Person of Christ. Without true unity the Body of Christ disintegrated (1 Co 12:12–26).

Ian Ker detected a question lurking in Newman's thought, 'But if this fundamental faith is prior to and superior to the Church, then who decides what this faith is?' 'The chief difficulty obviously lies', conceded the Anglican Newman, 'in determining what *is* the fundamental faith.'[20] Ker continued that 'this takes us back to the question to the question of whether Christianity means fundamentally a Church or a religion that is fundamentally distinct from any Church. To put it another way, is Christianity primarily a religion of the book (the Bible), that precedes any Church, or of the Eucharist, that presupposes the Church?'[21]

With regard to Newman's Catholicus letters, the notion of faith independent of the Church was what Peel, perhaps Brougham, and many English Christians believed. By 1841 Newman had utterly rejected this view. Faith was not individualistic, not simply of the Bible, or an inferred conclusion. Rather, faith was communal, traditional, and could not exist apart from the Church. Faith in 'the bosom of the Church' was Christianity, as he underscored in his 'Duty of Christian Educators':

> This is the faith of the Saints—the doctrine of the Blessed Trinity in Unity—the Incarnation of our Lord Jesus Christ—His immaculate conception—His birth, ministry, sufferings, death, atonement, resurrection, victory, Kingdom—the Mission of the Holy Ghost, the Holy Law, the privilege of prayer, the power of the Sacraments, the prerogatives of Holy Church, the unseen communion of all Saints,

---

19 Whether Nestorius actually held this is a matter for speculation; see David E. Wilhite, *The Gospel according to Heretics* (Grand Rapids, MI: Baker Academics, 2015), 145–68.

20 Ker, '"Mere Christianity" and Catholicism', 133; Newman, 'Palmer's *Treatise on the Church of Christ*', 368.

21 Ker, '"Mere Christianity" and Catholicism', 134.

the resurrection of the dead, the life everlasting, such I say is the faith of the Church throughout the whole world.[22]

Thus, when writing in the pages of *The Times*, Newman was not only seeking to reposition scientific knowledge and faith, but also to correct the errant view that faith stood apart from the Church. As his analysis in 1838 queried and his 'Duty of Christian Educators' revealed, Newman understood that once faith became unmoored from 'the bosom of the Church', as it was in Peel's thought, then purportedly it could be nurtured equally in mechanics' institutes. Newman, as Catholicus, vehemently opposed this assumption, for he knew that the healing power of grace and the mystery of faith must be found 'in graver and holier places than libraries and reading rooms.'[23]

The Form and Method of Newman's Sermons in *The Tamworth Reading Room*

In order to demonstrate to *The Times*' readers what he meant by these 'graver and holier places', Newman drew upon a form and method that he had developed in St. Mary's pulpit. Although his letters to *The Times* resembled several of the compositional styles that he developed in the course of the 1830s, for example editorials and tracts,[24] he knew that he was addressing a different audience, with a different purpose, and he adapted accordingly. Newman's sermons, especially his *Parochial and Plain Sermons*, provide the best analogue to the Catholicus letters. Burgis has noted this association:

---

22 *Sermons 1824–1843*, III, 405.
23 *LD*, VIII, 542.
24 *LD*, I, 102–5. Newman wrote his first editorial for the *Christian Observer* in May 1821. As a Tractarian he wrote 'a series of lengthy letters to the *Record* newspaper on the revival of church discipline' beginning in October 1833 (Ker, *Biography*, 85; *LD*, IV, 141). Newman also wrote an editorial to the *British Magazine* in October 1834 on 'Centralization' (*LD*, IV, 339–43). Newman countenanced the advantages and disadvantages of political centralization. Some of his concerns in this article resurfaced in the Catholicus letters (*LD*, IV, 341–3). On tracts: 'Advertisement', *Tracts for the Times* 3: vi, available at: http://www.newmanreader.org/works/times/advertisement3.html; Imberg, *Quest for Authority*, 44–125, has traced the development of Newman's ecclesiology in the *Tracts*.

> [The] separate Letters are organised in a way that resembles that of the series; that is to say he does not proceed by means of a chain of argument, but by circling round a subject clearly announced at the beginning, so that not even the most cursory reader could fail to make something of it while the more leisurely would find that from the consideration of particular instances and the use of quotation and comment upon it ... had some real content for him to take hold of. The method is not so much that of the early Tracts, which often consist of a short sharp sequence of admonitions; as of the *Parochial Sermons*.[25]

Newman had a personal way of composing the sermons, usually beginning with a particular passage from the daily Scripture readings found in the *Book of Common Prayer*.[26] This passage served to introduce a given theological subject, for example, baptism, the Holy Spirit, or the visible Church.[27] He then cultivated the topic in the form of a conversation—incorporating various arguments or perspectives into the sermon, providing concrete images from Scripture or from everyday life, and raising questions that engaged his listeners.[28] Tristram has noted that 'His manner of speaking was the same in the pulpit as on ordinary occasions; in fact, he was not preaching but conversing, very thoughtfully and earnestly, but still conversing.'[29]

Newman stumbled upon this conversational form in October of 1831; as he recorded in his diary: 'Walked back to Oxford, through clay fields, streams, and miry roads, about fifteen miles. [It was in this walk that I devised the mode of writing sermons which is my published mode].'[30] This new 'mode of writing' represented a significant change from an Evangelical form that had characterized his earlier preaching.

---

25 Burgis, *TRR*, 152.

26 See Paul V. Harrison, 'A Scriptural Index to Newman's *Parochial and Plain Sermons*', *Newman Studies Journal* 3/2 (Autumn 2006): 119–23. See also Francis J. Butler, 'John Henry Newman's Parochial and Plain Sermons Viewed as a Critique of Religious Evangelicalism' (Ph.D. diss., Catholic University of America, 1972), 98.

27 Ian Ker, *The Achievement of John Henry Newman* (Notre Dame: University of Notre Dame Press, 1990), 76.

28 Tolhurst, *The Church*, x.

29 *The Sermon Notes of John Henry Newman, 1849–1874*, ed. Henry Tristram (London: Longman, Green, 1914), vii.

30 *LD*, II, 366.

The 'Idea' of the Church

Prior to 1831 he had appropriated a style outlined by the great Anglican Evangelical, Charles Simeon.[31] He stressed a systematic approach to sermons and recommended that they have a singular purpose, clear organization, as well as utilize plain and common language. Finally, Simeon believed that sermons were dually meant to instruct and to raise the spirits and the moral awareness of the congregation.[32]

Although certain features of Simeon's style persisted in Newman's preaching, Simeon's exhortative method contrasted with Newman's conversational approach. While his sermons remained informative, inspiring, and simply worded, Newman also sought to draw his listeners into a theological dialogue; thus he avoided a rigorous method.

Newman knew that words could only do so much in 'preparing the way for the Gospel'; his priestly office and the Church's sacraments did far more than either the pulpit or the columns of a newspaper.[33] He nevertheless understood the evocative power of words spoken and printed. The 'idea' of the Church appeared in his sermons 'because they were preached Sunday after Sunday to a particular congregation rather in the manner of an extended conversation; and as in a conversation we can discover a thread which links the thoughts together and gradually becomes plain.'[34] For example, in 'The Spiritual Presence of Christ in the Church' (1838) Newman instructed his congregation to continually discern the visible from the invisible, for the fruit of this discernment is Christ's abiding call:

> Christ has come so close to us in the Christian Church (if I may so speak), that we cannot gaze on Him or discern Him. He enters into us, He claims and takes possession of His purchased inheritance; He does not present Himself to us, but He takes us to Him. He makes us His members. Our faces are, as it were, turned from Him; we see Him not, and know not of His presence, except by faith, because He is over us and within us.[35]

---

31 Ker, *Biography*, 90.
32 James Packer, 'Expository Preaching: Charles Simeon and Ourselves', *Churchman* 74/2 (1960): 94–101, at 94–5.
33 JHN to Samuel Wilberforce (4 February 1835), *LD*, V, 21.
34 *Ibid.*
35 *PPS*, VI, 121.

'An aristocracy of exalted spirits'

The letters to *The Times*, like the sermons given to St. Mary's congregation, attempted to coax his audience into a discourse about the Church. They were composed in a personal way, 'by circling round a subject', interjecting and asking questions.[36] For instance, in his third letter Newman remarked about the Church's tradition while also asking pointed questions about the Knowledge School's claims:

> Each one of us has lit his lamp from his neighbour, or received it from his fathers, and the lights thus transmitted are at this time as strong and as clear as if 1800 years had not passed since the kindling of the sacred flame. What has glory or knowledge been able to do like this? Can it raise the dead? can it create a polity? can it do more than testify man's need and typify God's remedy?[37]

Newman's sermons and his letters, were not ends in themselves, but as signs pointing readers to the Church, to faith, to Christ. However, they differed in several respects. First, the letters did not take their cue from the characters and images in Scripture; rather they began with the premises from Peel and the Knowledge School, popular idioms, and work-a-day portraits of common people. As a preacher, Newman attempted to unfurl the mysteries latent in Scripture for his congregation; as the pseudonymous Catholicus, he highlighted the struggles of the working class and the contradictions of the Knowledge School in the light of Christian truth. A second difference lay in audiences. Newman preached his sermons to members of the English Church who gathered each Sunday at St. Mary's. The letters were intended for anyone who read *The Times*—Christians of all denominations, other religious minorities, and non-believers. Thus, the Catholicus letters could not follow the assumptions and vernacular of a preacher in a pulpit. As Newman stated in his second letter, and in subsequent reflections, he was not 'exact in using theological language'.[38] The letters were crafted by Newman as a modern street evangelist, who like St. Paul shared the Gospel with any who might listen, only now upon Britain's Areopagus.

A final difference between the letters and sermons is manifest in a technique unique among Newman's Anglican corpus: the use of satire.

---

36 *DA*, iii.
37 *LD*, VIII, 544.
38 *LD*, VIII, 539.

According to Ker, 'From a literary point of view alone, the most important of Newman's Anglican writings is *The Tamworth Reading Room* ... It is also the one sustained work of satire that Newman wrote as an Anglican.'[39] Newman infused satire into his letters, because he found Peel and the Knowledge School wildly inconsistent in their assumptions: 'One of the most efficacious ways of winning an argument is show that one's opponent is inconsistent, but it is also one of the best ways of showing that his point of view is not only wrong but also absurd ... [It] is remarkable how pervasively the theme of inconsistency runs through Newman's satirical writings. Nothing seems to inspire so much amused contempt in him as the absence of or lack of consistency.'[40]

Newman's analysis of the Knowledge School demonstrated that its euphemisms and claims for scientific knowledge were inconsistent with how humans thought and acted. Moreover, politicians and pedagogues who advocated 'science' did not necessarily have credibility in extolling its virtue because they were not practioners. In order to expose these contradictions, Newman chose satire as Peel and the Knowledge School's 'substitution of knowledge for religious faith [was] so incongruous and absurd.'[41]

Newman viewed Peel's speech as a 6,500-word contradiction. For example, in his first letter Newman connected Peel to Brougham's infidel principle. His adoption of this principle showed that 'he [was] inconsistent enough to think highly of its application in the culture of the mind.'[42] He considered the Knowledge School's creation of an indiscriminate Pantheon of Science another incongruity: 'Nothing comes amiss to this author [Craik]; saints and sinners, the precious and the vile, are torn from their proper homes and recklessly thrown together under the category of Knowledge.'[43] Through satire, metaphor, and aphorism set within a conversational form, Newman exposed the postulations and wishes latent in Peel's address and in the Knowledge School's agenda.

39 Ker, 'Newman the Satirist', 12.
40 Ibid, 8.
41 Ibid., 13.
42 LD, VIII, 537.
43 LD, VIII, 553.

If the conversational form of the sermons anticipated Newman's Catholicus letters, so also their informal method. Mary Katherine Tillman described Newman's approach as using language to present an idea: 'Words, whole sermons, or an entire volume of sermons, like the artist's dabs of paint, whole canvases, and entire series of painting, are employed by Newman to portray a multi-faceted subject from a particular point of view'.[44] Many of Newman's sermons exhibited this method in order to reveal different theological ideas, especially the 'idea' of the Church. His Anglican sermons, offered 'a unique source of information on the development of Newman's ecclesiology precisely because they were preached week after week. The idea of the Church was not a literary exercise for Newman but a part of his very life which he gradually unfolded within the community of his parishioners.'[45]

Unlike his more focused and refined work on the Church such as the *Via Media*, Newman's sermons offered a way to understand the 'idea' of the Church, precisely because they did not offer a singular or systematic presentation. Newman figuratively walked his parishioners around the Scriptures, doctrines, sacraments, and exemplars of faith, allowing them to glimpse and assemble different views into a cohesive 'idea' of the Church. For example, in an 1835 sermon entitled 'The Church Visible and Invisible', Newman used this method to reveal two aspects of the 'idea' of the Church:

> It is allowable to speak of the Visible and of the Invisible Church, as two sides of one and the same thing, separated by our minds only, not in reality … No harm can come of the distinction of the Church into Visible and Invisible, while we view it as, on the whole, but one in different aspects; as Visible, because consisting (for instance) of clergy and laity—as Invisible, because resting for its life and strength upon unseen influences and gifts from Heaven.[46]

Newman performed a descriptive analysis of the visible or 'existing' Church in order to show his listeners how they may begin to discern the presence of the Holy Spirit already present in the ecclesial community, for example:

44 Tillman, 'An Introduction', OUS, xii–xxix.
45 Tolhurst, *Church*, ix, xii.
46 Newman, *PPS*, III, 221–2.

The 'Idea' of the Church

> Take the analogy of the human body by way of illustration. Considering man according to his animal nature, I might speak of him as having an organized visible frame sustained by an unseen spirit. When the soul leaves the body it ceases to be a body, it becomes a corpse. So the Church would cease to be the Church, did the Holy Spirit leave it; and it does not exist at all except in the Spirit.[47]

This serial method found in Newman's sermons moved his Catholicus letters. He used this to great effect in the fifth letter covering several vantage points to reveal the power of faith through the Church's influence upon society:

> Faith, once the soul of social union, is now but the spirit of division. Not a single doctrine but is 'controversial divinity;' not an abstraction can be imagined (could abstractions constrain), not a comprehension projected (could comprehensions connect), but will leave out one or other portion or element of the social fabric. We must abandon religion, if we aspire to be statesmen. Once, indeed, it was a living power, kindling hearts, leavening them with one idea, moulding them on one model, developing them into one polity. Ere now it has been the life of morality; it has given birth to heroes, it has wielded empire. But another age has come in, and faith is effete; let us submit to what we cannot change; let us not hang over our dead, but bury it out of sight. Seek we out some young and vigorous principle, rich in sap, and fierce in life, to give form to elements which are fast resolving into their inorganic chaos; and where shall we find such a principle but in knowledge?[48]

Passages like this arose throughout his letters and Newman guided readers of *The Times* around the various tenets of the Knowledge School in contrast to aspects of the Church: faith, education, salvation, and unity. These aspects gradually revealed the distinction between the 'idea' of the Church and the pretensions underlying the Tamworth Library and Reading Room. Satire vivified the letters, their conversational form allowed readers to question, ponder, and laugh along with him, and his serial method allowed them to see the 'idea' he hoped to reveal.

This unique combination differentiated *The Tamworth Reading Room* from Newman's sermons and other works, which stand alone as a

---

47 Ibid., III, 224.
48 LD, VIII, 551.

testament to a concise, persuasive, and popular way of doing theology akin to that of some of the Fathers of the Church.

Newman's Catholicus letters ultimately approached theology in a unique way, a way that Newman may not have appreciated at the time. Theology, speaking of things divine, did not have to deduce from Scripture and tradition or be speculatively rigorous to be effective. Editorials and scholarly articles have missed many theological themes and possibly the 'idea' of the Church in the letters because they seemed discordant with the use of satire and humor. Newman showed that theology did not have to be a dull or sobering exercise, but could begin from the ground and reach up to the divine. Humor, imagery, and a conversant tone were an innovative way to approach what many times seemed unapproachable theological topics.

Aspects that Reveal Newman's 'Idea'

The form, method, and ecclesial aspects found in Newman's sermons resurfaced in his Catholicus letters. When Newman tepidly, then lustily, embraced his role as Catholicus he was existentially in between his life in the Church of England—his 'idea' of the Apostolic and Catholic Church—and the Church of Rome (which he later identified with his 'idea'). His pilgrimage toward what he believed to be the true Church animated his letters. Faith informed, nurtured, and developed in 'the bosom of the Church', was in part a *crie de cœur* for himself and others. The offer from *The Times* to mount Britain's Areopagus and dispute with Peel and the Knowledge School provided him with the ultimate venue to illuminate the 'idea' of the Church.

Initially, the Catholicus letters were viewed by the press and individual observers in terms of British politics or as an outcry from the Tractarian faction of the Church against societal progress and change.[49] Others interpreted aspects such as education, faith and reason, or religious conservatism, as the heart of the letters. Many of those who have analyzed *The Tamworth Reading Room* have tended to follow Newman's summary in letter seven: his principal motive for writing was to clarify the proper relationship between religious faith and scientific knowledge

---

49 The main exception was the editorial of 12 February in the *Morning Chronicle*.

in education.⁵⁰ For example, Burgis wrote: '[The] single theme, the relation between knowledge, faith and action and popular misconceptions about that relation as seen particularly in the Address, does give them [the letters] a loose unity.'⁵¹ Keith Beaumont has concluded that the letters were concerned with the role of knowledge and religion in Victorian society.⁵² James Arthur and Guy Nichols have emphasized that Newman 'excoriated' Peel's 'idea of secular knowledge as a substitute for religion' and 'his approbation of the utility of education'.⁵³ These conclusions derive fittingly from the contents of the letters and from their 1872 titles. Education and faith in contrast to scientific knowledge appeared central to his letters. Others, however, such as Coats, have disagreed with this general consensus:

> 'The Tamworth Reading Room' cannot be appraised by the modern reader as a single work. It may not even be correct to say that they are a series of works since the concept of a 'work' can suggest an integrity of development that none but the first of the letters maintained. What *The Times* published after that initial letter was one part of a dialogue concerning a public discourse on the subjects of religion, education, society and politics. As with most conversations on volatile subjects, the Tamworth discussion changed throughout the debate.⁵⁴

Yet a holistic view of the letters and the circumstances surrounding them reveal that Newman had an 'idea' in mind greater than the sum of the various aspects and topics flitting about in the pages of *The Times*. *The Tamworth Reading Room* was a 'single work' and his 'idea' of the Church manifests this unity. There are several aspects, different from the those cited above, that illumine this 'idea.'

---

50 Kei Uno, 'The Views of Sir Robert Peel and John Henry Newman on the Establishment of the Tamworth Reading Room in 1841 and its Effect on Humankind and their Ideas of Adult Education', *Studies in Philosophical Anthropology* 37 (2007): 15–33.
51 Burgis, *TRR*, 151.
52 Beaumont, 'Savoir et foi', 56: 'Son objet dans *The Tamworth Reading-Room* est de denouncer les presupposes qui concernent la place et le rôle, respectivement, du "savoir" et de la religion, dans la culture et la société de l'époque.'
53 Arthur and Nichols, *John Henry Newman*, 100.
54 Coats, 'Rhetorical Approaches', 177.

I. Faith cannot be separate from the Church

Throughout his letters, Newman concentrated upon the problem of faith separated from the Church. He knew that Peel considered himself a loyal member of the Church of England—he adhered to basic Christian mores and observed the Church's rites. He also was aware that the Knowledge School consisted of an array of Christians, Deists, Skeptics, and a few nonbelievers. Newman thought it inconsistent and objectionable that Peel and many in the Knowledge School conceived of faith apart from doctrine and thus apart from the Church.

The separation of faith from the Church was clear in Peel's address—ministers, deprived of their office, could only act as advisors who recommended secular literature; the glory of science either led to or could be substituted for religious faith; scientific knowledge or faith could be discovered, free from religious institutions and the bigotries Peel believed they tended to impart. This separation also had been a key component of the mechanics' movement. Further, Peel, in line with the Knowledge School, believed that a human faith divorced from the Church and combined with the wonders of scientific knowledge could do what a doctrinal, traditional, and divine Christian faith could not—harmonize the classes in society.

Newman could not abide emasculated ministers or a rationalized human philosophy coequal with the Church's faith. As he declared in his sixth letter, 'I have no confidence then in philosophers who cannot help having religion, and are Christian by implication. They sit at home, and reach forward to distances which astonish us; but they hit without grasping, and are sometimes as confident about shadows as about realities.'[55]

A philosophy that appeared Christian, but truly lacked divine action, sacramental edification, and doctrinal content, was not real. In contrast, Christian faith was a grace given by Christ's Spirit through the Church, a gift that united believers and opened them to the fullness of God's saving power—through the sacraments, prayer, and even their quotidian experiences. Peel and the Knowledge School had misplaced 'what in its place is a divine gift'.[56] The fullness of grace was nurtured and edified

---

55 LD, VIII, 556.
56 LD, VIII, 545.

The 'Idea' of the Church

through the Church; faith divorced from grace and the Church could not save (Ep 2:8–9).[57]

II. Formed in faith and knowledgeable of the world

Newman saw the Church as a setting which allowed faith to coexist in harmony with knowledge. He demonstrated this by blending elements from his sermons into the Catholicus letters. For example, Newman noted in the 'Duty of Christian Educators' that humans were dependent upon each other—'Man is not sufficient for himself'[58]—and ultimately upon God. Humans needed to learn from others; an education through a community formed character and tamed rebellious human nature.[59] These principles were at times implicit and explicit in the letters—particularly in Newman's denunciation of the infidel principle.[60] A library, institute, or university devoid of Christianity could impart useful or interesting knowledge but could not form and elevate the whole person or community. A life without religious faith would not necessarily yield bold and intelligent persons. Rather, as Newman depicted in the third letter, they 'shall but mature into a mawkish, frivolous, and fastidious sentimentalism ... into a dry unamiable longheadedness ... into a polished outside, with hollowness within, in which vice has lost its grossness, and perhaps increased its malignity ... into an uppish supercilious temper, much inclined to scepticism.'[61] Newman knew that only Christian community and tradition could deeply touch then raise men and women from a life soaked in sin, sentiment, or doubt. This for him was the goal of 'direct Christian instruction'. In his third letter, he declared that:

> Christianity, and nothing short of it, must be made the element and principle of all education. Where it has been laid as the first stone, and acknowledged as the governing spirit, it will take up into itself, assimilate, and give a character to literature and science. Where revealed truth has given the aim and direction to knowledge, knowledge of

---

57 'For by grace are ye saved, through faith, and that not of your selves: it is the gift of God: Not of works, lest any man should boast.'
58 Newman, *Sermons 1824–1843*, III, 400.
59 *Ibid*.
60 *LD*, VIII, 536.
61 *LD*, VIII, 546.

all kinds will minister to revealed truth. The evidences of religion, natural theology, metaphysics,—or, again, poetry, history, and the classics,—or physics and mathematics, may all be grafted into the mind of a Christian, and give and take from the grafting.[62]

For Newman 'Christianity was faith', and faith was in 'the bosom of the Church', and this ecclesial faith was to be the priority in education. Faith did not interfere with knowledge but rather gave it 'character'. Moreover, faith was expressed in doctrine, which Newman identified in his fourth letter as 'Christian Knowledge'.[63] Christian Knowledge was open to and incorporated all the sciences and yet pointed to the God revealed in Christ through the Church.

He expressed his admiration of science and technology, and showed command of the classics and of current trends, while consistently putting faith first. Newman's Catholicus showed exactly the type of person he was hoping for: formed in the Church's faith *and* knowledgeable of the world. Whereas Peel and the Knowledge School envisioned a 'neutral ground, on which men of every shade of politics and religion may meet together, disabuse each other of their prejudices, form intimacies, and secure cooperation',[64] Newman inverted their idea—bigotry arose not from faith through the Church, but by using secular institutions (academic or political) to usurp and exclude faith formation.[65]

III. Sin and salvation: different visions

Newman used his letters to awaken his readers to the realities of sin and its remedy in salvation through the Church. He did so in order to respond to Peel's vision of human progress, one that implied salvation without divine faith or the Church. Newman assumed that he and Peel shared a similar belief that human nature was distorted by sin.[66] They also concurred that a formative education helped mitigate error. He agreed with Peel that knowledge or effort might yield technology useful to the community or amuse and distract many. However, human

---

62 LD, VIII, 546.
63 LD, VIII, 549.
64 LD, VIII, 534.
65 LD, VIII, 550–1.
66 LD, VIII, 539.

striving could not apply the necessary salve to the moral and spiritual conflicts that actually split persons and communities apart.

For Peel, individual effort—like the poor man who transcended his class through study—could save a person.[67] The idea of divine grace as necessary to elevate an individual was absent from Peel's address. For him and the Knowledge School, a 'neutral ground', free of dogma and ecclesial authority, like a library or a secular university could transform a person's life. Peel and the Knowledge School desired that the community support an individual's growth in knowledge—by providing materials or lectures to improve one's mind. Increase in knowledge was,[68] for Peel, a path to salvation for the individual and indirectly the community.

Newman challenged this secular soteriology and contended that Peel's proposal led to solipsistic idolatry:

> When we survey the marvellous truths of astronomy, we are first of all lost in the feeling of immense space, and of the comparative insignificance of this globe and its inhabitants. But there soon arises a sense of gratification and of new wonder at perceiving how so insignificant a creature has been able to reach such a knowledge of the unbounded system of the universe. So, this is the religion we are to gain from the study of nature; how miserable! The god we attain is our own mind; our veneration is even professedly the worship of self.[69]

For Newman, education through the Church not only allowed for enlightenment, but also renovation of heart and mind through Christ's grace. Grace was not only constitutive of the person, manifesting divine love and mercy, but also had the power to unite the community of faith. Knowledge had no such purchase.

> Now, independent of all other considerations, the great difference, in a practical light, between the objects of Christianity and of heathen belief, is this—that glory, science, knowledge, and whatever other fine names we use, never healed a wounded heart, nor changed a sinful one; but Christ's word is with power. The ideas which Christianity brings before us are in themselves full of influence, and they are endowed

---

67 *LD*, VIII, 529–31.
68 *LD*, VIII, 555.
69 *LD*, VIII, 559.

with a supernatural gift over and above, in order to meet the special exigencies of our nature ...

The Knowledge School does not contemplate raising man above himself; it merely aims at disposing of his existing powers and tastes, as is most convenient or practicable under circumstances ... It leaves man where it found him—a sinner, not a saint; but it tries to make him look as much like what he is not as ever it can ... Nay, every where, so far as human nature remains hardly or partially Christianized, the heathen law remains in force; as is felt in a measure even in the most religious places and societies ... You do not get rid of vice by human expedients; you can but use them according to circumstances, and in their place. You must go to a higher source for renovation of heart and will. You do but play a sort of 'hunt the slipper' with the sin of our nature till you go to Christianity.[70]

Faith through the ministry of the Church embraced both the wealthy and the working class, and women both virtuous and not, and had the ability to regenerate the drunkard, the thief, the insolent, and the angry. All other potential remedies were merely palliative.

IV. The Church as the 'soul of social union'

For Newman, ecclesial faith—the 'fulcrum of society ... and the soul of social union'[71]—was a true principle of unity: 'faith is the only known principle capable of subduing moral evil, educating the multitude, and organizing society'.[72] What Newman recognized in his letters, and as early as 1829, was that unity in faith was central to the life of the Church. In contrast, Peel and the Knowledge School believed that social unity could emerge from scientific knowledge or from industrial, commercial, or political advances. Newman's rejoinder was that science could not provide unity because it was always revisable.[73] Definitive commitments, the acts of Christian faith and love, were true ingredients for unity and science did not have this capacity.

Ecclesial faith did not create an artificial and universal harmony for which Peel and the Knowledge School had hoped. The Church, in

---

70 *LD*, VIII, 543–5.
71 *LD*, VIII, 551.
72 *LD*, VIII, 561.
73 *LD*, VIII, 555.

The 'Idea' of the Church

Newman's mind, was more dynamic. He acknowledged that the Church was broken at this time and real differences remained.[74] However, the faith and doctrines that flowed from the Church were truths that drew Christians toward unity, for this was the underlying principle commanded by Christ and found in the Spirit:

> Knowledge is not 'power,' nor is glory 'the first and only fair;' but 'grace,' or 'the word,' by whichever name we call it, has been from the first a quickening, renovating, organizing principle. It has new-created the individual, and diffused and knit him into a social body, composed of members each similarly created. It has cleansed man of his moral diseases, raised him to hope and energy, given him to propagate a brotherhood among his fellowmen, to form a large family or rather kingdom of saints all over the earth, and with wonderful vigour prolonged its original impulse down to this day.[75]

Unity achieved in faith had consequences: the Body of Christ allowed for differences but also engendered a distance from those who embraced only worldly ends. This was the same world, where in 1841, he found Peel's hope for unity and salvation in science and secular institutes to be so 'pitiable' and his call for the Church to be so exigent.

The 'Idea' of the Church in *The Tamworth Reading Room*

Political, theological, and pedagogical aspects of the 'idea' of the Church bloomed and developed in the course and composition of his letters. These various blossoms were how both detractors and admirers of Newman interpreted the Catholicus letters. As blossoms reveal flowers, so do aspects reveal ideas; the 'idea' of the Church arose from the variety of themes and images in *The Tamworth Reading Room*. Although the Church was presented with different images and at different times, Coulson saw that Newman consistently viewed the 'idea' of the Church as the visible Body of Christ:

> For Newman the starting point [of understanding the Church] must be the objectified presence or 'Body' of Christ existing in the world. It is to be identified by what Newman calls his 'method of personation,' a

---

74 *LD*, VIII, 537; 550.
75 *LD*, VIII, 543–4.

method [where] Christ is not encountered directly or introspectively as an *alter ego*, but always through the Church and it sacraments ... Christ is uniquely present to each Christian when the Church is gathered to form the Eucharistic community, since this is that special mode of approaching Him which he has bequeathed.[76]

The Church as a body perceptible, expressed in metaphors such as 'an aristocracy of exalted spirits', was the consistent counterpoint to the Knowledge School throughout the Catholicus letters. The tangible and social Church as 'idea', not an interior impression in one's mind or heart, was what Newman exhorted his readers to return to.[77] This was his 'idea', one that in this instance did not follow the Platonic *eidos*, but rather recapitulated an earlier meaning, related to the Latin *species*, of the concrete appearance of an entity. However, his 'idea' of the Church in his Catholicus letters has escaped most scholars' purview. For instance, Burgis correctly described the method of the letters, saw their inner coherence, and found them to have a 'loose unity'. Yet her excellent and careful study did not account sufficiently for Newman's theology or ecclesiology (to be fair, this was not her focus) and thus led to this conclusion: 'In the "Tamworth Reading Room" there is not, in the Letters as a series, or in most of them individually, the gradual unfolding of an idea that is the achievement of [for example] the *Grammar*.'[78] As the preceding chapters have shown, however, Newman's Catholicus letters were as he conceived—whole, complete in themselves, and yet adjusted for time and circumstance. He wanted his readers to glimpse the evolving 'idea' of the Church, its 'objectified presence in the world', in fresh and interesting ways. He later intimated this desire by remarking that even if persons read bits and pieces (aspects) of one or two letters: 'by the end of them the *idea* is created and *grown up*'.[79]

Only Rowlands recognized Newman's understanding of the Church, the 'idea' that integrated the letters, in his appraisal of *The Tamworth*

---

76 Coulson, 'Newman on the Church', 130.

77 Terrence Merrigan (*Clear Heads and Holy Hearts: The Religious and Theological Ideal of John Henry Newman* [Louvain: Peeters, 1991], 82–102), provides an excellent commentary on this notion of 'idea'.

78 Burgis, *TRR*, 179.

79 *LD*, XVII, 428–9; emphasis added.

The 'Idea' of the Church

Reading Room. Rowlands provided an excellent overview of the letters, and offered this insight:

> It was Newman's conviction that intellectual knowledge by itself was inimical to true religion ... Christianity had never emphasised the mind of man at the cost of minimising his other faculties ... Newman was always trying to join together what man had put asunder. By drawing many things into one, the human personality became an indivisible whole. As Newman's concern was with the whole Church, so too in social matters his interest was in the whole man ... In his Baptism man was originally made whole ... In the act of pure living, the heart, the passions, the senses, the emotions as well as the mind were involved. Newman's concern was to gather all things into one, in the totality of the Holy, Catholic and Apostolic Church and in the unique individuality of each human personality.[80]

The scope and focus of Rowlands's work curbed further explanation as to how the Church functioned in the letters. It was enough to show how Newman's notion of faith and knowledge were relational and traditional—they extended down through the Church to reach the whole person. This was precisely what Newman's Catholicus emphasized again and again.

That this 'idea' of the Church did not surface in other scholarly approaches to *The Tamworth Reading Room* may be accounted for in the following ways: perhaps Newman's concern with the Church in *Tract 90* eclipsed his other works in 1841; or because the term 'Church' was used only five times; or because Newman used 'Christianity', following 'The Duty of Christian Educators', to represent the Church and its faith. Coats, for example, claimed that Newman's letters were free of ecclesial concerns and were simply intended to attack Brougham's infidel principle.[81] Newman 'preferred [*sic*] here to argue not among religious values but in favor of faith as against unbelief'.[82] Newman did contrast faith with Brougham's equation of belief to opinion and he did not intend the letters to settle disputes between Tractarians and

---

80 Rowlands, *Church, State, and Society*, 170–1.
81 *Ibid.*, 175.
82 Coats, 'Rhetorical Approaches', 175.

the High or Broad Church.⁸³ However, Newman's attack upon the infidel principle sprung from his understanding of faith given through the Church. Finally, and most importantly, scholars may have missed the 'idea' of the Church because the conversational form and serial method moving the letters were not associated with Newman's developing ecclesiology.

Newman intended the images and arguments in the Catholicus letters to lead readers to question both the possibilities and the limitations of Peel's library and reading room and similar institutions. For him, the Church and its ministries complemented their capacity to educate and exceeded their human limitations because it was divine and not a wishful projection. The 'idea' he conveyed was the Church present in the world through good human beings weakened by sin, diverse yet unified, incarnate in various nations and cultures, and always divinely ordained and guided.

Coda: An Oratory for 'Exalted Spirits'

The Catholicus letters were a defense of the Church and an invitation to see it set within the cross currents of science, technology, and the politics of nineteenth-century Britain. Newman knew that the great theological axiom of faith within 'the bosom of the Church' needed to be recast for the modern world. The Church would do as it had done for 1800 years: heal, transform, unite, and also absorb and elevate culture.

For Newman, living in the Church, and not simply accepting the platitudes of a Christian society, engendered a robust faith. The Catholicus letters invited all to a conversation about the Church and the world and in this sense were a means to conversion. For the letters did not simply posit a stark choice of light and dark, sacred and profane. Rather, they proclaimed an embrace of the emerging knowledge of the world, while returning to the ground of faith: 'Instruction in the church, with all its defects and mistakes, came to some end, for it started from some

---

83 Although Newman's first letter alluded to, and his sixth letter acknowledged, ecclesial controversies between factions in the Anglican Church, he espoused various Tractarian views in these letters (*LD*, VIII, 537; 557).

beginning.'[84] The 'end' for harmonizing the innovations of knowledge was the Church; the 'beginning' was also the Church, found in the encounter between believers and their worship of the Trinity.

Although the Catholicus letters, and most of Newman's writings during this period, pointed to the 'idea' of the Church, he himself did not fully realize this until he entered the Roman Catholic Church in 1845. He considered his complex and varied spiritual journey 'like coming into port after a rough sea'.[85] The once rebellious Anglican minister and mysterious Catholicus eventually found a home. As a Catholic, Newman continued to debate atop the Areopagus, to offer various iterations of faith in 'the bosom of the Church' in his *Idea of a University*, the *Essay in Aid of a Grammar of Assent*, and the *Letter to the Duke of Norfolk*. In 1879, Newman also donned a cardinal's hat and recapitulated what Catholicus had warned of so many years earlier in his famous 'Bigletto Speech'.[86]

Although Newman combated spurious notions of faith, education, and the Church in his sermons, monographs, letters, and speeches, he also attempted put into practice how these errors could be overcome. He truly believed that the Church at its best complemented modern institutions of learning. His *Idea of a University* testified to this deep, abiding belief and represented his great but ultimately failed attempt at founding the University of Dublin. There he tried to establish a place of higher learning in which all forms of knowledge, distinct in their objects and methods, ultimately turned toward the unity of God proclaimed by the Church.

Another less conspicuous attempt, related to *The Tamworth Reading Room*, occurred soon after Newman returned to England from Rome in 1847. He knew that he had to reach out to workers and their families as he designed an oratory in Birmingham. Newman sought a way to creatively appropriate the mechanics' movement, which was very strong in this industrial city, with his new ministry. This concern echoed his Catholicus letters, where he challenged Peel's vision for

---

84 *LD*, VIII, 557.
85 Newman, *Apologia*, 238.
86 John Henry Newman, *Addresses to Cardinal Newman and his Replies, 1879–1881*, ed. Rev. W. P. Neville (London: Longman, Green, & Co., 1905), 63–5; 69–70.

'An aristocracy of exalted spirits'

the education of mechanics and their families. However, he did not propose how Christianity, the 'idea' of the Church, might accomplish this task in the letters:

> People say to me, that it is but a dream to suppose that Christianity should regain the organic power in human society which once it possessed. I cannot help that; I never said it could. I am not a politician; I am proposing no measures, but exposing a fallacy, and resisting a pretence ... The ascendancy of faith may be impracticable, but the reign of knowledge is impossible. The problem for statesmen of this age is how to educate the masses, and literature and science cannot give the solution.[87]

Although detractors then and now believed Newman hostile to progress for workers, his letters and subsequent actions demonstrate that he was never directly opposed to the mechanics' movement or mass education.[88] He desired only balance and the priority of the Church's faith over knowledge in the formation of persons. Although Newman mocked and inveighed against the Knowledge School in his Catholicus letters, he knew that their message, faith in knowledge, had in many ways eclipsed the Church's role in education. Mechanics' institutes had become a haven and a refuge for workers, no longer the Church.[89] However, after the controversy with Peel and his conversion to Rome, Newman still pondered, against 'the talent of the day', what might be done to educate the laboring classes. In the heady days of forming the Oratory, he wrote about some of his plans to John Dalgairns in January 1847:

> Next I conceive that the plan of the Oratory needs altering, in order to adapt it to the state of England, and this alteration would be in favour of study. St. Philip met with his brethren three hours a day, and all comers were admitted. A spiritual book gave rise first to some remark, then to a dialogue—then to a sermon. Now I should prefer meeting in this way only on Sundays and other festivals, and giving the discussion somewhat more of an intellectual character. On festivals it might also be, or at least embrace, the discussion which would be

---

87 *LD*, VIII, 555.
88 For example, Coats, 'Rhetorical Approaches', 176.
89 *LD*, XII, 38.

> found in a mechanics' institute, indeed I should wish at any rate the Oratorio to include the functions of a Mechanics' Institute among its duties. On Sundays, when English habit would not bear mere science or literature, the matter, which was the [*aphorme*] of the discussion, might be Butler's Lives, Ecclesiastical History, a spiritual book &c. &c. First then would come music, then the reading, then *an objection* upon it; e.g. '*This* saint gave up his property—I don't see the good of this'; or 'I can't make out that there was time enough between the deluge and Exodus for *this* formation of language'; or 'These Mahometans seem as good people as Catholics'; or '*These* discoveries in the stars seem to shake one's faith in the special connection of the human race with the Creator,' &c. &c. Then would follow a debate, ending perhaps in a sermon, if there was not too much of it. The whole should end either with the Rosary, or Litany, and with music too in some way or other. Out of the persons who came a confraternity should gradually be formed, chiefly of course of young persons, and confession and directions would come in.[90]

This was an ideal, an ideal full of hope (and a litte naivety), so characteristic of Newman. He wanted so much for people to enter into a relationship with the Church, with Christ, to share in the wounds and joy, as he had. Much like his University of Dublin, this ideal did not materialize according to his creative plan, but nevertheless he found subsequent ways to educate the Catholic laity in Birmingham and beyond.[91]

Admirers and critics alike have always seen in Newman an idealist or a dreamer, one who as a youth had a 'mistrust of the reality of material phenomena' and for whom the spiritual was greater than the physical.[92] For his votaries this was one of his greatest attributes—the ability to dream with the Church, to try and devise ways of understanding God and the economy of faith beyond the hard lines of the 'real' world. He *dreamed* about the *Idea of the University* and about the Birmingham Oratory as a Sunday Mechanics' Institute. His detractors, from Kingsley to Turner, saw in his dreams a man deceived and a deceiver. His

---

90 LD, XII, 17.
91 See Paul Shrimpton, *The 'Making of Men', The Idea and Reality of Newman's university in Oxford and Dublin* (Leominster: Gracewing, 2014), 42–4.
92 Newman, *Apologia*, 16.

love of the faith in 'the bosom of the Church' blinded him to its true actions—from persecutions fueled by bigotry to a rigidity unable to accept the onrush of modernity.

Newman, who felt the hardships of the actual Church as an Anglican and as a Catholic, saw the problems clearly, but did not abide such pessimism. He had watched his ecclesial theory dissolve into his 'idea' of the Church in 1845, and this 'idea' was visible, wracked with sin, and yet divine in origin. The grace transmitted through this 'idea' was able to 'heal [his] wounded heart' and others' as well.

A final illustration suffices to show how Newman came to regard his 'idea' of the Church. In January 1868 he responded to a question from a Mr. Bartholomew, who wondered if he had regretted leaving the Anglican Communion. Newman plainly stated that although he had had problems working with the hierarchy,

> there is a depth and a power in the Catholic religion, a fulness of satisfaction in its creed, its theology, its rites, its sacraments, its discipline, a freedom yet a support also, before which the neglect or the misapprehension about oneself on the part of individual living persons, however exalted, is as so much dust, when weighed in the balance. This is the true secret of the Church's strength, the principle of its indefectibility, and the bond of its indissoluble unity. It is the earnest and the beginning of the repose of heaven.[93]

The 'idea' of the Church that Newman raised as a question in the 1830s, intuited as he implicitly withdrew from the Anglican Communion, and was moving toward in his *Tamworth Reading Room* had now enveloped his life. As a Catholic he realized he was living the 'idea' and was joyful. Even with the Church's imperfect and sinful relations among the Body and with the world, he had been drawn into its divine purity and unity.[94] Newman had become his Catholicus, no longer hidden, but flush in the full light of the 'aristocracy of exalted spirits'.

---

93 *LD*, XXIV, 24–5.
94 Wilfrid Ward, *The Life of Cardinal Newman* (Longman, Green, & Co., 1912), 201.

APPENDICES

Appendix I. Peel's Address and the Catholicus Letters

The address and letters presented here can be found in *LD*, VIII, whose pagination is given in parentheses within the text. The text has been checked against the original publication in *The Times* (paragraph divisions in Peel's speech are, however, editorial).

Sir Robert Peel's Address

THE TIMES, TUESDAY, 26 JANUARY 1841

SIR ROBERT PEEL'S ADDRESS ON THE ESTABLISHMENT OF
A LIBRARY AND READING-ROOM AT TAMWORTH.

(From the *Staffordshire Advertiser*)

Our readers are aware that the Right Hon. Sir Robert Peel has come forward most liberally to assist in the establishment of a library and reading-room for Tamworth and its neighbourhood. (525) We understand that Sir Robert has given the munificent sum of 100*l*. towards the object, and has kindly accepted the office of president. The institution is founded on a comprehensive basis, without reference to rank or to political and religious distinctions. Sir Francis Lawley, Bart., is the chairman of the managing committee.

The committee of management and the book committee having been appointed, a public meeting was held on Tuesday last, the 19th inst., at the Town-hall, Tamworth, the Right Hon. President having consented to deliver on that day an address explanatory of the objects of the institution.

The Town-hall was crowded on the occasion.

Sir R. Peel was accompanied by Lady Peel and two sons. Amongst the company present were Sir F. Lawley, Bart., Sir J. C. B. Cave, Bart,

'An aristocracy of exalted spirits'

Mr. I I. J. Pye (High Sheriff of the county) and Mrs. Pye, Mr. S. P. Wolferstan, Mrs. and the Misses Wolferstan, Mr. J. Colville, Mr. E. W. Dickenson, Mr. W. Tongue, Mr. H. Stokes, Mr. W. Parsons, sen., Mr. W. Parsons, jun., Mr. F. Willington, Mr. T. Bramall, Mr. J. Hall, the Rev. Dr. Lally, and the Rev. Messrs. F. Blick, R. C. Savage, R. W. Lloyd, J. Hodge, T. Laugharn, C. Thompson, &c.

At 1 o'clock, the hour fixed for the purpose, Sir R. Peel rose, and addressed the assembly as follows:—

It has been usual, on the foundation of an institution similar to that which it is now proposed to establish in this town, to open the proceedings with an inaugural lecture or address, explanatory of the objects of the institution, and of the regulations on which it is proposed to conduct it; and in conformity with that practice, and because I am sincerely desirous of faithfully discharging the functions which belong to the appointment to which I have been recently elected, I have willingly undertaken to perform a duty which is generally assigned to the office of president. I feel that I shall best perform that duty by attempting to explain to you, in very simple and very perspicuous language, the views of those who have taken a leading part in the establishment of this institution, and the advantages which we think it holds out to those who are willing to become members of it. I feel perfectly convinced that on such subjects as the extension of knowledge and intellectual improvement it would be vain to hope to discover any novelty, either of argument or of expression. I conceive that on such an occasion, and in such a meeting as this, any parade of learning would be an idle affection; and if I do add anything to the simple explanation of the objects of this institution, it will be to recall to your minds truths which are very obvious and very trite, but which do not, generally speaking, exercise a practical influence upon the conduct of men that corresponds with their obviousness and with their importance. The printed paper which I hold in my hand, and which, probably, most of you have seen, explains so fully the basis on which the institution is founded, and the (526) fundamental rules by which it is proposed to govern it, that it is hardly necessary for me to enter into any minute detail; but perhaps a general summary of those regulations would be convenient.

It is proposed to establish a library and a reading-room, for the advantage of this town and neighbourhood—the reading-room to be open for certain hours of every day (with the exception of particular holydays and Sundays), under such regulations as the committee of management shall determine. It is proposed that the library shall be open to all persons, and that they shall be permitted, under certain regulations, to have books from the reading-room at their own houses, for the amusement and instruction of themselves and their families. We propose that the advantages of this institution shall be open to all persons of all descriptions, without reference to political opinions or to religious creed, who shall have attained the age of 14 years. We propose that the institution shall be open to the female as well as the male portion of the population of this town and neighbourhood; because we consider that we should have done great injustice to the well-educated and virtuous women of this town and neighbourhood, if we had supposed that they were less capable than their husbands or their brothers of benefiting by the instruction which we hope to give, or if we had supposed that they were less interested in the cause of rational recreation and intellectual improvement. We propose, also, that they shall have equal power and equal influence in the management of this institution with others, being well assured that the influence which a virtuous woman can hold (if it be necessary to call it into action) will always be exercised in favour of whatever is sound and profitable in respect of knowledge, and whatever is decorous and exemplary in respect to conduct.

It would be presumptuous in me to anticipate the decision of the committee of management on many points which are reserved for their consideration; but I do hope it may be possible hereafter, and at no distant period, to extend the advantages of this institution beyond those which are contemplated in the printed paper. I hope that it may be possible to make some arrangement, by which, at some hour of the day, not interfering with the hours set apart for reading, it may be possible for parents to take their children, below the age of 14, that they may benefit by access to the maps or globes, or books of reference, which may be deposited in the library. I hope, also, that we are laying the foundation of a great treasury of knowledge—of stores, more various and more rich than those we at present contemplate. For instance, I am not too sanguine in hoping to live to see the day when it may be possible in this district, not deficient itself in mineral productions, and

'An aristocracy of exalted spirits'

bordering upon a great division of England that is pregnant with iron and coal (the great incentives to human skill and industry), to form a collection of minerals most interesting to a mind inquisitive after knowledge, and facilitating the comprehension of such treatises as may be written, and such works as may be published, on mineralogy and such kindred subjects.

It is proposed, also, if our funds will permit, to cause the delivery of plain and popular lectures (comprehensible by all) on such subjects as astronomy, botany, and mineralogy—upon the recent improvements that may have been made in the arts and manufactures—upon the application of scientific discoveries, and on the result of the experience of practical observers as to agriculture and to those various trades and occupations which chiefly engross the attention of this district of the country.

These are not, I trust, over sanguine expectations. I think the acquisition of knowledge has a great tendency to multiply itself; and if I can only persuade you to enter upon that delightful path, I am sanguine enough to believe that there will be open to you gradual charms and temptations which will induce you to persevere. (Applause.)

But our immediate object is with the present rules and regulations of the society, and with that species of information which we can at once undertake to provide. [The right hon. baronet here proceeded to refer to the difficulties to be contended with in constituting such a society, explaining the course which he had thought proper to adopt in order to establish it, by calling a preliminary meeting for the purpose of considering, first, the policy of forming such an institution, and next, the regulations by which it should be conducted.] Sir Robert observed, that to that preliminary meeting he had invited all the chief authorities of the town—the ecclesiastical and the municipal authorities—the clergy, the mayor, the town-clerk, the aldermen, and all persons holding any public responsible employment. He also invited those who were chiefly concerned in manufactures, or in occupations which gave the greatest opportunity of employment to the working classes, without distinction of party, political opinion, or religious profession. A preliminary meeting must necessarily be limited as to numbers; and it was impossible to act upon any rule of selection without excluding many persons who, he was perfectly willing to admit, were quite as much entitled to be present as those who actually took a part in the preliminary proceedings; but he hoped he had said (527) enough to satisfy all that the exclusion was not a captious or an arbitrary one, but was unavoidable; and he therefore trusted no one would refuse his sanction to the institution on account of their exclusion from taking a part in the preliminary proceedings. (Applause.) The right hon. baronet proceeded to state, that at the preliminary meeting a very decided preponderance of opinion was in favour of the regulations which had been printed and circulated (applause), that in compliance with those regulations the subscribers entitled to vote had met and had appointed the officers of the institution, and the committee of management.

To the office of president Sir Robert Peel had been appointed (loud applause); to the office of treasurer, Mr. Bramall had been appointed; and to the office of honorary secretary, Mr. Gray. The committee of management consisted of the officers before mentioned, together with Sir Francis Lawley, Mr. John Hall, Mr. E. Hamel, Mr. W. Brindley, Mr. Francis Hunter, and Mr. S. Watton. It also consisted of three men who were entitled to exercise in the committee equal influence and equal power with those he had mentioned—namely, John Bailey, James Simmons, and Thomas Woodcock. The committee of management had met that morning, and had appointed the book committee. It consisted of the president, of the vicar, and one of the curates of Tamworth, to be named by the vicar (who were to hold their appointments *ex officio*, on account of their sacred functions), together with Mr. Pye, Mr. Wolferstan, and Mr. Stokes.

Now (said the right hon. baronet), I particularly call your attention to the appointment of this book committee, because I have reason to believe that the chief objection (I may almost say the only objection), which has been urged against these regulations is as to that particular rule which refers to the appointment of the book committee; and I should be particularly sorry, in addressing a public meeting of this nature, if I evaded, or on the other hand if I did not distinctly court, a reference to any regulation which has been the subject of doubt or objection. (Applause.) It is felt by some to be objectionable that two of the clergy of this great parish should, by virtue of their offices, be members of the book committee. I confess, for myself, that I do not feel the force of that objection. ('Hear' and applause.) I do not think it an unreasonable proposal that when we find public ministers of religion holding prominent and responsible offices, whose education necessarily implies that they are conversant with literary subjects and with literary works—who are endowed by the state for the performance of certain duties (those duties being immediately connected with the moral condition and improvement of the inhabitants of the districts committed to their charge)—I do say, it appears to me reasonable and just, not to invite them, but to require them, in the discharge of an important duty, to give us the advantage of their experience and their assistance. (Applause.) I know, at the same time, that it is perfectly right to be jealous of all power held by such a tenure, and I trust I am prepared to discuss with perfect temper, and in the spirit in which they ought to be discussed, any objections which intelligent and honourable men might make to any regulation of this institution. I say, then, it is right to consider whether the power given is liable to be abused, and what are the checks and restrictions upon this regulation. Now, it is quite true that two ministers of religion, and those of the established church, are, by a fundamental rule of this society, placed upon the book committee; but remember that they accept their appointments, and perform their duties, subject to this preliminary and fundamental rule, that no works of controversial divinity shall enter into the library. (Applause.) They accept their offices and perform their duties subject to this other rule, that, in the formation of the library, and in the selection of the subjects for public lectures, every thing calculated to excite religious or political animosity shall be excluded. (Applause.) They accept their powers subject to this other rule,—that no discussion on matters connected with religion, politics, or local party differences be permitted to take place in the reading room. However highly respectable and highly esteemed individuals may be, and however entitled to confidence, yet I am perfectly willing to admit that it is legitimate and right to be jealous of power. I ask you, however, not to consider detached regulations, but to look to the whole scope and tenor of the rules. The result of the regulations is, that two-thirds of the book committee are laymen—that the committee of management is wholly composed of laymen; and if, in the almost inconceivable case that these powers should be abused, an authority is reserved to the subscribers, by giving notice, of an alteration in the (528) fundamental regulations. Three-fifths of the subscribers have the power to alter these fundamental regulations;

and can I have a doubt that if the existing checks were not sufficient, that if the power were abused (as I hold it cannot be), the great body of the subscribers in this town would bring under consideration the propriety of altering the regulations? I do, therefore, hope, that when this subject is calmly considered, those who feel an objection (the force of which I have never seen) will not, on account of one single regulation, view that in a captious spirit, but look at the whole scope and tenor of these regulations, recollecting that we avow that in giving knowledge we wish to take every security against that knowledge being perverted to evil or immoral purposes.

We avow that as our great object; and, that being so, can any Dissenter from the establishment say that this is any interference with freedom of opinion, or that there is a chance, if this be the rule of the society, that his religious scruples can be invaded or be individually interfered with? My object has been to conciliate as much support as possible to an institution which I believe to be, if properly worked out, intimately connected with the rational amusement, recreation, and intellectual improvement of this neighbourhood. I have had objections to contend with of very opposite natures, and coming from very opposite directions. As far as I possibly could, consistently with my own convictions, I wished to pay every deference to those objections; all I ask in return is, that the whole scope of these regulations may be fairly and liberally considered, and that no one will refuse his sanction to this institution because there may be some one regulation which he thinks might possibly be omitted. (Applause.)

The library that we shall form will, I trust, contain works not merely connected with abstract science, but treatises coming home to the daily business and daily interests of those who are concerned in the pursuits of active industry. Now, let me take two departments of knowledge, on which I think most useful information might be deposited in a library of this kind. Let me first speak of works connected with agricultural improvement, and let me make an earnest appeal to that most valuable and respectable class of society, I mean the farmers of this country, to whom we are so much indebted for their general deportment, and whose respectability and success are intimately connected with the best interests of this country. (Applause.) I am perfectly prepared to hear from them that they receive with great distrust the advice of persons who are not practically connected with farming. No one is more deeply satisfied than I am that it is much easier to talk of farming than to farm. I am not surprised that they (the farmers) distrust the theories of speculative farmers. I am not surprised that they listen with distrust to the result of experiments much more extensive than their capital enables them to engage in. I consider those feelings to be perfectly rational and perfectly natural; but, on the other hand, if the farmers of this neighbourhood (because they are practical farmers) think that their experience is all-sufficient—if they think that they have nothing to learn—if they think they can safely neglect the opportunities of acquiring knowledge connected with their proper business, let me tell them that they labour under a greater and more dangerous delusion than the gentlemen who undertake to instruct them. (Applause.) If you are satisfied with the limited experience that your own farm affords—if you really believe that the farming in your particular parish admits of no improvement let me remind you, that these were the impressions entertained 50 years since, and 100 years since, by practical farmers, who then thought, I have no doubt, that there was nothing to be learned, and that there could be no advantage in attempting to benefit by the experience and experiments of others. Now, with respect to works on agriculture, which might be included in the library of this institution, let me ask any reasonable man, whatever might be his practical experience, whether he does not think it highly probable that advantages might be derived by his having access, on the payment of 1s. quarterly, to such information as may be deposited in this library? [The right hon. baronet referred to the information contained in treatises on agriculture, mentioning *Remarks on Thorough Draining and Deep Ploughing*, by Mr. James Smith.] Was it possible there could be any harm—not in a farmer being forced to adopt this system of farming—but in hearing what was the result of experiments? This little book was given to him (Sir R. Peel) by that eminent man, Dr. Buckland, the great geologist, on his return from Scotland, after having had an opportunity of witnessing the improvements on the farm of Mr. Smith. The right hon. baronet, in alluding to a treatise he had lately received, *A Report on the Diseases to which the Wheat Plant is Liable*, observed, that if the farmer told him that he had information on the subject already, he would inform him that Professor Henslow, the Professor of Botany at Cambridge, had stated, in reference to treatises written for a prize offered by the English Agricultural Society for the best essay on this subject, that it was evident to him (Professor Henslow) that the authors (529) were ignorant of many facts well known to scientific men for many years, respecting the nature of those diseases, and the causes producing them; and that in point of fact no one treatise sent was deemed deserving of the prize. It appeared to him (Sir R. Peel) that the farmer, whatever importance he might attach to practical experience, could not deny that he might derive great benefit from reading treatises on this and various other subjects—such as the proper time for laying manure on the ground, the chymical properties of that manure, and the liability of the volatile parts flying off into the atmosphere.

It has also been suggested that popular lectures might be given on a subject of the greatest importance—upon the simplest method of keeping a clear account of profit and loss. (Applause.) Now, he was informed that nothing could be more imperfect than the accounts which were kept by a farmer of the daily outgoings of his farm and the profit returned from actual outlay. Nor could he doubt that if a farmer were instructed as to the most simple method of keeping such an account, and was supplied with a book containing the proper form, the greatest advantages might be derived from his having the opportunity of judging of such improvements as the one he (Sir R. Peel) had been referring to.

The right hon. baronet next referred to the advantages which such a society might afford by containing within its library the most recent information upon the subject of colonization, as to the cost of emigration, the amount of capital required, and the comparative advantages held out in different colonies. But (said Sir R. Peel) these are merely examples of the information which might be made easily accessible. Every newspaper teems with notices of publications, written upon popular principles, detailing all the recent discoveries in science and their connexion with improvements in arts and manufactures.

Let me earnestly entreat you not to neglect the opportunity which we are now willing to afford you. It will not be our fault if the ample page of knowledge, rich with the spoils of time, is not unrolled to you. You will not be able to say that 'chill penury' has 'frozen the genial current' of your aspirations for knowledge and distinction. We tell you that here is access for you to that information which may at the same time facilitate your advance in your worldly occupations and lay the foundation for mental improvement. (Applause.) Do not be deceived by the sneers that you hear against knowledge, which are uttered by men who want to depress you, and keep you depressed, to the level of their own contented ignorance. (Renewed plaudits.) Do not believe that you have not time (that is what you will hear) for rational recreation. (Applause.) Now, believe me, that it is the idle man who wants time for everything. (Laughter and applause.) The industrious man, the man who is persevering in his pursuits, is the man who knows the value of the economy of time, and can find leisure for rational recreation as well as for his attention to his business. (Continued applause.) Do not believe that the acquisition of knowledge, of such knowledge as we shall offer you, is inconsistent with the success of your worldly pursuits. Depend upon it you cannot exercise and sharpen your intellectual faculties in one branch of knowledge without becoming better men of business in consequence. (Applause.) Depend also upon this, that there is a spirit of inquiry afloat, and that there is a degree of competition requiring the utmost mental activity and exertion. Every steamboat, every railroad, all the facilities of intercourse, are operating as premiums upon skill and intelligence. (Applause.) They are shortening the distance between the producer and the consumer; it is not safe for you to remain behindhand; for, depend upon it, if you are inferior in point of skill, in point of intelligence, in point of general knowledge, to the manufacturers and producers of other districts, those increased facilities of intercourse to which I have been referring will transfer the demand from you to others; and you will be labouring under a fatal delusion if you place confidence in those sneers to which I have alluded, and if you believe that increased intelligence is incompatible with worldly success. On the contrary, I believe that society is now in the position that increased intelligence and increased knowledge are absolutely essential to success in your worldly pursuits. (Applause.)

Again, do not believe that science is not a field which is perfectly open to you, whatever may be your occupations and conditions in life. I ask you to consider the names of those men who, at the present moment, or within your own memory, have acquired for themselves immortal fame by their eminence in the arts and sciences. I ask you to call to mind the names of Mr. Rennie, the great engineer, of Sir Humphry Davy, of Professor Faraday, of Sir Francis Chantry, of Mr. Wheatstone, the inventor of the electrical telegraphs, and of a hundred others I might name—to consider their first position in life, the difficulties which they had to struggle with and to search out in their early origin—not for the purpose of despising it, but of admiring the more the interval between their origin and the eminence to which they subsequently attained. (Applause.)

I have made inquiry upon the subject, and I (530) cannot help reading to you one or two of the answers I have received on the subject of eminent men of the present day who acquired knowledge, and by the simple determination to overcome every difficulty that poverty or a low condition might oppose, and to raise themselves from it. (Applause.) [The right hon. baronet here read a letter, dated the 5th of January, stating that Mr. Grainger, the great architect, who had rebuilt the town of Newcastle-upon-Tyne, within a few years, in a style infinitely superior to Regent-street, and whom he (the writer) met at the Duke of Northumberland's a short time since, began his career as a poor mason's boy carrying a hod of mortar.] In the interval between 1834 and 1838 he converted Newcastle from a black and thick cluster of brick to a condition exceeding anything he (the writer) had seen, except in the best parts of Edinburgh. In a postscript to the letter it was also stated, that the late Mr. Harvey, who died at an early age, a Professor at Woolwich, published an excellent work on meteorology: he worked for many years as a carpenter in the dockyard at Plymouth, afterwards became a teacher of mathematics, and was advanced to the professorship abovementioned. The right hon. baronet observed, that he had in his possession a letter from the writer of this treatise on meteorology to one of the most eminent men of the present day. That letter was indeed to his (Sir R. Peel's) purpose, and he would not withhold from the meeting its contents. The author of it was cold in the grave, but it was a voice from the grave, and entitled on that account to the highest authority. Sir Robert Peel here read the letter, dated the 31st of March, 1834, of which the following is the substance:—

'In forwarding these papers for acceptance to men bred and educated at Oxford, he (Mr. Harvey) confessed he felt much diffidence and fear; and nothing but the great and unexampled personal kindness he had experienced during the visits of the British Association, and the kind indulgence shown towards him, could have got the better of those feelings. He would, therefore, be pleased to regard the work as the production of one blessed at that time with nothing like unbroken leisure, and all whose early days were lost amidst vulgar associates in a carpenter's workshop, and whose education never reached beyond reading and writing. He wrote this in all the fullness of those feelings which beat high, and which looked back with the most poignant regret on the years that were spent in heartless labour, and without a friend to open to him a path which might have led to academical distinction, and by consequence to some higher and brighter prospects in the world.'

Why (said the hon. baronet), if we should have some such kindred spirit in this town that should be drawn from these heartless associates, and, instead of spending his time among vulgar amusements, should have the means of procuring access to those treatises which this man wanted, and the absence of which he lamented, shall we not be tenfold repaid by the reflection that we have given such a man an opportunity of rescuing himself from such associations, and of enabling him to walk in early life in a path that leads to virtuous fame. (Applause.)

But if you still want any additional proof that the heights of science are not closed to the humblest amongst you, look around, I say, at this neighbourhood. If you go to Lichfield, you see the statue of Dr. Johnson. If you go to Handsworth, you see the statue of Mr. Watt. Look in this very town, and who is the man that is now engaged in extensive works for the purpose of bringing coal and lime under your immediate command? Mr. Stephenson, the engineer. Mr. Stephenson, I am assured, worked for three years as a boy in the meanest capacity in a colliery at Newcastle. He saved 100 *l*. by mending the watches of his fellow-workmen for half-a-crown a piece; and he devoted that 100 *l*. to provision for his indigent parents, and set out with a light heart and conscience for the purpose of accumulating more. The result has been that he presents a daily example of encouragement to our eyes, and brought within our immediate contemplation in this town. He presents another example, where, from the lowest origin, merit has been able to raise itself to high eminence and great respect. (Applause.)

My appeal in my recent observations has been addressed chiefly to you who compose the working classes, or to men engaged in the pursuits of active industry, to induce you to enroll yourselves as members of this institution. I now make an appeal to others in more prosperous circumstances, who probably have had an education which enables them fully to appreciate the advantages of knowledge, and who are enabled, if they will exercise their power out of their affluent means, to spare what may be sufficient to insure the perfect success of this institution. I hope they will not be deterred from it by any belief that they are risking injurious consequences, either to the moral or religious character of the people, by giving them the opportunity of acquiring such knowledge, and such only, as that which we profess to give. For myself, I cannot believe that we shall be interfering with any legitimate object of human policy; or that we shall be counteracting any of the purposes of that Almighty Being, who has intrusted us with faculties which (531) distinguish us from the beasts that perish, and who will demand from us a severe account of the manner in which those faculties have been employed.

I cannot think that we shall dissatisfy men with their lot, by proving to them that avenues of distinction are open to merit alone (whatever be the lot and condition of men) can secure access and gain the prize. I cannot help thinking that by bringing together, in an institution of this kind, intelligent men of all classes and all conditions in life, by uniting together, as we have united, in the committee of this institution the gentleman of ancient family and great landed possessions with the skilful mechanic and artificer of good character.—I cannot help thinking that we are all establishing a bond of social connexion that will derive more than common strength from the pure motives that influence us, and from the cause in which we are engaged. (Applause.) I cannot help believing that we are harmonizing the gradations of society, and binding men together by a new bond, which, as I said before, will have more than ordinary strength on account of the object which unites us. (Loud applause.) Nay, I am sanguine enough to believe that this very institution will afford the opportunity of honourable and appropriate reward to humble merit.

In a society limited like this, small in point of numbers, it is very difficult to find any distinctions of an honourable nature; but I must say, that I was forcibly struck on Saturday last by a distinction which was paid, and which I cannot help thinking must have a powerful effect in encouraging men to honourable conduct, and also to intellectual improvement. The subscribers to this institution on Saturday last were called upon to give their votes in favour of those who should be placed upon the committee of management. There was one individual who united, without exception, every vote which was given. There being 57 votes to give, those votes were given (in a single case only) unanimously in favour of one individual. I did think it was a remarkable and most honourable and encouraging compliment, on chancing to cast my eyes on the voting papers, to find that every man (whatever was his condition) had delivered in a paper which contained the name of 'James Simmons' (applause): and I think you will agree with me, that that man must be dead to every impulse of honourable fame who did not envy the feelings of James Simmons, when, by the unanimous voice of every one entitled to vote, he was called upon to take his place on the committee of management of this institution. (Applause.)

I cannot believe that there is any risk to religious impressions and religious belief by opening the avenues to literary acquirements. I agree with the Bishop of London in the opinions which he has delivered upon that subject in the sermon which he preached on the opening of King's College. He expressed sentiments, in language worthy of the sentiments which it conveyed, and in which I for one cordially concur. [The right hon. baronet here read an extract from the sermon alluded to, in which the Bishop of London observed, that there was nothing in the revealed will of God which limited and restrained the inquiries and conclusions of man in any branch of knowledge properly so called, or which interfered with the freest exercise of his faculties; but that the very constitution of man, which led him to indefinite inquiry, and which was adapted to it, afforded a sufficient reason for believing that its Divine Author intended it for that purpose. The principle of curiosity was almost the first which manifested itself in the human mind. The sagacity of the elephant, though it might differ in different individuals of the same species, and although by some it might be differently exerted, was at all times a definite quality; whereas the faculties of man were sharpened and strengthened by exercise, the capacities of his mind were enlarged, and past experience was made the ground of future improvement. Under proper limitations, they might join in the praises lavished upon philosophy and science, and go forth with their votaries in the various paths of research by which the mind of man was enlightened and instructed. Such studies removed the veil which to the ignorant or careless observer obscured the traces of God's glory in the works of his hands.] That (said the (532) hon. baronet) I firmly believe. I never can think it possible that a mind can be so constituted that, after being familiarized with the great truth of observing in every object of contemplation that nature presents the manifest proofs of a Divine intelligence—if you range even from the organization of the meanest weed you trample upon, or of the insect that lives but for an hour, up to the magnificent structure of the heavens, and the still more wonderful phenomena of the soul, and reason, and conscience of man—I cannot believe that any man accustomed to such contemplations can retire from them with any other feelings than those of enlarged conceptions of the Divine power, and greater reverence for the name of the Almighty Creator of the Universe.

We believe, on the contrary, that the man accustomed to such contemplations will feel the moral dignity of his own nature exalted; and, struck with awe by the manifold proofs of infinite power and infinite wisdom, will yield more ready and hearty assent—yes, the assent of the heart, and not only of the understanding—to the pious exclamation, 'Oh, Lord, how glorious are Thy works; Thy thoughts are very deep. An unwise man doth not consider, and a fool doth not understand.' (Applause.) It is the unwise man, and the fool, that form unworthy conceptions of the Divine nature and the Divine power. Far different were the impressions of those mighty spirits who have the most considered this, and have made the greatest (however imperfect) advances towards the understanding of it. These are the thoughts with which Sir Isaac Newton concludes his profound speculations into the material causes which produce and into the laws which regulate the motions of the heavens; he says, 'This beautiful system of sun, planets, and comets, can have its origin in no other way than by the purpose and command of an intelligent and powerful Being. He governs all things not as the sovereign of this world, but as the Lord of the Universe. He is not only God but Lord or Governor. We know him only by his properties and attributes—by the wise and admirable structure of things around us. We admire Him on account of his perfections—we venerate and worship Him on account of His government.' These are the thoughts from which Sir Humphry Davy, in his last illness, derived according to his own expression, pleasure and consolation, when every other source of pleasure and consolation had failed him. He is speaking of the moral and intellectual qualities of the true scientific inquirer into natural philosophy. He says—'His mind should always be awake to devotional feeling; and in contemplating the variety and beauty of the external world, and developing its scientific wonder, he will always refer to that Infinite Wisdom through whose beneficence he is permitted to enjoy knowledge. In becoming wiser he will become better; he will rise at once in the scale of intellectual and moral existence; his increased sagacity will be subservient to a more exalted faith; and, in proportion as the veil becomes thinner through which he sees the causes of things, he will admire more the brightness of the Divine light by which they are rendered perceptible.' That (said the right hon. baronet) is my belief.

My belief and hope are that an increased sagacity will administer to an exalted fame—that it will make men not merely believe in the cold doctrines of natural religion, but that it will so prepare and temper the spirit and understanding, that they will be better qualified to comprehend the great scheme of human redemption. (Loud applause.) My firm belief is, that that superior sagacity which is most conversant with the course and constitution of nature, which sees the wonderful preparations that are made for the subsistence and enjoyment of the meanest animal, will be the first to believe that that Almighty Being who has made such preparation for mere physical enjoyments has not left in neglect and indifference the immortal soul of man. Knowing the difficulties that attend every object which we can see, observing the gradual system of progression and change, and that one course of existence is made preparatory for another, I am sanguine enough to believe that that superior sagacity will be the first to turn a deaf ear to objections and presumptions against revealed religion, will be the first to acknowledge the complete harmony of the Christian dispensation with all that reason, assisted by revelation, tells us of the course and constitution of nature. These are serious and solemn subjects, but I hope not unfitted for an occasion when we contemplate an institution of this nature. (Applause.) They contain at least an exposition of my views and hopes, with respect to the progress of knowledge, which alone could induce me to take a part in an establishment of this kind.

I will now release you. I shall shortly leave you, for the purpose of engaging in the scenes of warfare on the great arena of political contention; but if I can believe that before my departure I have laid the foundation stone of an edifice in which men of all political opinions and of all religious feelings may unite in the furtherance of knowledge without the asperities of party feeling—if I can entertain the hope that there will be the means afforded of useful occupation and rational recreation—that men will prefer the pleasures of knowledge above (533) the indulgence of sensual appetite that there is a prospect of contributing to the intellectual and moral improvement of this town and neighbourhood, then I can safely say that I shall be repaid, with tenfold interest, for any time I have spent or any attention I have given to the formation of this institution. (The right hon. baronet resumed his seat amid loud and general plaudits.)

Sir F. LAWLEY, Bart., then rose and said, that high and elevated as must have been their gratification in listening to the speech which they had just heard, he was quite sure they could not depart to their homes with any degree of satisfaction if they had not an opportunity of expressing to Sir R. Peel their heartfelt acknowledgments for that address—an address distinguished by so much kindness, good feeling, and friendship, but above all, by that deeply religious feeling which he had instilled into all their hearts and minds upon the present interesting occasion. (Applause.) He now proposed to that meeting that they should all rise from their seats in token of thanks to Sir R. Peel.

The company simultaneously rose, and expressed their approbation amid loud and general applause.

Sir R. PEEL said he was deeply grateful for the very kind manner in which they had received his humble exertions. Every effort of his life should be directed towards the improvement, in every sense, of that town and neighbourhood, with the welfare of which his own interests were immediately connected, and which, from every circumstance of neighbourhood, residence, of early association, and intimacy of kind friends, commanded his warmest and most affectionate attachment.

The meeting then broke up.

'An aristocracy of exalted spirits'

Newman's Letters of Catholicus

THE TIMES, FRIDAY, 5 FEBRUARY 1841

SIR ROBERT PEEL'S LATE ADDRESS AT TAMWORTH.

LETTER I.

TO THE EDITOR OF THE TIMES.

Sir,—Sir Robert Peel's (534) position in the country and his high character render it impossible that his words and deeds should be other than public property. This alone would furnish an apology for my calling the attention of your readers to the startling language, which many of them doubtless have already observed, in the Address which this most excellent and distinguished man has lately delivered, upon the establishment of a Library and Reading-room at Tamworth: but he has superseded the need of apology altogether, by proceeding to present it to the public in the form of a pamphlet. His speech, then, becomes important, both from the name and the express act of its author. At the same time I must allow that he has not published it in the fulness in which it was spoken. Still it seems to me right and fair, or rather imperative, to animadvert upon it as it has appeared in your columns, since in that shape it will have the widest circulation. A public man must not claim to harangue the whole world in newspapers, and then to offer his second thoughts to such as choose to buy them at a bookseller's.

I shall surprise no one who has carefully read Sir Robert's Address, and perhaps all who have not, by stating my conviction, that, did a person take it up without looking at the title-page, he would to a certainty set it down to be a production of the years 1827 and 1828, the scene Gower-street, the speaker Mr. Brougham or Dr. Lushington, and the occasion, the laying the first stone or the inauguration of the then called London University. I profess myself quite unable to draw any satisfactory line of difference between the Gower-street and the Tamworth exhibition, except, of course, that Sir Robert's personal religious feeling breaks out in his Address across his assumed philosophy. I say assumed; I might say affected—for I think too well of him to believe it genuine.

On the occasion in question Sir Robert gave expression to a theory of morals and religion, which of course, in a popular speech, was not put out in a very dogmatic form, but which, when analyzed and fitted together, reads somewhat as follows:—

Human nature, he seems to say, if left to itself, becomes sensual and degraded. Uneducated men live in the indulgence of their passions, or, if they are merely taught to read, they dissipate and debase their minds by trifling on vicious publications. Education is the cultivation of the intellect and heart, and useful knowledge is the great instrument of education. It is the parent of virtue, the nurse of religion; it exalts man to his highest perfection, and is the sufficient scope of his most earnest exertions.

Physical and moral science rouses, transports, exalts, enlarges, tranquillizes, and satisfies the mind. Its attractiveness obtains a hold over us; the excitement attending it supersedes grosser excitements; it makes us know our duty, and thereby enables us to do it; by taking the mind off itself, it destroys anxiety; and by providing objects of admiration, it soothes and subdues us.

And, in addition, it is a kind of neutral ground, on which men of every shade of politics and religion may meet together, disabuse each other of their prejudices, form intimacies, and practise co-operation.

This, it is almost needless to say, is the very theory, expressed temperately, in which Mr. Brougham once expatiated in the Glasgow and London Universities. Sir R. Peel, indeed, has spoken with somewhat of his characteristic moderation; but for his closeness in sentiment to the Brougham of other days, a few parallels from their respective discourses will be a sufficient voucher.

For instance, Mr. Brougham, in his Discourse upon Science, and his Pursuit of Knowledge under Difficulties, wrote about the 'pure delight' of physical knowledge, of its 'pure gratification,' of its tendency 'to purify and elevate man's nature,' of its 'elevating and refining it,' of its 'giving a dignity and *importance* to the enjoyment of life.' Sir Robert, pursuing the idea, shows us its importance even in death, observing, that physical knowledge supplies the thoughts from which 'a great experimentalist professed *in his last illness* to derive some pleasure and some consolation, when most other sources of consolation and pleasure were closed to him.'

Mr. Brougham talked much and eloquently of 'the *sweetness* of knowledge' and 'the *charms* of philosophy,' of students 'smitten with the love of knowledge,' of 'wooing truth with the unwearying ardour of a lover,' of 'keen and overpowering emotion,' of 'ecstacy,' of 'the absorbing passion of knowledge,' of 'the strength of the passion, and the exquisite pleasure of its gratification.' And Sir Robert, in less glowing language, but even in a more tender strain than Mr. Brougham, exclaims, 'If I can only persuade you to enter upon that *delightful* path, I am sanguine enough to believe that there *will be open to you gradual charms and temptations* which will induce you to persevere.'

Mr. Brougham naturally went on to enlarge upon 'bold and successful adventures in the pursuit;' such, perhaps, as in the story of 'Paris and Helen,' or 'Hero and Leander;' of 'daring ambition in its course to greatness,' of 'enterprising spirits,' and their 'brilliant feats,' 'adventures of the world of intellect,' and of 'the illustrious vanquishers of fortune.' And Sir Robert, not to be outdone, echoes back '*aspirations* for knowledge and distinction,' 'simple determination of overcoming difficulties,' 'premiums on skill and intelligence,' 'mental activity,' 'steamboats and railroads,' 'producer and consumer,' 'spirit of inquiry afloat;' and he breaks out into almost conventicle eloquence—'Every newspaper *teems with notices* of publications written upon *popular principles*, detailing all the recent discoveries of science, and their connexion with improvements in arts and manufactures. *Let me earnestly entreat* you not to neglect the *opportunity* which we are now willing to afford you! *It will not be our fault* if the ample page of knowledge, rich with the spoils of time, is not unrolled to you! *We tell you*,' &c. &c.

Mr. Brougham pronounces that a man by 'learning truths wholly new to him,' and by 'satisfying himself of the grounds on which known truths rest,' 'will enjoy a *proud consciousness* of having, by his own exertions, become a *wiser*, and *therefore* a more *exalted*, creature.' Sir Robert runs abreast of this great sentiment. He tells us, in words which he adopts as his own, that a man 'in becoming *wiser* will become *better*:' he will 'rise *at once* in the scale of intellectual and moral existence, and by being accustomed to such contemplations, he will feel the *moral dignity* of his nature *exalted*.'

Peel's Address and the Catholicus Letters

Mr. Brougham, on his Inauguration at Glasgow, spoke to the ingenuous youth assembled on the occasion, of 'the benefactors of mankind, when they rest from their pious labours, looking down upon the blessings with which their toils and sufferings have clothed the scene of their former existence;' and in his Discourse upon Science he declared it to be 'no mean reward of our labour to become acquainted with the prodigious genius of those who have almost exalted the nature of man above his destined sphere;' and who 'hold a station apart, rising over *all* the great teachers of mankind, and spoken of reverently,' as if Newton and La Place were not the names of mortal men. Sir Robert cannot of course equal this sublime flight: but he succeeds in calling Newton and others 'those mighty spirits which have made the *greatest* (though imperfect) advances towards the understanding' of 'the divine nature and power.'

Mr. Brougham talked at Glasgow about putting to flight the 'evil spirits of *tyranny and persecution* which haunted the long night now gone down the sky,' and about men 'no longer suffering themselves to be led *blindfold in ignorance;*' and in his Pursuit of Knowledge he speaks of Pascal having, 'under the influence of certain religious views, during a period of *depression*, conceived' scientific pursuits 'to be little better than abuse of his time and faculties.' Sir Robert, fainter in tone, but true to the key, warns his hearers—'Do not be deceived by the sneers that you *hear* against knowledge, which are uttered by men who *want to depress you*, and keep you depressed to the level of their *own contented ignorance.*'

Mr. Brougham laid down at Glasgow the infidel principle, or, as he styles it, 'the great truth,' which 'has gone forth to all the ends of the earth, that man shall no more render account to man for his belief, over which he has himself no control.' And Dr. Lushington applied it in Gower-street to the case of the college then and there rising, by asking, 'Will any one argue for establishing a *monopoly* to be enjoyed by the few who are of one *denomination* of the Christian church only?' And he went on to speak of the association and union of all *without exclusion or restriction*, of 'friendships cementing the bond of charity, and softening the *asperities* which (537) ignorance and separation have fostered.' Long may it be before Sir Robert Peel professes the great principle itself! even though, as the following passages show, he is inconsistent enough to think highly of its *application* in the culture of the mind. For instance, he speaks of 'this preliminary and fundamental rule, that no works of *controversial divinity* shall enter into the library (applause),'—of 'the institution being open to all persons of all descriptions, without reference to political opinions or *religious creed*,'—and of 'an edifice in which men of all political opinions and *all religious* feelings may unite in the furtherance of knowledge, without the *asperities* of party feeling.' Now, that British society should consist of persons of different religions, is this a positive standing evil, to be endured at best as unavoidable, or a topic of exultation? Of exultation[,] answers[;] Sir Robert; the greater differences the better, the more the merrier. So we interpret his tone.

It is reserved for few to witness the triumph of their own opinions; much less to witness it in the instance of their own direct and personal opponents. Whether the Lord Brougham of this day feels all that satisfaction and inward peace which he attributes to success of whatever kind in intellectual efforts, it is not for me to decide; but that he has achieved, to speak in his own style, a mighty victory, and is leading in chains behind his chariot-wheels a great captive, is a fact beyond question. Such is the reward in 1841 for unpopularity in 1827.

What, however, is a boast to Lord Brougham, is in the same proportion a slur upon the fair fame of Sir Robert Peel, at least in the judgment of those who have hitherto been his friends. Were there no other reason against the doctrines propounded in the Address which has been the subject of these remarks (but I hope to be allowed an opportunity of assigning others), its parentage would be a grave *primâ facie* difficulty in receiving it. It is, indeed, most melancholy to see so sober and experienced a thinker practising the antics of one of the wildest performers of this wild age; and taking off the tone, manner, and gesture of the versatile ex-Chancellor, with a versatility almost equal to his own. Yet let him be assured that the task of rivalling him is hopeless as well as unprofitable. No one can equal the great sophist. Lord Brougham is inimitable in his own line.

Peel's Address and the Catholicus Letters

THE TIMES, TUESDAY, 9 FEBRUARY 1841

SIR R. PEEL'S ADDRESS AT TAMWORTH.

———•—•———

LETTER II.
TO THE EDITOR OF THE TIMES.

Sir,—A distinguished Conservative statesman (538) tells us from the Town-hall of Tamworth, that 'in becoming wiser a man will become better;' meaning by wiser, more conversant with the facts and theories of physical science; and that such a man will 'rise *at once* into the scale of intellectual and *moral* existence.' 'That,' he adds, 'is my belief.' He avows also, that the fortunate individual whom he is describing, by being 'accustomed to such contemplations, will feel the *moral dignity of his nature exalted;*' which I suppose is intended to imply that it *is* exalted, as well as is felt to be. He speaks also of physical knowledge as 'being the means of useful occupation and rational recreation;' of 'the pleasures of knowledge' superseding 'the indulgence of sensual appetite,' and of its 'contributing to the intellectual and *moral improvement* of the community.' Accordingly, he very consistently wishes it to be set before 'the female as well as the male portion of the population;' otherwise, as he truly observes, 'great injustice would be done to the well-educated and virtuous women' of the place. They, then, are to 'have equal power and equal influence with others.' It will be difficult to exhaust the reflections which rise in the mind on reading avowals of this nature.

The first question which obviously suggests itself, is *how* these wonderful moral effects are to be wrought under the instrumentality of the physical sciences. Can the process be analysed and drawn out, or does it act like a dose or a charm which comes into general use empirically? Does Sir Robert Peel mean to say, that whatever be the occult reasons for the result, so it is—you have but to drench the popular mind with physics, and moral and religious advancement follows on the whole, in spite of individual failures? Yet when has the experiment been tried on so large a scale as to justify such anticipations? Or rather, does he mean, that from the nature of the case, he who is imbued with science and literature, unless adverse influences interfere, cannot but be a better man? It is natural and becoming to seek for some clear idea of the meaning of so dark an oracle. To know is one thing, to do is another; the two things are altogether distinct. A man knows he should get up in the morning—he lies a-bed; he knows he should not lose his temper, yet he cannot keep it. A labouring man knows he should not go to the ale-house, and his wife knows she should not filch when she goes out charing; but, nevertheless, in these cases the consciousness of a duty is not all one with the performance of it. There are, then, large families of instances, to say the least, in which men may become wiser, without becoming better; what, then, is the meaning of this great maxim in the mouth of its promulgators?

Mr. Bentham would answer, that the knowledge which involves virtue is the knowledge how to take care of number one—a clear appreciation of what is pleasurable, what painful, and what promotes the one and averts the other. An uneducated man is ever mistaking his own interest, and standing in the way of his (539) own enjoyments. Useful knowledge is that which tends to make us more useful to ourselves—a most definite and intelligible account of the matter, and needing no explanation. But it would be a great injustice, both to Lord Brougham and to Sir Robert, to suppose, when they talk of knowledge being virtue, that they are Benthamising. Bentham had not a spark of poetry in him; on the contrary, there is much of high aspiration, generous sentiment, and impassioned feeling, in the tone of Lord Brougham and Sir Robert. They speak of knowledge as something 'pulchrum,' fair and glorious, exalted above the range of ordinary humanity, and so little connected with the personal interest of its votaries, that, though Sir Robert does *obiter* talk of improved modes of draining and the chymical properties of manure, yet he must not be supposed to come short of the lofty enthusiasm of Lord Brougham, who expressly panegyrises certain ancient philosophers who gave up riches, retired into solitude, or embraced a life of travel, smit with a sacred curiosity about physical or mathematical truth.

Here Mr. Bentham, did it fall to him to offer a criticism, doubtless would take leave to inquire whether such fine language was any better than a set of words representing nothing—flowers of rhetoric, which bloom, smell sweet, and die. But it is impossible to suspect so grave and practical a man as Sir Robert Peel of using words literally without any meaning at all; and though I think at best they have not a very profound meaning, yet, such as it is, we ought to attempt to draw it out.

Now, without being exact in using theological language, we may surely take it for granted, from the experience of facts, that the human mind is at best in a very unformed or disordered state; passions and conscience, likings and reason, being in conflict, might against right, and the prospect of getting worse. Under these circumstances, what is it that the school of philosophy in which Sir Robert has enrolled himself proposes to accomplish? Not a victory of the mind over itself—not the supremacy of the law—not the education[1] of the rebels—not the unity of our complex nature—not an harmonizing of the chaos— but the mere *lulling* of the passions by *turning* the course of thought; not a change of character, but a removal of temptation. This should be carefully observed. When a husband is gloomy, or an old woman peevish and fretful, persons about them do all they can to keep dangerous topics and causes of offence out of the way, and think themselves lucky if, by such careful management, they get through the day without an outbreak. When a child cries, the nurserymaid dances it about, or points out the pretty black horses out of window, or shows how ashamed poll parrot or poor puss is of its tantarums. Such is the sort of prescription which Sir Robert Peel offers to the good people of Tamworth. He makes no pretence of subduing the giant nature in which we were born, of smiting the loins of the domestic enemies of our peace, of overthrowing passion and fortifying reason; he does but offer to bribe the foe with gifts which will avail for the purpose just so long as they *will* avail and no longer. This was mainly the philosophy of the great Tully, except when he spoke as a stoic. Cicero handed the recipe to Brougham, and Brougham has passed it on (540) to Peel. If we examine the old Roman's meaning in 'O *philosophia, vitæ dux*,' it was neither more nor less than this—that *while* we were thinking of philosophy, we were not thinking of anything else; we did not feel grief, or anxiety, or passion, or ambition, or hatred; and the only point was to keep thinking of it. *How* to keep thinking of it was *extra artem*. If a man was in grief, he was to be amused; if disappointed, to be excited; if in a rage, to be soothed; if in love, to be roused to the pursuit of glory.

---

[1] Erratum for 'reduction' (*The Times*, 11 February 1841).

No inward change was contemplated, but a change of external objects; as if we were all White Ladies or Undines, our moral life being one of impulse and emotion, not subjected to laws, not consisting in habits, not capable of growth. When Cicero was outwitted by Cæsar, he solaced himself with Plato; when he lost his daughter, he wrote a treatise on consolation. Such, too, was the philosophy of that Lydian city, mentioned by the historian, who in a famine played at dice to stay their stomachs. And such is the rule of life advocated by Lord Brougham; and though, of course, he protests that knowledge 'must invigorate the mind as well as entertain it, and refine and elevate the character, while it gives listlessness and weariness their most agreeable excitement and relaxation,' yet his notions of vigour and elevation, when analyzed, will be found to resolve themselves into a mere preternatural excitement under the influence of some stimulating object, or the peace which is attained by there being nothing to quarrel with. He speaks of philosophers leaving the care of their estates, or declining public honours, from the greater desirableness of knowledge, envies the shelter enjoyed in the University of Glasgow from the noise and bustle of the world, and, *apropos* of Pascal and Cowper, 'so mighty,' says he, 'is the power of intellectual occupation, to make the heart forget, *for the time*, its most prevailing griefs, and to change its deepest gloom to sunshine.'

Whether Sir Robert Peel meant all this, which others have meant before him, it is impossible to say; but I will be bound, if he did not mean this, he meant nothing else, and his words will certainly insinuate this meaning, wherever a reader is not content to go without any at all. They will countenance, with his high authority, what in one form or other is a chief error of the day, in very distinct schools of opinion— that our true excellence comes not from within, but from without; not wrought out through personal struggles and sufferings, but following upon a passive exposure to influences over which we have no control. They will countenance the theory that diversion is the instrument of improvement, and excitement the condition of right action; and whereas diversions cease to be diversions if they are constant, and excitements by their very nature have a crisis and run through a (541) course, they will tend to make novelty ever in request, and will set the great teachers of morals upon the incessant search after stimulants and sedatives, by which unruly nature may, *pro re natâ*, be kept in order.

Hence, be it observed, Lord Brougham, in the last quoted sentence, tells us with much accuracy of statement, that 'intellectual occupation made the heart' of Pascal or Cowper *for the time forget its griefs.'* He frankly offers us a philosophy of expedients: he shows us how to live by medicine. Digestive pills half an hour before dinner, and a posset at bed-time at the best; and at the last, dram-drinking and opium—the very remedy against broken fortunes or remorse of conscience which is in request among the many in gin palaces *not* intellectual.

And if these remedies be but of temporary effect at the utmost, more commonly they will have none effect at all. Strong liquors do for a time succeed in their object; but who was ever consoled in real trouble by the small beer of literature or science? 'Sir,' said Rasselas, to the philosopher who had lost his daughter, 'mortality is an event by which a wise man can never be surprised.' 'Young man,' answered the mourner, 'you speak like one that hath never felt the pangs of separation. What comfort can truth or reason afford me? Of what effect are they now but to tell me that my daughter will not be restored?' Or who was ever made more humble or more benevolent by being told, as the same practical moralist words it, 'to concur with the great and unchangeable scheme of universal felicity, and co-operate with the general dispensation and tendency of the present system of things?' Or who was made to do any secret sort of self-denial, or was steeled against pain or peril, by all the lore of the infidel La Place, or those other 'mighty spirits' which Lord Brougham and Sir Robert eulogize? Or when was a choleric temperament ever brought under by a scientific King Canute planting his professor's chair before the rising waves? And as to the keen and ecstatic pleasures which Lord Brougham, not to say Sir Robert, ascribes to intellectual pursuit and conquest, I cannot help thinking that in that line they will find themselves outbid in the market by ratifications much closer at hand, and more level to the meanest capacity. Sir Robert makes it a boast that women are to be members of his institution; it is hardly necessary to remind so accomplished a classic, that Aspasia and other learned ladies of Greece are no very encouraging precedents in favour of the purifying effects of science. But the strangest and most painful topic which he urges, is one which Lord Brougham has had the good taste altogether to avoid—the power, not of religion, but of scientific knowledge on a death bed; a subject which Sir Robert treats in language which it is far better to believe is mere oratory than has a meaning in it.

If anything were necessary *in cumulum* to complete the folly and nonsense of the whole affair, it is found in the circumstance that this new art of living is offered to the labouring classes—for instance, in a severe winter, snow on the ground, glass falling, bread rising, coal at 20d. the cwt., and no work. (542)

It does not require many words, then, to determine, that taking human nature as it is actually found, and assuming that there is an art of life, to say that it consists, or in any essential manner is placed, in the cultivation of knowledge—that the mind is changed by a discovery, or saved by a diversion, or amused into immortality—that grief, anger, cowardice, self-conceit, pride, or passion, can be subdued by an examination of shells or grasses, or inhaling of gasses, or a chipping of rocks, or observing the barometer, or calculating the longitude, is the veriest pretence which sophist or mountebank ever professed to a gaping auditory. If virtue be a mastery over the mind, if its end be action, if its perfection be inward order, harmony, and peace, we must seek it in graver and holier places than libraries and reading rooms.

CATHOLICUS.

Peel's Address and the Catholicus Letters

THE TIMES, WEDNESDAY, 10 FEBRUARY 1841

SIR ROBERT PEEL'S ADDRESS *at* TAMWORTH.

LETTER III.
TO THE EDITOR OF THE TIMES.

Sir,—There are (543) two schools of philosophy, flourishing at this day, as at others, neither of these accepting Christian principles as the guide of life, yet both of them unhappily patronized by persons whom it would be the worst and most cruel uncharitableness to suspect of unbelief. Mr. Bentham is the master of the one; and Sir Robert Peel is a disciple of the other. Mr. Bentham's system has nothing ideal about it; he is a stern realist, and he limits his realism to things which he can see, hear, taste, touch, and handle. He does not acknowledge the existence of anything which he cannot ascertain for himself. Exist it may nevertheless, but, till it make itself felt, to him it exists not; till it comes down to him, and he is very short-sighted, it is not recognized by him, as having a co-existence with himself, any more than the Emperor of China by the European family of Kings. With him a being out of sight is a being out of mind; nay, he allows not the claims of traces or glimpses to regard, but to know a little and not much is to know nothing at all. With him to speak truth is to speak with a meaning; and to imagine, to guess, to doubt, or to falter, is much the same as to lie. What opinion will such an iron thinker entertain of Cicero's 'glory,' or Lord Brougham's 'truth,' and Sir Robert's 'scientific consolations,' and all those other airy nothings which are my proper subject of remark, and which I have in view, when by way of contrast I make mention of the philosophy of Bentham?

And yet the doctrine of the three eminent orators whom I have ventured to criticise has in it much that is far nobler than Benthamism, their misfortune being, not that they look for an excellence above the beaten path of life, but that whereas Christianity has told us what that excellence is, Cicero lived before it was given, and Lord Brougham and Sir Robert Peel prefer his involuntary error to their own inherited truth. Surely, there is something unearthly and superhuman in spite of Bentham; but it is not glory, or knowledge, or any abstract idea of virtue, but great and good tidings which need not here be particularly mentioned, and the pity is, that these Christian statesmen cannot be content with what is divine without hankering after what was heathen.

Now, independent of all other considerations, the great difference, in a practical light, between the objects of Christianity and of heathen belief, is this—that glory, science, knowledge, and whatever other fine names we use, never healed a wounded heart, nor changed a sinful one; but Christ's word is with power. The ideas which Christianity brings before us are in themselves full of influence, and they are endowed with a supernatural gift over and above, in order to meet the special exigencies of our nature. Knowledge is not 'power,' nor is glory 'the first and only fair;' but 'grace,' or 'the word,' by whichever name we call it, has been from the first a quickening, renovating, organizing principle. It has new-created the individual, and diffused and knit him into a social body, composed of members (544) each similarly created. It has cleansed man of his moral diseases, raised him to hope and energy, given him to propagate a brotherhood among his fellowmen, to form a large family or rather kingdom of saints all over the earth, and with wonderful vigour prolonged its original impulse down to this day. Each one of us has lit his lamp from his neighbour, or received it from his fathers, and the lights thus kindled are to-day as strong and as clear as if 1,800 years had not passed since the original of the sacred flame. What has glory or knowledge done like this? Can it raise the dead? can it create a polity? can it do more than testify man's need and typify God's remedy?

And yet, in spite of this, when we have an instrument given us, capable of changing the heart, great orators and statesmen are busy, forsooth, with their heathen charms and nostrums, their sedatives, correctives, or restoratives; as preposterously as if we were to build our men of war, or conduct our iron works, on the principles approved in Cicero's day. The utmost that Lord Brougham seems to propose to himself in the education of the mind, is to keep out bad ideas by good—a great object, doubtless, but not so great in conception, as is the destruction of the appetency for bad in Christian fact. 'Every one,' he says in his Discourse upon the Objects and Advantages of Science, 'is *amused* with reading a story, a romance may please some, and a fairy tale may entertain others; but no *benefit* beyond the amusement is derived from this source; the imagination is gratified. Accidents, adventures, anecdotes, crimes, and a variety of other things amuse us, independent of the information respecting public affairs, in which we feel interested as citizens of the State, or as members of a particular body. Most persons who take delight in reading tales of ghosts, which they know to be false, and feel all the whole to be silly in the extreme, are *merely* gratified, or rather occupied, with the *strong emotions* of horror excited by the momentary belief, for it can only last an instant. *Such* reading is a degrading waste of precious time, and has even bad effect on the feelings and the judgment. But true stories of horrid crimes, as murders, and pitiable misfortunes—as shipwrecks, are not much more instructive. It may be better to read these than to sit yawning and idle; much better than to sit drinking or gaming, which, when carried to the last excess, are crimes in themselves, and the fruitful parents of many more. But this is nearly as much as can be said of such vain and unprofitable reading. If it can be a *pleasure to gratify curiosity*, to know what we were ignorant of, to have our *feelings of wonder* called forth, *how pure a delight of this very kind* does natural science hold out to its students? ... Akin to this pleasure of contemplating new and extraordinary truths is the *gratification of a more learned curiosity*, by tracing resemblances and relations between things which to common apprehension seem widely different.' And in the same way Sir Robert tells us of a *devout* curiosity. In all cases *curiosity* is the means, *diversion* of mind the highest end; and though of course I will not assert that Lord Brougham, and certainly not that Sir Robert Peel, denies any higher kind of morality, yet when he rises above Benthamism, in which he often indulges, into what may be called *Broughamism proper*, he commonly grasps at nothing more real and substantial than these Ciceronian ethics. (545)

In morals, as in physics, the spring[2] cannot rise higher than its source. Christianity raises men from earth, for it comes from Heaven; but human morality creeps, struts, or frets upon the earth's level, without wings to rise. The Knowledge School does not contemplate raising man above himself; it merely aims at disposing of his existing powers and tastes, as is most convenient or practicable under circumstances.

2 Erratum for 'stream' (*The Times*, 11 February 1841).

It finds him, like the victims of the French Tyrant, doubled up in a cage in which he can neither lie, stand, sit, nor kneel, and its highest desire is to find an attitude in which his unrest may be least. Or it finds him, like some musical instrument, of great power and compass, but imperfect; from its very structure some keys must ever be out of tune, and the object, when ambition is highest, is to throw the fault of its nature where least it will be observed. It leaves man where it found him—man, and not an angel—a sinner, not a saint; but it tries to make him look as much like what he is not as ever it can. The poor indulge in low pleasures; they use bad language, swear loudly and profanely, laugh at coarse jests, and are rude and boorish. Sir Robert would open on them a wider range of thought and more intellectual objects, by teaching them science; but what warrant will be given us that, if his object could be achieved, what they would gain in decency they would not lose in natural humility and awe? If so, he has exchanged a gross fault for a more subtle one. 'Temperance topics' stop drinking; let us suppose it; but will much be gained, if those who give up spirits take to opium? *Naturam expellas furcâ, tamen usque recurret*, is a heathen truth, though a Christian fable; and universities and libraries which recur to heathenism may reclaim it from the heathen for their motto. Nay, every where, so far as human nature remains hardly or partially Christianized, the heathen law remains in force; as is felt in a measure even in the most religious places and societies. Even there where Christianity has power, the venom of the old Adam is not subdued. Those who have to do with our colleges give us their experience, that in the case of the young committed to their care, external discipline can but change the fashionable sin, but cannot allay the principle of sinning. Stop cigars, they will take to drinking parties; stop drinking, they gamble; stop gambling, and a worse license follows. You do not get rid of vice by human expedients; you can but use them according to circumstances, and in their place. You must go to a higher source for renovation of heart and will. You do but play a sort of 'hunt the slipper' with the sin of our nature till you go to Christianity.

I say, you must use human methods *in this place*, and there they are useful; but they are worse than useless out of their place. I have no fanatical wish to deny to any subject of thought or method of reason a place altogether, if it chooses to claim it, in the cultivation of the mind. Mr. Bentham may despise verse making, or Mr. Dugald Stewart logic, but the great and true maxim is to sacrifice none—to combine, and therefore to adjust all. All cannot be first, and therefore each has its place, and the problem is to find it. It is at least not a lighter fault to make what is secondary first than to leave it out altogether. Here then it is that the Knowledge (546) Society, Gower-street College, Tamworth Reading-room, Lord Brougham, and Sir Robert Peel, are all so deplorably mistaken. Christianity, and nothing short of it, must be made the element and principle of all education. Where it has been laid as the first stone, and acknowledged as the governing spirit, it will take up into itself, assimilate, and give a character to literature and science. Where revealed truth has given the aim and direction to knowledge, knowledge of all kinds will minister to revealed truth. The evidences of religion, natural theology, metaphysics,—or, again, poetry, history, and the classics,—or physics and mathematics, may all be grafted into the mind of a Christian, and give and take from the grafting. But if in education we begin with nature before grace, with evidences before faith, with science before conscience, with poetry before practice, we shall be doing much the same as if we were to indulge the passions and turn a deaf ear to the reason. In each case we misplace what in its place is a divine gift. If we attempt to effect a moral improvement by means of poetry, we shall but mature into a mawkish, frivolous, and fastidious sentimentalism—if by means of argument, into a dry unamiable long-headedness—if by good society, into a polished outside, with hollowness within, in which vice has lost its grossness, and perhaps increased its malignity—if by experimental science, into an uppish supercilious temper, much inclined to scepticism. But reverse the order of things; put faith first and knowledge second; let the university minister to the church, and then classical poetry becomes the type of gospel truth, and physical science a comment on Genesis or Job, and Aristotle changes into Butler, and Arcesilas into Berkeley.

Far from recognizing this principle, the teachers of the knowledge school would educate from natural theology up to Christianity, and would amend the heart through literature and philosophy. Lord Brougham gives out that 'henceforth nothing shall prevail over us to praise or to blame any one for' his belief, 'which he can no more change than he can the hue of his skin or the height of his stature.' And Sir

'An aristocracy of exalted spirits'

Robert, whose profession and life give the lie to his philosophy, founds a library into which 'no works of controversial divinity shall enter,' that is, no doctrinal works at all; and he tells us that 'an increased sagacity will make men not merely believe in the cold doctrines of natural religion, but that it will *so prepare and temper the spirit* and understanding that they will be better *qualified to comprehend the great scheme of human redemption.*' And again, Lord Brougham considers that 'the pleasures of science tend not only to make our lives more agreeable but better;' and Sir Robert responds, that 'he entertains the hope that there will be the means afforded of useful occupation and rational recreation; that men will prefer the pleasures of knowledge above the indulgence of sensual appetite, and that there is a prospect of contributing to the intellectual and moral improvement of the neighbourhood.'

Can the 19th century produce no more robust and creative philosophy than this?

CATHOLICUS.

THE TIMES, FRIDAY, 12 FEBRUARY 1841

SIR R. PEEL'S ADDRESS AT TAMWORTH.

LETTER IV.
TO THE EDITOR OF THE TIMES.

Sir,—Human nature (547) wants recasting, but Lord Brougham is all for tinkering it. He does not despair of making something of it yet. He is not indeed of those who think that reason, passion, and whatever else is in us are made right and tight by the principle of self-interest. He understands that something more is necessary for man's happiness than self-love; he feels that man has affections and aspirations which Bentham does not account of, and he looks about for their legitimate objects. Christianity has provided these; but, unhappily, he passes them by. He libels them with the name of dogmatism, and conjures up instead the phantoms of glory and knowledge; *idola theatri*, as his famous predecessor calls them. 'There are idols,' says Lord Bacon, 'which have got into the human mind, from the different tenets of philosophers, and the perverted laws of demonstration. And these we denominate idols of the theatre; because all the philosophies that have been hitherto invented or received are but so many stage plays, written or acted, as having shown nothing but fictitious and theatrical worlds. Idols of the theatre, or theories, are many, and will probably grow much more numerous; for if men had not, through many ages, *been prepossessed with religion and theology*, and *if civil governments*, but particularly monarchies,' and, I suppose, their ministers, counsellors, functionaries, inclusive,'*had not been averse to innovations of this kind*, though but intended, so as to make it dangerous and prejudicial to the private fortunes of such as take the bent of innovating, not only by depriving them of advantages, but also by exposing them to contempt and hatred, there would doubtless have been *numerous other sects* of philosophies and theories introduced, of kin to those that in great variety formerly flourished among the Greeks. And these theatrical fables have this in common with dramatic pieces, that the fictitious narrative is neater, more elegant and pleasing, than the true history.'

'An aristocracy of exalted spirits'

I suppose we may readily grant that the science of the day is attended by more lively interest, and issues in more entertaining knowledge, than the study of the New Testament. Accordingly Lord Brougham fixes upon it as the great desideratum of human nature, and puts aside faith under the nickname of opinion. I wish Sir Robert Peel had not fallen into the snare—by insulting doctrine under the name of 'controversial divinity.'

However, it will be said that Sir Robert, in spite of such forms of speech, differs essentially from Lord Brougham; for he goes on in the latter part of the address which has occasioned these remarks to speak of science as leading to Christianity. 'I can never think it possible,' he says, 'that a mind can be so constituted, that after being familiarized with the great truth of observing in every object of contemplation that nature presents the manifest proofs of a Divine Intelligence, if you range even from the organization of the meanest weed you trample upon, or of the insect (548) that lives but for an hour, up to the magnificent structure of the heavens, and the still more wonderful phenomena of the soul, reason, and conscience of man; I cannot believe that any man, accustomed to such contemplations, can return from them with any other feelings than those of enlarged conceptions of the Divine Power, and greater reverence for the name of the Almighty Creator of the universe.' A long and complicated sentence, and no unfitting emblem of the demonstration it promises. It expresses a process and deduction. Depend on it, it is not so safe a road and so expeditious a journey from premis and conclusion as Sir Robert anticipates. The way is long, and there are not a few halfway houses and travellers' rests along it; and who is to warrant that the members of the reading-room and library will go steadily on? and when at length they come to 'Christianity,' pray how do the roads lie between it and 'controversial divinity?' Or, grant the Tamworth readers to *begin* with 'Christianity' as well as science, the same question suggests itself. What is Christianity?—Universal benevolence? Exalted morality? Supremacy of law? Conservatism? An age of light? An age of reason?—which of them all?

Most cheerfully do I render to so religious a man as Sir Robert Peel the justice of disclaiming, on my part, the idea that he has any intention at all to put aside religion; yet his words either mean nothing, or they do, both on their surface and when carried into effect, mean something very irreligious.

Peel's Address and the Catholicus Letters

And now for one plain proof of this.

It is certain, then, that the multitude of men have neither time nor capacity for attending to many subjects. If they attend to one, they will not attend to the other; if they give their leisure and curiosity to this world, they will have none left for the next. We cannot be everything, as the poet says. We must make up our minds to be ignorant of much, if we would know ought. And we must make our choice between risking science and risking religion. This I consider to be a plain fact, not a theory,[3] for the truth of which I appeal, not to argument but to the proper judges of facts, common sense and practical experience; and if they pronounce it to be a fact, then Sir Robert Peel, little as he means it, does unite with Lord Brougham in taking from Christianity what he gives to science.

I will make this fair offer to both of them. Every member of the church established shall be eligible to the Tamworth library on one condition—that he brings from the 'public minister of religion,' to use Sir Robert's phrase, a ticket in witness of his proficiency in Christian knowledge. We will have no 'controversial divinity' in the library, but a little out of it. If the gentlemen of the knowledge school will but agree to teach town and country religion first, they shall have a *carte blanche* from me to teach anything or everything else second. Not a word has been uttered or intended in these letters against science; I would treat it, as they do *not* treat 'controversial divinity,' with respect and gratitude. They caricature doctrine under the (549) name of controversy. I do not call science infidelity. I call it by their own name, 'useful and entertaining knowledge;' and I call doctrine 'Christian knowledge;' and, as thinking Christianity something more than useful and entertaining, I want faith to come first, and utility and amusement to follow.

That persons indeed are found in all classes, high and low, busy and idle, capable of proceeding from sacred to profane knowledge, is undeniable; and it is desirable that they should do so. It is desirable that talent for particular departments in literature and science should

---

3 This I consider to be a plain fact, not a theory] *The Tamworth Reading Room pamphlet reads*: Sir Robert indeed says, 'Do not believe that you have not time for rational recreation. It is the idle man who wants time for every thing.' However, this seems to me rhetoric; and what I have said to be the matter of fact,

be fostered and turned to account, wherever it is found. But what has this to do with this general canvass of *all* persons of *all* descriptions, without reference to religious creed, who shall have attained *the age of fourteen?* Why solicit 'the working classes, without distinction of party, political opinion, or religious profession;' that is, whether they have heard of a God or no? Whence these cries rising on our ears, of 'Let me entreat you!' 'Neglect not the opportunity!' 'It will not be our fault!' 'Here is an access for you!'—very like the tones of a street preacher, or of the cad of an omnibus, little worthy of a great statesman and a religious philosopher?

However, the Tamworth reading-room admits one restriction, which is not a little curious, and has no very liberal sound. It seems that all '*virtuous* women' may be members of the library; that 'great injustice would be done to the *well educated and virtuous* women of the town and neighbourhood,' had they been excluded. A very emphatic silence is maintained about women not virtuous. What does this mean? Does it mean to exlude them, while bad *men* are admitted? Is this accident or design, sinister and insidious, against a portion of the community? What has virtue to do with a reading-room? It is to *make* its members virtuous; it is to 'exalt the *moral dignity* of their nature.' It is to provide 'charms and temptations' to allure them from sensuality and riot. To whom but to the vicious ought Sir Robert to discourse about 'opportunities,' and 'access,' and 'moral improvement;' and who else would prove a fitter experiment, and a more glorious triumph of scientific influences? And yet he shuts out all but the well-educated and virtuous.

Alas, that bigotry should have left the mark of its hoof in the great 'fundamental principle of the Tamworth Institution!' Sir Robert Peel is bound in consistency to attempt its obliteration. But if that is impossible, as many will anticipate, why, O why, while he is about it, why will he not give us just a little more of it? *Cannot* we prevail on him to modify his principle, and to admit into his library none but 'well-educated and virtuous' men?

CATHOLICUS.

Peel's Address and the Catholicus Letters

THE TIMES, SATURDAY, 20 FEBRUARY 1841

SIR ROBERT PEEL'S ADDRESS AT TAMWORTH.

LETTER V.
TO THE EDITOR OF THE TIMES.

Sir,—Sir Robert Peel (550) proposes to establish a library which 'shall be open to all persons of all descriptions, without reference to political opinions or to religious creed.' He invites those who are concerned in manufactories, or who have many workmen, 'without distinction of party, political opinions, *or* religious profession.' He promises that 'in the selection of subjects for public lectures everything calculated to excite religious *or* political animosity shall be excluded.' Nor is any 'discussion on matters connected with religion, politics, *or* local party differences' to be permitted in the reading-room. And he congratulates himself that he has 'laid the foundation of an edifice in which men of all political opinions *and* of all religious feelings may unite in furtherance of knowledge, without the asperities of party feeling.' In these statements religious differences are made synonymous with 'party feeling;' and, whereas the tree is known by its fruit, their characteristic symptoms are felicitously described as 'asperities,' and 'animosities.' And, in order to teach us more precisely what these differences are worth, they are compared to differences between Whig and Tory—nay, even to '*local* party differences;' as, for instance, about a municipal election, or a hole-and-corner meeting, or a parish job, or a bill for a railway.

But, to give him the advantage of the more honourable parallel of the two, are religious principles to be put upon a level even with political? Is it as bad to be a republican as an unbeliever? Is it as magnanimous to humour a scoffer as to spare an opponent in the House? Is a difference about the Reform Bill all one with a difference about the Creed? Is it as polluting to hear arguments for Lord Melbourne as against the Apostles? To a statesman, indeed, like Sir Robert, to abandon one's party is a far greater sacrifice than to unparliamentary persons; and it would be uncandid to doubt that he is rather magnifying politics than degrading religion in throwing them together; but still, when he advocates concessions in theology *and* politics, he must be plainly told to make presents of things that belong to him, nor seek to be generous with other people's substance. There are entails in more matters than parks and old places. He made his politics for himself, but Another made theology.

Christianity is faith, faith implies a doctrine, a doctrine propositions, propositions yes or no, yes or no differences. Differences, then, are the natural attendants on Christianity, and you cannot have Christianity, and not have differences. When, then, Sir Robert Peel calls such differences points of 'party feeling,' what is this but to insult Christianity? Yet so cautious, so correct a man, cannot have made such a sacrifice for nothing; nor does he long leave us in doubt what is his inducement. He tells us that his great aim is the peace and good order of the community, (551) and the easy working of the national machine. With this in view, any price is cheap, everything is marketable; all impediments are a nuisance. He does not undo for undoing's sake; he gains more than an equivalent. It is a mistake, too, to say that he considers all differences of opinion as equal in importance; no, they are only equally in the way. He only compares them together where they are comparable,—in their common inconvenience to a Minister of State. They may be as little homogeneous as chalk is to cheese, or Macedon to Monmouth, but they agree in interfering with social harmony; and, since that harmony is the first of goods and the end of life, what is left us but to discard all that disunites us, and to cultivate all that may amalgamate?

Could Sir Robert have set a more remarkable example of self-sacrifice than in becoming the disciple of his political foe, accepting from Lord Brougham his new principle of combination, rejecting faith for the fulcrum of society, and proceeding to rest it upon knowledge?

'I cannot help thinking,' he exclaims at Tamworth, 'that *by bringing together in an institution of this kind* intelligent men of all classes and conditions of life, by uniting together, in the committee of this institution, the gentleman of ancient family and great landed possessions with the skilful mechanic and artificer of good character, I cannot help believing that we are *harmonizing* the gradations of society, and binding men together by a *new* bond, which will have *more than ordinary* strength on account of the object which unites us.' The old and ordinary bond, he seems to say, was religion; Lord Brougham's, and at length I agree with him, is knowledge. Faith, once the soul of social union, is now but the spirit of division. Not a single doctrine but is 'controversial divinity;' not an abstraction can be imagined (could abstractions constrain), not a comprehension projected (could comprehensions connect), but will leave out one or other portion or element of the social fabric. We must abandon religion, if we aspire to be statesmen. Once, indeed, it was a living power, kindling hearts, leavening them with one idea, moulding them on one model, developing them into one polity. Ere now it has been the life of morality; it has given birth to heroes; it has wielded empire. But another age has come in, and faith is effete; let us submit to what we cannot change; let us not hang over our dead, but bury it out of sight. Seek we out some young and vigorous principle, rich in sap, and fierce in life, to give form to elements which are fast resolving into their unorganic chaos; and where shall we find such a principle but in knowledge? (552)[4]

Lord Brougham will make all this clearer to us. A work of high interest and varied information is attributed to him, to which I have in former letters alluded, and in which the ingenious author shows how knowledge can do for society what has hitherto been supposed the prerogative of faith. As to faith and its preachers, he had already complimented them at Glasgow, as 'the evil spirits of tyranny and

---

4 *The Tamworth Reading Room pamphlet adds*: Accordingly, though Sir Robert somewhat chivalrously battles for the appointment upon the Book Committee of what he calls two 'public ministers of religion, holding prominent and responsible offices, endowed by the State,' and that ex officio, yet he is untrue to his new principle only in appearance: for he couples his concession with explanations and restrictions quite sufficient to prevent old faith becoming insurgent against young knowledge. First he takes his Vicar and Curate as 'conversant with literary subjects and with literary works,' and then as having duties 'immediately connected with the moral condition and improvement' of the place. Further he admits 'it is perfectly right to be jealous of all power held by such a tenure:' and he insists on the 'fundamental' condition that these sacred functionaries shall permit no doctrinal works to be introduced or lectures to be delivered.

Lastly, he reserves in the general body the power of withdrawing this indulgence 'if the existing checks be not sufficient, and the power be abused;' and apropos of 'abuse,' he desires 'to take every security in giving knowledge against that knowledge being perverted to evil or immoral purposes;' for instance, any contraband introduction of the doctrines of faith.

persecution,' and had bid them good day as the scared and dazzled creatures of the 'long night now gone down the sky.' 'The great truth,' he proclaimed in language borrowed from the records of faith (for after parsons no men quote Scripture more familiarly than Liberals and Whigs), 'has finally *gone forth to all the ends of the earth*, that man shall no more render account to man for his belief, over which he has himself no control. Henceforth nothing shall prevail upon us to *praise or to blame* any one for that which he can no more change than he can the hue of his skin or the height of his stature.' And then he proceeds to his new *Vitæ Sanctorum*, or, as he calls it, Illustrations of the 'Pursuit of Knowledge;' and, whereas the badge of Christian saintliness is conflict, he writes of the 'pursuit of knowledge *under difficulties*;' and, whereas this knowledge is to stand in the place of religion, he assumes a hortatory tone, in which decidedly he has no equal but Sir Robert. 'Knowledge,' he says, 'is happiness, as well as power and virtue;' and he demands 'the dedication of our faculties' to it. 'The *struggle*,' he gravely observes, which its disciple 'has to wage may be a protracted, but it ought not to be a *cheerless* one; for, if he do not *relax his exertions*, every movement he makes is necessarily a *step forward*, if not towards that distinction which intellectual attainments sometimes confer, at least to that *inward satisfaction and enjoyment* which is always their reward. No one stands in the way of another, or can deprive him of any part of his chance, we should rather say of his certainty, of success; on the contrary, they are all *fellow-workers*, and may materially *help each other forward*.' And he enumerates in various places the virtues which adorn the children of knowledge—ardour united to humility, child-like alacrity, teachableness, truthfulness, patience, concentration of attention, husbandry of time, self-denial, self-command, and heroism.

Faith, viewed in its history through past ages, presents us with the fulfilment of one great idea in particular—that, namely, of an aristocracy of exalted spirits, drawn together out of all countries, ranks, and ages, raised above the condition of humanity, specimens of the capabilities of our race, incentives to rivalry and patterns for imitation. This Christian idea Lord Brougham has borrowed for his new pantheon, which is equally various in all attributes and appendages of mind, with the one characteristic in all its specimens—the pursuit of knowledge. Some of his worthies are low born, others of high degree; some are in

Europe, others in the Antipodes; some in the dark ages, others in the ages of light; some exercise a (553) voluntary, others an involuntary toil; some give up riches, and others gain them; some are fixtures, and others in adventure; some are profligate, and others ascetic; and some are believers, and others are infidels.

Alfred, severely good and Christian, takes his place in this new canon beside the gay and graceful Lorenzo de Medicis; for did not the one 'import civilization into England,' and was not the other 'the wealthy and munificent patron of all the liberal arts?' Edward VI. and Haroun al Raschid, Dr. Johnson and Dr. Franklin, Newton and Protagoras, Pascal and Julian the apostate, Joseph Milner and Lord Byron, Cromwell and Ovid, Bayle and Boyle, Adrian pope and Adrian emperor, Lady Jane Grey and Madame Roland, human beings who agreed in nothing but in their humanity and their love of knowledge, are all admitted by Lord Brougham to one beatification, in proof of the Catholic character of his substitute for faith.[5]

Nothing comes amiss to this author; saints and sinners, the precious and the vile, are torn from their proper homes and recklessly thrown together under the category of intellectualists. 'Tis a pity he did not extend his view, as Christianity has done, to beings out of sight of man. Milton could have helped him to some angelic personages, as patrons

---

5 *The Tamworth Reading Room pamphlet adds*: The persecuting Marcus is a 'good and enlightened emperor,' and a 'delightful' spectacle when 'mixing in the religious processions and ceremonies' of Athens, and 're-building and re-endowing the schools,' whence St. Paul was driven in derision. The royal Alphery on the contrary 'preferred his humble parsonage' to the throne of the Czars. West was 'nurtured among the quiet and gentle affections of a Quaker family.' Kirk White's 'feelings became ardently devotional, and he determined to give up his life to the preaching of Christianity.' Roger Bacon was 'a brother of the Franciscan Order, at that time the great support and ornament of both Universities.' Belzoni seized 'the opportunity' of Buonaparte's arrival in Italy to 'throw off his monastic habit,' its 'idleness and obscurity,' and engaged himself as a performer at Astley's. Duval, 'a very able antiquarian of the last century,' began his studies as a peasant boy, and finished them in a Jesuit's College. Mr Davy, 'having written a system of divinity,' effected the printing of it in thirteen years 'with a press of his own construction,' and the assistance of his female servant, working off page by page for twenty-six volumes 8 vo. of nearly 500 pages each. Raleigh, in spite of an 'immoderate ambition,' was 'one of the very chief glories of an age crowded with towering spirits.'

'An aristocracy of exalted spirits'

and guardians of his intellectual temple, who of old time, before faith had birth,

> 'reasoned high
> 'Of providence, foreknowledge, will, and fate,
> 'Passion and apathy, and glory, and shame,—
> 'Vain wisdom all, and false philosophy.'

And, indeed, he does make some guesses that way, speaking most catholically of being 'admitted to a fellowship with those loftier minds' who 'by universal consent held (554) a station apart,' and are 'spoken of reverently,' as if their names were not those 'of mortal men;' and he speaks of these 'benefactors of mankind, when they rest from their pious labours,' looking down 'upon the blessings with which their 'toils and sufferings have clothed the scene of their former existence.'

Such is the oratory which has fascinated Sir Robert; yet we must recollect that in the year 1832, even the venerable Society for Promoting Christian Knowledge herself, catching its sounds and hearing something about sublimity, and universality, and brotherhood, and effort, and felicity, was beguiled into an admission of this singularly irreligious bud into the list of publications which she had delegated to a committee to select *in usum laicorum*.

That a venerable society should be caught by the vision of a Church Catholic is not wonderful; but what could possess philosophers and statesmen to dazzle her with it, but the urgent need of human nature[6] and the divine excellence and sovereign virtue of the remedy which faith once realized against it?[7]

CATHOLICUS

---

6 the urgent need of human nature] *The Tamworth Reading Room pamphlet reads*: man's need of some such support

7 of the remedy ... against it?] *The Tamworth Reading Room pamphlet reads*: of that which faith once created?

Peel's Address and the Catholicus Letters

THE TIMES, MONDAY, 22 FEBRUARY 1841

SIR R. PEEL'S ADDRESS AT TAMWORTH.

LETTER VI.
TO THE EDITOR OF THE TIMES.

Sir,—People (555) say to me, that it is but a dream to suppose that Christianity should regain the organic power in human society which once it possessed. I cannot help that; I never said it could. I am not a politician; I am proposing no measures, but exposing a fallacy, and resisting a pretence. Let Benthamism reign if men have no aspirations; but do not tell them to be romantic, and then solace them with glory; do not attempt by philosophy what once was done by religion. The ascendancy of faith may be impracticable, but the reign of knowledge is impossible. The problem for statesmen of this age is how to educate the masses, and literature and science cannot give the solution.

Not so deems Sir Robert Peel; his firm belief and hope is, 'that an increased sagacity will administer to an exalted faith; that it will make men not merely believe in the cold doctrines of natural religion, but that it will so prepare and temper the spirit and understanding, that they will be better qualified to comprehend the great scheme of human redemption.' He certainly thinks that scientific pursuits have some considerable power of impressing religion upon the mind of the multitude. I think not, and will now say why.

Science gives us the grounds or premises from which religious truths are to be inferred; but it does not set about inferring, much less does it reach the inference—that is, not its province. It brings before us phenomena, and it leaves us, if we will, to call them works of design, wisdom, or benevolence; and further still, if we will, to proceed to confess an Intelligent Creator. We have to take its facts, and to give them a meaning, and to draw our conclusions from them. First comes knowledge, then a view, then reasoning, and then belief. This is why science has so little of a religious tendency; deductions have no power or persuasion. The heart is commonly reached, not through the reason, but through the imagination, by means of direct impressions, by the testimony of facts and events, by history, by description. Persons influence us, voices melt us, looks subdue us, deeds inflame us. Many a man will live and die upon a dogma; no one will be a martyr for a conclusion. A conclusion is but an opinion; it is not a thing which *is*, but which *we are certain* about; and it has often been observed, that we never say that we are certain, without implying that we doubt. To say that a thing *must* be, is to admit that it *may not* be. No one, I say, will die for his own calculations; he dies for realities. This is why a literary religion is so little to be depended upon; it looks well in fair weather; but its doctrines are opinions, and when called to suffer for them, it slips them between its folios, or burns them at its hearth. And this again is the secret of the distrust and the raillery with which moralists have been so commonly visited. They say, and do not: why? Because they are contemplating the fitness of things, and they live by the square when they should be realizing their high maxims in the concrete. Now Sir Robert thinks better of natural history, chymistry, and astronomy, but what are (556) they too, but divinity *in posse*? He protests against 'controversial divinity;' is *inferential* much better?

I have no confidence then in philosophers who are forced to have[8] religion, and are Christian by implication. They sit at home, and reach forward to distances which astonish us; but they hit without grasping, and are sometimes as confident about shadows as about realities. They have worked out by a calculation the lie of a country which they never saw, and mapped it by a gazetteer; and like blind men, though they can put a stranger on his way, they cannot walk straight, and do not feel it quite their business to walk at all.

Logic makes but a sorry rhetoric;[9] first shoot round corners, and you may not despair of converting by a syllogism. Tell men to gain notions of a Creator from His works, and if they were to set about it (which nobody does), they would be jaded and wearied by the labyrinth they were tracing. Their minds would be gorged and surfeited by the logical operation. Logicians are more set on concluding rightly than on drawing right conclusions. They cannot see the end for the process. Few men have that power of mind which may hold fast and firmly a

---

8 are forced to have] *The Tamworth Reading Room pamphlet reads*: cannot help having
9 rhetoric] *The Tamworth Reading Room pamphlet adds*: with the multitude

variety of thoughts. We ridicule 'men of one idea,' but a great many of us are born to be such, and we should be happier if we knew it. To most men argument makes the point in hand only more doubtful, and considerably less impressive. After all, man is not a reasoning animal; he is a seeing, feeling, contemplating, acting animal. He is influenced by what is direct and precise. It is very well to freshen our impressions and convictions from physics, but to create them we must go elsewhere. Sir Robert Peel 'never can think it possible that a mind can be so constituted that after being familiarized with the wonderful discoveries which have been made in every part of experimental science, it can retire from such contemplations without more enlarged conceptions of God's providence and a higher reverence for His Name.' If he speaks of religious minds, he perpetrates a truism; if of irreligious, he insinuates a paradox.

Life is not long enough for a religion of inferences; we shall never have done beginning if we determine to begin with proof. We shall ever be laying our foundations, we shall turn theology into evidences, and divines into textuaries. We shall never get at our first principles. Resolve to believe nothing, and you must prove your proof and analyze your elements, sinking further and further, and finding 'in the lowest deep a lower deep,' till you come to the broad bosom of scepticism. I would rather be bound to defend the assumption that Christianity is true, than to prove a moral governance from the physical world. Life is for action. If we insist on proof for everything, we shall never come to action; to act you must assume, and that assumption is faith.

Let no one suppose that in saying this I am maintaining that all proofs are equally difficult, and all propositions equally debatable. Some assumptions are greater than others, and some doctrines involve postulates larger than others, and more numerous. I only say that impressions lead to action, and that reasonings (557) lead from it. Knowledge of premises, and inferences upon them, this is not to *live*. It is very well as a matter of liberal curiosity and of philosophy to analyze our modes of thought; but let this come second, and where there is leisure for it, and then our examinations will in many ways even be subservient to action. But if we commence with scientific knowledge and argumentative proof, or lay any great stress on it as the basis of Christianity, or attempt to make men moral and religious by libraries and museums, let us in consistency take chymists for our cooks, and mineralogists for our masons.

Now I wish to state all this as matter of fact, to be judged by the candid testimony of any persons whatever. Why we are so constituted that faith not knowledge or argument is our principle of action, is a question with which I have nothing to do; but I think it is a fact, and if it be such, we must resign ourselves to it as we best may, unless we take refuge in the intolerable paradox, that the mass of men are created for nothing, and are meant to leave life as they entered it.

So well has this practically been understood in all ages of the world, that no religion yet has been a religion of physics or philosophy. It has ever been synonymous with revelation. It never has been a deduction from what we know; it has ever been an assertion of something to be believed. It has never lived in a conclusion; it has ever been a message, a history, or a vision. No legislator or priest ever dreamed of educating our moral nature by science or by argument. There is no difference here between true religions and pretended. Moses was instructed not to reason from the creation, but to work miracles. Christianity is a history supernatural and almost scenic; it tells us what its Author is by telling us what He has done.

I have no wish at all to speak otherwise than respectfully of conscientious Dissenters; but I have heard it said by those who were not their enemies, and who had known much of their preaching, that they had often heard narrow-minded and bigotted clergymen, and often dissenting ministers of a far more intellectual cast, but that dissenting teaching came to nothing—that it was dissipated in thoughts which had no point, and inquiries which converged to no centre; that it ended as it began, and sent away its hearers as it found them. Whereas, the instruction in the church, with all its defects and mistakes, came to some end, for it started from some beginning.

Nay, Lord Brougham himself, as we have already seen, has recognized the force of the principle. He has not left his philosophical religion to argument, but committed it to the keeping of the imagination. Why should he depict a great republic of letters and an intellectual pantheon, but that he feels instances and patterns to be the living conclusions which alone have a hold over the affections and can form the character?

CATHOLICUS.

Peel's Address and the Catholicus Letters

THE TIMES, SATURDAY, 27 FEBRUARY 1841

SIR R. PEEL'S ADDRESS AT TAMWORTH.

TO THE EDITOR OF THE TIMES.
LETTER VII.

Sir,—When (558) Sir Robert Peel assures us from the Town-hall at Tamworth that physical science must lead to religion, it is no bad compliment to him to say that he is unreal. He speaks of what he knows nothing about. To a religious man like him science has ever suggested religious thoughts; he colours the phenomena of physics with the hue of his own mind, and mistakes an interpretation for a deduction. 'I am sanguine enough to believe,' he says, 'that that superior sagacity which is most conversant with the course and constitution of nature will be first to turn a deaf ear to objections and presumptions against revealed religion, and to acknowledge the complete harmony of the Christian dispensation with all that reason, assisted by revelation, tells us of the course and constitution of nature.' Now, considering that we are all of us educated as Christians from infancy, it is not easy to decide at this day whether science creates faith, or only confirms it; but we have this remarkable fact in the history of heathen Greece against the former supposition, that her most eminent experimentalists were atheists, and that it was their atheism which was the cause of their eminence. 'The natural philosophies of Democritus and others,' says Lord Bacon, '*who allow no God or mind* in the frame of things, but attribute the structure of the universe to infinite essays and trials of nature, or what they call fate or fortune, and assigned the causes of particular things to the necessity of matter, *without any intermixture of final causes*, seem, as far as we can judge from the remains of their philosophy, *much more solid*, and to have *gone deeper into nature*, with regard to physical causes, than the philosophies of Aristotle or Plato: and this only because they *never meddled with final causes*, which the others were perpetually inculcating.'

Lord Bacon gives us both the fact and the reason of it. Physical philosophers are ever inquiring *whence* things are, not *why*; referring them to nature, not to mind; and thus they tend to make a system a substitute for a God. Each pursuit or calling has its own dangers, and each numbers among its professors men who rise superior to them. As the soldier is tempted to dissipation, and the merchant to acquisitiveness, and the lawyer to the unreal, and the statesman to the expedient, and the clergyman to ease, yet there are good clergymen, statesmen, lawyers, merchants, and soldiers, notwithstanding; so there are religious experimentalists, yet physics tend to infidelity; and to have recourse to physics to *make* men religious is like recommending a canonry as a cure for the gout, or giving a youngster a commission as a penance for irregularities.

The whole framework of nature is confessedly a tissue of antecedents and consequents; we may refer all things forwards to design, or backwards on some physical cause. La Place is said to have considered he had a formula which solved all the motions of the solar system; shall we say that those motions were from this (559) formula or from a Divine fiat? Shall we have recourse for our theory to physics or to theology? Shall we assume matter and its necessary properties to be eternal, or mind with its divine attributes? Does the sun shine to warm the earth, or is the earth warmed because the sun shines? The one hypothesis will solve the phenomena as well as the other. Say not it is but a puzzle in argument, and that no one ever felt it in fact. So far from it, I believe that the study of nature, when religious feeling is away, leads the mind, rightly or wrongly, to acquiesce in the atheistic theory, as the simplest and easiest. It is but parallel to that tendency in anatomical studies, which no one will deny, to solve all the phenomena of the human frame into material elements and powers, and to dispense with the soul. To those who are conscious of matter, but not conscious of mind, it seems more rational to refer all things to one origin, such as they know, than to assume the existence of a second origin, such as they know not. It is religion, then, which suggests to science its true conclusions; the facts come from knowledge, but the principles come of faith.

There are two ways, then, of reading nature—as a machine and as a work; if we come to it with the assumption that it is a creation, we shall study it with awe; if assuming it to be a system, with mere curiosity. Sir Robert does not make this distinction. He subscribes to the belief that the man accustomed to such contemplations, *struck with awe* by the manifold proofs of infinite power and infinite wisdom, will yield more ready and hearty assent—yes, the assent of the heart, and not only of the understanding, to the pious exclamation, 'O, Lord, how glorious are thy works!' He considers that greater insight into nature will lead a man to say, 'How great and wise is the Creator, who has done this!' True; but it is possible that his thoughts may take the form of 'How clever is the creature who has discovered it!' and self-conceit may stand proxy for adoration. This is no idle apprehension. Sir Robert himself, religious as he is, gives cause for it; for the first reflection that rises in his mind, as expressed in the above passage, *before* his notice of Divine power and wisdom, is, that 'the man accustomed to such contemplations will feel the *moral dignity of his nature exalted*.' But Lord Brougham speaks out. 'The delight,' he says, 'is inexpressible of *being able to follow*, as it were, with our eyes, the marvellous works of the Great Architect of Nature.' And more clearly still: 'One of the most *gratifying treats* which science affords us is *the knowledge of the extraordinary powers* with which the human mind is endowed. No man, until he has studied philosophy, can have a just idea of the great things for which Providence has fitted his understanding, the extraordinary disproportion which there is between his natural strength and the powers of his mind, and the force which he derives from these powers. When we survey the marvellous truths of astronomy, we are first of all lost in the feeling of immense space, and of the comparative insignificance of this globe and its inhabitants. But there soon arises a *sense of gratification and of new wonder* at perceiving how so insignificant a creature has been *able to reach such a knowledge* of the unbounded system of the universe.' So, this is the religion we are to gain from the study of nature; how miserable! The god we attain is our own mind; our veneration is even professedly the worship of self.

The truth is, that the system of nature is just as much connected with religion, (560) where minds are not religious, as a watch or a steam-carriage. The material world, indeed, is infinitely more wonderful than any human contrivance; but wonder is not religion, or we should be worshipping our railroads. What the physical creation presents to us in itself is a piece of machinery, and when men speak of a Divine Intelligence as its author, this God of theirs is not the living and true, unless the spring is the god of a watch, or steam the creator of the engine. Their idol, taken at advantage (though it is *not* an idol, for they do not worship it), is the animating principle of a vast and complicated system; it is subjected to laws, and it is connatural and coextensive with matter. Well does Lord Brougham call it 'the great architect of nature;' it is an instinct, or a soul of the world, or a vital power: it is not the Almighty God.

It is observable that Lord Brougham does not allude to any *relations* as existing between his *God* and ourselves. He is filled with awe, it seems, at the powers of the human mind, as displayed in their analysis of the vast creation. Is not this a fitting time to say a word about gratitude towards Him who gave them? Not a syllable. What we gain from his contemplation of nature is 'a gratifying treat,' the knowledge of the 'great things for which Providence has fitted man's understanding;' our admiration terminates in man; it passes on to no prototype. I am not quarrelling with his result;[10] it is but consistent with the principles with which he started. Take the system of nature by itself, detached from religion, and I am willing to confess—nay, I have been expressly urging, that it does not force us to take it for *more* than a system; but why, then, persist in calling the study of it religious, when it can be treated and is treated thus atheistically? Say that religion hallows the study, not that the study is a true ground of religion. The essence of religion is the idea of a Moral Governor; now let me ask, is the doctrine of moral governance conveyed to us through the physical sciences at all? Would they be physical sciences if they treated of morals? Can physics teach moral matters without ceasing to be physics? But are not virtue and vice, and responsibility, and reward and punishment, nothing but moral matters, and are *they* not of the essence of religion? In what department, then, of physics are they to be found? Can the problems and principles they involve be expressed in the differential calculus? Is the galvanic battery a whit more akin to conscience and will than the mechanical powers? What we seek is what concerns us, the traces of a Moral Governor; even religious minds cannot discern these in the physical sciences; astronomy witnesses divine power, and physiology divine skill; and all of them divine beneficence; but which teaches of divine holiness, truth, justice, or mercy? Is that much of a religion which is silent about duty, sin, and its remedies? Was there ever a religion which was without the idea of an expiation?

10 result] *The Tamworth Reading Room pamphlet adds*: as illogical or unfair

Peel's Address and the Catholicus Letters

Sir Robert Peel tells us, that physical science imparts 'pleasure and *consolation*' on a deathbed. Lord Brougham confines himself to the 'gratifying treat;' but Sir Robert ventures to speak of 'consolation.' Now, if we are on trial in this life, and if death be the time when our account is gathered in, is it at all real or serious to be talking of 'consoling' ourselves at such a time with scientific subjects? Are these topics to suggest to us the thought of the Creator or not? If not, are they better (561) than story books, to beguile the mind from what lies before it? But, if they are to speak of Him, can a dying man find rest in the mere notion of his Creator, when he knows Him also so awfully as his Moral Governor and his Judge?[11]

But enough on this most painful portion of Sir Robert's address. As I am coming to an end, I suppose I ought to sum up in a few words what I have been saying. I consider, then, that intrinsically excellent and noble as are scientific pursuits, and worthy of a place in a liberal education, and fruitful in temporal benefits to the community; still they are not, and cannot be, the instrument of education; that physics do not supply a basis, but only materials for religious feeling; that knowledge does but occupy, instead of forming the mind; that faith is the only known principle capable of subduing moral evil, educating the multitude, and organizing society; and that whereas man is born for action, action flows not from inferences, but from impressions; not from reasonings, but from faith.

That Sir Robert would deny these propositions I am far from contending. I do not even contend that he has asserted the contrary at Tamworth. It matters little to me whether he spoke boldly and intelligibly as the newspapers represent, or guarded his strong sayings with the contradictory matter with which they are intercalated in his own report. In either case the drift and the effect of his address are the same. He has given his respected name to a sophistical school, and condescended to mimic the gestures and tones of Lord Brougham. How melancholy it is that a man of such exemplary life, such cultivated tastes, such political distinction, such Parliamentary tact, and

---

11 *The Tamworth Reading Room pamphlet adds*: Meditate indeed on the wonders of nature on a death-bed! rather stay your hunger with corn grown in Jupiter, and warm yourself by the Moon.

'An aristocracy of exalted spirits'

such varied experience, should have so little confidence in himself, so little faith in his own principles, so little hope of sympathy in others, so little heart for a great venture, so little of romantic aspiration, and of firm resolve, and stern dutifulness to the Unseen! How sad that he who might have had the affections of many, should have thought in a day like this that a statesman's praise lay in preserving the mean, not in aiming at the high; that to be safe was his first merit, and to kindle enthusiasm his most disgraceful blunder! How pitiable that such a man should not have understood that a body without a soul has no life, and a political party without an idea no unity!

CATHOLICUS.

Appendix II.
Material Relevant to *The Tamworth Reading Room*

1. Newman's letter to his mother in the wake of Catholic Emancipation

March 1. 1829

[To my Mother]

We have achieved a glorious Victory. It is the first public event I have been concerned in, and I thank God from my heart both for my cause and its success. We have proved the independence of the Church and of Oxford. So rarely is either of the two in opposition to Government, that not once in fifty years can independent principle be shown; yet in these times, when its existence has been generally doubted, the moral power we shall gain by it cannot be overestimated. We had the influence of government in unrelenting activity against us—the 'talent' so called of the University, the Town Lawyers, who care little for our credit, the distance off and the slender means of our voters ... The 'rank and talent' of London came down superciliously to remove any impediment to the quiet passing of the Great Duke's bill, confessing at the same time that of course the University would lose credit by turning about, whatever the Government might gain by it. They would make use of their suffrage, as members of the University to degrade the University. No wonder that such as I, who have not, and others who have, definite opinions in favour of Catholic Emancipation, should feel we have a much nearer and holier interest than the pacification of Ireland, and should with all our might resist the attempt to put us under the feet of the Duke and Mr Brougham.

Their insolence has been intolerable; not that we have done more than laugh at it. They have every where styled themselves the 'talent' of the University—that they have rank and station on their side, I know; and that we have the inferior Colleges and the humbler style of men; but as to talent, Whately with perhaps Hawkins is the only man of talent among the—as to the rest, any one of us in the Oriel Common Room will fight a dozen of them apiece—and Keble is a host—Balliol too gives us a tough set—and we have all the practical talent, for they

'An aristocracy of exalted spirits'

have shown they are mere sucking pigs in their canvass and their calculations. Their excessive confidence amounted to infatuation. Several days since their London chairman wrote to Mr Peel assuring him of complete and certain success. They strutted about (peacocks!) telling our men who passed through London that they should beat by eight to one, and they wondered we should bring the matter to a poll. We endured all this, scarcely hoping for success, but determining, as good Churchmen and true, to fight for the principle, not consenting to our own degradation. I am sure I would have opposed Mr Peel, had there been only just enough with me to take off the appearance of egotism and ostentation, and we seriously contemplated, about ten days since, when we seemed to have too slight hopes of victory to put men to the expense of coming up, we, the residents seventy, simply and solemnly to vote against Mr Peel, though the majority against us might be many hundreds. How much of the Church's credit depended on us residents! and how inexcusable we should have been, if by drawing back we had deprived our country friends of the opportunity of voting, and had thus in some sort betrayed them!

Well, the poor defenceless Church has borne the brunt of it—and I see in it the strength and unity of Churchmen—An hostile account in one of the Papers says, 'High and Low Church have joined, being set on ejecting Mr Peel. I am glad to say I have seen no ill humour any where. We have been merry all through it.[1]

2. *Newman's Letter to Jemima Newman in the wake of Catholic Emancipation*

Oriel College. Mar 4. 1829

My dear no, I will send this to you Jemima, and another to my Mother soon, for you have not had one on this grave business. However, since this is to be my famous 'reason' letter, you must be kind enough to read it to her, thanking her withal for her letter received yesterday morning.

1. Well then—take the case—Mr Peel changes his mind on the Catholic Question, resigns his seat—and is not re-proposed by his Society. Meddling individuals put him up again, the Anti Catholic lead-

---

1 *LD*, II, 125–6.

ers (old Die-in-the-breach and others) shrink back, the Town lawyers say it will be a bad thing for the success of their Political Schemes if he is not re-elected acknowledging the while Oxford will lose credit by his re-election, and all the influence of Government and the Aristocracy is brought into play. Now is not it hard that because a Minister chooses deliberately to change his opinion, that Oxford must suddenly in a few days change too?—And changing with a Minister incur the imputation of changing from interested motives? It is rather too much that MP's change is to be sheltered by our change and that we are to whitewash him by our own disgrace. What is the reputation of the whole cabinet, great Captain and all, put together, compared with that of Oxford, built up (as it is) in the lapse of centuries. Oxford has never turned with the turn of fortune. Mistaken we may have been, but never inconstant. We kept to the Stuarts in misfortune. Better be bigoted than time-serving.—Our opinion of the Catholic Question is a fact of times gone by—it is a thing done—if a bigoted opinion, it remains so—we do not undo it, by now changing—we do no good—we only get the blame of worldly-mindedness. I am in the condition of one who opposes a measure (e.g.) when under deliberation, but resolves to act on it vigorously when determined on. While the petition was under debate, (we will say) I oppose it—but when it is carried and presented to the House, to reject Mr Peel is the step which necessarily follows. And I take it. But the truth is I am not for Catholic Emancipation—and I did not (128) oppose the Petition. I am in principal Anti Catholic—i.e. I think there is a grand attack on the Church in progress from the Utilitarians and Schismatics—and the first step in a long train of events is accidentally the granting these claims. Thus it is to me a matter of subordinate consequence whether they are granted or not—if granted, something fresh will be asked; say, the unestablishing of the Irish Protestant Church. If then I am for Catholic Emancipation it is not because I expect a 'settling of the Question', but because I think that when the claims are granted, I shall fight the enemy on better ground and to more advantage. While then, on the one hand, my view of the Question enables me without much or even any repugnance to imply that opposition to the Claims which an opposition to Mr Peel seemed to intimate, on the other observe how vastly important is the maintenance of the credit of the University. In these perilous times the influence of the Church depends on its Character. It is not once in a Century that Oxford and the Church are in opposition to Government. I would not have lost this opportunity of showing our independence for the world. I look upon that opportunity as providential, and intended (probably) to bear upon times to come and events as yet undisclosed. Even had I a strong opinion of the political advantage resulting for the Emancipation, yet the mere political advantage resulting from a display of integrity such as this is infinitely greater. And when we further think that we are appointed Guardians and Guides of Christ's Church, I am sure I cannot understand how any one soul (viewing things as we do) could do otherwise than reject Mr Peel even though the political evil were very great. In such cases we have no right to look to consequences. We must do our duty straightforward, and be faithful Servants to the Church, even could it be proved that commotions would arise in Ireland from our conduct; tho' such a prospect, if probable (which it is not at all) should of course make us more circumspect and wary before we decided on our line of conduct

Dear me, when shall I get through my 'reasons'—I have barely finished No 1 now. I hope you all are well ...[1]

3. Newman's Letter to his Mother Concerning 'Universal Education'

13 March 1829

[To my Mother]

What a scribler I am become! but the fact is, my mind is so full of ideas [in consequence of this important event], and my views have so much enlarged and expanded ...

We live in a novel era—one in which there is an advance towards universal education. Men have hitherto depended on others, and especially on the Clergy, for religious truth; now each man attempts to judge for himself. Now, without meaning of course that Christianity is in itself opposed to free inquiry, still I think it in fact at the present time opposed to the particular form which that liberty of thought has now assumed. Christianity is of faith, modesty, lowliness, subordination; but the spirit

---

1 *LD*, II, 127

at work against it is one of (130) latitudinarianism, indifferentism, republicanism, and schism, a spirit which tends to overthrow doctrine, as if the fruit of bigotry, and discipline as if the instrument of priestcraft. All parties seem to acknowledge that the stream of opinion is setting against the Church. I do believe it will ultimately be separated from the State, and at this prospect I look with apprehension, 1. because all revolutions are awful things, and the effect of this revolution is unknown. 2. because the upper classes will be left almost religionless. 3 because there will not be that security for sound doctrine without change which is given by an Act of Parliament. 4 because the Clergy will be thrown on their Congregations for voluntary contributions. It is no reply to say that the majesty of Truth will triumph, for man's nature is corrupt; also, even should it triumph, still this will only be ultimately, and the meanwhile may last for centuries. Yet I do still think there is a promise of preservation to the Church, and, in its sacraments preceding and attending religious education, there are such means of heavenly grace, that I do not doubt it will live on in the most irreligious and atheistical times.

Its enemies at present are 1. the uneducated or partially educated mass in towns, whose organs are Wooler's, Carlisle's publications etc. They are almost professedly deistical or worse. 2 The Utilitarians, political economists, useful knowledge people—their organs the Westminster Review, the London University, etc. 3 The schismatics, in and out of the Church, whose organs are the E[c]lectic Review, the Christian Guardian, etc. 4. The Baptists, whose system is consistent Calvinism, for, as far as I can see, Thomas Scott†1 etc are inconsistent, and such inconsistent men would in times of commotion split, and go over to this side or that. 5 the high circles in London. 6. I might add the political indifferentists, but I do not know enough to speak, like men who join Roman Catholics on one hand and Socinians on the other. Now you must not understand me as speaking harshly of individuals; I am speaking of bodies and principles.

And now I come to another phenomenon; the talent of the day is against the Church. The Church party, (visibly at least, for there may be latent talent, and great times give birth to great men,) is poor in mental endowments. It has not activity, shrewdness, dexterity, eloquence, practical powers. On what then does it depend? on prejudice and bigotry. This is hardly an exaggeration; yet I have good meaning and one honorable to the Church. Listen to my theory. As each individual has certain instincts of right and wrong, antecedently to reasoning, on which he acts and rightly so, which perverse reasoning may supplant, which then can hardly be regained, but, if regained, will be regained from a different source, from reasoning, not from nature, so, I think, has the world of men collectively. God gave them truths in His miraculous revelations, and other truths, in the unsophisticated infancy of notions, scarcely less necessary and divine. These are transmitted as 'the wisdom of our ancestors', through men, many of whom (131) cannot enter into them, or receive them themselves, still on, on, from age to age, not the less truths, because many of the generations, through which they are transmitted, are unable to prove them, but hold them either from pious and honest feeling (it may be) or from bigotry or from prejudice. That they are truths, it is most difficult to prove; for great men alone can prove great ideas or grasp them—Such a mind was Hooker's, such Butler's; and, as moral evil triumphs over good on a small field of action, so in the argument of an hour, or the compass of a volume would men like Brougham, or again Wesley show to far greater advantage than Hooker or Butler—Moral truth is gained by patient study, by calm reflection, silently as the dew falls, unless miraculously given, and, when gained, it is transmitted by faith and by 'prejudice.' Keble's book is full of such truths; which any Cambridge man might refute with the γρεατεστ εασε[2]

4. Excerpt of Henry Brougham's Speech at the University of Glasgow

To those, too, who feel alarmed as statesmen, and friends of existing establishments, I would address a few words of comfort. Real knowledge never promoted either turbulence or unbelief; but its progress is the forerunner of liberality and enlightened toleration. Whoso dreads these, let him tremble; for he may be well assured that their day is at length come and must put to sudden flight the evil spirits of tyranny and persecution, which haunted the long night now gone down the sky. As men will no longer suffer themselves to be led blindfold in ignorance, so will they no more yield to the vile principle of judging and treating their fellow creatures, not according to the intrinsic merit of their actions, but according to the accidental and involuntary coincidence of their

---

2 LD, II, 129

opinions. The Great Truth has finally gone forth to all the ends of the earth, THAT MAN SHALL NO MORE RENDER ACCOUNT TO MAN FOR HIS BELIEF, OVER WHICH HE HAS HIMSELF NO CONTROL. Henceforward, nothing shall prevail upon us to praise or to blame any one for that which he can no more change than he can the hue of his skin or the height of his stature. Henceforward, treating with entire respect those who conscientiously differ from ourselves, the only practical effect of the difference will be, to make us enlighten the ignorance on one side or the other from which it springs, by instructing them, if it be theirs; ourselves, if it be our own, to the end that the only kind of unanimity may be produced which is desirable among rational beings the agreement proceeding from full conviction after the freest discussion.³

5. Excerpt of Stephen Lushington's Speech at the Opening of the University of London

Though the Metropolis of almost every country in Europe, has enjoyed and appreciated the benefits of an University she [London], the queen of cities, the emporium of the world ... has had to lament the want of an establishment, where her sons might obtain that liberal acquaintance with learning and science, which is the best guide to the honourable acquisition of wealth, contributes most to its due enjoyment, and is its proudest ornament when attained.

England has indeed to boast of those venerable seats of learning the Universities of Oxford and Cambridge, which the munificence of our forefathers prepared for us: but the demand for public instruction, the desire, nay, I may add the necessity of obtaining knowledge, classical and scientific, have increased so rapidly, that Oxford and Cambridge are utterly inadequate to supply the wants of the nation. The great expense attending education in those Universities, the distance from the home of the parent, the exclusion of all who do not conform to the Established Church, necessarily prevent a large proportion of the youth of this kingdom from resorting thither. Can any man contend that an Institution which diminishes the expense, which brings the means of acquiring knowledge closer to the home of the parent, which expands

---

3 Brougham, *Speeches*, 128.

its portals with equal hospitality to all without distinction, will not confer an inestimable boon on learning and science? Have we not with one common consent of all parties and denominations agreed to educate the whole population of the country? Are we to stop short in this splendid career? Will any one argue for limiting the degree of cultivation which the human intellect shall receive, or establishing a monopoly to be enjoyed only by the few, whose wealth renders expense undeserving of consideration, and who are of one denomination of the Christian Church only? ... Amongst the many benefits likely to arise, my mind dwells with peculiar satisfaction on the expectation, that in this place, by the association and union of all, without exclusion or restriction, friendships will be formed in early days, which long remembered, as our youth are embarked on the ocean of life, will cement the bond of charity, and soften those asperities which ignorance and separation have fostered.[4]

6. Acts of the Apostles (17:16–34, KJV)

Now while Paul waited for them at Athens, his spirit was stirred in him, when he saw the city wholly given to idolatry. Therefore disputed he in the synagogue with the Jews, and with the devout persons, and in the market daily with them that met with him. Then certain philosophers of the Epicureans, and of the Stoicks, encountered him. And some said, What will this babbler say? other some, He seemeth to be a setter forth of strange gods: because he preached unto them Jesus, and the resurrection. And they took him, and brought him unto Areopagus, saying, May we know what this new doctrine, whereof thou speakest, is? For thou bringest certain strange things to our ears: we would know therefore what these things mean. (For all the Athenians and strangers which were there spent their time in nothing else, but either to tell, or to hear some new thing.) Then Paul stood in the midst of Mars' hill, and said, Ye men of Athens, I perceive that in all things ye are too superstitious. For as I passed by, and beheld your devotions, I found an altar with this inscription, TO THE UNKNOWN GOD.

Whom therefore ye ignorantly worship, him declare I unto you. God that made the world and all things therein, seeing that he is Lord of

---

4 Lushington, *Statement by the Council of the University of London*, 52–4.

heaven and earth, dwelleth not in temples made with hands; Neither is worshipped with men's hands, as though he needed any thing, seeing he giveth to all life, and breath, and all things; And hath made of one blood all nations of men for to dwell on all the face of the earth, and hath determined the times before appointed, and the bounds of their habitation; That they should seek the Lord, if haply they might feel after him, and find him, though he be not far from every one of us: For in him we live, and move, and have our being; as certain also of your own poets have said, For we are also his offspring. Forasmuch then as we are the offspring of God, we ought not to think that the Godhead is like unto gold, or silver, or stone, graven by art and man's device.

And the times of this ignorance God winked at; but now commandeth all men every where to repent: Because he hath appointed a day, in the which he will judge the world in righteousness by that man whom he hath ordained; whereof he hath given assurance unto all men, in that he hath raised him from the dead. And when they heard of the resurrection of the dead, some mocked: and others said, We will hear thee again of this matter. So Paul departed from among them. Howbeit certain men clave unto him, and believed: among them which was Dionysius the Areopagite, and a woman named Damaris, and others with them.

7. The Morning Chronicle's review of the Catholicus Letters

The growing spirit of Puseyism in the Church appears thus far to have worked tolerably well in harness with Toryism. But the symptoms of restiveness are beginning to show themselves, which plainly indicate that such will not be the case long. Nor is it difficult to foresee that eventually this Popish heresy in a Protestant Establishment will split the Tory faction into fragments incapable of any further re-union.

With the Toryism of two centuries ago, Puseyism might have permanently amalgamated. But it has come too late into the world. Modern Toryism is quite a different affair from the absolutism and Jacobitism to which it has succeeded. The vitality of principle is gone; and the carcass is only animated by the demon of expediency. The professed attachment of Toryism to national institutions never regards the idea and final cause of those institutions, but some sinister class interest which, in them it would conserve. In Democracy, it only beholds the materials for corruption. In Sovereignty, not the personified unity of the state, but an agency for securing the ascendancy of a party. And its church is a fat provision for the juniors of great families and their toadeaters; or a useful organization for electioneering and other influences, but not an institution for the spiritual culture of the community. The party wants the middle classes, and has occasional need of the multitude. It coquets with all popular notions. It temporizes and accommodates. It dabbles and traffics in reforms and emancipations. It is great in tricks and tactics. It is a thing of shreds and patches.

Not so Puseyism. That is earnest and uncompromising. It disclaims and disdains expediency. The vigour of old Papal Rome is in the cohesion and boldness of its pretensions. Whatever is incongruous with itself it smites and spares not. It claims to be god upon earth, and commands intelligence like a slave. It heeds not interests. Its moralists tell us that men are born slaves; that slavery is the necessity of their nature. The one duty of its education is obedience; first to the parent, then to the State; above all to the Church. Such is its Jacob's ladder up to the heights of its own supremacy. The union of Puseyism and Toryism is that of Don Quixote and Sancho Panza rolled into one fat single gentleman. The particles must fly off. Else there is no such power in the nature of things as repulsion.

Were the Tories reinstated, they could never get through the work of office with Puseyism on their backs. Their appointments in the Church, dictated by worldly policy; their tampering with Dissenters and their concessions on such points as education would all be sacrilege to the Puseyites. And they would be annoyed, on the other hand, with more propositions for depopulating the large towns, for enforcing the observance of fast days and saints' days, and for the revival of obsolete ceremonies to the unbounded horror and alarm of all the evangelical population. But Puseyism is an iron mace; Toryism, a rope of sand...

The columns of the *Times* itself are thrown open to this sect for attacks upon Sir ROBERT PEEL. We do not say the attacks are not well founded. His sincerity of speech is impeached in the form of a compliment to his understanding. His philosophy is shown to be superficial. The low-toned character of his morality is exposed. His shiftings, turnings, and inconsistencies, to catch this or that class, are laid bare unmercifully. The conviction of his thorough want of mental honesty is enforced. Now this is all very sound and true. We have not now to learn what sort of person it pleases the Tories to follow, or rather to drive before them, as their leader. The instructive part of the matter is in such an exhibition of the portrait-painting power of Puseyism. The sect speaks out; while other Tories conceal their lack of respect, because they think PEEL convenient. Puseyism is insurgent against the first law of Tory union and co-operation. It forbids the use of plausibilities to the man who lives by plausibilities; who is himself only one great plausibility. Will not doings like this make havoc in the camp? Another of the stern fraternity was yesterday introduced by the *Times* with a flourish of trumpets, to make proclamation to the House of Lords against duelling. The Puseyites work out their morality into politics and practice. They do not play at religion and righteousness according to the good old conventional ways of the Church. They are all for realities. We like their spirit. But it will never do with the Tories …

[We] are mistaken in the Puseyites if they will either put up with a rebuff or consent to a compromise. With the exception of their dishonest participation in the moneys of the National Church—and they, doubtless, make that out, somehow, to their own consciences—they have all the marks of the most right-down earnestness that the world has seen, in religion, since the times of the Puritans and the Reformers. The genuine ecclesiastical spirit is strong in them. They are as obstinate as THOMAS à BECKETT. The soft, slimy substance is already squashing beneath their feet. They are the iron of the composite image, and woe betide its clay.

But for the entire party, as a party, the position is rather a ridiculous one. Its own principle is at war with its own policy. By its unprincipledness it has fished for the alliance of Puseyism and Puseyism comes into the alliance to denounce its unprincipledness. The incongruous compound cannot long hold together; but its momentary existence is one of the strangest novelties of the nineteenth century.[5]

---

5 *The Morning Chronicle*, 12 February 1841.

8. Excerpt on the Catholicus Letters in The Rambler

We have now reached the year of hottest warfare, when the movement suddenly shewed itself before the world in its true colours ... How strange and unexpected had been its progress up to 1841, was proved by a singular step taken in its regard by a no less acute observer than the proprietor of the Times newspaper. Another acute observer of the signs of the age, the late Sir Robert Peel, had just issued a manifesto of his opinions on the influence of secular knowledge on the wellbeing of man. The 'Address' ... exhibited the great baronet as a patron of principles hitherto supposed peculiar to the school of Brougham, of the Whigs and the Radicals. With all his characteristic complacency, Sir Robert announced his adhesion to the system which advocates mental cultivation apart from religion; or, as he would have stated it, in connexion with such comprehensive ideas on religion as would embrace alike the Catholic and the Socinian, the Anglican and the Quaker. The liberal press of the day was fairly thrown into ecstacy at the conversion of so illustrious an individual; Tories and High Churchmen looked askance, or frowned severe; and the Address was read and commented on with no little marvel as to the ultimate development of its authors' views.

Among other journalists, the late Mr. Walter, chief proprietor and manager of the Times considered that the time was come for 'taking up' Puseyism, and for striking a heavy blow at the latitudinarian Peel in the columns of his paper. Little foreseeing what a manifestation of the tendencies of the movement was on the eve of appearing, and still less anticipating that a day was at hand when he would treat the outward marks and works of Puseyism as a personal insult to himself, Mr. Walter visited Mr. Newman at Oriel College, and urged him again and again to write against Peel's Address in the *Times* newspaper. This was in the month of February, and but one month before the publication of Tract 90, and supplies perhaps as curious an instance as could be named of the miscalculations into which the most accomplished watchers of public opinion are frequently betrayed. At length Mr. Newman consented to the request, and a series of letters speedily appeared, with the signature of 'Catholicus,' which set the *quidnuncs* gossiping throughout the kingdom, and handled Sir Robert with a delicacy and severity of satire and argumentative dissection, compared to which the

Material Relevant to The Tamworth Reading Room

ruder attacks of which he had been the frequent subject in the House of Commons were as a game of play. Some few knew the authorship of the letters; others guessed it, for it was difficult indeed not to detect the well-known style; but of the innumerable readers of the *Times*, on the whole, comparatively few ever learnt whose was the hand that inflicted the scourging.[6]

---

6 Capes, 'The Rise, Progress, and Results of Puseyism', 81–2.

Appendix III.
Sample Press Reception of Peel's Address and the Catholicus Letters

DATE	Peel speeches	The Times and Catholicus	The Staffordshire Advertiser	The Spectator	The Morning Post	The Standard	The Globe	The Morning Herald	The Morning Chronicle	The Sun
19.1	X									
23.1		X		X						
25.1					X					
26.1	X				X					
29.1									X	
30.1			X							
31.1										
2.2										
5.2	X									
8.2	X					X		X		
9.2	X									
10.2	X								X	
11.2	X						X			
12.2	X					X		X		
13.2			X						X	
14.2									X	
15.2									X	
20.2	X									
22.2	X									
25.2	X					X		X		
27.2	X				X	X		X		
28.2										
2.3					X					
3.3						X		X		
4.3	X					X	X			

'An aristocracy of exalted spirits'

DATE	Peel speeches	The Times and Catholicus	The Staffordshire Advertiser	The Spectator	The Morning Post	The Standard	The Globe	The Morning Herald	The Morning Chronicle	The Sun
6.3										
10.3	×					×				
11.3	×									
12.3						×		×		
13.3			×	×	×				×	
15.3							×			
16.3						×				
19.3								×		
20.3										
21.3										
26.3	×							×		
28.3										
3.4										
4.4										
8.7						×		×		
2.10								×		
2.12								×		

330

Appendix IV. Biographical Entries

George **Berkeley** (1685–1753), Anglican Bishop of Cloyne (Ireland), was a proponent of a philosophical movement that has been labeled 'subjective idealism'; the city where the University of California is located was named after him.

Napoléon **Bonaparte** (15 August 1769, Ajaccio, Corsica – 5 May 1821, Saint Helena), Emperor of the French (20 March 1804 – 6 April 1814; Exile on Island of Elba 'One Hundred Days': 1 March 1815 – 22 June 1815).

Samuel **Bosanquet** (1800–82) 'educated at Eton and Christ Church, B.A. 1822. He was called to the bar at the Inner Temple in 1826 and he was one of the revising barristers appointed on the passing of the Reform Act of 1832. He contributed many leading articles to *The Times* and three articles to the *British Critic*, two of which he worked up into his volume on The Rights of the Poor and Christian Almsgiving vindicated, London 1841, in which he showed a strong sympathy for the poor and disillusionment with the Poor Laws. He published a number of miscellaneous works during his life, and was for thirty-five years Chairman of the Monmouthshire Quarter Sessions' (*DNB*) (*LD*, VII, 510).

John William **Bowden** (1798–1844), Newman's close friend at Trinity College. (*LD*, I, 328)

Henry Peter **Brougham** (1778–1868), First Baron Brougham and Vaux, a British writer, scientist, lawyer, abolitionist, educational reformer, and Whig politician, was also a found of the *Edinburgh Review*, the University of London, and the Society for the Diffusion of Useful Knowledge (*DNB*).

William **Buckland** (1784–1856), Waynflete Professor Mineralogy and Professor of Geology at Oxford (*LD* I, 329).

Bishop Joseph **Butler** (1692–1752), Anglican Bishop of Bristol (1738–50) and Durham (1750–2), influenced Newman through his *Analogy of Religion, Natural and Revealed* (1736).

'An aristocracy of exalted spirits'

George **Canning** (1770–1827) a follower of the younger Pitt and staunch Tory, served briefly as Prime Minister (1827) but died four months into his tenure (*SMB*, 188).

John Moore **Capes** (1812–89) became a Roman Catholic in 1845, founded the *Rambler* in 1848, but rejoined the Church of England in 1870 and criticized Newman for accepting the definition of infallibility; Capes returned to the Roman Catholic Church a dozen years later (*LD*, XI, 336).

Thomas **Carlyle** (1795–1881) was a leading essayist, historian, satirist and social critic in the Victorian era (http://www.dumfries-and-galloway.co.uk/people/carlyle.htm).

John Frederick **Christie** (1808–60), student and Fellow of Oriel (1829–48), was rector of Ufton-Nervet, Berkshire (1847–60). (*LD*, II, 403)

Richard William **Church** (1815–90), Fellow of Oriel, junior proctor who vetoed the condemnation of *Tract 90*, later Dean of St. Paul's (London).

Samuel Taylor **Coleridge** (1772–1834), philosopher and poet ('The Rime of the Ancient Mariner' and 'Kubla Khan').

William **Cowper** (1731–1800) poet and hymnodist.

Paul Cardinal **Cullen** (1803–78) was rector of the Irish College in Rome (1832–50) before being named Archbishop of Armagh in 1850 and Archbishop of Dublin in 1852 and in 1866 was the first Irish bishop to be named a cardinal.

Charles **Darwin** (1809–82), a geologist and naturalist, whose *On the Origins of Species* (1859) explained the diversity of in nature by the evolution of species through natural selection.

Thomas **Erastus** (1524–83), a Swiss physician and theologian, gave his name to 'Erastianism', the doctrine that the State is supreme in religious matters.

Frederick William **Faber** (1814–63), a graduate of Balliol College, Oxford, and later a Scholar (1835) and Fellow (1837) of University College, won the Newdigate Poetry Prize (1836); an Anglican deacon (1837) and priest (1839), he entered the Roman Catholic Church (November 1845) and was ordained a priest in 1847; he established the Wilfridians,

Biographical Entries

who soon merged with the Oratorians; when an Oratorian house was founded in London (1849), first at King William Street and later in Brompton Road, Faber was superior, as well as being an indefatigable preacher, prolific author and hymn-writer.

Godfrey **Fausset** (1780/81–1853) entered Corpus Christi College in 1797, BA 1801, and gained a Fellowship at Magdalen in 1802. He was appointed Lady Margaret Professor of Divinity in 1827, and a Canon of Christ Church in 1840.

James Anthony **Froude** (1818–94), son of Robert Hurrell Froude, was educated at Westminster School and Oriel College, Oxford; his publication of *Nemesis of Faith* led to his resignation of his fellowship at Exeter College; subsequently, he was editor of *Fraser's Magazine*, rector of St. Andrew's University and Regius Professor of Modern History at Oxford.

Richard Hurrell **Froude** (1803–36), son of Robert Hurrell Froude, was like Newman a Fellow of Oriel and one of the leaders of the Oxford Movement until his early death (*LD*, XI, 340).

William **Froude** (1810–79), son of Robert Hurrell Froude, graduated from Oxford with a first in mathematics and then worked for the South-Eastern Railway before becoming a naval architect; his correspondence with Newman is reflected in the *Grammar of Assent*.

William Ewart **Gladstone** (1809–98) was Chancellor of the Exchequer (1852–5, 1859–66, 1873–4, 1880–2) and Prime Minister (December 1868 – February 1874; April 1880 – June 1885; February–July 1886; August 1892 – March 1894).

Edward **Hawkins** (1789–1882), a student at St. John's, who graduated with a double first in 1811, was Newman's predecessor as vicar of St. Mary's (1823–8) and provost of Oriel College (1828–82). (*LD*, I, 334).

David **Hume** (1711–76), Scottish philosopher and skeptic, author of *Essays Moral and Political* and *Philosophical Essays*.

William **Huskisson** (1770–1830), a Tory MP and supporter of the younger Pitt, was a leader in the Liverpool administration with economic policies such as a return to the gold standard and free trade (*SMB*, 164).

'An aristocracy of exalted spirits'

Richard Holt **Hutton** (1826–97), journalist, joint editor of *The Spectator*, and biographer of Cardinal Newman (www.newmanreader.org/biography/hutton/index.html)

Sir Robert **Inglis** (1786–1855), MP for Dundalk (1824–6) and Ripon (1828–9), with the support of Newman defeated Sir Robert Peel in the Oxford University by-election of 1829, and represented Oxford for the rest of his life (*LD*, II, 408).

Robert Banks **Jenkinson**, second Earl of Liverpool (1770–1828), a politician and Prime Minister during the rise of 'Liberal Toryism' in the 1820s (*SMB*, 153–4).

John **Keble** (1792–1866), Professor of Poetry at Oxford (1831–41) and like Newman a Fellow of Oriel College, gave the Assize Sermon on 14 July 1833, which Newman considered the beginning of the Oxford Movement; in 1836, Keble became vicar of Hursley, a post that he would hold for the rest of his life (*LD*, XI, 343).

Charles **Kingsley** (1819–75), educated at Magdalene College, Cambridge ... He had religious doubts, resolved by reading the works of F. D. Maurice and others, reacted strongly against the Oxford Movement, and took Orders in 1842. In 1844 he married Fanny Grenfell, and was made rector of Eversley, Hampshire. He became one of the Christian Socialists in 1848, and his first novels (for example, *Westward Ho!*) were written under their influence. Later he developed a xenophobic patriotism and became an advocate of muscular Christianity ... After his death Newman wrote that he could not feel resentment towards Kingsley, who had accidentally given him the opportunity to vindicate his career. He had hoped they might have met, and felt sure that he, Newman, would have felt no embarrassment (*LD*, XXI, 550).

William **Lamb**, Viscount **Melbourne** (1779–1848) A Whig politician who was Prime Minister (1834–5; 1835–41), at other times represented loyal opposition to the Conservative party, and was an important advisor to the young Queen Victoria (*SMB*, 226).

Pierre-Simone **Laplace** (1749–1827), a French mathematician and astronomer, was a leading intellectual during the French Enlightenment.

Biographical Entries

Felicité Robert de **Lamennais** (1782–1854), a Roman Catholic priest who felt that the Church in France could have no real liberty under a royal government, was a co-founder of *L'Avenir*; after his views were rejected by Pope Gregory XVI (b. 1765, r. 1831–46), he left the Church and died excommunicated.

Charles **Lloyd** (1784–1829), Regius Professor of Divinity at Oxford, was appointed Bishop of Oxford in 1827 (*LD*, I, 337)

John **Locke** (1632–1704), a philosopher, who is considered the first of the British Empiricists.

Stephen **Lushington** (1782–1873), a prominent judge and MP, was a liberal political and social reformer who was a founder of the SDUK and spoke at the inauguration of London University (*DNB*).

Thomas Babington **Macaulay**, First Baron Macaulay (1800–59), was a poet, prominent historian, essayist, and Whig politician (*DNB*).

Henry Edward **Manning** (1808–92), graduate of Balliol, Fellow of Merton, rector of Wool Lavington and then of Graffham, Sussex, became a Roman Catholic and later Archbishop of Westminster (1865) and a cardinal (1875) (*LD*, II, 409).

Walter **Mayers** (1790–1828), an Evangelical Anglican clergyman, was senior classical master at Ealing School (1814–22) while Newman was a student there; in his *Apologia* (4), Newman described Mayers as 'the human means of the beginning of divine faith' (*LD*, I, 337); Mayers later became curate of Over Worton, where Newman preached his first sermon on 23 June 1824; four years later, Newman would preach the sermon at Mayers's funeral.

James **Mill** (1773–1836), a utilitarian philosopher and political economist, and member of the 'Philosophical Radicals', who promoted widespread social and political change in England (*SMB*, 20)

John Stuart **Mill** (1806–73), British philosopher, political economist, civil servant and MP, was an influential liberal thinker.

Henry Hart **Milman** (1791–1868), an Anglican cleric, professor of poetry (1821) and Bampton lecturer (1827) at Oxford, was the author of many historical works, including *History of Christianity to the*

Abolition of Paganism in the Roman Empire (1840) and *History of Latin Christianity* (1855).

Anne **Mozley** (1809–91), sister-in-law of Newman's sisters, was asked by Newman to edit the letters of his Anglican years—a project which she was able to complete within a few weeks of his death: *Letters and Correspondence of John Henry Newman during his Life in the English Church with a Brief Autobiography* (*LD*, XXV, 488).

Thomas **Mozley** (1806–93), a pupil of Newman and later Fellow of Oriel, married Newman's sister Harriet in 1836 and became a writer for *The Times* in 1844; his *Reminiscences, Chiefly of Oriel College and Oxford Movement* (1882) was severely criticized by Newman (*LD*, I, 338).

Horatio **Nelson** (1758–1805), a British admiral and Duke of Bronté, was victor over the French fleet at the Battle of Cape Trafalgar, Spain (*SMB*, 130).

Isaac **Newton** (1643–1727), English philosopher, mathematician, scientist, wrote *Philosophiae Naturalis Principia Mathematica* (1687).

Charles Robert **Newman** (1802–84), Newman's younger brother, after working for the Bank of England (1825–32) was supported by his family and lived in seclusion the last decades of his life in Tenby (*LD*, I, 338).

Francis William **Newman** (1805–97), Newman's youngest brother, attended Worcester College and obtained a double first and was elected Fellow of Balliol; from 1830 to 1833, he was a missionary in Persia; he was later Professor of Classical Literature at Manchester (1840–6) and Professor of Latin at London (1846–69); his *Early History of Cardinal Newman* (1891) was an indignant account of his elder brother (*LD*, I, 339).

Harriet **Newman** (1803–52), Newman's oldest sister, married Thomas Mozley in 1836 and broke off relations with her brother before his entrance into the Roman Catholic Church (*LD*, I, 339).

Jemima **Newman** (1808–79), Newman's second sister, married John Mozley, a printer and publisher at Derby; while disapproving of Newman's entrance into the Roman Catholic Church, she remained on relatively friendly terms with him. (*LD*, I, 339)

Biographical Entries

Jemima Fourdrinier **Newman** (1772–1836), Newman's mother, who married John Newman in 1799.

John **Newman** (1767–1824), Newman's father, a banker, who married Jemima Fourdrinier in 1799 (*LD*, I, 339).

Mary **Newman** (1809–28) was Newman's youngest sister (*LD*, I, 339).

Daniel **O'Connell** / Dónal Ó Conaill (1775–1847), known as 'The Liberator' and 'The Emancipator'; his election to Parliament led to the Emancipation Act (1829).

Thomas **Paine** (1737–1809), deist and pamphleteer, author of *The Age of Reason* (*SMB*, 109).

William **Paley** (1743–1805), Christian utilitarian, author of *Principles of Moral and Political Philosophy* (1785) as well as *Natural Theology* (1802). This latter book provided an inferential method of correlation between new scientific theories and deist principles. The premise of the book rested heavily on the argument from design. Paley's utilitarian and inferential approach was attacked by Newman (see Fletcher, 'Newman and Natural Theology', 28–9).

Roundell **Palmer** (1812–96), brother of William Palmer of Magdalen, served as Solicitor General (1861–3), Attorney General (1863–6) and Lord Chancellor (1872–4, 1880–5); created Baron Selborne (1872), he was later named Earl of Selborne and Viscount Wolmer.

James Laird **Patterson** (1822–1902), a student at Trinity College, Oxford, who became a Roman Catholic in 1850; he was president of St. Edmund's College, Ware (1870–80) and then auxiliary bishop of Westminster (1880–1901) (*LD*, XXI, 560).

Dionysius **Petavius**, the Latinized name of Denis **Pétau**, SJ (1583–1652), was a professor at various French universities and author of *De Theologicis Dogmatibus* and *Opus de Doctrina Temporum*; a crater on the Moon is named in his honor.

Edward Bouverie **Pusey** (1800–82), like Newman a Fellow of Oriel College and a leader of the Oxford Movement, was appointed Regius Professor of Hebrew and a canon of Christ Church in 1828 (*LD*, XI, 353).

'An aristocracy of exalted spirits'

David **Ricardo** (1772–1823), British economist who followed Adam Smith. He provided persuasive arguments for free trade that were implemented by the liberal Tories in the 1820s (http://www.policonomics.com/david-ricardo/; *SMB*, 176).

Frederic **Rogers** (1811–89), a pupil of Newman, who took a double first and was a Fellow of Oriel (1833–45), served in the government and was created Lord Blachford; after a falling out with Newman (1843–63), they were reconciled (*LD*, II, 413).

Hugh James **Rose** (1795–1838) of Trinity College, Cambridge, a friend of Newman and founder of the *British Magazine* (*LD*, II, 413).

Thomas **Scott** (1747–1821), rector of Aston Sandford and a founder of the Church Missionary Society, was famous for his *Commentary on the Whole Bible* (1788–92); Scott was described by Newman in his *Apologia* as the person 'to whom (humanly speaking), I almost owe my soul' (*LD*, I, 342)

Thomas **Short** (1789–1879), formerly a tutor at Rugby, became a Fellow of Trinity College, Oxford, in 1816, where he served as tutor for four decades (1816–56) and lived to see Newman named Trinity's first Honorary Fellow (1878) (*LD*, I, 342–3).

Charles **Simeon** (1759–1836), vicar of Holy Trinity, Cambridge, and one of the founders of the Church Missionary Society, has been considered one of the founders of the Evangelical movement.

Queen **Victoria** (1819–1901), arguably the most powerful politician of the nineteenth century, helped shape and direct England throughout her reign (*SMB*, 341–2).

Arthur **Wellesley** (1769–1852), Duke of **Wellington**, was victor over Napoloon at the Battle of Waterloo (1815) and served as Prime Minister (1828–30, 1834).

Richard **Whately** (1787–1863), Fellow of Oriel and Principal of St. Alban Hall, where Newman was Vice-Principal, was appointed Anglican Archbishop of Dublin in 1831 (*LD*, I, 345).

Henry William **Wilberforce** (1807–73), fourth and youngest son of William Wilberforce, was Newman's pupil at Oriel and graduated with a first in classics and a second in mathematics; married to a daughter of John Sargent, he became a Roman Catholic in 1850; after serving as secretary of the Catholic Defence Association in Dublin he became proprietor and editor of the *Catholic Standard* (*LD*, II, 415).

Samuel **Wilberforce** (1805–73), third son of William Wilberforce, went up to Oriel in 1823; married to the oldest daughter of John Sargent, he was appointed Bishop of Oxford in 1845 and Bishop of Winchester in 1869 (*LD*, II, 415).

Nicholas **Wiseman** (1802–65), rector of the English College in Rome (1828–40), president of Oscott College and coadjutor bishop of the Midland district (1840–7) and bishop of the London district (1847–50), was named cardinal and Archbishop of Westminster in 1850 (*LD*, III, 344).

Henry Arthur **Woodgate** (1801–74), a student and Fellow of St. John's with a first in classics, who dedicated his Bampton lectures (*The Authoritative Teaching of the Church*) to Newman in 1839; the *Apologia* brought them together again (*LD*, I, 345–6).

BIBLIOGRAPHY

Primary Sources

Anonymous. 'Ure's Philosophy of Manufactures'. *Mechanics' Magazine and Journal of the Mechanics' Institute* 9. New York: D. K. Minor and George C. Schaeffer, 1837.

Bacon, Francis. *The Works of Francis Bacon: Minor Latin Works*, ed. Basil Montague. Vol. XI. London: William Pickering, 1829.

Blomfield, Charles. *A Memoir of Charles James Blomfield*, ed. A. Blomfield. Vol. I. London: 1863.

Bosanquet, Samuel. 'Pauperism and Almsgiving'. *The British Critic* 28 (July 1840): 195–257.

—— 'Private Alms and Poor-Law Relief'. *The British Critic* 28 (October 1840): 441–70.

Brougham, Henry. *A Discourse of the Objects, Advantages, and Pleasures of Science*. London: Baldwin, Craddock, and Joy, 1827.

—— 'Inaugural Discourse of Henry Brougham, Esq., M.P., on being installed Lord Rector of the University of Glasgow', Wednesday, 6 April 1825. *Speeches of Henry Lord Brougham: upon Questions relating to Public Rights, Duties, and Interests with Historical Introductions*. Vol. II. Philadelphia: Lea and Blanchard, 1841.

Capes, John Moore. 'The Rise, Progress and Results of Puseyism'. *The Rambler: A Catholic Journal and Review* 7:37 (January 1851): 60–89.

Craik, George Lille. *The Pursuit of Knowledge under Difficulties*. London: Charles Knight, 1830.

Croker, John Wilson. *The Croker Papers: The Correspondences and Diaries*, ed. Louis J. Jennings. London: John Murray, 1884.

Davy, Sir Humphry. 'Consolation in Travel'. *The Collected Works of Sir Humphry Davy*, ed. John Davy. Vol. IX. London: Smith, Elder, & Co., 1840.

Gray, Thomas. *An Elegy Written in a Country Churchyard*. New York: Appleton & Co., 1854.

Greville, Charles. *Greville Memoirs: A Journal of the Reign of Queen Victoria. 1837–1852*. Vols. I and III. London: Longman, Green, & Co.; New York: Appleton & Co., 1885.

Haly, W. T. *The Opinions of Sir Robert Peel: Expressed in Parliament and in Public*. London: Whittaker & Co., 1843.

Hansard's Parliamentary Debates. Available at: http://hansard.millbanksystems.com/.

Horace. *The Epistles of Horace*, ed. Augustus S. Wilkins. Vol. I. London: MacMillan & Co., 1888.

Lushington, Stephen. *Statement by the Council of the University of London, Explanatory of the Nature and Objects of the Institution*, ed. Thomas Coats. London: Richard Taylor, 1827.

Milman, Henry H. *The History of Christianity: From the Birth of Christ to the Abolition of Paganism in the Roman Empire*. 3 vols. London: John Murray, 1840.

—— *The History of the Jews*. London: John Murray, 1829.

Mozley, John. *The Letters of Rev. J. B. Mozley, DD*, ed. Anne Mozley. London: Rivingtons, 1885.

Mozley, Thomas. 'Religion of the Manufacturing Poor'. *The British Critic* 28 (October, 1840): 334–71.

—— *Reminiscences Chiefly of Oriel and the Oxford Movement*. London: Longman, Green, & Co., 1882.

—— 'Tamworth Reading Room', *The British Critic* 30 (July 1841): 46–99.

Newman, John Henry. *Addresses to Cardinal Newman and his Replies, 1879–1881*, ed. Rev. W. P. Neville. London: Longman, Green, & Co., 1905.

—— *Apologia pro Vita Sua*, ed. David J. Delaura. New York: W. W. Norton & Co., 1968. [Original: London: Longman & Co., 1864.]

—— *Arians of the Fourth Century*. London: Longman, Green, & Co., 1908.

—— *Autobiographical Writings*. Edited by Henry Tristram. New York: Sheed and Ward, 1957.

—— 'The Catholicity of the English Church'. *The British Critic* 27 (January, 1840): 40–88.

—— 'Catholicus'. Letters to the Editor. *The Times*. 5 February; 9 February; 10 February; 12 February; 20 February; 22 February; 27 February, 1841.

Bibliography

Newman, John Henry. *Certain Difficulties Felt by Anglicans in Catholic Teaching*. Vol. 1. London: Longman, Green, & Co., 1901.
—— *The Correspondence of John Henry Newman with John Keble and Others*. London: Longman, Green, & Co., 1917.
—— *Discussions and Arguments*. London: Longman, Green, & Co., 1907.
—— *An Essay in Aid of a Grammar of Assent*. Introduction by Nicholas Lash. Notre Dame: University of Notre Dame Press, 1979.
—— *An Essay on the Development of Christian Doctrine*. Notre Dame: University of Notre Dame Press, 2005.
—— *Fifteen Sermons Preached before the Oxford University between A.D. 1826 and 1843*. Edited with Introduction and Notes by James David Earnest and Gerard Tracey. Oxford: Oxford University Press, 2006.
—— *Historical Sketches*. Vol. I. London: Longman, Green, & Co., 1908.
—— 'Jacobson's *Apostolical Fathers*'. *British Critic* 25 (January, 1839): 49–76.
—— *The Idea of a University*. Introduction and Notes by Martin J. Svaglic. Notre Dame: University of Notre Dame Press, 2003.
—— 'A Letter Addressed to the Duke of Norfolk on Occasion of Mr. Gladstone's Recent Expostulation'. *Certain Difficulties Felt by Anglicans in Catholic Teaching Considered*. Vol. II. London: Longman, Green, & Co., 1900.
—— *Letters and Correspondence of John Henry Newman to 1845*, ed. Anne Mozley. London: Longman, Green, & Co., 1890.
—— *The Letters and Diaries of John Henry Newman*, ed. Charles Dessain et al. 32 vols. Various Publishers, 1961–2009.
—— 'Milman's *History of Christianity*'. *The British Critic* 29 (January, 1841): 71–114.
—— 'Palmer's *Treatise on the Church of Christ*', *The British Critic* 24 (October, 1838): 347–72.
—— *Parochial and Plain Sermons*. 8 vols. London: Longman & Co., 1907.
—— 'The Personal and Literary Character of Cicero'. *Historical Sketches*. Vol. 1. London: Longman, Green, & Co., 1909.
—— *Remarks on Certain Passages in the Thirty-Nine Articles*. London: Rivington, 1841.
—— *The Sermon Notes of John Henry Newman, 1849–1874*, ed. Henry Tristram. London: Longman, Green, & Co., 1914.
—— *Sermons 1824–1843*, ed. Placid Murray. Vol. I. Oxford: Clarendon Press, 1991.

Newman, John Henry. *Sermons 1824–1843*, ed. Placid Murray and Francis McGrath. Vol. III. Oxford: Clarendon Press, 2010.

—— *Sermons 1824–1843*, ed. Francis McGrath. Vol. IV. Oxford: Clarendon Press, 2011.

—— 'The State of Religious Parties', *The British Critic* 25 (April 1839): 396–426.

—— *Verses on Various Occasions*. London: Longman, Green, & Co., 1903.

—— *The Via Media of the Anglican Church*. London: Longman, Green, & Co., 1908.

Palmer, Roundell. 'English Public Schools' *The British Critic* 29 (January 1841): 151–73.

Peel, Sir Robert. Peel Papers. British Library. London.

—— *An Inaugural Address Delivered by the Right Hon. Sir Robert Peel, Bart. M.P., President of the Tamworth Library and Reading Room on Tuesday, 19th January, 1841*. Second edition. London: James Bain, 1841.

—— *The Peel Banquet: Speeches of the Rt. Hon. Sir Robert Peel, Bart., Lord Stanley, and Sir James Graham, Bart., at Merchant Taylors' Hall, May 12, 1838*. London: Robert Tyas; Edinburgh: J. Menzies, 1838.

—— *The Private Letters of Sir Robert Peel*, ed. George Peel. London: John Murray, 1920.

—— *The Speeches of the Late Right Honorable Sir Robert Peel, Bart.* London: George Rutledge & Co., 1853.

Rogers, Frederick. 'Sewell's *Christian Morals*/Utilitarian Moral Philosophy'. *The British Critic* 29 (January, 1841): 1–44.

—— 'Utilitarian Moral Philosophy'. *The British Critic* 28 (July, 1840): 93–125.

Scott, Sir Walter. *The Poetical Works of Sir Walter Scott: with a Memoir of the Author*. Vol. VII. Boston: Little, Brown, & Co., 1861.

Whately, Richard. 'Logic'. *Encyclopaedia Metropolitana* Edited by Edward Smedly *et al*. London: B. Fellowes and J. Rivington, 1845.

Wiseman, Nicholas. 'The Anglican Claim of Apostolical Succession'. *Dublin Review* 7 (August, 1839): 139–80.

Bibliography

Secondary Sources

Achten, Rik. *First Principles and Our Way to Faith: A Fundamental-Theological Study of John Henry Newman's Notion of First Principles.* New York: Peter Lang, 1995.

Aldrich, Richard. 'Peel, Politics and Education, 1839–46', *The Journal of Educational Administration and History* 13 (1981): 11–23.

Amico, Charles, R. *The Natural Knowability of God according to John Henry Newman with Special Reference to the Argument from Design to the Universe.* Rome: Urbaniana University Press, 1986.

Anonymous. *The History of the Times: 'The Thunderer' in the Making, 1785–1841.* Nendeln, Liechtenstein: Kraus-Thompson, 1971.

Arendt, Hannah. *The Human Condition.* Chicago: University of Chicago Press, 1998.

Armytage, W. H. G. *Four Hundred Years of English Education.* Cambridge: Cambridge University Press, 1964.

Artz, Johannes. 'Newman as Philosopher', *International Philosophical Quarterly* 16 (1976): 263–87.

Authur, James, and Guy Nichols. *John Henry Newman*, ed. Richard Bailey. Continuum Library of Educational Thought. London: Continuum, 2007.

Barnard, Howard Clive. *A Short History of English Education from 1760 to 1844.* London: University of London Press, 1961.

Beaumont, Kenneth. 'The Tamworth Reading Room: rapports entre «savoir profane» et foi Chrétienne', *Études Newmaniennes* 16 (2000): 55–68.

Bouyer, Louis. *Newman: His Life and Spirituality*, trans. by J. Lewis May. San Francisco: Ignatius Press, 2011.

Burgis, Nina Fay. 'An Edition of Newman's *Tamworth Reading Room*, with Introduction and Textual and Expository Apparatus'. MA diss., University of London, Birkbeck College, 1964.

Butler, Francis J. 'John Henry Newman's Parochial and Plain Sermons Viewed as a Critique of Religious Evangelicalism'. Ph.D. diss., Catholic University of America, 1972.

Chadwick, Henry. *The Early Church.* London: Penguin Books, 1993.

Christie, Robert. 'The Clash of Evangelical Doctrine with Parish Experience: The Overlooked Catalyst to Newman's "Great Change in his Religious Opinions" in 1824–5', *Newman Studies Journal* 1/2 (Autumn 1995): 90–101.

Coats, Jerry. 'John Henry Newman's "Tamworth Reading Room": Adjusted Rhetorical Approaches for the Periodical Press', *Victorian Periodicals Review* 24 (1991): 173–80.

Colby, Robert A. 'The Structure of Newman's *Apologia pro Vita Sua* in Relation to his Theory of Assent', *The Dublin Review* (1953): 140–56.

Cordasco, Francesco. 'Junius' (1768–73) in *DNB*.

Coulson, John. 'Newman on the Church—His Final View, its Origins and Influence'. In *The Rediscovery of Newman: An Oxford Symposium*. Edited by John Coulson and A. M. Allchin. London and Melbourne: Sheed and Ward, 1967; London: SPCK, 1967.

Crimmins, James E. 'Religion, Utility, and Politics: Bentham versus Paley'. In *Religion, Secularization, and Political Thought: Thomas Hobbes to J. S. Mill*, ed. James E. Crimmins. London: Routledge, 1990.

Crosby, John F. 'Newman on the Personal', *First Things* 13/125 (August/September 2002): 43–9.

Culler, Dwight. *The Imperial Intellect*. New Haven: Yale University Press, 1955.

Delio, David. 'A Multitude of Subtle Influences: Faith, Reason, and Conversion in Newman's Thirteenth Oxford University Sermon', *Newman Studies Journal* 5/1 (Spring 2008): 77–86.

—— 'Calculated to Undermine Things Established: Newman's Fourteenth Oxford University Sermon', *Newman Studies Journal* 5/2 (Fall 2008): 69–83.

Dulles, Avery, SJ. 'Newman: The Anatomy of a Conversion'. In *Newman and Conversion*, ed. Ian Ker. Edinburgh: T & T Clark, 1997.

Dunne, Joseph. *Back to the Rough Ground: Practical Judgment and the Lure of Technique*. Notre Dame: University of Notre Dame Press, 1993.

Earnest, James David. 'A Study of John Henry Newman's Oxford University Sermons'. Ph.D. diss., Yale University, 1978.

Elliott-Binns, L. E. *Religion in the Victorian Era*. London: Lutterworth Press, 1946.

Evans, Eric J. *Sir Robert Peel: Statesmanship, Power and Party*. 2nd edn. London: Routledge, 2006.

Bibliography

Evans, Eric J. *The Shaping of Modern Britain: Identity, Industry and Empire, 1780–1914.* Harlow: Pearson Educational, 2011.

Fell, M. L. 'Erastianism'. In *New Catholic Encyclopedia.* 2nd edn. Detroit: Gale, 2003.

Fey, William R. *Faith and Doubt: The Unfolding of Newman's Thought on Certainty.* Shepherdstown, WV: Patmos Press, 1976.

Fletcher, Patrick J. 'Newman and Natural Theology', *Newman Studies Journal* 5/2 (Fall 2008): 26–42.

Ford, John T. 'John Henry Newman as Contextual Theologian', *Newman Studies Journal* 2:2 (Fall 2005): 60–76.

—— 'Newman's View of Education; The Oxford Background'. In *The Literary and Educational Effects of the Thought of John Henry Newman,* ed. Michael Sundermeier and Robert Churchill. Lewiston, New York: The Edwin Mellon Press, 1995.

—— 'Recent Studies on Newman: Two Review Articles', *The Thomist* 38 (1977): 424–40.

Gash, Norman. *Aristocracy and the People: Britain 1815–1865.* Cambridge: Harvard University Press, 1979.

—— *Mr. Secretary Peel: the Life of Sir Robert Peel to 1830.* London: Longman, Green, & Co., 1961.

—— *Sir Robert Peel: The Life of Sir Robert Peel after 1830.* London: Longman, 1972.

Gilley, Sheridan. *Newman and his Age.* London: Dartmon, Longman, & Todd, 1990.

Gregory, Brad. *The Unintended Reformation: How a Religious Revolution Secularized Society.* Cambridge, MA: Belknap Press, 2012.

Griffin, John R. *The Oxford Movement: A Revision.* Edinburgh: Pentland Press, 1984.

Guarino, Thomas. *Vincent of Lerins and the Development of Christian Doctrine.* Grand Rapids, MI: Baker Academic, 2013.

Harris, Wendell V. 'Newman, Peel, Tamworth, and the Concurrence of Historical Forces', *Victorian Studies* 32 (1989): 189–208.

Harrison, Paul V. 'A Scriptural Index to Newman's *Parochial and Plain Sermons*', *Newman Studies Journal* 3/2 (Fall 2006): 119–23.

Harrold, Charles Frederick. 'Introduction' to John Henry Newman, *Essays and Sketches,* ed. Charles Frederick Harrold. London: Longman, Green, & Co., 1948.

Harrold, Charles Frederick. *John Henry Newman: An Expository and Critical Study of his Mind, Thought and Art.* London: Longman, Green, & Co., 1945.

Hill, Richard Leslie. *From Toryism to the People.* London: Constable & Co., 1929.

Hilton, Boyd. 'Peel: A Reappraisal', *The Historical Journal* 22/3 (September 1979): 585–614.

Houghton, Esther Rhoads. '*The British Critic* and the Oxford Movement', *Studies in Bibliography* 16 (1963): 119–37.

Imberg, Rune. *In Quest for Authority.* Sweden: Lund University Press, 1987.

Jaki, Stanley L. 'Newman and Science', *The Downside Review* 108 (October 1990): 282–94.

Jay, Elisabeth. *Evangelical and Oxford Movements*, ed. Elizabeth Jay. Cambridge: Cambridge University Press, 1983.

Jost, Walter. *Rhetorical Thought in John Henry Newman.* Columbia, SC: University of South Carolina Press, 1989.

Kelly, Thomas. *George Birkbeck: Pioneer of Adult Education.* Liverpool: Liverpool University Press, 1957.

—— *A History of Adult Education in Great Britain.* 3rd edn. Liverpool: Liverpool University Press, 1992.

Kenny, Terence. *The Political Thought of John Henry Newman.* Westport, CT: Greenwood Press, 1974.

Ker, Ian. *The Achievement of John Henry Newman.* Notre Dame: University of Notre Dame Press, 1990.

—— *John Henry Newman: A Biography.* Oxford: Oxford University Press, 1988.

—— '"Mere Christianity" and Catholicism'. In *C. S. Lewis and the Church: Essays in Honor of Walter Hooper*, ed. Judith E. Wolfe and Brendan N. Wolfe. London: T & T Clarke, 1988, 129–34.

—— *Newman and Faith.* Louvain Theological and Pastoral Monographs 31. Louvain: Peeters, 2004.

—— 'Newman's Conversion to the Catholic Church: Another Perspective', *Renascence* 43/1–2 (Fall 1990/Winter 1991): 17–28.

—— 'Newman the Satirist'. In *Newman after a Hundred Years*, ed. Ian Ker and Alan G. Hill. Oxford: Clarendon Press, 1990.

—— *Newman and Truth.* Louvain Theological and Pastoral Monographs 39. Louvain: Peeters, 2008.

Ker, Ian. *Newman and the Word*. Louvain Theological and Pastoral Monographs 27. Louvain: Peeters, 2000.

—— and Terrence Merrigan, ed. *The Cambridge Companion to John Henry Newman*. Cambridge: Cambridge University Press, 2009.

Komonchak, Joseph A. 'John Henry Newman's Discovery of the Visible Church (1816–1828)'. Ph.D. diss., Union Theological Seminary, New York, 1976.

Lang, Jessica, and Jennifer Speake. 'Buses and Coaches'. In *Literature of Travel and Exploration: An Encyclopedia*, ed. Jennifer Speake. New York: Taylor and Francis Group, 2003.

Lawson, M. K. 'Cnut', Canute (d.1035). In *DNB*.

Lobban, Michael. 'Henry Brougham' (1778–1868). In *DNB*.

Machin, G. I. T. *Politics and the Churches in Great Britain: 1832–1868*. Oxford: Clarendon Press, 1977.

MacIntyre, Alasdair. 'The Idea of an Educated Public'. In *Education and Values: The Richard Peters Lectures*, ed. Graham Haydon. London: Institute of Education, 1987.

—— *Whose Justice? Which Rationality?*. Notre Dame: Notre Dame Press, 1988.

Mandel, W. F. 'Newman and his Audiences: 1825–1845', *Journal of Religious History* 24 (2000): 143–58.

Martin, Brian. *John Henry Newman: His Life and Work*. Leominster: Gracewing, 2012.

McGrath, Fergal. *Newman's University: Idea and Reality*. London: Longman, Green, 1951.

McGrath, Francis: *see under Newman*.

McKenna, Joseph H. 'Honesty in Theology?', *Heythrop Journal* 62 (2001): 49–60.

Merrigan, Terrence. *Clear Heads and Holy Hearts: The Religious and Theological Ideal of John Henry Newman*. Louvain: Peeters, 1991.

Murray, Placid: *see under Newman*.

Nockles, '"Church and King": Tractarian Politics Reappraised'. In *From Oxford to the People*, ed. Paul Vaiss. Leominster: Fowler Wright Books, 1996.

Packer, James. 'Expository Preaching: Charles Simeon and Ourselves', *Churchman* 74/2 (1960): 94–101.

Pattison, Robert. *The Great Dissent: John Henry Newman and the Liberal*

Heresy. Oxford: Oxford University Press, 1991.
Porter, Dilwyn. 'John Walter III' (1818–94). In *DNB*.
Prest, John. 'Sir Robert Peel' (1788–1850). In *DNB*.
Prothero, Stephen. *Why Liberals Win the Culture Wars (Even when they Lose Elections): The Battles that Define America from Jefferson's Heresies to Gay Marriage.* San Francisco, HarperOne, 2016.
Quang, Vin Boa Luu. 'Newman's Theology of the Immanent Trinity in his Parochial and Plain Sermons 1829–1834', *Newman Studies Journal* 7:1 (Spring 2010): 73–97.
Read, Donald. *Peel and the Victorians.* Oxford: Blackwell, 1987.
Rowlands, John Henry Lewis. *Church, State, and Society: The Attitudes of John Keble, Richard Hurrell Froude, and John Henry Newman, 1827–1845.* Worthing: Churchman Publishing, 1989.
Rupert, Jane M. 'John Henry Newman on Education'. Ph.D. diss., University of Toronto, 1998.
Rupert, M. Jane. 'Newman and Bacon', *The Downside Review* 118 (2000): 45–70.
Sack, James J. 'The Quarterly Review and the Baptism of the "Conservative Party"—A Conundrum Resolved', *Victorian Periodicals Review* 24/4 (Winter 1991): 170–2.
Salmon, Philip. *Electoral Reform at Work: Local Politics and National Parties, 1832–1841.* Rochester, NY: Boydell and Brewer, 2002.
Shrimpton, Paul. *The 'Making of Men', The Idea and Reality of Newman's University in Oxford and Dublin.* Leominster: Gracewing, 2015.
Sillem, Edward J. *The Philosophical Notebook of John Henry Newman.* Vol. I. Louvain: Nauwelaerts Publishing House, 1969.
Skinner, Simon. 'Liberalism and Mammon: Tractarian Reaction in the Age of Reform', *Journal of Victorian Culture* 4/2 (Autumn 1999): 197–227.
—— 'Mozley, Thomas' (1806–93). In *DNB*.
—— *Tractarians and the 'Condition of England': The Social and Political Thought of the Oxford Movement.* Oxford: Clarendon Press, 2004.
Smith, Christian, and Melinda Ludquist Denton. *Soul Searching: The Religious and Spiritual Lives of American Teenagers.* Oxford: Oxford University Press, 2005.
Stephen, Leslie. *The English Utilitarians.* Vol. II. London: Duckworth & Co., 1900.

Bibliography

Taylor, Charles. *A Secular Age*. Cambridge, MA: Belknap Press, 2007.

'Thirty-Nine Articles'. In *The Concise Oxford Dictionary of the Christian Church*, ed. E. A. Livingstone. Oxford: Oxford University Press, 2006.

Tillman, Mary Katherine. 'Introduction'. In John Henry Newman, *Fifteen Sermons Preached before the Oxford University between A.D. 1826 and 1843*. Notre Dame: University of Notre Dame Press, 1997.

——— '"Realizing" the Classical Authors: Newman's Epic Journey in the Mediterranean', *Newman Studies Journal* 3:2 (Fall 2006): 60–77.

Tolhurst, James K. *The Church ... A Communion in the Preaching and Thought of John Henry Newman*. Leominster: Fowler Wright Books, 1988.

——— 'The Idea of the Church as a Community in the Anglican Sermons of John Henry Newman', *The Downside Review* 101/343 (July 1983): 140–64.

Trevor, Meriol. *Newman: The Pillar of the Cloud*. New York: Double Day & Co., 1962.

Tuckwell, William, *Pre-Tractarian Oxford: A Reminiscence of the Oriel 'Noetics'*. London: Smith, Elder, & Co., 1909.

Turner, Frank. *John Henry Newman: The Challenge to Evangelical Religion*. New Haven: Yale University Press, 2002.

Uno, Kei. 'The Views of Sir Robert Peel and John Henry Newman on the Establishment of the Tamworth Reading Room in 1841 and its Effect on Humankind and their Ideas of Adult Education', *Studies in Philosophical Anthropology* 37 (2007): 15–33.

Vargish, Thomas. *Newman: The Contemplation of Mind*. Oxford: Clarendon Press, 1970.

Walgrave, Jan H., OP. *Newman the Theologian*, trans. by A.V. Littledale. New York: Sheed and Ward, 1960.

Ward, Wilfrid. *The Life of Cardinal Newman*. 2 vols. London: Longman, Green, & Co., 1912.

Wilhite, David E. *The Gospel according to Heretics*. Grand Rapids, MI: Baker Academics, 2015.

Williams, Francis. *Dangerous Estate: The Anatomy of Newspapers*. New York: MacMillan, 1958

Williams, Rowan. 'Introduction'. In *The Works of Blessed John Henry Newman*, The Birmingham Oratory Millennium Edition, vol. IV, *The Arians of the Fourth Century*. Leominster: Gracewing, 2002.

INDEX

A

Act of Emancipation 23, 353
Act of Union 10, 17
Adam 126, 292
America 8, 64, 65, 240
Amiens, Peace of 10
Anderson Institute 45
Anglican Church 7, 16, 28, 35, 39, 78, 81, 213, 256
Anglicanism 28, 36
Anglicans xii, xiv, xv, xix, 1, 7, 13, 16, 17, 20, 27, 28, 35, 37, 38, 39, 40, 47, 48, 78, 80, 81, 83, 101, 119, 125, 147, 150, 151, 170, 173, 202, 211, 213, 215, 218, 221, 231, 235, 236, 237, 238, 241, 242, 243, 244, 256, 257, 260, 326
Apostles 85, 179, 237, 299, 322
Apostolic tradition 3, 6, 26, 28, 78, 82, 88, 157, 181, 182, 236, 246, 255
Arcesilas 128, 293
Areopagus 2, 175, 177, 178, 179, 180, 181, 182, 183, 209, 232, 233, 242, 246, 257, 322
Arianism xiv
Aristotelian philosophy 21, 112, 159, 162, 169
Aristotle 126, 128, 160, 162, 163, 169, 170, 293, 309
Athanasius 125
Atomists 234
Augustine 37, 125
Aurelius, Marcus 178

B

Bacon, Francis 121, 122, 126, 134, 169, 234, 295, 303, 309
Baptism 86, 87, 151, 240
Baptists 165, 319
Barnes, Thomas (editor of *The Times*) 105, 124, 128, 132, 133, 140, 184, 185, 186, 187, 194
Belaney, Robert 89, 90
Bentham, Jeremy (philosopher) 19, 51, 70, 75, 108, 109, 112, 118, 119, 120, 123, 124, 134, 143, 144, 230, 234, 284, 289, 290, 293, 295
Berkeley 128, 293
Biblical references
 1 Corinthians xix, 83, 120, 122, 238, 353
 1 Peter 88
 Acts 2, 177, 178, 180, 183
 Exodus 4
 Genesis 4, 128, 353
 Hebrews 134
 Job 128, 293
Birkbeck, George 45, 121
Birmingham 214, 216, 257, 259
Blomfield, C. J. 58
Body of Christ 84, 86, 122, 238, 253
Bolton 9
Book of Common Prayer 240
Bosanquet, Samuel 70
Britannia 198
British Critic xii, 35, 38, 41, 67, 69, 70, 71, 75, 76, 78, 99, 101, 108, 138, 178, 192, 201, 202, 207, 208, 237

'An aristocracy of exalted spirits'

Brougham, Henry 23, 24, 44, 15, 16, 47, 51, 58, 60, 62, 92, 94, 96, 97, 99, 100, 101, 102, 104, 105, 108, 111, 112, 113, 114, 118, 119, 120, 121, 122, 123, 124, 127, 128, 134, 135, 136, 137, 138, 139, 143, 144, 147, 151, 152, 153, 154, 155, 156, 158, 166, 172, 175, 178, 182, 184, 193, 199, 200, 204, 206, 216, 222, 228, 230, 234, 235, 238, 243, 255, 278, 279, 280, 281, 282, 284, 285, 286, 287, 289, 290, 291, 293, 294, 295, 296, 297, 300, 301, 302, 303, 308, 311, 312, 313, 315, 320, 321, 326

Buckland, William 48, 49, 56, 57, 63, 64, 93, 94, 108, 268

Burke, Edmund 12, 18, 44

Butler, Joseph 128, 240, 259, 293, 320

C

Caesar 111

Calvinism 319

Cambridge 100, 268, 320, 321

Canning, George 21, 44

Capes, John Moore 91, 219, 220, 221, 327

Carbutt, Dr, of Manchester 56

Cashel 11

Catholic Emancipation 21, 22, 23, 315, 316, 317

Catholicism xii, xix, 3, 6, 7, 8, 10, 12, 17, 18, 21, 22, 23, 24, 25, 27, 28, 34, 36, 37, 38, 40, 41, 58, 62, 65, 74, 77, 78, 79, 80, 82, 84, 85, 86, 87, 88, 89, 90, 94, 106, 125, 131, 150, 154, 156, 157, 165, 171, 173, 179, 182, 198, 204, 206, 211, 214, 215, 216, 219, 221, 222, 223, 224, 225, 226, 230, 231, 235, 236, 237, 240, 246, 255, 257, 259, 260, 303, 304, 315, 316, 317, 326, 353

Catholics 10, 13, 17, 22, 23, 28, 37, 77, 80, 101, 200, 259, 319

Catholic Standard 223

Catholic University of Ireland 222

Catholicus xix

Catholicus (John Henry Newman) xv, xvi, xix, 1, 2, 3, 4, 6, 49, 58, 61, 64, 66, 71, 76, 90, 92, 103, 105, 106, 107, 108, 109, 110, 111, 112, 113, 114, 115, 116, 118, 119, 120, 121, 122, 123, 124, 125, 126, 127, 128, 131, 132, 133, 134, 135, 136, 137, 138, 139, 140, 142, 143, 147, 148, 149, 150, 152, 153, 154, 155, 156, 157, 158, 159, 160, 161, 162, 163, 164, 165, 166, 167, 168, 169, 170, 171, 172, 173, 174, 175, 176, 177, 178, 180, 181, 182, 183, 184, 185, 186, 187, 188, 189, 192, 193, 194, 195, 196, 197, 198, 199, 200, 201, 202, 203, 204, 205, 206, 207, 208, 209, 211, 212, 213, 215, 216, 218, 219, 220, 221, 222, 223, 224, 225, 227, 228, 229, 231, 232, 233, 234, 235, 238, 239, 242, 244, 245, 246, 249, 250, 253, 254, 255, 256, 257, 258, 260, 261, 278, 323, 326, 329, 330, 353

Chalcedon, council of 36, 215

Church of England xv, 6, 7, 17, 18, 21, 22, 40, 46, 53, 64, 77, 81, 83, 86, 125, 150, 214, 215, 246, 248

Church of Rome 35, 38, 40, 214, 215, 246

Cicero 110, 111, 119, 120, 124, 143, 234, 285, 286, 289, 290

Conservative Journal 198

Conservatives 1, 29, 30, 43, 51, 61, 63, 107, 129, 133, 184, 189, 198, 203, 204, 283

Craik, George Lille 57, 96, 97, 108, 111, 113, 122, 152, 154, 155, 156, 166, 178, 243

Creed 14, 86, 299

Crocker, John Wilson 31, 33

Cyril of Alexandria 36

Index

D

Dalgairns 216
Darwinism 165
Davy, Humphrey 56, 58, 59, 97, 114, 123, 174, 270, 275, 303
Deism 169
de La Motte Fouqué, F. H. (author) 111, 112
Democritus 154, 169, 309
Dioscorus 36
Dissenters 22, 33, 83, 165, 308, 324
Donatism 35, 37
Dublin Review 35, 37, 215, 226

E

Ealing School 13, 14
England xv, 1, 2, 3, 4, 6, 7, 8, 10, 17, 18, 21, 22, 27, 40, 43, 44, 45, 46, 53, 64, 65, 66, 69, 77, 81, 83, 86, 94, 111, 112, 113, 125, 131, 138, 150, 168, 180, 192, 214, 215, 216, 223, 246, 248, 257, 258, 264, 303, 321
Enlightenment 2, 3, 4, 24, 44, 152, 155
Ephesus, council of 36
Established Church 32, 33, 90, 165, 321
Eucharist 238
Eutyches 36
Evangelicalism 13, 20, 46, 81, 88, 93, 107, 113, 128, 135, 136, 137, 154, 195, 234, 240, 241
Evangelicals 77

F

Faber, Frederick 218, 332, 333
Fairbairn, A. M. (Protestant theologian) 160
Faraday, Michael 56, 271
Fitzgerald, Vesey 22
Floyd, Julia (wife of Robert Peel) 18
France 8, 9, 10, 12

Froude, Catherine 81, 214
Froude, Hurrell 5, 27, 34, 81, 214, 215, 226, 353

G

George III 8, 10, 185
George IV 21, 199
Gilpin verses 192
Glasgow University 45, 50, 56, 99, 279, 281, 286, 301, 320
The Globe 61, 167, 186, 187, 191, 194, 198, 199, 200, 329, 330
Gnosticism 74
Gospel 2, 68, 73, 118, 120, 149, 178, 179, 182, 183, 234, 238, 241, 242
Gower Street (i.e. University of London) 94, 95, 127, 278, 281, 293, 353
Grace 118, 122, 123, 251
Greece 114, 169, 287, 309
Greek drama 114
Greville, Charles 55, 199, 207, 208

H

Hamilton, Hans Henry 16
Harrow School 10, 11
Hawkins, Edward 21, 238, 315
Heaven 4, 124, 244, 260, 291, 323
High Church 23, 25, 34, 46, 65, 71, 77, 106, 150, 182, 188, 189, 201, 224, 316, 354
Holmes, Mary 40
Holy Spirit xix, 86, 148, 234, 238, 240, 244, 245
Hooker 320
House of Commons 30, 43, 204, 327
House of Lords 43, 325
Hume, David 13
Huskinsson, William 18

I

Idolatry 172, 180, 251, 311, 322

Ireland 7, 10, 11, 12, 13, 17, 22, 23, 190, 193, 222, 315, 318, 353
Italy 303

J

Jacobinism 44
Judaism 72

K

Keble, John 5, 26, 27, 34, 39, 40, 41, 71, 72, 167, 208, 209, 315, 320
King's College, London 57, 58, 274
Kingsley, Charles (author) 225, 259
Knowledge School 124, 125, 128, 131, 133, 134, 147, 148, 153, 156, 157, 160, 161, 166, 168, 172, 173, 175, 176, 177, 178, 186, 203, 206, 222, 223, 230, 234, 235, 242, 243, 245, 246, 248, 250, 251, 252, 254, 258, 291

L

Lambeth Conferences xx
Lancashire 9
Lausanne xx
Leo, Pope 36
Liberals 65, 152, 302
Liberal Tories 22
Littlemore (Newman's church) 38, 39, 194
Locke 13
London xix, 1, 10, 19, 57, 94, 100, 107, 116, 121, 138, 167, 183, 186, 201, 206, 218, 222, 274, 278, 279, 315, 316, 319, 321
   London University 5, 44, 58, 94, 100, 107, 116, 222, 278, 319, 321, 322
Lord's Prayer 86
Low Church 23, 46, 65, 316, 354
Lushington, Stephen 94, 100, 278, 281, 321, 322, 354

M

Macedon 150, 300
Mayers, Walter 14
Mechanics' Institutes 51, 54, 60, 121, 204, 228, 259
Mechanics' Magazine 55, 56, 121
Melbourne, Lord 32, 68, 82, 201, 299
Merchant Taylors' Hall 31, 32
Midlands xiv, 44, 49, 52
Milman, Henry Hart 71, 72, 73, 74, 75, 76, 77, 88
Milton, John (poet) 155, 163, 303
Monmouth 150, 186, 300
Monophysitism 36, 37, 215
Moral Governor 75, 173, 174, 312, 313
Morning Chronicle 104, 132, 167, 186, 187, 188, 193, 200, 201, 209, 246, 323, 325, 329, 330
Morning Herald 61, 186, 329, 330
Morning Post 50, 60, 61, 198, 329, 330
Moses 165, 308
Mozley, Anne 70, 200
Mozley, Thomas 70, 71, 175, 200, 202, 203, 204, 205, 206, 207, 208, 212, 354

N

Napoleon 14, 18
Napoleonic Wars 10, 12
Near East 74
Nestorians 36
Newman, Jemima 11, 48, 162, 316
Newman, John Henry
   Apologia pro Vita Sua xi, xv, 2, 13, 14, 15, 21, 27, 29, 35, 36, 37, 38, 39, 41, 72, 77, 78, 79, 80, 88, 89, 105, 213, 215, 224, 225, 226, 236, 237, 257, 259
   Arians of the Fourth Century xiii, 179
   Discourses on the Nature and Scope of University Education 213
   Discussions and Arguments xv, 2, 3,

Index

78, 92, 96, 104, 114, 118, 121, 124, 154, 158, 166, 171, 173, 174, 213, 223, 225, 228, 230, 231, 242
'The Duty of Christian Educators' 69, 149, 238, 239, 249
An Essay in Aid of a Grammar of Assent xi, xvi, xix, 161, 164, 179, 213, 214, 220, 225, 227, 228, 235, 254, 257, 354
An Essay on the Development of Christian Doctrine xi, 88, 231
The Idea of a University xi, xv, xvi, 115, 134, 179, 221, 222, 223, 257
'The Influence of Natural and Revealed Religion Respectively' 181
'Lead, Kindly Light' 4
Letter to the Duke of Norfolk 257
Oxford University Sermons 68, 70, 88, 179, 180, 181, 182, 226, 234, 236, 244
Parochial and Plain Sermons 69, 149, 176, 177, 178, 179, 236, 239, 240, 241, 244
'The Religion of the Day' 68
The Tamworth Reading Room xv, xvi, xix, xx, 1, 2, 3, 4, 5, 6, 26, 46, 60, 63, 91, 106, 135, 142, 156, 194, 199, 201, 202, 204, 206, 207, 208, 216, 218, 223, 225, 228, 230, 231, 232, 239, 243, 245, 246, 247, 253, 254, 255, 257, 260, 297, 301, 303, 304, 306, 312, 313, 315
'The Church Visible and Invisible' 244
'Spiritual Presence of Christ in the Church' 241
Tract 85 78
Tract 90 xv, 69, 72, 77, 78, 79, 80, 81, 82, 88, 89, 101, 102, 106, 141, 168, 176, 177, 193, 194, 195, 199, 200, 201, 213, 216, 218, 220, 221, 229, 232, 255, 326
Verses on Various Occasions 4
Via Media 231, 244
Newton, Isaac 58, 113, 154, 275, 281, 303

Nicaea, council of xiii
Nonconformists 22

O

O'Connell, Daniel 22
Oriel College, Oxford xiii, 7, 20, 21, 38, 67, 72, 167, 187, 202, 203, 219, 315, 316, 326
Orthodox 6, 28, 40
Owen, Robert 46
Oxford 26, 27, 28, 30, 38, 39, 40, 67, 90, 91, 140, 142, 160, 167, 182, 194, 235, 240, 271, 315, 317, 318, 321
Oxford Movement xii, 1, 3, 5, 7, 26, 27, 28, 34, 35, 64, 67, 69, 70, 78, 80, 188, 194, 202, 203, 215, 216, 219, 220, 225, 232

P

Paine, Thomas 12, 13
Paley, William 108, 119, 127, 135, 165
Pall Mall 63
Palmer, Roundell 27, 67, 75, 76, 221, 237, 238
Pascal, Blaise 99, 154, 281, 286, 287, 303
Peel, Robert xiv, xv, xvi, xix, xx, 1, 2, 3, 4, 5, 6, 7, 8, 9, 10, 11, 12, 13, 16, 17, 18, 19, 21, 22, 23, 24, 25, 26, 29, 30, 31, 32, 33, 34, 41, 43, 44, 46, 47, 48, 49, 50, 51, 52, 53, 54, 55, 56, 57, 58, 59, 60, 61, 62, 63, 64, 65, 66, 67, 68, 71, 76, 82, 90, 91, 92, 93, 94, 95, 96, 97, 98, 99, 100, 101, 102, 104, 105, 106, 107, 108, 109, 110, 111, 112, 113, 114, 116, 117, 118, 119, 120, 123, 124, 125, 127, 128, 129, 131, 132, 133, 134, 135, 136, 137, 138, 139, 140, 142, 143, 144, 147, 148, 150, 151, 156, 158, 163, 166, 168, 169, 170, 171, 172, 173, 174, 175, 176, 177, 178, 179, 182, 183, 184, 186, 187, 189, 190, 192, 193, 195, 196, 197, 198, 199, 200, 201, 202, 203, 204, 205, 206, 207, 208, 209, 211, 212, 213, 216, 217, 218,

219, 220, 221, 222, 223, 225, 228, 229, 230, 232, 233, 234, 235, 238, 239, 242, 243, 244, 246, 247, 248, 249, 250, 251, 252, 253, 256, 258, 261, 262, 265, 268, 269, 271, 277, 278, 279, 282, 283, 285, 286, 289, 290, 291, 293, 296, 297, 298, 299, 300, 305, 307, 309, 313, 316, 317, 318, 326, 329, 330, 354
   Bain pamphlet 92
Pentecost 179
Pitt, William, the Younger 8, 9, 10, 12, 18, 19
Plato 111, 169, 170, 286, 309
Platonism 74, 254
Plymouth 49, 271
Poor Law 30, 70
Protagoras 154, 303
Protestantism 6, 12, 17, 27, 28, 31, 32, 72, 78, 81, 160, 165, 188, 230, 236, 237, 317, 323
Protestants 13, 23, 28, 36, 37, 80
Pusey, Edward 7, 192
Puseyism 8, 67, 167, 168, 187, 188, 191, 194, 199, 200, 219, 323, 324, 325, 326, 327
Pythagorean philosophy 75

Q

Queen's Colleges 222
Queen's Colleges, Ireland 222, 354
Queen's Letter 83, 354

R

Radicals 30, 61, 64, 326
The Rambler xii, 219, 326
Reform Act 26, 27, 29, 83
Ricardo, David 18
Rogers, Frederick 70, 75, 89, 108, 109, 187, 194, 199, 200, 220
Romanism 72
Royal Society 44, 123

S

Savage, R. C. (vicar of Tamworth) 211, 262
Scotland 43, 44, 46, 56, 268
Scott, Thomas 14, 111, 112, 125, 319
Second Vatican Council xx
Sheldonian Theatre, Oxford 17
Shillibeer, George 138
Short, Thomas 19, 44
Smith, Adam 18
Smith, James 268
Society for the Diffusion of Useful Knowledge 44, 45, 62, 96, 122
Socinians 319
The Spectator 49, 61, 62, 94, 97, 101, 128, 133, 190, 198, 329, 330
Staffordshire Advertiser 49, 50, 60, 61, 63, 261, 329, 330
Staffordshire Examiner 61
The Standard 50, 189, 190, 198, 199, 223, 224, 329, 330
The Statesman 61
St. Clement's church, Oxford 20, 125
St. Mary's church, Oxford 28, 39, 40, 41, 72, 82, 177, 226, 239, 242
Stoicism 169
The Sun 61, 97, 186, 198

T

Tamworth xiv, xv, xvi, xix, xx, 1, 2, 3, 4, 5, 6, 9, 25, 26, 29, 30, 34, 41, 43, 44, 46, 48, 49, 50, 52, 53, 55, 56, 57, 60, 61, 63, 64, 67, 68, 80, 91, 94, 95, 106, 114, 116, 117, 124, 127, 132, 133, 135, 136, 139, 142, 147, 156, 170, 175, 179, 180, 189, 190, 193, 194, 197, 198, 199, 201, 202, 203, 204, 205, 206, 207, 208, 211, 213, 216, 217, 218, 223, 225, 228, 230, 231, 232, 233, 239, 243, 245, 246, 247, 253, 254, 255, 257, 260, 261, 265, 278,

283, 285, 293, 296, 297, 298, 300, 301, 303, 304, 306, 309, 312, 313, 315
Library xiv, 4, 6, 44, 46, 50, 63, 218, 245
Ten Commandments 86
Thirty-Nine Articles 69, 77, 78, 79, 88
The Thunderer 67, 68, 130, 156, 184, 185
The Times xiv, xv, xvi, xix, 1, 2, 3, 4, 6, 16, 33, 49, 50, 61, 63, 66, 67, 68, 69, 70, 72, 75, 78, 80, 81, 82, 83, 88, 90, 92, 93, 103, 104, 105, 107, 110, 115, 116, 117, 118, 128, 130, 131, 132, 133, 137, 139, 140, 141, 142, 143, 144, 147, 151, 154, 157, 159, 168, 175, 176, 178, 182, 183, 184, 185, 186, 187, 189, 190, 192, 193, 194, 195, 196, 197, 199, 200, 201, 203, 209, 217, 218, 219, 220, 221, 229, 231, 232, 233, 239, 242, 245, 246, 247, 261, 285, 291, 329, 330
Tories xix, 1, 3, 7, 11, 12, 17, 19, 22, 23, 25, 29, 30, 32, 41, 43, 46, 47, 51, 55, 60, 63, 64, 116, 128, 129, 131, 133, 136, 137, 150, 156, 182, 184, 186, 188, 189, 190, 199, 208, 224, 299, 323, 324, 325, 326
Toryism 18, 19, 47, 60, 132, 187, 188, 200, 323, 324
Tractarianism 21, 26, 67, 68, 69, 70, 71, 77, 89, 90, 131, 156, 182, 188, 189, 194, 199, 203, 212, 213, 221, 238, 239, 246, 256
Tractarians 26, 53, 68, 69, 70, 90, 108, 191, 208, 217, 220, 255
Tracts for the Times xii, xv, 26, 69, 77, 89, 239
Trafalgar 11
Trinity 74, 86, 87, 236, 238, 257
Trinity College, Cambridge 16, 19

U

Ultra-Tories 23, 25, 27, 32, 33, 53, 55, 62, 137
Undine 111, 112, 286
Utilitarians 119, 317, 319

V

Victoria, Queen 32

W

Walter II, John 67, 68, 91, 103, 104, 105, 106, 128, 129, 130, 131, 133, 139, 140, 141, 142, 144, 145, 157, 167, 168, 183, 184, 185, 186, 187, 194, 195, 220
Walter III, John 67, 82, 90, 91, 96, 103, 104, 130, 131, 142, 167, 184, 219, 220, 221
Waterloo 14, 21
Weekly Chronicle 193
Weekly Dispatch 198
Wellesley, Arthur, Duke of Wellington 11, 21, 22, 58, 212
Westminster 17, 48, 319
Whately, Richard 21, 158, 315
Whigs 12, 17, 19, 22, 26, 30, 32, 33, 43, 51, 61, 62, 63, 64, 119, 128, 144, 152, 156, 184, 186, 187, 189, 190, 198, 199, 207, 211, 299, 302, 326
White Lady 111, 112, 286
Wilberforce, Henry 91, 131, 142, 167, 168, 186, 187, 191, 192, 194, 220, 223, 241
William IV 30, 199
Wiseman, Nicholas 35, 37, 215, 218
Woolwich 49, 271

www.ingramcontent.com/pod-product-compliance
Lightning Source LLC
Chambersburg PA
CBHW030332240426
43661CB00052B/1610